CULTURE AND ENVIRONMENT

THE BROOKS/COLE BASIC CONCEPTS IN ENVIRONMENT AND BEHAVIOR SERIES

Series Editors:

Irwin Altman, The University of Utah
Daniel Stokols, University of California, Irvine
Lawrence S. Wrightsman, The University of Kansas

AN INTRODUCTION TO ECOLOGICAL PSYCHOLOGY
Allan W. Wicker, Claremont Graduate School

CULTURE AND ENVIRONMENT
Irwin Altman, The University of Utah
Martin Chemers, The University of Utah

INQUIRY BY DESIGN: TOOLS FOR ENVIRONMENT-BEHAVIOR RESEARCH
John Zeisel, Harvard University

ENVIRONMENTAL EVALUATION: PERCEPTION AND PUBLIC POLICY
Ervin H. Zube, University of Arizona

ENVIRONMENTAL PROBLEMS/BEHAVIORAL SOLUTIONS
John D. Cone, West Virginia University
Steven C. Hayes, University of North Carolina

CULTURE AND ENVIRONMENT

IRWIN ALTMAN
The University of Utah

MARTIN CHEMERS
The University of Utah

BROOKS/COLE PUBLISHING COMPANY
MONTEREY, CALIFORNIA
A Division of Wadsworth, Inc.

Published by the Press Syndicate of the University of Cambridge
The Pitt Building, Trumpington Street, Cambridge CB2 1RP
32 East 57th Street, New York, NY 10022, USA
10 Stamford Road, Oakleigh, Melbourne 3166, Australia

First published 1980 by Wadsworth, Inc.
First published by Cambridge University Press 1984
Reprinted 1984

Printed in the United States of America

ISBN 0 521 31970 6

To
Louis L. Altman and Ethel Schonberg Altman
and
to the memory of
Meyer Chemers and Hannah Lesnevsky Chemers,
our parents.

SERIES FOREWORD

The study of environment and behavior has shown a rapid development in recent decades; we expect that interest in this field will continue at a high level in the future. As a young and informative area, it has many exciting qualities. For example, the analysis of the relationship between human behavior and the physical environment has attracted researchers from many fields in the *social sciences,* such as psychology, sociology, geography, and anthropology, and from the *environmental design* fields, such as architecture, urban and regional planning, and interior design. The multidisciplinary character of this field has led to an atmosphere of stimulation, cross-fertilization, and, yes, even confusion and difficulty in communication. Furthermore, because of the diversity in intellectual styles and goals of its participants, research on environment and behavior has as often dealt with applied, real-world problems of environmental design as it has treated basic and theoretical issues.

These factors, coupled with the relatively young stage of development of the field, led us to believe that a series of short books on different areas of the environment and behavior field would be useful to students, researchers, and practitioners. Our view was that the study of environment and behavior had not yet firmed up to the point that a single volume would do justice to the wide range of topics now being studied or to the variety of audiences interested in the field. Furthermore, it became clear to us that new topical areas have emerged over the past decade and that some vehicle is necessary to facilitate the evolutionary growth of the field.

For these reasons, Brooks/Cole established the present series of books on environment and behavior with the following goals in mind: first, we endeavored to develop a series of short volumes on areas of research and knowledge that are relatively well established and are characterized by a reasonably substantial body of knowledge. Second, we have recruited authors from a diversity of disciplines who bring to bear a variety of perspectives on various subjects in the field. Third, we asked authors not only to summarize research and knowledge on their topic but also to set forth a "point of view," if not a theoretical orientation, in their book. It was our intention, therefore, that these volumes be more than textbooks in the usual sense of the term—that they not only summarize existing knowledge in an understandable way but also, we hope, advance the field intellectually. Fourth, we wanted the books in the series to be useful to a broad range of students and readers. We planned for the volumes to be educationally valuable to students and professionals from different fields in the social sciences and environmental-design fields and to be of interest to readers with different levels of formal professional training. As part of our broad and flexible strategy, the series will allow instructors in a variety of fields teaching a variety of courses to select different combinations of volumes to meet their particular course needs. In so doing, an instructor might select several books for a course or use a small number of volumes as supplementary reading material.

Because the series is open-ended and not restricted to a particular body of content, we hope that it will not only serve to summarize knowledge in the field of environment and behavior but also contribute to the growth and development of this exciting area of study.

Irwin Altman
Daniel Stokols
Lawrence S. Wrightsman

PREFACE

The idea for this book grew out of a chapter on culture and environment that we coauthored for a forthcoming *Handbook of Cross-Cultural Psychology*. Having explored briefly how the environment is used and adapted to by different cultures, we decided that the time was ripe to pursue the subject in more detail. Although the study of environment and behavior has become popular in the last ten years, very little attention has been given to cultural similarities and differences in orientations to the physical environment. It occurred to us that this was a major gap in research on environment and behavior, for an understanding of human behavior is not wholly achieved through the study of physical settings within one's own culture; it also requires that we identify similarities and differences among cultures. Not only is cross-cultural analysis fascinating in its own right, but it can help make vivid certain facets of behavior that we often take for granted, such as uses and design of homes, communities, and other places. Cross-cultural analysis is also an excellent vehicle for testing and extending hypotheses in a greater range of settings. Perhaps even more important, cross-cultural analysis can help generate new hypotheses and ideas about relations between environment and behavior, because it allows the researcher to see and think about settings that are not part of his or her own everyday environment. For these reasons, the study of culture and environment can have an important impact on the study of general environment/behavior relations.

An exciting feature of our analysis of culture and environment was that it took us further and further afield from our parent discipline of social psychology. Although we had always espoused the value of multidisciplinary knowledge, we had never realized before how truly fertile such a quest could be. Within psychology, and even in the fields currently identified with the study of environment and behavior, such as geography, sociology, architecture, and urban planning, we discovered how little cross-cultural work had been done. Our search for information took us well beyond even these fields to anthropology, history, philosophy, religion, and literature. To our perhaps naive surprise, there existed a vast wealth of information, some quantitative and some qualitative, some anecdotal and some speculative, about how people and cultures around the world relate to their physical environments. As we absorbed this information, our perspective on environment and behavior broadened, our appreciation of the importance and excitement of culture in relation to the environment increased, and we reveled in the new topics and new information that we had uncovered. But cross-cultural analysis is not always easy. It is hard to locate information, one is often not certain about the accuracy or validity of the information, one sometimes has difficulty learning about a new field. Nevertheless, the process has been exciting, and this book gives you a glimpse—and only a glimpse—into possibilities for studying, from a multidisciplinary perspective, how different cultures relate to their physical environments. Much more remains to be done, and there are vast untapped bodies of knowledge presently available for others to explore.

After the Introduction (Chapter 1), the book is organized into three sections, each of which contains several chapters. The Introduction spells out the conceptual framework we used to explore environment and behavior in a cultural context, and it sets down the organization and main themes of the book. Part 1 of the book contains Chapters 2 and 3, which examine some basic psychological processes in a cross-cultural perspective. In these chapters, we describe environmental cognition and perception, or how people respond perceptually to the physical environment and what world views and conceptions they hold about the environment, from the small-scale aspects of their environments to those of cities, regions, and even the world. Part 2 of the book, Chapters 4 through 6, focuses on behavioral processes in relation to the environment. Here we consider how people in different cultures are similar and different in their regulation of privacy, use of personal space, and territorial behavior. The third part of the book, Chapters 7 through 11, shifts focus and deals with environmental places in an attempt to understand how the environments that people create reflect the cultures in which they live. The places that we examine include homes and their interiors and communities ranging in size from temporary encampments to villages to large urban centers. As part of this analysis, we also examine a few visionary plans for cities and communities in the future.

The book ends with a chapter that highlights the central themes of our analysis and suggests some ways to apply knowledge of culture/environment relations to the design of better environments for people in different cultures.

This has been an exciting adventure for us, if only a modest beginning to a complex and far-reaching topic. Our plan is to continue this work, extending the analysis to other processes and places and to a broader range of cultures and disciplines. There is considerable room for creative work, and it is hoped that our efforts will stimulate others to study culture and environment.

Many people helped in many ways in the preparation of this book. We are especially indebted to Daniel Stokols and Lawrence Wrightsman, our long-time colleagues, friends, and consulting editors for Brooks/Cole Publishing Company. They provided extensive comments and pushed us to our intellectual limits in this venture. For their technical help and for their constant encouragement and patience, we are most appreciative. We also thank others who commented on all or parts of the book or on materials that appeared in other places and were included in the book: Lawrence Loeb, Seymour Parker, and Barbara Rogoff, University of Utah; Stephen Margulis, National Bureau of Standards; M. Brewster Smith, University of California, Santa Cruz; and the members of an environmental-psychology seminar at the University of Utah, Spring 1978 (Audrey Alvarado, Roya Ayman, Ellen Baker, Barbara Brown, David Dodd, Barbara Goza, Polly Hough, Dorothy Kagehiro, Bijan Marashi, Patricia Parmelee, and Anne Vinsel).

We also appreciate the perseverance and patience of the many people who assisted us as typists and editorial assistants. In particular, we wish to thank Susan Grant and Joan Larscheid for their efforts on the later versions of the manuscript and several others who worked on earlier drafts and reference materials. A special word of apppreciation goes to Judith Turner, who was with us from the very beginning and who guided the manuscript through many drafts. As sole proprietor, manager, editorial assistant, and typist for "Mother's Manuscripts," Judie Turner nurtured, cajoled, encouraged, and disciplined us with a fine maternal hand.

A special word of thanks is directed to administrators and colleagues at the University of Utah who provided us with the facilities, support, and time to work on this project in the form of sabbatical leaves and a fellowship to one of us. We also owe a great deal to the Brooks/Cole staff. Once again they demonstrated patience, commitment, and professionalism. In particular, we wish to thank William Hicks and Claire Verduin for their managerial skills. Sally Schuman squired us through the editing and production process with a gracious and competent hand. And we are particularly indebted to Rephah Berg for her delicate, conscientious, and incisive editing of the manuscript.

Finally, a word of thanks to our families. Gloria, Bill, and Dave Altman once again provided a fine balance of encouragement, good humor, and reality. Arlene, Michael, and Holden Chemers were, as always, patient and understanding under trying circumstances.

Irwin Altman
Martin Chemers

CONTENTS

Chapter 1

INTRODUCTION

This is a book about people, culture, and the physical environment. We are interested in how people and cultures affect their environments and how the physical environment affects cultures and people. Most important, the book emphasizes the theme that we cannot understand any member of this trio separately: we must consider the three as a unity. In the same way that, for example, automobile driving involves an inseparable linkage of many components—drivers, automobiles, roads, and laws—so people, cultures, and physical environments form a social "system," all of whose parts work together in an integrated way. Consider a few examples of this theme:

1. Different cultures see the physical environment in very different ways. The Oglala Sioux Indians have a circular conception of the world and design their homes and communities accordingly. To them the sky is round, the sun moves in a circle, and people's lives cycle through different periods. But ancient Chinese societies emphasized the rectangular quality of the world and designed their communities accordingly. How did these differences arise? Did differences in the environments and cultures of the ancient Chinese and the Sioux Indians lead these societies to see and act on the world so differently? This is one issue that we will pursue in the book.

2. The Mbuti Pygmies of Zaire, Africa, live in a rain forest so heavily vegetated that they can hardly see the sun or stars. For them the world is primarily horizontal, and the sun and sky have little religious or symbolic meaning in their life. Many other cultures, however, emphasize a vertical dimension of the universe in the form of heaven, earth, and, often, an underworld. It is easy to see how the physical environment shaped the Pygmy conception of nature. But what can be said about the beliefs of other cultures? Are they, too, affected by qualities of the physical environment? Do cultural values also affect how people perceive the environment? Or do cultural and environmental factors combine in some way? These are also questions that we shall wrestle with throughout the book.

3. Take a tangible example in the form of environments that people create, such as homes. Homes are designed in very different ways around the world. In the Middle East they have high ceilings to overcome the heat of the climate; in the South Pacific they are designed to capitalize on prevailing breezes; in Alaska Eskimo igloos effectively conserve heat and withstand wind and the elements. So housing design is often responsive to the demands of the environment. But there are also some strange exceptions (Rapoport, 1969a). Houses in certain parts of India are oriented toward sacred directions, often counter to the topography of the land. A culture in the jungles of Brazil has heavily roofed and thick-walled dwellings, which are uncomfortable in a tropical climate. And people often transplant housing designs to new environments where they may be inappropriate. For example, the English of the 19th century built traditional English cottages and mansions in India, often at odds with the climate.

How is it that environmental demands sometimes affect culture, whereas at other times cultural influences seem to influence what people do to the environment? Once again we see an interesting interplay of culture and environment, each influencing the other, as they function as parts of a single system.

4. We will also discuss a number of behavioral processes in relation to the environment, such as privacy and territoriality. Some cultures seem to have considerable privacy; others seem to have no privacy whatever. For example, some people in Java live in houses surrounded by walls, and outsiders do not enter others' homes without an invitation—much as in our own culture. Yet in other societies—for example, certain Chinese groups in Malaysia and the !Kung Bushmen in Africa—people live in extremely close and communal quarters, with little apparent privacy. A closer look at such cultures, however, reveals strategies that they have evolved to regulate social interaction. Such techniques do not always include the physical environment but may involve cultural styles, etiquette, and customs. So understanding a process like privacy requires an examination of whole social systems—not just environments alone, cultures alone, or individual characteristics alone. Once again the physical environment and culture blend together as a unity, each affecting and being affected by the other.

The preceding examples are intended to whet your imagination about the complex, exciting relations among people, culture, and environments that this book will discuss. Before proceeding, however, it is important to have consensus about language and terms, and so we will next give some definitions. Following that, we will discuss some theoretical properties of the relation between culture and the environment. Finally, we will outline the conceptual framework around which the book is organized.

SOME DEFINITIONS: CULTURE, ENVIRONMENT, AND PSYCHOLOGICAL PROCESSES

Culture

The term *culture* is commonly used in sociology, anthropology, and social psychology (see Kroeber and Kluckhohn, 1952, for a collection of 150 definitions of *culture*). It has been applied to many different-sized units of society, from "Western culture" down through "U.S. culture," "Southern culture," "suburban culture," "gang culture," and perhaps even "family culture." Thus, there are many levels of culture, from broad aspects of society to very small social units. A simple and broad definition of culture was offered by the anthropologist Herskovits (1952), who stated that culture is the man-made part of the human environment.

For our purposes the term *culture* has several key components. First, it refers to *beliefs and perceptions, values and norms, customs and behaviors of a group or society*. Culture includes what people believe to be true of the world, their lives, and the environment. It also includes their values, or what they hold to be good and bad, acceptable and unacceptable. Still another part of culture is a set of rules and beliefs about how to behave or do things. Thus, cognitions, perceptions, values, and modes of appropriate behavior constitute a cluster of characteristics implied in the concept of culture.

Second, the term *culture* is used to indicate that *cognitions, feelings, and behaviors are shared among a group of people in a consensual way*. That is, for a culture to exist, people must agree, with or without verbalizing their agreement, that there are common ways to view the world and to behave. This does not mean that they agree in all respects, but only that they share a common core of consensus. Thus, Western cultures more or less agree on a Judeo-Christian religious value system; Americans agree on the principle of a democratically elected government (even if they are sometimes apathetic about candidates). Americans also share principles of "fair play," "justice," and "equality" (even if they do not always practice these virtues). And urban gangs often exhibit extreme group loyalty, avoid squealing to the authorities, and respect other gangs' territories. Thus, consensus is a central feature of the concept of culture.

Third, the term *culture* implies that *these shared beliefs, values, and styles of behavior are passed on to others, especially children, and that the socialization and education of new members of the culture help preserve consensus from one generation to the next*. Thus, children learn eating manners appropriate to a family and to the larger society; they learn to share and compete, work and play. Social virtues are also taught, along with other beliefs and practices, including prejudices toward other groups, male and female sex roles, and sexual and other taboos. Through the socialization process cultures preserve themselves, even though successive generations may produce some changes. Except for dramatic events, such as revolutions or major upheavals, cultural changes are slow and evolutionary, partly because so much of a culture is implicit, taken for granted, and difficult to label.

Fourth, a society's values, beliefs, and practices involve more than "mental" and "behavioral" processes; *culture appears in objects and in the physical environment*. Home designs, community layouts, and public buildings often explicitly reflect the values and beliefs of a culture.

In summary, the concept of culture reflects a multifaceted set of things, from abstract principles about how to view the world to more concrete actions, such as ways of behaving and relating to the environment and ways of raising children. The question for us is how these different aspects of culture affect and are affected by the physical environment. Part of our strategy will be to adopt a cross-cultural perspective, to see how different societies relate to their physical environments. Comparative, cross-cultural analysis is rewarding in itself, and it also provides a vehicle for learning about one's own culture through the window of other cultures. For example, by understanding the Pygmies' beliefs about the nature of the universe, coupled with how they build homes, live communally, and rear their children, we can gain better leverage on understanding how our own culture and other cultures relate to the physical environment.

Environment

Physical environment is also a term with several dimensions. The physical environment can be subdivided into (1) the natural environment and (2) the built environment. *Natural environment* refers to places and geographical features, such as mountains, valleys, and oceans; environmental conditions, such as temperature and rainfall; and flora and fauna. *Built environment* refers to the results of people's alterations of environments—for example, homes, cities, communities, and farms. In some cases the built environment includes alterations of natural environmental conditions, such as artificial rainfall or pollution of air, water, and food.

A third dimension concerns the *scale of environments*. There are very small built environments, such as bathrooms, kitchens, and homes, and rather large built environments, such as communities and cities. Similarly, natural environments vary in scale from relatively small places, like streams and particular forests, to large places, such as wilderness regions, oceans, and continents. These different levels of scale are all important parts of the environment, and each can be a separate field of study.

Although this book cannot deal with all natural and built environments or with all levels of scale, try to keep these dimensions in mind, so that you will be sensitive to similarities and differences among cultures in relation to these and other facets of the environment.

Psychological Processes

Cultures and physical environments are linked with people and various psychological processes, which comprise two main classes: *mental activities* and *behavioral activities*. Mental activities include things that occur in the minds of people—what they see, hear, and smell and their interpretations about the physical environment. Mental activities also include beliefs and attitudes, positive or negative, concerning environments. These psychological processes are affected by the physical environment. For instance, a blinding snowstorm affects one's ability to discriminate distance and direction; a chronic food shortage influences cultural attitudes toward nature. But the way we perceive and feel about our environments also affects how we act to change and create physical environments. Thus, people may learn to build different structures as a result of their understanding of and feelings about climate, or they may drastically alter the physical environment as a result of cultural views about the functions of the environment in the lives of people—as in strip mining. So once again cultures, environments, and psychological processes operate in an interdependent system.

A second facet of psychological processes involves *overt behaviors*, or what people do and how they act in relation to the environment. Such behaviors include—among a host of others—attempts to achieve privacy and to establish and control territories, migrations, and uses of the land. We are particularly interested in how people in different cultures behave in similar and different ways with respect to the physical environment and in how overt behaviors are related to perceptions, cognitions, attitudes, and values about the environment.

THEORETICAL PERSPECTIVES ON CULTURE AND ENVIRONMENT

The relation among people, culture, and environment is certainly not a new topic of study. In fact, it forms the backbone of several disciplines in the social and behavioral sciences. Political scientists interested in geopolitics, for example, are very much concerned about the relation between political processes and geographic/cultural factors. Human ecologists who examine migration and settlement patterns focus on culture and environment. Anthropologists and archeologists are quite interested in how people in different cultures and at different periods in history have shaped their homes, communities, and cities in relation to cultural and environmental variables. But our approach differs in emphasis from these: namely, we will adopt a social-psychological perspective on the relation between culture and environment. That is, we plan to examine interpersonal relations and social interaction in the context of the physical environment, along with perceptions, cognitions, and attitudes that bear on social relations. Thus our interest will be in interpersonal, people-to-people processes, even though we will draw heavily on research and theory from other disciplines.

There have been several psychological and anthropological analyses that bear on relations between culture and environment. These fall under the label of studies of *cultural ecology* (Vayda, 1969; see Berry, 1975, for a review of illustrative research and thinking in this tradition). In general, the cultural-ecology viewpoint emphasizes the role of the physical environment as one powerful determinant of customs, life-style, and behaviors in different cultures. Some cultural ecologists adopt what Berry (1975) has termed a "strong" version of culture/environment relations. This view is that "environmental phenomena are responsible in some manner for the origin or development of the cultural behavior under investigation" (Vayda, 1969, p. xi). In this approach, environment is seen as strongly determining, limiting, and affecting behavior and cultural processes. Another approach, a "weak" orientation to culture and environment, is less firm in its view about how the environment affects social systems. Rather, it focuses on the interrelations of cultural and environmental variables in networks and patterns of dependencies and is less concerned with establishing hard and fast causal relations.

Consider some examples of these theoretical orientations. One example of the strong approach to culture/environment relations deals with child-rearing practices. Whiting (1964) observed that the circumcision of boys at puberty was quite prevalent in the rainy, tropical climates of Africa and certain South Pacific islands. His analysis of a number of cultures led to the hypothesis of a long causal chain by which climate—a physical environmental variable—affected the practice of circumcision. First, in tropical climates, food supplies are often low in protein, and the diet consists largely of fruits and roots. As a result, people often suffer a severe protein deficiency. Since mother's milk is a rich source of protein, there is a tendency in many of these societies to avoid pregnancy soon after childbirth, as a way of ensuring that nursing children receive adequate supplies of milk. Since sexual abstinence is an effective way to avoid pregnancy, the next link in the chain appears in the form of taboos on sexual activity during the extended nursing periods that occur in such societies. However, long periods of sexual abstinence may be an unstabilizing force in a society. As a compensatory practice, Whiting reasoned, such cultures may have adopted polygamy as an acceptable mode of life. Furthermore, because of the extended nursing period, it is also a practice in many of these cultures that a mother and child spend a great deal of time together for several years, including sleeping, which results in a very close mother/child relationship. As males approach adolescence, however, they need to break away from the mother and to begin identification with the male role. Whiting hypothesized that circumcision at puberty serves to enhance the male role and provides a dramatic vehicle for breaking the long-term psychological association between a boy and his mother.

Although one may wonder about the validity of this long causal chain, in which an environmental condition—climate—is hypothesized to result eventually in a circumcision ritual, Whiting's analysis is a good example of a strong approach to cultural ecology.

Leeds (1969, reported in Vayda, 1969) provides another instance of the strong cultural-ecology perspective in his analysis of the impact of environmental factors on the leadership structure of the Yaruro Indians of south central Venezuela. In this group there is apparently very little formal leadership, and when leaders do appear, they often seem to be ignored or play only a minor role in the life of the people. Leeds attributed this fact to the Yaruro agricultural system and to the seasonal climate that prevails in their environment. Agricultural practices are quite simple among the Yaruro and involve "slash and burn" techniques, with irregular rotation of crops to new pieces of land. In addition, these people live on naturally growing roots, game, fish, and domesticated pigs. Their food-production activities are performed with simple implements by one or two persons working alone and hence require little organization or leadership. Leeds hypothesized that ecological, geographical, and climatological features of Yaruro life led, over the years, to a system in which leaders were not especially powerful or influential because they were simply not needed. Once again we see an example of a strong cultural-ecology position that argues that environment strongly determines culture in a one-way causal process.

In an alternative perspective, Berry (1975) proposed a "weak" version of culture/environment relations. This view states that there are "functional interdependencies" among environmental and cultural variables and that it is not always easy to establish precise directions of what caused what. This position holds that it is more fruitful to examine culture/environment relations as part of an interdependent ecosystem, without always trying to establish exact causes and effects. It argues that culture/environment relations have, over the course of time, become such a complex web that it is not always possible to establish single-direction, chainlike relations between variables. The weak version of a cultural-ecology orientation suggests that it is best to examine culture/environment relations as a *network* of related factors, each of which can have an impact on another. Rather than thinking in terms of a long, involved causal chain, such as A causes B causes C, the alternative is to view $A \ldots C$ as a web of mutually related factors of the form $(A \leftrightarrow B, A \leftrightarrow C, B \leftrightarrow C)$.

An example of this way of thinking is Turnbull's analyses of the Mbuti Pygmies of the Ituri Forest of northeastern Zaire, Africa (Turnbull, 1961, 1968). The Pygmies live in a heavily vegetated rain forest, gather food that grows readily in the forest, and hunt the abundant wild game of the region. Turnbull observed different hunting styles among various Pygmy bands. Some bands worked in a cooperative arrangement involving many people and captured animals in large nets, while others used bows and arrows and hunted in small groups.

Two aspects of the difference in hunting styles were perplexing to Turnbull. First, members of each group, when visiting a member of the other, easily adopted the hunting techniques of their host. Second, and more important for our discussion, Turnbull observed that there were no apparent environmental reasons that these different hunting styles should exist. The terrain, climate, and food sources were all exactly the same, and the environment did not seem to place differential demands on net hunters and archer hunters. Turnbull speculated that the difference in hunting technique may have arisen *because* so few environmental demands were placed on the people that they had the freedom to develop individualistic styles. He stated that "part of the explanation may lie in the fact that in both cases, the environment is generous enough to allow alternative hunting techniques . . . thus a common basis of abundant vegetable food sources may make possible alternative and equally felicitous styles of hunting" (Turnbull, 1968, p. 135). This example nicely illustrates the principle that, although the environment may be an important contributor to cultural practices, its influence is not simple, and it does not generally operate in a strict, one-way, wholly causal fashion.

In another analysis compatible with a weak cultural-ecology approach, Berry (1976) integrated research from a variety of sources on the relation among environmental characteristics, management and accumulation of food resources, residential and community settlement practices, and family structure. He argued that climate, geography, and other environmental considerations may help determine the mode of food production, such as farming or hunting and gathering, which in turn may contribute to differences in family structure, child rearing, and personality. However, Berry also stated that such relations are highly probabilistic and often involve complex interrelations among variables.

As one example, Berry (1976) cited Murdock's (1969) analysis of 322 societies, which indicated the following: Food-gathering, hunting, and pastoral (herding) cultures tend to be nomadic, whereas fishing and agricultural societies tend to be more sedentary. Furthermore, the population of settled societies is usually larger than that of nomadic groups. Thus, style of food gathering, presumably related to environmental factors, is also related to settlement patterns. In addition, other data suggest that migratory hunting-and-gathering peoples have simpler social organizations and weaker leadership systems than settled societies, which tend to organize administratively and to have systematic leadership arrangements and political structures. Thus the Pygmies, a seminomadic group, have few rules and regulations about how to live and few strong leadership hierarchies.

Other work also suggests differences in child-rearing patterns between settled and nomadic groups (Barry, Bacon, & Child, 1957). Agricultural and settled groups seem to emphasize responsibility, obedience, and compliance, perhaps because people who live together and work in organized communities require more-structured social practices. Nomadic peoples often socialize children with an emphasis on independence and resourcefulness, which prepares them well for the unpredictable and sometimes harsh demands of their environment.

Thus, although the physical environment is obviously important in relation to cultural practices, its exact cause/effect role is often hard to pinpoint. Rather, cultural practices in relation to the environment seem to involve a complex network of events, not a simple chain of causation that begins with one variable and ends at another.

OUR CONCEPTUAL FRAMEWORK

Although some of our biases about the relation between environment and culture are probably already evident, let us now spell out the orientation that will guide the discussion in the rest of the book. We will not propose a full "theory" but only a framework of relevant variables and a general statement of their relations. What we will provide is more a way to view the field than it is a precise statement of exact relations among variables.

Figure 1-1 outlines our approach, a "social systems" orientation that is quite compatible with the "weak" version of the cultural-ecology perspective just described. The figure first suggests that several classes of factors, some of which were described above, are important to understanding the relation between culture and environment. These are the natural environment, environmental orientations and world views, environmental cognitions, environmental behaviors and processes, and environmental outcomes, or end products of behavior.

The natural environment includes such features of the physical environment as temperature, rainfall, terrain and geographic features, and flora and fauna. *Environmental orientations and world views* are global

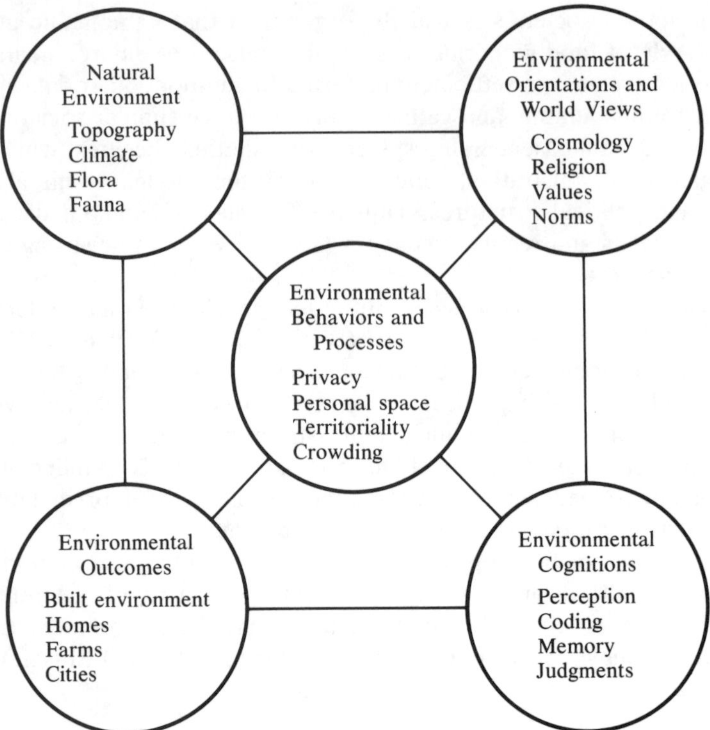

Figure 1-1. A framework of culture/environment relations.

views of the environment that relate to religions, values, and dominant modes of thought. *Environmental cognitions* are perceptions, beliefs, and judgments that people make about environments. *Environmental behaviors and processes*, such as personal space, territorial behavior, and privacy, are the ways that people use the environment in the course of social relations. *Environmental outcomes,* or products of behavior, include the results of people's actions—namely, (1) the built environment of homes, communities, and cities and (2) modifications of the natural environment, such as farms, dams, and climate changes.

Another feature of our social-systems approach is that simple linear, chainlike cause/effect relations are not always easy to identify, since every variable can theoretically serve as either a cause or an effect. For example, the strong environmental-determinist view described earlier often states that the physical environment affects culture in a one-way, linear fashion (*A* leads to *B*, which leads to *C*). Although environmental factors such as terrain and climate may indeed play an important role, the reverse can also occur: cultural practices and attitudes can result in drastic alterations of the environment. And people in the same environment often have totally different cultural practices. Thus, culture can affect environment, environment can affect culture, or the two may be independent. Accordingly, almost any variable in Figure 1-1 is capable of being a cause or an effect in relation to any other variable.

In short, our social-systems approach implies multiple directions of causation. By presenting variables in a network format with multidirectional connections between them, we wish to suggest that causes and effects can occur almost anywhere. This does not rule out the need to track particular cause/effect relations in particular research studies; that endeavor is quite necessary for scientific understanding. However, we should not forget that a directional relation found in a particular research study is not necessarily the universe of all possible relations. That is, the same variables in another context may be reversed in their roles as causes and effects.

A third feature of our systems orientation is that interventions in any part of the system can reverberate throughout the system. For example, environmental behaviors and processes (privacy, personal space, and territory) may be a cumulative result of perceptions and cognitions, cultural factors, environmental factors, and outcomes of earlier behaviors, or vice versa. A change in one part of this network of variables can have impacts throughout the system. If the physical environment changes, there can be impacts anywhere; or if there is a dramatic cultural change, there may well be a rippling effect throughout the system. Thus, a social-systems approach means that we are dealing with interrelated elements that have an interdependent relationship such that, at any given time, one part of the system can be a cause of changes in other parts of the system, and they all fit together as a network or pattern of events. We have placed behavior at the center of our network because such processes are central to the analyses that we, as social psychologists, generate. A systems approach implies, however, that any other concept could serve as the focus, depending on the particular interests of the author or investigator.

To summarize, we will adopt an orientation to the relation among environment, culture, and people that views them as an integrated and interdependent system—each part necessary to understand the others, each affecting the others in complex ways, and all parts contributing to a social system that has meaning only insofar as all the components are described together, simultaneously, and as a unity.

ORGANIZATION OF THE BOOK

This book is organized into three general parts. Part 1 contains two chapters that deal with the right-hand side of Figure 1-1. These chapters discuss subjective and mental aspects of culture/environment relations.

Chapter 2 describes general *environmental orientations and world views* that people from different cultures hold about their environments, including their positive and negative attitudes toward nature and their conceptions of the world and the universe. Chapter 3 examines *environmental cognition*. It describes recent empirical work on how people perceive and think about their environments, developmental processes in children, the knowledge held about different aspects of environments, environmental preferences, and how people perceptually and cognitively organize environments.

Part 2 comprises three chapters that deal with the middle part of Figure 1-1 and focus on *environmental behaviors and processes*. These include privacy regulation as a central process in different cultures (Chapter 4), personal space (Chapter 5), and territorial behavior (Chapter 6) as major vehicles by which people in groups regulate their contact and interaction.

Chapters 7 through 11 constitute Part 3 and deal with *environmental outcomes* depicted in Figure 1-1. Chapters 7 and 8 focus on the home as one outcome, or product, of people/environment relations. Chapter 7 examines homes from a cultural and historical perspective, and Chapter 8 focuses on the American home and its features, including size, design, and use of various rooms. Chapters 9 through 11 move to a different level of scale and consider small communities, towns, and cities. Chapter 9 addresses cultural and historical factors associated with community and city design. Chapter 10 examines adaptation to urban life, and Chapter 11 describes some futuristic city and community designs proposed by architects and urban planners.

Chapter 12, the final chapter, discusses practical, environmental design considerations, such as the design of homes and communities for different cultural groups. This chapter also summarizes some of the general themes of the volume.

As you read the various chapters, be sure to keep Figure 1-1 and the overall organization of the book in mind. We see all parts of the figure as constituting a unified system, but each part must necessarily be written about separately. So be sure to refer occasionally to the figure and our organizational plan so that you have the systems idea clearly before you.

Before reading the remainder of the book, you should also be aware that we cannot, and did not intend to, cover *all* possible topics relevant to culture/environment relations. Neglected topics include institutional environments, such as schools, prisons, and hospitals; workplaces; and recreational and leisure environments—to name just a few. Our goal was to focus in reasonable depth on selected issues rather than to scatter our energies and words across many topics. So it is important to realize that there are gaps in the book and that you can fill these in with your own research and analysis.

PART ONE

ENVIRONMENTAL ORIENTATIONS AND COGNITIONS

This section of the book presents two chapters that deal with the way people think and feel about their environment. Chapter 2 takes a broad look at cultural and historical differences in world views, or the general values that people hold about nature and about particular features of the natural environment. Chapter 3 is concerned with more specific cognitive and perceptual processes, such as thinking and categorization, learning and memory, and emotionality, in relation to the physical environment.

Since language, perceptions, and thought are central aspects of human functioning, how people perceive, think about, and remember their environments can be very illuminating. The ways people think and feel about the environment reflect mediating psychological processes that can give clues to the behaviors and actions that people may take with respect to the environment and to the shaping and influencing demands that the environment has placed on them.

You will see that in different cultures and at different times in history people have liked or disliked, felt close to or distant from, and ignored or attended to various aspects of their environments. How and why such differences exist is rather complex. Some cultures may change their physical environments, by technology and other means, while other cultures may try to mesh and blend with their environments. We assume that such differences are partly related to values and life-styles that evolved because they were adaptive for the survival of different societies in their unique environments. If some people are more sensitive to, know more about, and feel more positively toward certain features of their environments, it may be that successful adaptation in a particular ecocultural niche requires that knowledge and attention. In general, underlying our analysis of cognitive and perceptual orientations to the environment is the idea that these psychological processes are functional and became part and parcel of a given culture because they contribute to the well-being of that culture and its people.

Chapter 2

WORLD VIEWS OF THE ENVIRONMENT

This chapter examines the general orientations, attitudes and beliefs that different cultures have about nature and the environment. Different cultures see themselves as subordinate or dominant in relation to nature; people have positive and negative feelings about cities and the wilderness; they have diverse attitudes toward various places, such as mountains and oceans, and diverse perceptions and cognitions about horizontal and vertical dimensions of the world and the universe. The goal of the chapter is to explore the world views of people from different societies and historical periods and to analyze factors that contributed to their orientations to the environment.

The chapter is organized along a dimension of scale. We begin with very broad environmental orientations held by different cultures and gradually narrow the focus to more-specific attitudes and beliefs.

GENERAL ORIENTATIONS TO NATURE AND THE ENVIRONMENT

Florence Kluckhohn (1953), an anthropologist, described three general orientations to nature held by people in different cultures and at different times in history: (1) *people as subjugated to nature*, living at the mercy of a powerful and uncompromising nature; (2) *people as over nature*, dominating, exploiting, and controlling the environment; and (3) *people as an inherent part of nature*, like animals, trees, and rivers, trying to live in harmony with the environment.

Naturally, cultures are not singular in their orientation to nature, and it is likely that, although one of these views may predominate in a given society, any orientation may have elements of the other two. Thus, it is possible that societies hold aspects of all these orientations to one degree or another, although one may be a more salient force.

People as Subjugated to Nature

In many societies and periods of history, especially societies having little industrial technology or living in excessively harsh and unpredictable climates, people feel that they live under the control of nature. The environment is viewed as powerful, uncontrollable, and unpredictable, and all that people can do is adapt as best they can, be fatalistic, and accept the good and the bad from the environment. This world view implies that people can only act in a subordinate and submissive fashion in the face of all-powerful and all-dominating natural forces over which they have little direct control. People who live in earthquake regions, whether in Los Angeles, Italy, or Guatemala, exhibit elements of this orientation—a kind of resigned acceptance of a powerful nature. Farmers in dust-bowl regions and South Pacific islanders exposed to hurricanes and tidal waves often reflect a fatalistic value system that says "There will be good years and bad years; we must accept what comes and do the best we can; one must simply wait things out and hope for the best." People may interpret a serious disaster, such as an earthquake, as "the will of God" or as a punishment or warning from God to mend their ways. They may believe that they can exert some influence on a deity by praying and behaving properly, but they still often feel that they are relatively powerless and are subject to the will of God(s) or nature.

A vivid example of this orientation appears in medieval attitudes toward forests and the wilderness, attitudes that are richly conveyed in fairy tales and myths of Western Europe during the 12th through 15th centuries (Ittelson, Proshansky, Rivlin, & Winkel, 1974; Nash, 1967). In these writings the forest is the personification of evil. It is foreboding, dangerous, and uncontrollable. Forests and the wilderness are to be avoided or hurried through, and they are to be respected, feared, and accepted in a fatalistic way. Little Red Riding Hood hurried through the forest, quaking in her boots all the way; Hansel and Gretel were abused by a forest witch; story after story conveys the subjugation of people to the dark, gloomy, foreboding, and dangerous forests of the Middle Ages.

The medieval forest was also the habitat of demons and monsters who preyed on people. Nash (1967) stated:

> The most important imaginary denizen of the wildernesses of Medieval Europe was the semi-human Wild Man. His naked figure, covered completely with thick hair, appeared widely in the art, literature, and drama of the period. . . . According to folk tradition, the Wild Man lived in the heart of the forest as far as possible from civilization. He was regarded as a kind of ogre who devoured children and ravished maidens. The character of his mate varied from place to place. In the Austrian Tyrol and Bavarian Alps, the Wild Woman was imagined to have enormous size, tough bristles, immense pendulous breasts, and a hideous mouth that stretched from ear to ear. . . Her principal offense was stealing human babies and leaving her own offspring in their place [p. 13].[1]

[1] This and all other quotations from this source are from *Wilderness and the American Mind,* by R. Nash. Copyright 1967 by Yale University Press. Reprinted by permission.

Other monsters included werewolves, man-eating ogres, witches, and bizarre figures, such as one who had the face of a woman, the body of a pig, and the legs of a horse (Nash, 1967).

This fearful and submissive view of nature goes back even further in history, according to Nash (1967), and is based on the inability of people to control nature and on the association of nature with the supernatural and demonic. The early Romans looked upon forests as dangerous; classical Greek mythology referred to Pan, Lord of the Woods, who

> was pictured as having the legs, ears, and tail of a goat and the body of a man. He combined gross sensuality with boundless, sportive energy. Greeks who had to pass through forests or mountains dreaded an encounter with Pan. Indeed, the word "panic" originated from the blinding fear that seized travelers upon hearing strange cries in the wilderness and assuming them to signify Pan's approach. Related to Pan was the tribe of satyrs—goat-men of a demoniacal character devoted to wine, dancing, and lust. . . . According to Hellenic folklore, satyrs ravished women and carried off children who ventured into their wilderness lairs. Sileni and centaurs completed the Greek collection of forest spirits. These monsters had the torso and head of a man and the body, legs, and tail of a horse [p. 11].

A similar orientation appears in the early Judeo-Christian feelings toward the desert. People were afraid of and hated the desert because of its uncompromising demands, its uncontrollability, and its threat to human survival. For these people, Nash states, life was under the control of God, who could provide water and good crops or could punish them with drought. Thus, the desert and God were all-powerful, and people's only recourse was to adapt and to hope that good behavior would bring forth positive treatment. The ancient Hebrews also believed that there were monsters in the desert, such as winged female monsters and man-goats.

Although such views are not typical in modern societies, they do crop up from time to time. Farmers feel a sense of subjugation to nature in times of drought; skiers caught in a blinding snowstorm or hikers lost in the mountains often feel powerless in the face of nature; flood and earthquake victims often report a feeling of inferiority and inability to control nature. And we have our own "monsters" to match those of the Middle Ages. For example, there is "Bigfoot," or "Sasquatch," who shares a remarkable number of features with the medieval forest monsters. Rather than trembling in apprehension at the existence of such beings, though, our society sends out expeditions to study or capture the creature.

Thus, from the early Hebrews to the Greeks, to the Romans, to the Middle Ages, and even to the present, there are aspects of our lives—minor for some people, major for others—in which the natural environment is powerful, uncontrollable, and uncompromising. Such features lead us, to varying degrees, to see nature as something to which we must adapt, bend, and be respectful—something larger than ourselves.

People as above Nature

The second world view of nature is diametrically opposed to the preceding perspective. As described by Ittelson et al. (1974), Kluckhohn (1953), Nash (1967), and Tuan (1974), this world view states that people are "above" nature. That is, humans are separate from nature, are superior to it, and have a right and even a responsibility to control, subjugate, and bend the environment in accordance with human needs. This orientation has predominated in Western cultures and is especially characteristic of American life. It appears in many facets of our lives—food production, use of natural resources, land use, and exploitation of the earth. Farmers have eagerly adopted pesticides, fertilizers, and other forms of technology to generate higher quality and greater crop yields. Rather than allowing nature to take its course—for example, through natural ecological relationships between insects—we have created more-effective insecticides to overpower "pests." In the area of natural resources, such as mining, a value exists that we have the obligation and the right to draw from the earth that which is beneficial to people, and in some instances we have carried it to the extreme of strip mining, deforestation, and resource depletion. Clearly, such activities reflect our view that nature exists to serve people and that almost any form of "progress" that makes life easier or more pleasant is acceptable.

Perhaps the areas of exploration and science most vividly typify Western views of nature as being subordinate to people. We speak of "conquering the wilderness" or of climbing Mount Everest "because it is there" and because the act symbolizes people's special place in the world. We revel in the "conquest" of space, and the phrase "a giant step for mankind," uttered by the first astronaut to walk on the moon, implies that we have overcome the forces of nature on earth and can now begin to control the universe. Scientists speak of "cracking" the genetic code, "unlocking" nature's secrets; engineers and dam builders refer to "harnessing" nature and "exploiting" untapped resources—all of which symbolizes the modern view that people are different from nature, are superior to it, and have the right and the responsibility to overcome nature.

What are the historical and cultural roots of this orientation? According to several writers (Ittelson et al., 1974; Nash, 1967; Tuan, 1974), there are at least two major origins of this world view: the Judeo-Christian heritage of Western society and the scientific and industrial revolution of the past 200 years.

As described earlier, uncontrolled nature and the wilderness were historically viewed in Western society as dangerous and to be feared, although they sometimes served a purification and penance function (when religious leaders like Moses and Jesus spent time in the desert alone, communing with God and cleansing their souls). There also was the belief among early Judeo-Christian peoples that "controlled" and "conquered" nature, in the form of farms and cities, was desirable and that God would help them create such places if they conscientiously practiced religious values. To multiply, to grow food, to build temples, to convert the wilds to civilization became an important value. This set of values was reinforced by the theological doctrine that man was created in God's image and, as such, was chosen to represent God on earth in a unique way. A capstone thought that crystallizes the point appears in Genesis 1:28: "The first commandment of God to man stated that mankind should increase, conquer the earth, and have dominion over all living things" (Nash, 1967, p. 31).

It was an easy next step to the idea that people are somehow separate from and above animals and other things in nature and that people were placed on earth by God to regulate and to bring order to the earth. The idea of evil in unsettled nature began with Adam and Eve and their expulsion into the "bad" world outside the Garden of Eden. From then on people had the religious duty to control and tame the wilderness into which Adam and Eve had been thrust:

> In early and Medieval Christianity, wilderness kept its significance as the earthly realm of the powers of evil that the Church had to overcome . . . Christians judged their work to be successful when they cleared away the wild forests and cut down the sacred groves where the pagans held their rites [Nash, 1967, p. 17].

This theme carried over to the settlement of the United States, beginning with the early Puritans, extending through the development of the West, and even holding to the present day. The wilderness was feared by the Pilgrims but was also something to be overcome and conquered, as a religious obligation. The goal was "to carve a garden from the wilds; to make an island of spiritual light in the surrounding darkness" (Nash, 1967, p. 35). The Pilgrims were to break the stranglehold of evil that lurked in the darkness of the wilderness and to make the light of the Gospel shine through and be evident everywhere. Building cities, towns, farms, and gardens was doing God's work and fulfilled the destiny of humans as God's agents. One can easily see how such values served a young and growing society located in a natural environment of unparalleled abundance and potential.

This world view was sustained throughout the development of the American frontier. As Nash states, the frontier was described during this period as "the enemy," which had to be subdued and conquered. There was an ever-present struggle with nature, the object of which was to create a prosperous society. Reclaiming nature, transforming the wilderness into fruitful and productive land, creating a Garden of Eden are a few seminal ideas that were central in one of Andrew Jackson's inaugural addresses (cited in Nash, 1967, p. 41): "What good man would prefer a country covered with forests and ranged by a few thousand savages to our extensive Republic, studded with cities, towns and prosperous farms, embellished with all the improvements which art can devise or industry execute?"

These views were further perpetuated in modern Western society under the aegis of the scientific and industrial revolution (Ittelson et al., 1974). Science and technology rapidly produced vehicles for conquering nature and reinforced the idea that people were above and separate from nature. To control temperature, to cure illness, to raise food efficiently, to be able to kill animals and people in large numbers, to explore outer space, to build bridges over seemingly uncrossable rivers, to construct dams and massive irrigation systems, to settle "uninhabitable" land, and to mine the earth's resources all attested to the superiority and uniqueness of people.

The feeling of omnipotence grew and grew, as human accomplishments meshed with the Judeo-Christian value of people as something special and above all other creatures. Beauty was found not in untended nature but in the transformation of nature into farms and cities, the unlocking of nature's secrets, and the ability to change the course of nature on a dramatic scale, all of which is reflected in recent genetic experiments, nuclear energy, lasers, and other 20th-century exploits.

Two other facets of Judeo-Christian values and the scientific revolution contributed to the predominant Western view of people as separate from and above nature: a linear view of the universe and the scientific philosophy of experimentation.

Judeo-Christian values and modern Western societies have a linear view of life. There is, in this view, a beginning to history, as reflected in the text "In the beginning God created the heaven and the earth." There is also a hypothesized end of life or continuation of life in a new form, in the eventual appearance (or reappearance) of the Messiah and the Messianic Age and in an afterlife in heaven or hell. The Western sense of history is continuous and progressive, with a value that we must strive toward some distant, long-term goal. As discussed below, this is not a universal value, for many cultures currently and throughout history have held a cyclical view of nature and people, whereas we in Western society think more about movement forward, progress, and a long-term expectation of a future full of glory or suffering (depending on our actions). This value system has permitted us to act on and subdue nature, to control it and alter it, because doing so fits with the idea of a future optimal state that depends on our fulfilling God's dictum to multiply and alter the earth.

The value of experimentation and change also pervades Western science, as typified in the premium we place on experimentation as a scientific method. Learning by changing things—by experimenting—is valued more than learning by observation and noninterference. Although there are aspects of science that call for less experimentation and more observation, the central ethos in Western science is change, control, and experimentation. For this reason, Western science and technology fit perfectly with the Judeo-Christian ethic of people as above nature, as controllers of nature, and as separate from it.

Naturally, we have overstated the case of Western values in relation to the environment, for there have been, and are today, many countertrends. However, Western society has had a long tradition of viewing people as separate from and superior to nature, and this orientation derives from a host of sources, not the least of which are our religious and scientific heritages.

People as Part of Nature

A third world view, prevalent in many contemporary and historical cultures, states that humans are an intrinsic part of nature in the same way as animals, trees and flowers, thunder and lightning. For example, Ittelson et al. (1974) describe how the early Greeks, in spite of certain feelings of subjugation to nature, viewed the universe as a harmonious unity, of which people were part. For the Greeks, nature was a stable, orderly, and smoothly operating system. Events moved in a systematic and cyclical fashion—days and nights progressing regularly, seasons following one another, natural events occurring predictably, and people's lives flowing in a clocklike and orderly way. Even life and death had a quality of harmony and cycling.

Perhaps the best-known examples of harmony with nature appear in Oriental philosophy and religion. Although there are many varieties of Oriental thought, these ways of thinking have a common core: All things in nature are sacred and are not to be unduly exploited by people. Moreover, people's lives, including their moods and feelings, are intertwined with nature. One cannot impose oneself on nature; rather, one must flow with it, be part of it, understand its changing patterns, and adapt to natural events. This does not mean passivity or surrendering; it means understanding nature's flow and changes and working within its boundaries. Most essential is the idea that people are not the center of a natural universe that revolves around them, but that people are part of nature and must blend with it and be responsible for it.

Other examples of this orientation come from the Pygmies of the Ituri Forest of Zaire and several American Indian groups (Ortiz, 1972; Rapoport, 1969b; White, 1964). As noted in Chapter 1, the Pygmies live in a tropical rain forest that is heavily vegetated and abundant in food (Turnbull, 1961). The Pygmies see themselves as an intrinsic part of the forest, no less so than the animals and plants. Because they live in such a benign environment, they have little fear of the forest. Their feelings are well captured in the statement made by a Pygmy: "The forest is a father and a mother to us, and like a father or mother it gives us everything we need—food, clothing, shelter, warmth . . . and affection. Normally everything goes well, because the forest is good to its children" (p. 92). When misfortune happens, the Pygmies believe that the forest must have been sleeping and was therefore not able to take care of them. So they seek its help: "We wake it up by singing to it, and we do this because we want it to awaken happy. Then everything will be well and good again" (p. 92).

Thus, the Pygmies exist in harmony with the natural environment, see it as alive and concerned about them, and conceive of themselves as children of the forest, living with other parts of nature as a family.

Many American Indian cultures similarly think of themselves as children of nature. Some consider the earth and land to be the mother, the sky the father, the animals brothers and sisters, all of whom live together as a family. People are no better and no worse than the other members of the earth's family; they are all part of the family (Neihardt, 1961).

There is also a strong feeling among American Indians that people and nature are interdependent. Nature is to be preserved and cared for, and one must take only what one really needs, whether it be food, water, or some other resource. In some groups this value is carried to the extent of apologizing to nature when one takes something from it. Little wonder that the American Indians were mystified by the White people's large-scale slaughter of buffalo during the 19th century. The massive killing was a clear violation of the principle of taking only what one needed to survive. The fact that only skins and fur were used and meat was left to rot was an even greater transgression and wasting of nature's resources.

Harmony with nature is also reflected in the beliefs of the Pueblo Indians of the southwestern United States (Ortiz, 1972; White, 1964). According to Ortiz, the Pueblo Indians consider the sun to be their father and the earth their mother. Earth and sun govern life and create an endless series of cycles—summer and winter, spring and fall, day and night, life and death, growth and decay. Thus, beginnings and endings are unimportant; rather, there is a process of emergence and reemergence, a cycling through and around of life. As Ortiz (1972) put it:

> Within this general metaphysical order, the human life cycle might be portrayed metaphorically as a slowly revolving giant cylinder on which are

> imprinted the generations. Thus to die in a pueblo is not to become dead but to return to the only real life there is; one "changes houses" and rejoins the ancestors, but one can come back later [p.145].

The Pueblo Indians' harmonious and unending relationship with nature is also reflected in their mythology about the origin of people on earth, described in more detail later in this chapter. They believed that the earth had four layers and the people first lived deep inside, at the most central layer. The people gradually moved upward as Mother Earth caused trees and food to grow at successively higher strata. At each layer there was a hard crust, and Mother Earth asked various insects and other animals that she had created to make holes so that people could climb to the next layer. Thus, under the guidance and control of Mother Earth, all creatures took part in the emergence of life from the lower levels of earth.

Furthermore, Pueblo cosmology viewed the world as flat, with four corners and several cardinal points. Each place had a god—of leaves, of winter and summer, of agriculture, and others. And the key directions each had its own animal—the puma lived in the north, the bear in the west, the bobcat in the south. Thus, everything had its place in the scheme of things, and people, animals, resources, and seasons were part of the family of Mother Earth and Father Sun. People were part of nature, not above it or subjugated to it.

Many of us nowadays sometimes experience such oneness with nature. Being near the ocean and experiencing the crashing of waves against rocks or the ebb and flow of tides can arouse a sense of unity with nature. Or hiking alone in the mountains can produce a feeling of awe and a sense that one is a part of nature, albeit a relatively insignificant part. Very often, when we leave the built environments of cities and suburbs and go to natural environments, we experience an almost unverbalizable feeling of being part of the natural environment, not being separate from it. The upsurge of interest in camping and backpacking in recent years may reflect a desire to experience such links with nature. We take our families or go alone to wilderness areas, we visit natural parks, hiking, eating, and living in nature, ofttimes rejecting technology and being proud of the "primitive" way in which we live on a backpacking trip. Many people have joined survival-training classes to learn how to live off the land and to survive in wilderness settings. Following such experiences, people often say that they have rediscovered themselves, understand nature and their role in it better, and realize that they are part of the natural environment, not separate from it. Does all this reflect an attempt to alter the long-standing Western value of people as above nature?

The modern ecology movement may also reflect the idea of people in harmony with nature. Attempts to preserve wilderness areas, to recycle resources, to take part in reforestation projects, to argue vociferously against pollution of the air and water—all reinforce the idea that people should not unduly exploit nature. Rather, ecology advocates argue that we must recognize our reliance on nature and our interdependence with the environment. It is hard to assess, however, whether recent sensitivity to ecological concerns reflects a deeply rooted value system of the type espoused by Eastern philosophies and by American Indians or whether it is really only a statement of the need to exploit nature more carefully, while still holding to the basic superiority of people over nature. After all, even modern-day ecologists are children of 2000 years of Judeo-Christian values and 200 years of the scientific/industrial revolution.

The three general world views described above are somewhat overstated. Most cultures, especially technologically complex ones, are apt to have elements of all three perspectives embedded in their value systems, and so what we have presented should be taken as a highlighting of alternative perspectives, not a categorical classification system.

ATTITUDES TOWARD THE NATURAL AND THE BUILT ENVIRONMENT

The preceding section dealt with very general views of nature. In this section we examine people's orientations to particular parts of the environment—namely, the city in comparison with the "garden," or rural, environment and these two in comparison with the wilderness, or untamed, environment. Yi-Fu Tuan (1971, 1974), a humanistically oriented geographer, has provided an excellent analysis of attitudes toward these three aspects of the environment, and the following discussion is based heavily on his writings.

At different periods in history and in different cultures, people have held a variety of attitudes toward the wilderness, the city, and the developed landscape of farms, villages, and rural areas. There often have been conflicting attitudes toward these environments, people sometimes having positive, sometimes negative, and sometimes ambivalent feelings toward the same environmental feature. We often speak of both the advantages and disadvantages of city life, in the form of availability of facilities and the stimulating quality of cities, on the one hand, and noise, pollution, and crowding, on the other. The farmer's love and appreciation of the soil are often mingled with fear and concern about the unpredictability of weather and seasons. And we often speak of the beauty of being alone in undeveloped wilderness, away from the hubbub of our daily lives, yet we also have strong needs for the company of others. Thus, many of our attitudes toward the built, natural, and modified landscape are an intermingling of positive and negative feelings, one or the other feeling dominating at different times. So it is with cultural and historically based views toward the built, modified, and natural environment, as reflected in Figure 2-1, adopted from Tuan (1971, 1974).

The *Edenic ideal* reflects a value that has appeared at different times throughout history. The biblical Garden of Eden, the monastery, and the utopian communities of the 19th century are examples of this value. Here, nature that has been groomed is "good," as in pastoral settings of gardens, farms, and planned communities. Uncontrolled, wild, and primitive nature, in contrast, is "bad." The biblical account of the casting out of Adam and Eve from the benign Garden of Eden into the "cursed ground overgrown with thorns and thistles" and the later promise of "a land flowing with milk and honey" reflect the value of "developed nature" (but not too developed) as being better than the wilderness.

While this value system has predominated at certain periods of history, there has also often been some feeling that the wilderness had some positive features. Biblical characters, such as Moses, Jesus, and early ascetics such as the Essenes, often went into the wilderness alone to purify themselves and to clarify their thoughts, to better experience the Almighty, and to confront God and evil in a setting unencumbered by distractions.

At other times in history, attitudes toward city, rural, and wilderness environments had a different configuration. For example, in certain biblical periods, cities were held in esteem because of their symbolic value. Many ancient cities were monuments to political and religious values and represented the cohesion of societies. At other times, cities were treasured as centers of art, culture, politics, and economics. Very often the city was seen as the center and epitome of civilization, as in Plato's Republic and biblical Jerusalem. For many cultures, then, the city was a very desirable place, and it stood in sharp contrast to the wild, untamed wilderness of forests and deserts. In many present-day developing nations, such as Ghana and Tanzania, cities are seen as very positive places (Gould, 1973b).

Still another orientation appears in what is called the "*juxtaposed ideals*" of city and nature, in which both were held in esteem simultaneously or positive and negative attitudes alternated over time. For example, in medieval China there was a mixture of feelings about the city and the countryside, especially among the scholar-politicians who administered the Chinese Empire. The great cities of that period offered a life of culture, politics, and power; the rural life offered the opportunity for study and reflection. Many leaders of this period spent part of their time in the city and part in the country, shifting back and forth as political and personal needs demanded. Similarly, writers in 18th- and 19th-century England referred to the mixed blessings of cities and the countryside. Cities offered stimulation, camaraderie, arts, good food, and exciting living. But they were also cluttered, noisy, distracting, and dirty. The countryside was idyllic, sheltered, calm, and close to nature, but it was also unstimulating, lonely, and limited in intellectual possibilities.

1. The Edenic ideal

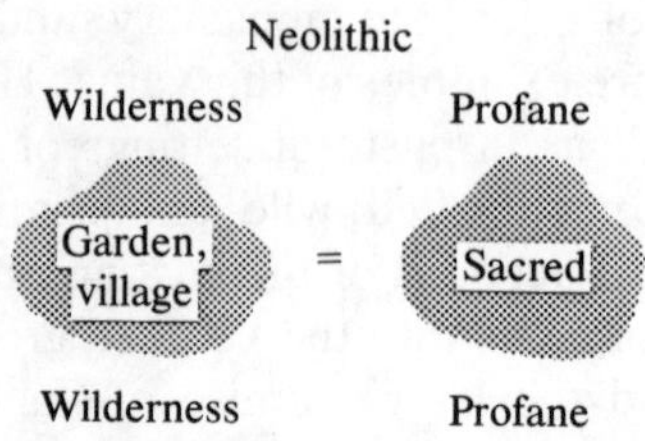

Historical Examples

a. Eden and wilderness
b. Monastery and wilderness
c. The New England town and wilderness
d. The American seminary or college and wilderness
e. American utopian communities (first half of 19th century)

---

2. Urban revolution and the cosmic ideal

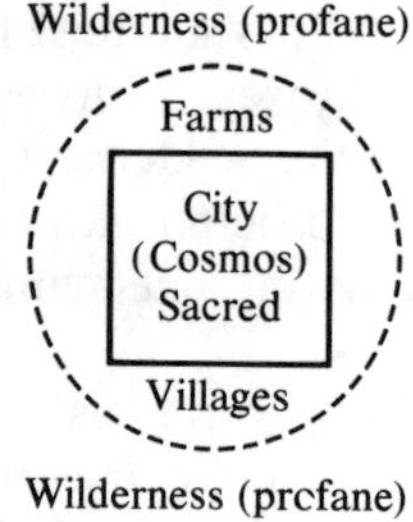

Utopia

a. Plato's Republic
b. New Jerusalem

---

3. The two juxtaposed ideals

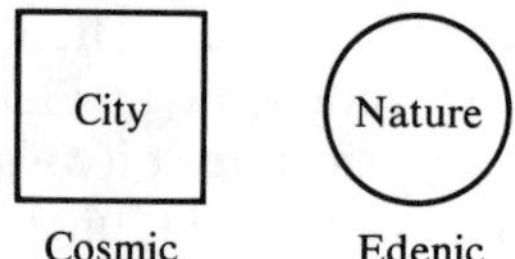

Pastoral (bucolic) { a. Alexandrian Greece
b. Augustan Rome

Garden { c. T'ang-Sung China
d. Renaissance Europe

Countryside e. 18th- and 19th-century England

---

4. The ideal of the "Middle Landscape" (Jeffersonian ideal: late 18th to mid-19th century)

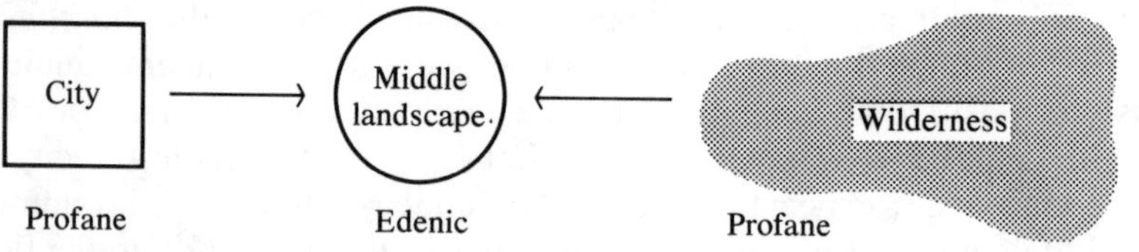

The "Middle landscape" of yeoman farmers is seen as threatened by the city on the one side and by wilderness on the other. In fact, this was a time when both the city and the middle landscape were expanding at the expense of wilderness. Thus:

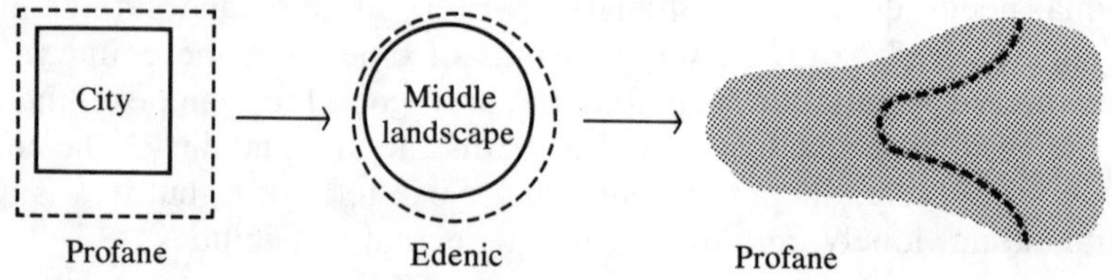

5. Late 19th-century values

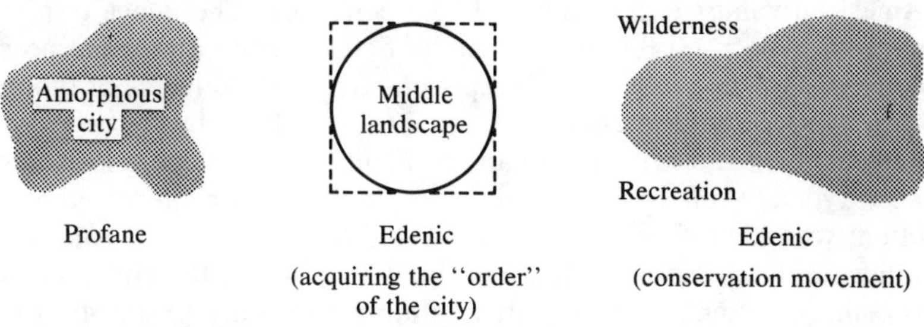

6. Middle- and late-20th-century values

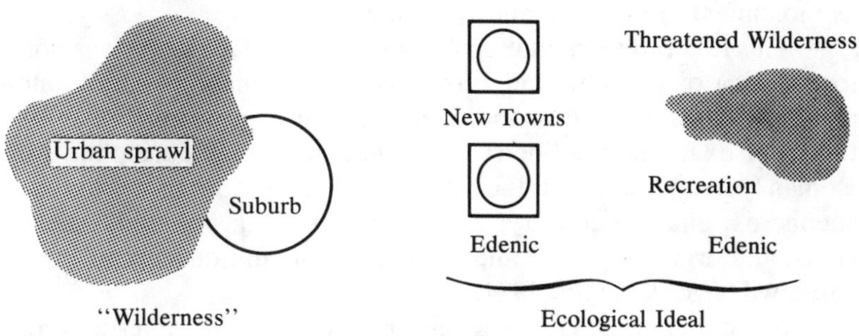

Figure 2-1. Wilderness, garden, city. From "Man and Nature," by Y. F. Yuan, Resource Paper No. 10 of the Commission on College Geography, 36–37. Copyright 1971 by the Association of American Geographers. Reprinted by permission.

Still another orientation, the so-called *Jeffersonian ideal*, involved strong negative feelings toward both the city and the wilderness, coupled with the upholding of the rural, garden, pastoral "middle landscape" as the ideal environmental setting. Thomas Jefferson (cited in Tuan, 1971, 1974) stated this value succinctly:

> Those who labour in the earth are the chosen people of God. . . . The mobs of great cities add just as much to the support of pure government as sores do to the strength of the human body [1974, p. 108].[2]

> I should wish [Americans] to practice neither commerce nor navigation. . . . We should avoid thus all wars, and all our citizens would be husbandmen [1971, p. 35].

[2]This and all other quotations from this source are from *Topophilia: A Study of Environmental Perception, Attitudes, and Values*, by Y. F. Tuan. Copyright © 1974 by Prentice-Hall, Inc. Reprinted by permission.

The virtues of the rural life and the disdain for cities were central American values in the 18th and 19th centuries. The image of a simple, hard-working rural family plowing its fields, taming the wilderness, and adhering to basic religious precepts embodied basic ideals of the period. Cities and the wilderness were viewed negatively and were believed to be the loci of sin and evil. American presidents of the 18th and 19th centuries were typically of the landed gentry or were from rural areas, and they often were identified with, and appealed to, the image of Americans as solid, rural, agricultural folk. Yet the vilification of the city was not universal. For example, Jefferson was not drawn only to the rural life; he also appreciated civilization and culture. Although he deplored the evils of city life, he supported the development of cities like Washington, D.C., as monuments to culture and sophistication.

This favorable orientation toward the rural landscape was not unique to America of the 18th and 19th centuries. It also appeared among the ancient Chinese, the Romans, and Western Europeans of the 19th century. For example, the poetry of Virgil and Horace during the Augustan Roman period reflected the ideal pastoral scene of secluded farms, shepherds, and the countryside, in contrast with polluted, ostentatious, crass, and orgiastic Rome and the desolation and dangers of the uncultivated wilderness (Tuan, 1974).

Beginning in the late 19th century, especially in America, a dramatic shift occurred in attitudes toward the undeveloped wilderness. No longer was it viewed as wholly evil and as something to be conquered. Instead, early conservationists (like members of the current ecology movement) viewed the wilderness as beautiful, as serving esthetic and recreational needs, and as having an almost religious quality. At the same time, cities were perceived to be more and more undesirable. They took on the image of a new form of wilderness—uncontrolled, dangerous, and harboring demons (criminals).

A further shift in values occurred in the 20th century, as people began to seek a kind of technologically advanced Jeffersonian middle landscape, in the form of suburban communities. In such places people could have gardens, a patch of greenery, and their own homes—a modern-day equivalent of the Jeffersonian ideal. But with the extraordinary growth of population in the United States during the 20th century, we have even come to view many suburban developments with disfavor. Many such developments are seen as a new form of wilderness—sprawling, unplanned, depersonalized tracts of houses with no sense of individuality or respect for quality of life.

This concern with the negative qualities of cities and suburban life has given rise to a new ideal life-style, reflected in the so-called "new towns" of Reston, Va., Columbia, Md., and other places (see Chapter

11). These are planned communities that combine green space and open space with urban services and cultural resources. Many see these communities as being ideal in the sense of combining the virtues of cities with those of the pastoral life; for example, they offer stimulation but serenity, availability of amenities but proximity to nature. For many people the concept of planned communities coupled with the appreciation and protection of wilderness represents the new millennium.

In the discussion thus far, we have seen how people throughout history and in different cultures viewed nature and the built environment at a broad, cosmological level, and we have examined the balance between their positive and negative feelings toward nature, the pastoral environment, and the built environment. You should keep in mind several themes of the discussion:

1. Cultures vary considerably in their orientations to the environment. This diversity can be attributed to a variety of factors, such as the properties of the environment itself, religious and social values, and available technology. It is rarely likely that any of these factors by itself is "the cause" of differences in world views. Rather, such factors probably form a network of influences that jointly affect orientations to the environment.

2. Attitudes toward the environment are not fixed. Because of the limited span of our own cultural perspective, we tend to view present-day attitudes and relationships with the environment as permanent. But, as shown earlier in this chapter, environmental orientations change even within our own lifetimes, and it is likely that those of us living in fast-moving modern societies will continue to see dramatic changes in environmental values.

3. Although the general cultural and historical world views described thus far are often salient, their complexity should not be overlooked. For example, although a negative attitude toward the wilderness might have prevailed at one time in history or for a particular culture, it is also likely that there were often simultaneously positive feelings. Thus, world views are probably a mixture of positive and negative attitudes, although one feeling may dominate to some degree at a given moment in history.

ORIENTATIONS TO PARTICULAR PLACES

There are also many places in the environment that have been viewed with positive or negative feelings. These include mountains, the sea, islands, and valleys. Tuan (1974) did interesting analyses of attitudes held toward such places, and we will rely heavily on his writings.

Mountains

Early people looked upon mountains with intermingled fear, respect and wonder. Mountains were remote, majestic, mysterious, impenetrable, and threatening, and they often were symbols of the power and dominance of nature. As a result, mountains played an important role in the religion and cosmology of many cultures. For some religions, the mountains served as a central axis of the earth—the place where sky and earth came together, the place where the human spirit could feel closest to the sky and to God and the universe. Thus, Moses received the Ten Commandments and had contact with God on Mount Sinai; Mount Olympus, in Greece, was believed to be the home of the gods; Mount Fuji has considerable religious significance to the Japanese. The idea of mountains as central axes of the earth and as a link with heaven appears in many cultures—Chinese, Korean, Iranian, Asian Indian, German. Even small hills and elevated points were often used to symbolize the cosmic and religious importance of mountains. For example, the Greeks located their temples on the Acropolis, the highest point in Athens, and on similar sites in other cities. Furthermore, people often built symbols of mountains, such as the stepped pyramids of the Middle East, the ziggurats of Sumeria, and the gigantic pyramids of Egypt. In addition, cathedrals and temples of Western Europe are often the tallest structures in a community, perhaps to symbolize their reaching toward the heavens, as mountains do.

In some cultures reverence for mountains was accompanied by fear and hostility, whereas in others feelings of awe were blended with love and favorable attitudes. For example, the biblical Hebrews viewed mountains with respect and love. Mountains were peaceful, symbolized strength and righteousness, and signaled the presence of God. Among the ancient Greeks, however, mountains had a mixed message. They were the home of gods and were places of infinite beauty; yet they also had elements of wildness, desolation, and terror. To the later Romans, mountains were largely negative and undesirable places. Thus, over the course of early Western civilization, attitudes toward mountains covered the gamut from very positive to very negative views.

Among Western cultures, negative attitudes toward mountains lasted well into the 18th century, and not until the 19th century did feelings toward mountains begin to be more positive (Tuan, 1974). From then on, mountains have been described as "sublime," "spectacular," "exquisite," and "the essence of natural beauty." With the development of the western United States and the increased ease of transportation, mountains were looked upon in a very positive way. They became places in which to relax, to restore one's health, and to escape the pressures of day-to-day living. Among Jews who immigrated to the United States between 1890 and 1930 and among their children, the mountains of upstate New York were places to relax, recuperate, and become rejuvenated. Even though many of these people were born and bred in urban settings, there was still a certain magic associated with the mountains and countryside (Howe, 1976).

In summary, mountains have always been special places, often associated with religious and cosmological beliefs. Present-day attitudes toward them—in the Western world, at least—seem to be mainly favorable. Perhaps this fact is due to technological developments that have made mountains more accessible and less mysterious, or it may reflect a historical phase in a cycle of positive and negative orientations toward mountains and other aspects of the natural environment.

Seashores, Valleys, Islands

Tuan observed that some places have been almost universally viewed in a positive way. These include seashores, valleys, and islands.

Beaches, seashores, and river sites were probably original habitats of people. Many cultures developed near oceans, which in moderate climates provided a number of virtues—food, transportation, and security. The seashore also offers stimulation in the form of waves, changing tides and currents, a sense of the unending and infinite, and some danger if one is not careful. The seashore has also been praised for its healthful characteristics and its recreational possibilities.

The valley or basin, coupled with streams and rivers that flow through it, has also frequently been perceived as a desirable place. As Tuan noted, the valley may symbolically represent a womb or shelter and may be a place protected from the elements by surrounding mountains and hills and a site where one can easily farm and grow food. Valleys and their water supplies provide a continual source of new and rich soil and are generally a placid and secure place. Although some valleys have poor drainage and inconsistent water supplies and occasionally flood, valleys have generally been viewed throughout history as favorable and nurturant places.

The island has also been perceived historically with good feelings—as an idyllic place where one could live in abundance, in simplicity, and away from the burdens of complex societies. Islands often have an imaginative and romantic quality. In some mythologies they were the land of immortals and were places where afflictions of the body and soul were absent. The early Greeks saw islands as the habitats of heroes; medieval Europeans saw them as paradises of ease and abundance. Especially popular throughout medieval Europe was the legend of Saint Brendan. In a 12th-century Anglo-Norman version of the tale, Brendan searched for an island that could be a home for the pious, a place "where no tempest revels, where for nourishment one inhales the perfume of flowers from paradise" (Tuan, 1974, p. 119).

The idea of island paradises also existed in the period of European exploration of the New World. Ponce de León, in his search for the Fountain of Youth, thought Florida was an island; Columbus and others saw the New World "as small delectable island gardens" (Tuan, 1974, p. 119). Furthermore, such South Sea islands as Tahiti, the Hawaiian Islands, and Borneo have always loomed in Western people's imaginations as idyllic places. Even today our images of tropical islands are vividly portrayed in the travel sections of magazines—swaying palms, sun-drenched beaches, crystal-blue lagoons, happy and impeccably beautiful natives lolling in their tropical gardens. We ignore or downplay problems of hurricanes, tidal waves, hostile sea life, protein-poor diets, and innumerable diseases that are rampant in such places, and we ignore the restricted quality of such environments. Instead, islands are viewed with anticipation, as places where we can escape the pressures and stresses of our ordinary social and physical environments.

DIMENSIONS OF ORIENTATION TO THE ENVIRONMENT

So far we have examined attitudes and orientations to geographic places. Here our focus shifts to some of the dimensions that underlie these orientations. For example, we will describe how different cultures view the world along a central/peripheral dimension of closeness to or distance from themselves and along the vertical dimension, seen in the division of the cosmos into sky, earth, and underworld. We will also describe systems of orientation developed in different cultures, such as the four cardinal directions of north, south, east, and west.

The Vertical

Heaven, earth, and hell represent a vertical dimension of the universe which we in the Western world learn early and which continues to be vivid and real throughout our lives. We see the endless sky, and it is easy to speculate about heaven. We are on the earth, and it is all around us every day. Hell is not so visually evident, but it is easy to extend the vertical dimension downward, especially when we use a negative pole as a counterpoint to the positive heaven. Thus, for Westerners the universe has a vertical dimension anchored by positive and negative places at its ends. The belief of an upper world, a middle world (the earth), and an underworld is not unique to Western culture or to modern times. Tuan (1974) found such a perspective throughout history among the ancient

Sumerians (3000 B.C.) of the Middle East, the ancient Chinese, the Pueblo Indians, and others.

It is also interesting that we refer to the heavens and stars as "above" (rather than "distant"), and we tend to equate "above" with "good." That which is above is a place of freedom and the good life, perhaps also symbolized by birds in free flight; the sun rises to provide warmth and help nature supply us with food. And "below" is typically "bad"—as the sun drops below the earth, cold and fearful night prevails, and caves and subterranean places are often seen with disfavor and as threatening. Thus, for many cultures, not only is the vertical dimension important, but distinct values are associated with the poles of the dimension. For example, certain nomads of Siberia and central Asia believe that the world is organized in three layers (in fact, some of these groups believe that there are up to 12 layers) in the form of hemispheres stacked on one another. For some of these groups, the heavens are stretched skins; for others the sky is an overturned caldron; for others it is a tent roof protecting the earth, and "the stars are holes through which the light of heaven penetrates. . . . Heaven's roof is supported by a pillar, which is also the axis of the rotating stars around Polaris" (Tuan, 1974, p. 131). These nomads believe that a central axis connects the three levels of the universe and that it is along this axis that gods come down to earth and the dead go to the underworld. Furthermore, this people's own tents are symbolic microcosms of the universe, the smoke hole representing sky holes and the tent pole being a vertical axis leading up to the stars and heavens.

The importance of the vertical dimension, "up" being idealized, has already been implied in our discussion of the awe in which mountains were held during various historical periods. The positive connotations of high places are also evident in other aspects of people's lives: in the arrangement of offices, in building design, and in religious architecture. The medieval cathedrals of Europe were designed with tall towers, spires, and pointed arches that gave a feeling of "reaching upward." And, as noted earlier, the pyramids of Egypt, the ancient Greek temples on the Acropolis, and other examples all illustrate the importance of the vertical dimension in cultural beliefs about the nature of the world and the universe.

Height is also associated with status and positive things. The "top" executives of many present-day organizations have offices located in the highest places, often referred to as "upstairs," the "tower," the "penthouse." In Salt Lake City, for example, the leadership of the Mormon Church is located on the top floor of a new 27-story church office building (incidentally, the building itself is the tallest one in the city, and so the church leadership occupies the highest place in the whole geographical region). Kings sit on elevated thrones above their subjects, and in some cultures it is impolite to be higher than a person with more status. Furthermore, we use expressions such as "to look up to" another person as a symbol of respect, and we "look down on" someone to signify disrespect or disdain. So it is that the vertical dimension has been woven into the fabric of social processes in many ways.

But lest we become carried away with the universality of this dimension, it is important to realize that not all people attach meaning to verticality. For example, recall the Pygmies of Zaire, who live in a heavily vegetated rain forest (Turnbull, 1961). The forest growth is so thick that the Pygmies can barely see more than a hundred yards in any direction. The sun is no more than scattered light rays; the stars are barely visible. Pygmy legends contain little reference to the heavens or to the sky and stars. For the Pygmies, the forest surrounds them in all directions, and the vertical dimension is not visible or important in their lives.

The vertical dimension is evident in many societies; what can be said about its origins? Undoubtedly many factors contribute to sensitivity to the vertical dimension, some of which are obvious. For example, the sheer presence of the sky, sun, moon, and stars points to a visible and ever-present vertical dimension. The unreachability of these objects enhances the attribution of symbolic and religious qualities to the vertical. This is further reinforced by the concept of growth along a vertical dimension—trees and flowers, children and other living things grow upward and become stronger. Besides, the simple fact of gravity adds to the idea of "up" as not easily reached, since things always fall back to earth rather than going up endlessly.

Our sensitivity to the vertical also derives from cycles in nature (Tuan, 1974). The daily "rising" and "setting" of the sun easily suggest an upper world and an underworld, as the sun seems to rise *above* and set *below* the earth. The cycles of seasons and the changing positions of stars also sensitize people to the vertical qualities of the universe. Furthermore, Tuan (1968) noted how the hydrologic properties of the earth (the properties pertaining to water) emphasize a vertical dimension. The rising of water *up* into vapors to form clouds and the release of raindrops *down* onto earth was seen by some cultures as reflecting the idea of god(s) in heaven who provided sustenance to people on earth below.

The Horizontal Dimension and the Concept of Center

The horizontal dimension is also quite evident in our day-to-day lives, perhaps so much so that we are less aware of it than of the vertical dimension. We readily see things and places on the earth's surface that are "near" or "far," "close" or "distant." Clouds move across the sky toward and away from us, mountains appear in the distance, cars and trains traverse the landscape. From airplanes or in satellite photographs we see the land stretching out on a horizontal dimension. Maps also vividly convey the horizontal features of the world. And for most cultures the horizontal plane of the earth is very important in day-to-day life. After all, it is the surface of the earth that is crucial to much of our survival; food is grown on the horizontal, most animals move about on the horizontal plane, our lives are typically restricted to the horizontal.

One very pervasive aspect of the horizontal dimension is the idea of "center" and "periphery." Just as the vertical perspective had as anchoring points earth, heaven, and the underworld, so it is that many cultures organize the horizontal world around the idea of "center/periphery." In addition, there is widespread bias that the center, usually focused around the self or one's society or nation, is "good" and that successively more distant places and people are less and less desirable. Thus, the perception of self-at-center is linked with an egocentrism and ethnocentrism about what is desirable and undesirable in the world.

As described in the following chapter, current theories of children's cognitive and perceptual development involve an initially egocentric view. The child's world is first organized with the self at center, and only gradually is space organized around a more flexible perspective. Yet culture after culture and historical civilization after civilization seem to have a horizontal conception of the world, with their own culture and geographical location as central in the scheme of things. Furthermore, a center place is often sacred and has religious or mythical importance to its people—a temple, a palace, a rock, river, or valley. Consider several examples presented by Tuan (1974).

The Chinese of the fourth to sixth centuries B.C., and perhaps even further back in history, divided the world into a series of horizontal, concentric belts. In one version of this belief system, the imperial capital was located at the center, the next ring being the royal domains, followed by successively less sophisticated and less desirable lands, extending eventually to the domains of barbarians and savages.

An analogous conception appeared among the ancient Egyptians and Persians. The Egyptians looked on themselves as a superior culture, and they believed that the Nile Valley was the center of the civilized world and that beyond it were less civilized people. So it was with the Persians, whom the Greek historian Herodotus described: "Of nations, they honour most their nearest neighbors, whom they esteem next to themselves; those who live beyond these they honour in the second degree; and so with the remainder, the further they are removed the less the esteem in which they hold them" (cited in Tuan, 1974, p. 31).

Geographical and horizontal ethnocentrism also appears in ancient Greek maps. Some of these maps, dating to the fifth century B.C., depicted the world as surrounded by a belt of water. In different versions of these maps, the world was sometimes subdivided into general areas by the

Mediterranean and Caspian seas, sometimes by Europe, Africa, or Asia, and/or by the Nile River in the south and the Danube in the north. But in all perspectives Greece was more or less at the center of the civilized world (and for some maps, the holy city of Delphi or Mount Olympus was at the center of Greece).

With the rise of Christianity in the Middle Ages, European maps of the world conveyed the same sort of ethnocentrism, with the difference that the important religious city of Jerusalem was at a central position. In the so-called T-O maps of the medieval period, the world was believed to be girdled by the oceans, as in the early Greek maps. In one variant, the land mass of the world was divided by a T, one leg of which was variously represented by the Nile or Don river and the other by the Mediterranean Sea, to yield the land masses of Asia, Africa, and Europe, with Jerusalem at the center. There were many versions of these maps over a thousand years of European history, even into the period of sophisticated navigation, when it was well known that such maps were of little value in actual navigation. However, the central role of Christianity undoubtedly influenced the form of such maps, and they served to illustrate the importance of Jerusalem as a symbol of Christianity.

A shift in the "center" of the world from Jerusalem to Europe in the minds and maps of Western people occurred during the great age of exploration from the Middle Ages to the 20th century. Maps were drawn with Europe at the center, and everyday language conveyed the central location of Europe. Such terms as *Near East, Middle East,* and *Far East* are all implicitly based on Europe as center, with other parts of the world described in terms of their distance from Europe. (Surely the people of China and Japan do not see themselves as living in the Far East.) The American continents were, and are still, called the "New World" by Europeans to suggest that they were extensions of Europe as the center, old, and parent world.

Ethnocentric organization along a horizontal dimension is not always on the scale of the whole earth, but often involves localized geography. For example, the Yurok Indians of northern California mentally organized their world into a region of about 150 miles in diameter that was centrally bisected by the Klamath River (a crucial food source) and surrounded by the ocean. The "center" of the earth was located somewhere on the banks of the Klamath at a place where the sky was made and where there remained a ladder connecting the earth and sky. Thus, the concept of one's own place as center occurs on a small, as well as a large, scale.

The Keresan Pueblo Indian cosmology, described in more detail below, sees the earth as central in the universe and the Pueblo community site as the center of the earthly world. The Navajo Indians, however, have a more individualized center that is focused at the individual hogan (residence). This also holds for nomadic Mongol groups described earlier:

each tent is symbolically a central place, so that there are as many centers as there are hogans or tents.

We sometimes think that the beliefs held by other cultures regarding the horizontal dimension are quaint and curious. But we too anchor our lives around centers and peripheries, and we often hold egocentric and ethnocentric views about the world. Consider the headlines and newspaper accounts of the United States as the center of the free world, the United States as a central power in the United Nations, the United States as the main guardian of democracy. And maps produced in the United States inevitably have North and South America at the center. (It is also characteristic of maps produced in other parts of the world that each nation puts itself at the center.)

Moreover, modern centers are often associated with religious and symbolic significance, just as they were in ancient civilizations. In Washington, D.C., the Capitol Building of the United States is at the geographic and symbolic center of the city, and all street designations stem from that site. So it is in many other cities and communities, where the seat of government serves as the center. A religious place can instead serve as the center, as in Salt Lake City, Utah, where the Mormon Temple serves as center and all street locations derive from it. (Interestingly, the capitol building of the State of Utah, a few blocks from the Mormon Temple, is not the center, a fact that can be traced to the early history of the state.)

Furthermore, many present-day centers possess a sacred quality and are restricted to use by certain people. For example, we cannot go into the center of the U.S. Capitol, the House and Senate chambers, unless we have tickets. One can enter the Mormon Temple only if one is a member in good standing. And in ancient Egypt, Sumeria, and Mesoamerica only special priests or important people could enter the centers of temples and shrines.

The importance of center is also evident in the way we refer to places, such as cities: New York is the "center" of the clothing world, the banking world, and the theater world. Washington, D.C., is the "political center" of the United States. Chicago is the "hub" of the airline, railroad, and stockyard worlds. Innumerable other cities are called "centers," "hubs," and "capitals." Tuan (1974) says: "There are at least two hundred forty variants of nicknames in which the word 'capitol' appears, and the number rises several-fold if we also include the 'hub,' the 'home,' the 'center,' the 'heart,' the 'cradle,' the 'crossroads' and the 'birthplace' "(p.204).

This is not to say that one's own place is center in all respects or that it is always desirable. For many Americans the 1960s led to disillusionment with the United States as desirable and central. Many ghetto residents do not always see their communities or nations as favorable or sacred. Many Orthodox Jews and Zionists around the world consider Israel, not their national homes, sacred and central. It is likely that modern-day people carry around a variety of "centers" in their world cosmologies. For the mobile American, Washington, D.C., is a center of politics; a birthplace and early home may be another center; the company's "home" office may serve as still another center; Jerusalem or Rome may be a religious center; Paris, Florence, or Rome may function as a cultural center. Perhaps modern persons have a multitude of geographically dispersed centers, each serving a different facet of their lives, whereas members of less technologically complex or mobile societies have fewer and more geographically proximate centers.

SOME GENERAL WORLD VIEWS

In the preceding sections of this chapter, we described various spatial orientations of different cultures. In this final section, we adopt a more holistic approach and examine how cultures have ordered their universe through simultaneous use of several dimensions.

The fabric of a culture often contains a rich blending of vertical and horizontal dimensions and general orientation to nature. Directionality is often interwoven with stories of the origin of the earth or of people, seasons of the year, and religious values. This meshing of environment and culture illustrates well the theme of this book—namely, that environment, culture, and psychological processes function as a unity and that one cannot easily determine which factors "caused" certain outcomes. Often, all one can know is that an orderly pattern of relations among variables exists. Consider some examples from American Indian, ancient Egyptian, and ancient Chinese cultures.

White (1964) and Ortiz (1972) analyzed the cosmology, or world view, of the Pueblo Indians of the southwestern United States. The Pueblos' story of the origin of people on earth vividly reflects their conceptions of time and space and the intermingling of horizontal and vertical dimensions, seasons, animals, and nature. The following excerpts from White (1964) tell the story.[3]

> The world of the Pueblo Indians was not created in the beginning; it was always there—or here. But it was somewhat different in the beginning than it is now. The earth was square and flat; it had four corners and a middle. Below the surface of the earth there were four horizontal layers; each one was a world. The lowest world was a white one. Above that lay the red

[3]This and all other quotations from this source are from "The World View of the Keresan Pueblo Indians," by L. A. White. In S. Diamond (Ed.), *Primitive Views of the World*. Copyright 1964 by Columbia University Press. Reprinted by permission.

> world and then the blue one. Above the blue world, and just beneath this world that we are living in today, was the yellow world.
>
> In the beginning the people were living deep down inside the earth, in the white world, with their mother, Iyatiku. Finally it was time for them to come out, to ascend to this world. Iyatiku caused a great evergreen tree, a spruce or a fir, to grow so that the people could climb up its trunk and boughs and move to the next world. But when the tree reached the next world above it found its way blocked by a hard layer of earth and rock. So Iyatiku had Woodpecker make a hole through the layer into the next world. The people climbed up into the red world and lived there for four years. Then it was time to climb up into the blue world. Again Iyatiku had a tree reach up to the world above, and again she had someone make a hole through the hard layer so the tree and the people could pass through.
>
> At last the people were ready to ascend into this world. Iyatiku had Badger make a hole through the hard crust. He made so much dust in his work that there was danger that the people might be blinded, so Whirlwind Old Man went up and held the dust in his arms until Badger got through. Then, Cicada was asked to line the opening so it would be smooth and safe to pass through.
>
> They came out in a place in the north called Shipap. Everything was new and "raw." The earth was too soft for people to walk upon so Iyatiku had the mountain lion use his magic power to harden it. When it was sufficiently hard, the people came out. They stayed near the opening at Shipap for a time, but it was too sacred a place for permanent residence, so Iyatiku told them they were to migrate toward the south. She said: "I shall not go with you. I am going to return to my home in the white world, but I will be with you always in spirit. You can pray to me and I will always help you." . . . Iyatiku returned to the lower world and the people began their journey to the South. They stopped at a place and established a pueblo. They called it Kashikatchrutiya, or White House. They lived here a long time. . . .
>
> While the people were living at White House they came to know all about the world they were living in, and how to behave toward it. First of all there was the Earth, . . . "Mother Earth." It was the Earth that we live on. It was square and flat, although marked with mountains and valleys here and there. It was very large, also; one could not reach its edges in many days' journey, although one could easily see them on the distant horizons. Above the earth was Howake, "the Sky". This was not merely empty space, but a real something, a structure that arched like a great dome above the earth on which it rested [pp. 85–87].

The Pueblo cosmology also involves the sun (Tuan, 1974), which, for many American Indian cultures, is acknowledged as a "father" who helps the crops grow and who makes a journey every day across the sky to his house in the west.

The horizontal dimension of the Pueblo world included the four corners of the earth, the cardinal points, and the zenith and nadir. For example, at each corner of the earth was the house of a god—the house of leaves of the woman god who could make things happen by merely thinking about them, the house of spider grandmother, the turquoise house of the butterfly, the house of mockingbird youth. At each of the cardinal points—north, south, east, and west—and at the zenith and nadir, there also lived a god, such as the god of winter and snow at the north, or the god of crops and food growth at the south. And each of these directions had its own animal—such as the puma, the bear, the bobcat, and the badger. Each cardinal point also had a woman, a tree, a snake, and a warrior.

Another element in the Pueblo cosmology is that time is not linear, but works in cycles (Ortiz, 1972; White, 1964).

> When people died their bodies were buried, but their souls went back to Shipap, the place of emergence, and returned to their mother in the fourfold womb of the earth. Every year they would come back to White House to visit their relatives. But when the time came for them to return, the living people wanted to accompany them. But Iyatiku told them that they could not do this, that they would have to wait until they died and became like little children again before they could reenter the place of their birth. So every year, now, the souls of the dead come back to the pueblos of the living and visit their relatives and eat the food that has been placed for them on their graves and on the road toward the north. The living entertain their dead relatives, but do not accompany them when they leave [White, p. 89].

Thus, the Pueblo culture possesses a rich, well-ordered cosmology involving vertical and horizontal dimensions of the environment and close links with features of the natural environment—animals, seasons, and directionality. As such, this cosmology is an excellent example of the complex patterning of cultural and environmental factors.

In an analogous vein, the Oglala Sioux also orient their lives to the horizontal and vertical dimensions and to various natural events. Tuan (1971) cited from Neihardt's description of Black Elk, a Sioux medicine man, who, pointing to the four ribbons on his sacred pipe, said:

> These . . . are the four quarters of the universe.
>
> The black one is for the west, where the thunder beings live to send us rains; the white one for the north, whence comes the great white cleansing winds; the red one for the east, whence springs the light and where the morning star lives to give man wisdom; the yellow for the south, whence comes the summer and the power to grow [p. 24].[4]

[4]This and all other quotations from this source are from *Black Elk Speaks,* by John G. Neihardt, copyright 1932, 1959, 1961, 1972. Published by Pocket Books, a division of Simon and Schuster.

In another statement from Black Elk, it is made clear that the Oglala Sioux see the world as circular:

> The sky is round . . . the wind . . . whirls. Birds make their nests in circles, for theirs is the same religion as ours. The sun comes forth and goes down again in a circle. The moon does the same. Even the seasons . . . always come back again to where they were. The life of a man is a circle from childhood to childhood and so it is in everything where power moves. Our tepees were round like the nests of birds, and these were always set in a circle, the nation's hoop, a nest of many nests, where the Great Spirit meant for us to hatch our children [p. 24].

The cosmology of ancient Egypt is in some ways different from but in other ways similar to those of these American Indian cultures (Tuan, 1974). In ancient Egypt the Nile River, running north and south, was of crucial importance to the survival of the people because of irrigation. The Nile had fertile lands on each side of its banks, and deserts beyond, yielding a cosmology with strong symmetrical values. The earth was believed to be the center of the cosmos. Above it was the domain of the sky goddess, and below it was the underworld—each like a symmetrical pan that faced the earth in the center. The sun was crucial to the lives of the Egyptians, and a solar theology evolved along with a reverence for the Nile. The result was a north-south axis (Nile) and an east-west axis (movement of the sun). Such strongly held symmetrical orientations were carried over into Egyptian architecture. The pyramid, for example,

> is made up of four equal isosceles triangles converging on a single point. The base is an exact square . . . oriented precisely to the cardinal directions. . . . The interplay between pyramid and cosmos is stressed by the precision of orientation. The square base and the isosceles triangle emphasize the urge toward symmetry that appears also in other expressive domains of Egyptian life [Tuan, 1974, p. 87].

The blending of culture and environment is also reflected in cosmological orderings of nature (Tuan, 1974). For example, ancient Chinese cosmology unified seasons, resources, colors, and human emotions. For the Chinese, the east was associated with spring, wood, the color green, and the emotion anger; the south was associated with fire, summer, red, and joy and the north with winter, water, black, and fear. The Pueblo Indians also associated cardinal directions with animals, gods, and colors; for example, the east was associated with the color white, with a bird-like god, and with the wolf; the south was associated with the color red, a god who helps crops grow, and the bobcat.

So cultures have complex orderings of the world that reflect the vertical and horizontal dimensions of their environments, the colors and seasons, emotions, important animals and things that grow, and various social values. All come together in a coherent pattern that permits people to better understand and live in the world about them.

SUMMARY

This chapter discussed attitudes, beliefs, and orientations of cultures to the world and to the physical environment. Our analysis ranged over several levels of scale, from general orientations to nature and the environment to specific perceptions of horizontal and vertical dimensions of the world.

We noted that people in different cultures and throughout history have held different perspectives about their relation to the natural environment, sometimes feeling a sense of subjugation to nature, sometimes believing themselves to be superior to nature, and at other times feeling at one with and a part of nature. Differing views toward the undeveloped wilderness, the city, and the developed rural landscape have also occurred in a myriad of forms over the centuries and in different cultures. From these broad orientations, we then examined people's values and beliefs about particular places in the environment—mountains, islands, seashores—noting once again the range of historical and cultural variation in attitudes toward such places.

The chapter also examined specific aspects of environmental orientation, particularly the horizontal and vertical dimensions. We noted that both horizontal and vertical dimensions are prevalent in many societies. The vertical dimension usually involves a concept of heaven, earth, and underworld. The horizontal dimension includes not only a consistent use of cardinal directions of north, south, east, and west but also, frequently, a notion of center/periphery, with center as "good" and increasingly distant locations as "bad." The horizontal dimension also often has an egocentric component: the world is ordered on the basis of the geographic location of a particular culture.

Finally, the chapter described how all these environmental orientations have been woven together into a complex fabric of beliefs and values that include directionality, the relation of people to nature, color, emotions, animal and plant life, seasons, life and death, and views of the origin of people and the world. Thus, examination of the world views of different cultures highlights the theme of this book—namely, that people, culture, and environment operate as a unified system, each influencing and being influenced by the others, each as much a cause as an effect of the others, and each understandable only if considered in light of the others.

Chapter 3

ENVIRONMENTAL COGNITION AND PERCEPTION

Before reading this chapter, take a few minutes to do the following exercises. Then, as you read different parts of the chapter, analyze your responses in terms of the concepts discussed there.

1. Draw a map of the town or city in which you live. Include the important features of the community in your drawing.
2. Name as many New England states as you can in 30 seconds. Then do the same thing for one or more of the Western, Southwestern, Midwestern, and Eastern regions of the United States.
3. Name five states in the United States where you would most like to live permanently. List five states where you would least like to live.

These simple exercises illustrate the types of mental images that people have of environments—which aspects of places are salient and easily remembered; which aspects of environments have positive or negative connotations; and which parts of the environment we know more or know less about. The exercises also illustrate the point that environments can be depicted in more than one way—through spatial representations, or so-called cognitive maps, and through verbal memories of places. Furthermore, these exercises show that perceptions and cognitions of environments can have an emotional component—liking or disliking a place. Finally, the exercises highlight the concept of scale as a feature of our cognitions and perceptions, from the smaller scale of a town to the larger scale of a city, state, and nation.

The focus of the present chapter is at an individual psychological level of analysis, in contrast with the sociological, historical, and anthropological perspectives of the preceding chapter. Rather than describing how a whole culture views the physical environment, we will examine research and theory on individuals, to see how they psychologically respond to and organize the environment around them. In addition, the material to be discussed here has a more quantitative and empirical base than the analyses in Chapter 2, which relied largely on qualitative anthropological and historical descriptions. Furthermore, the present chapter will be somewhat more analytical in its orientation and less global and general than Chapter 2. As we shall illustrate, however, the anthropological, historical, and sociological perspective of that chapter fits nicely with the psychological perspective taken here.

The first part of the chapter offers some basic definitions and addresses the meaning of environmental cognitions and perceptions from a psychological perspective. The middle sections of the chapter describe the dynamics of environmental cognition and perception and of knowledge of, differentiation of, and preferences for environmental places and properties. The final section examines the development of environmental cognition and perception in childhood.

A DEFINITIONAL FRAMEWORK

The process of environmental perception and cognition (or cognitive mapping, to use a term from Downs and Stea, 1973) is defined as "a process composed of a series of psychological transformations by which an individual acquires, codes, stores, recalls, and decodes information about the relative locations and attributes of phenomena in his everyday spatial environment" (p. 9).

Figure 3-1 identifies the elements of this definition. The figure will serve as the basis for the following discussion, much of which is based on the analysis by Downs and Stea (1973).

Before we begin the discussion, however, it is important to come to some agreement on terms. The literature has used interchangeably the terms *environmental cognition, environmental perception, environmental image,* and *cognitive map*. Downs and Stea use the term *cognitive map* to mean momentary perceptions of stimuli and the cognitive beliefs that people hold about the environment. The "map" aspect of the term reflects its location and its attributes or properties. Downs and Stea also distinguish the attitudes, or likes and dislikes, that people have about environments. The following nomenclature will be adopted in this chapter. *Environmental orientation* will be the general term used to refer to all the elements of Figure 3-1 and to the general tendency for people to have attitudes and feelings about the environment. The term *environmental cognition* (analogous to Downs and Stea's *cognitive map*) will refer to perceptions, cognitions, and beliefs about the environment. *Environmental attitudes* or *environmental preferences* will refer to positive and negative evaluations, feelings, and preferences about the environment.

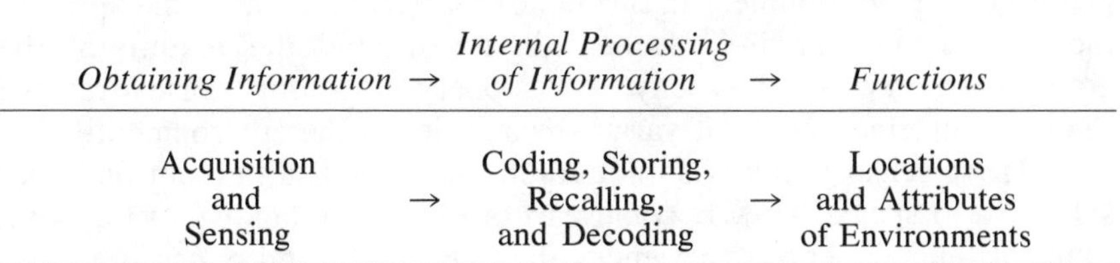

Obtaining Information	→	*Internal Processing of Information*	→	*Functions*
Acquisition and Sensing	→	Coding, Storing, Recalling, and Decoding	→	Locations and Attributes of Environments

Figure 3-1. The elements of environmental cognition and perception.

Let us begin with the process of *environmental cognition*, depicted in Figure 3-1. The basic questions are: "How do people acquire and process information about their environments?" To get a feel for these issues, imagine yourself in any of the following circumstances: (1) You are suddenly and without preparation thrust into the world of the Mbuti Pygmies, in the rain forest of Zaire. (2) You are a born and bred city-dweller who moves to a small town, or vice versa: you were raised in a small town and move to a large urban area. (3) You move suddenly to a tropical island in the South Pacific, an island no larger than 3 miles by 1 mile. (4) Or choose a personal example in which your life changed dramatically because of a move to a strange and novel environment.

In the face of such radical transformations, a person must be concerned with some very basic questions, such as "How do I find out about the environment? How do I get around? Where are things located? How do I find my way from place to place? Where do I seek food, supplies, people, and facilities?" Thus, one has to get information about locations and attributes of the environment, sort it out, organize it, and build environmental orientations that consist of ideas and feelings about different parts of the new and strange environment. Figure 3-1 and the following discussion portray aspects of this process.

The first stage in coping with a new environment is to obtain information about it. How is this done? Obviously this happens through the various sensory modalities—vision, hearing, smell, touch, taste, and kinesthesis (the sense of position and movement of body parts). We acquire information about a place by looking around—at the paths, landmarks, boundaries, and other features of the environment. We try to see how things are related to one another, we try to learn about the distances between places, whether and how we can go from place A to place B. We listen to things—the sounds of animals, the ocean, the wind rustling through the trees, desert sand blowing, the approach and departure of various noises, traffic sounds, people coming and going. We smell things, such as flowers and greenery, animal life, cooking from homes and public places, all of which tell us something about the location of things and the attributes of the environment. We touch and feel objects to help build a picture of the environment in our minds. We feel the wind, the spray of the ocean, the humidity of the rain forest, and the texture of the ground—spongy, hard, rocky, or slippery. All our senses receive firsthand information about various properties of the environment.

These sensory inputs do not enter our heads and "go out the other side," so to speak. They become part of our understanding of the environment, and they are experiences that we call on and remember again and again. They are registered in our minds and are available for later use in a variety of circumstances. Put another way, we gradually come to "know" the environment, to remember things about it, to be able to locate places rapidly and efficiently. As depicted in Figure 3-1, places gradually become familiar because of a complex series of *information processing* events that have taken place in our minds as we received and dealt with information pouring in from our senses. These information-processing events include the *coding and sorting* of information into categories that fit our past experience or personality. Thus, a new site is implicitly labeled as "something similar to X in that other place." Smells are sorted out as similar or different from one another or from other smells we know about, as when we say "It smells somewhat like a rose." Or we code locations, like "near the large rock," "to the left of the supermarket," "beyond the stand of aspen." Information is grouped and organized, compared with experiences with similar or dissimilar environments, and related to other features of the environment. Furthermore, information is *stored* in our minds, and it is remembered. It can be *recalled and decoded* as we need it; it is used in moving about the environment, in telling others about it, or in locating things and places. All these psychological information-processing activities permit us to piece together images, mental maps, or cognitions of various features of the environment.

Downs and Stea (1973) also observed that environmental cognitions are often inaccurate and incomplete, and they sometimes differ from person to person and from group to group. Environmental cognitions are often incomplete in that they are not exact replicas of the actual physical environment. They are selective and include elements that are important to people or that people are able to discriminate. For example, Eskimos distinguish many more types of snow than do residents of Tucson, Arizona, for whom snow is a rarity and for whom there may be only one or two varieties. The skier, however, like the Eskimo, is sensitive to many types of snow—heavy snow, powder snow, broken snow, icy snow, "crud" snow, new snow, skied-out snow. Similarly, people around the world develop differentially complicated cognitions about events, depending on how important various parts of the environment are to them.

In addition, Downs and Stea (1973) state that cognitive representations of the physical environment are often distorted and schematized.

For example, many maps drawn by amateurs overemphasize or underemphasize certain features of places. Distances and directions may be represented erroneously; paths and routes may be accentuated and blown up out of proportion to their size or may be in the wrong place. Thus, as part of the process of coding and storage, we tend to distort aspects of the environment. In the same way that people often say "All those people look alike," we also tend to shorthand our environmental cognitions. Thus, Rome *is* the Vatican; Greece *is* the Acropolis; the western United States *are* the Rocky Mountains. So simplifications, labels, and schematics are typical features of environmental cognitions.

Another characteristic of environmental cognitions is that they are augmented and often contain surplus information. We sometimes fill in the blanks, as in the early maps of the ancients that contained monsters and fictitious places, which mapmakers assumed to exist in various parts of the world. As another example, Appleyard (1970) found that maps drawn by residents of a city in Venezuela had a railway in a particular place even though the rail line did not extend that far. It is as if people assumed it belonged there and included it in their cognitive images of the city. In our environmental cognitions we infer the existence of things to round out our beliefs and perceptions and to make them rational and consistent.

In summary, environmental cognitions are truly "psychological" in that we interpret the environment and we are selective and incomplete in our portrayal of it. We receive information about the environment from our senses, we process and organize it in ways that are meaningful to us and to our lives, and the results are represented in and carried about in our minds. What is meaningful, consistent, and appropriate is, of course, heavily influenced by our cultural experiences.

What purposes or functions are served by environmental orientations? The right-hand side of Figure 3-1 indicates two basic types of information that we need about the environment: (1) the locations of places and objects and (2) the attributes, or characteristics, of the environment.

Location deals with where things are in terms of *distance* and *direction*. Distance has to do with how far away a place is, often measured in linear units, such as inches, feet, or miles. But even such an apparently straightforward feature of the environment as distance is cognitively very rich. For example, it is customary in the northeastern United States and in the urban areas of California to refer to distance in terms of travel time—for example, people measure the distance between New York City and Washington, D.C., in hours of driving time—whereas in much of the western United States one refers to distance in terms of miles. Why is this so? Perhaps because the distance covered per hour is so variable in the East and in urban centers, as one encounters slowdowns here and there;

or perhaps because the mileage is less important than travel time. This is an interesting example of how the features of the physical environment can affect the cognitive and perceptual measure one employs. We suspect that a similar process occurred among the early pioneers who crossed the United States. They probably judged distances in terms of days to a place rather than miles, since how long it took to arrive was far more important than how many miles away a place was. Perhaps, as the gasoline shortage becomes more severe, a new form of distance measurement will emerge, such as "That place is about three gallons of gas away," illustrating again the relation between important commodities such as time and gas and our cognitive orientations to the environment. So distance, a seemingly straightforward measure, can be quite complex and is closely linked with other aspects of environmental cognition and orientation.

The other dimension of location, *direction*, is equally complex. Maps are usually oriented toward the cardinal directions of north, south, east, and west, and, when traveling, we often rely on these directions. But in day-to-day life directions take many forms. In some instances all directions are based on a well-known landmark—a street, statue, or monument. One of the authors grew up in an urban area, the Bronx, New York, where direction was based on a major street called the Grand Concourse. Every place of importance was oriented to that thoroughfare, and we used such directional information as "two blocks *this* side of the Grand Concourse, five blocks *that* side of the Grand Concourse." If we wanted to refer to another direction, we used the term *uptown* or *downtown*. Thus, a precise designation of a place could be "five blocks uptown and three blocks this side of the Grand Concourse." This two-axis system was totally independent of the cardinal directions, the sun (which one hardly ever saw), or any other natural designations, but it was a complete system and was nicely geared to the culture and to the properties of the physical environment.

In Salt Lake City, Utah, the basic anchors for direction are the Wasatch mountains on the east and the Oquirrh mountains on the west. One speaks of directions in terms of east and west, north and south, with the mountains as ever-present anchoring points. Within that framework, the city is laid out with the Mormon Temple at the zero, zero coordinates of a Cartesian system, and the street designations are oriented toward the four cardinal directions, with the temple as center. Another type of system is used by the Tikopia, a people that lives on a small South Pacific island (Lynch, 1960). The ocean is an important and ever-present part of their lives, and direction is based on concepts of "landward" and "seaward"; the Tikopia will go so far, for example, as to refer to the "seaward side" of a person's face.

As another instance of the complexity of directionality and distance, Downs and Stea (1973) indicate that we often link distances, direction and time, as when we say "You go left past the second traffic light for about ten minutes, and you can't miss it.'' In summary, distance and direction are aspects of environmental orientation that serve the goal of helping us locate places and objects. But the variety of ways in which we use distance and direction attests to the idea that the environment and culture play an important role in our cognitive orientations.

The second function of sensing, storing, and coding processes is to inform us of environmental *attributes*, or properties. Knowledge of the attributes of a place supplements our knowledge of locations. For example, knowing that a particular house or movie theater will be at a given location or that a lake will be at the end of the road (attributes of the environment) contributes to our cognitive orientations. Downs and Stea (1973) also suggest that attributional phenomena can be of a *descriptive* or an *evaluative* type. Descriptions are neutral: the house at the end of the street; the mountains 25 miles away. Evaluations involve an affective, judgmental quality: the *dangerous* mountains, the *excellent* movie, the *filthy* home.

Given that we need information about the location and attributes of things and places in the environment, the question arises how we develop skills to build such cognitive representations. Do we start as infants with no such skills and learn them only by trial and error? Or do we possess a biological heritage that sets the stage for the ability to mentally organize the environment?

A great deal is learned in response to the particular demands of the environment and culture in which we grow up and live. However, Kaplan (1973) has also argued that a considerable segment of skills in environmental orientation derives from our evolutionary and biological history. Kaplan's idea is that over the course of evolution those who survived and reproduced had the necessary cognitive and perceptual skills for adaptation to the rigors of living. These skills are, according to Kaplan, (1) the ability to know where one is, (2) the ability to know what is likely to happen next, (3) the ability to determine the goodness or badness of what is likely to happen next, and (4) the ability to decide on and take alternative courses of action. The hunter who tracks game through the forest must be able to keep track simultaneously of his own movement and that of his prey, a process that requires a complex set of spatial cognitions. Those who could do such things well, Kaplan says, survived and reproduced, so that there is an evolutionary basis for skills associated with effective environmental orientation.

The first step of the process, knowing where one is, is accomplished by skills related to location, distance, and direction, discussed above. Such skills require a good sensing system, an ability to code, store, and recall information effectively and quickly, and an ability to integrate information. The ability to predict and to determine the positive or negative qualities of an environment likewise requires a good information-processing system and the ability to integrate large amounts of new and old information. Furthermore, decision making about alternative courses of action and finally selecting a specific action require similar skills—namely, the skills of linking past and present knowledge with an accurate prediction of the impact of one's reponses on future events.

Kaplan's (1973) provocative statement of the postulated evolutionary basis of our ability to develop successful environmental orientations is summarized as follows:

> Man is not a "tabula rasa." He is a kind of animal that has lived by his wits over millions of years. He is a kind of animal that lives by what he knows and by what he can guess and by the plans he makes. He is a restless, searching animal. He has been selected for speed; he is quick to perceive and quick to decide [p. 77].

The validity of this evolutionary approach is a matter for future research and discussion. The point is that people have extraordinary skills for developing cognitive orientations to the physical environment, and this highly organized process may be deeply ingrained in the evolutionary history of the species. But we have also seen how particular aspects of these cognitive and perceptual processes are affected by learning and culture.

DIMENSIONS OF ORIENTATION TO THE ENVIRONMENT

We have described the general process of how people orient to environmental attributes and locations. Let us now be more specific and examine this process in terms of particular dimensions of places.

Kevin Lynch (1960), a city planner, asked people a variety of questions about the "images" they held of cities like Boston, Jersey City, and Los Angeles. From his work he concluded that people use five key dimensions to construct a mental image of a city. These dimensions are *paths*, *edges, districts, nodes,* and *landmarks*. These five dimensions, Lynch stated, may vary in their specifics from city to city, but people seem to use them frequently when asked to describe a place. Other research described below suggests that people around the world also conceive of cities according to some of Lynch's five dimensions.

Paths

According to Lynch (1960), "Paths are channels along which the observer customarily, occasionally, or potentially moves" (p. 47).[1] Paths are well known to everyone; they include streets, highways, rivers, and

[1]This and all other quotations from this source are from *The Image of the City,* by K. Lynch. Copyright 1960 by M.I.T. Press. Reprinted by permission.

canals. They are the routes we take to go from one place to another, and they appear in a variety of forms, from narrow dirt trails to eight-lane superhighways. Paths can be narrow or wide; they can serve walkers, animal-pulled vehicles, and motor-driven vehicles. They can lead to central places, such as the Capitol Building of the United States, or they can connect relatively unimportant places. Paths usually have a directional quality and lead somewhere, to an origin or destination (except for the famous West Virginia Turnpike, a highway that ended abruptly and led nowhere because of a lack of funds). Paths also usually fit into a larger network, such as the California freeway system, which consists of numerous connecting highways that come together and separate, each leading in a different direction.

Lynch's analysis of paths was based primarily on the scale of a city and included streets, highways, and railroad and transit lines. One might also apply the concept of path at a smaller scale, as within the home (hallways, routes through and around rooms) or a neighborhood, including the informal paths of children and animals through backyards, over and under fences, and through vacant lots.

Edges

Lynch (1960) described a second dimension of environments:

> Edges are the linear elements not used or considered as paths. . . . They are boundaries between two phases, linear breaks in continuity: shores, railroad cuts, edges of development, walls. . . . Such edges may be barriers, more or less penetrable, which close one region off from another; or they may be seams, lines along which two regions are related and joined together [p. 47].

Edges can be easily seen in aerial views. The lakefront of Chicago forms a clearly demarcated edge to the city; a major river running alongside or through a city sharply distinguishes its areas; the roads forming rectangular patterns in the midwestern United States serve as edges to separate one plot of land from another; a forest adjacent to developed farmland forms an edge. Places are sometimes both paths and edges, such as a road that also serves as a boundary separating two areas. Even on the ground one can easily notice edges. Railroad tracks often serve as a sharp boundary for different sections of town, as when we speak of "the other side of the tracks"; certain streets demarcate the well-to-do from the not-so-well-to-do or residential areas from shopping areas. At a smaller scale, neighbors sometimes define the boundaries of their property through the use of easily visible edges, such as a hedge, a fence, a line of trees, or a path.

Like paths, edges can apply to large-scale features of the environment, such as the boundary between a continent and the ocean or a border separating nations or states. They can also apply to moderate levels of scale, such as boundaries within cities, or to the small scale of neighbors' yards or even of areas within homes, such as the imaginary (or often not so imaginary) boundaries that roommates use to delineate sides of the room.

Districts

Lynch (1960) defined districts as "the medium-to-large sections of the city, . . . having two dimensional extent, which the observer mentally enters 'inside of,' and which are recognizable as having some common, identifying character" (p. 47).

Districts have a thematic quality, often a combination of physical, sociological, and psychological qualities. Chinatown in San Francisco, the garment district in New York, theater or shopping areas of a city, Times Square in New York, Capitol Hill in Washington, D.C., and the Vatican in Rome are examples of districts. Such places often have a network of internal paths and have edges surrounding them. Inside, a district has a certain homogeneity or thematic quality that can take many forms: activities, such as shopping, theatergoing, or eating; characteristics of the inhabitants (for example, Black, Chinese, or Greek); poor people, rich people; or the style of architecture, as in colonial Georgetown, Washington, D.C. Frequently, districts have a distinctive flavor that involves some combination of activities, people, and physical qualities.

With these three elements in mind—paths, edges, and districts—one can begin to see how people develop cognitive images of places. Paths connect and run through districts, boundaries define areas and often surround districts, and the three types of elements help to organize in one's mind the nature of a particular place or city.

Nodes

Lynch (1960, p. 47) defined nodes as "points, the strategic spots in a city into which an observer can enter, and which are the intensive foci to and from which he is traveling. They may be primarily junctions, places of a break in transportation, a crossing or converging of paths." Or nodes may be concentrations of events, activities, and places, a kind of core that symbolizes a place, such as Times Square or the Vatican Plaza. Nodes are also sometimes clearly visible in aerial views. Highway cloverleafs and intersections are good examples of nodes; they are collection points and the intersection of paths. Large squares, such as the Vatican Plaza in Rome, the Marienplatz in Munich, and the Place de la Concorde in Paris, are nodes or collection points that have paths leading to and from them.

Subway stations, intersections, traffic circles all function as nodes; that is, they are connectors of paths and choice points for travelers. Most college campuses also have one or more nodes in the form of a quadrangle area, a plaza, or some other collection and intersection point. Once again we can conceive of nodes at many levels of scale, from the large cities as air and rail centers down to corner drugstores, family kitchens, and choice points in hiking trails.

Landmarks

Landmarks are the final elements that Lynch hypothesized as contributing to the image of cities. These are physical objects

> whose key physical characteristic . . . is singularity, some aspect that is unique or memorable in the context. Landmarks become more easily identifiable, more likely to be chosen as significant, if they have a clear form; if they contrast with their background; and if there is some prominence of spatial location. Figure-background contrast seems to be the principal factor [p. 79].

Some obvious landmarks known to almost everyone are the Capitol Building of the United States, the Washington Monument, the pyramids of Egypt, and the Leaning Tower of Pisa. But landmarks are not always widely known. They are often local and small, such as a statue in the town square, a courthouse, or an American Legion hall. As Lynch noted, a single traffic light or distinctive store can be a landmark. Within a home, an antique clock on the mantlepiece, a favorite chair, or some other object may serve as a landmark that is unique to a particular family. Furthermore, a landmark, such as a traffic circle, may also be a node or path, and so these elements are not mutually exclusive.

According to Lynch, these five elements contribute to the "images" that people have of cities. Although the elements are described one at a time, Lynch says that they should be treated as a set of interrelated features that affect our cognitions of places. They are integrated into a profile and, taken together, lend a sense of coherence to places. They also permit us to *locate* distances and directions and to understand the various *attributes* of places—whether the places be large- or small-scale. Thus, we move about and identify distances and directions in terms of paths, edges, nodes, districts, and landmarks, as in the following hypothetical example. One of the authors tells a stranger how to get to the Mormon Temple in Salt Lake City from the author's home: "You ride north on Foothill Boulevard (a major path) alongside the mountain (edge) past the shopping center (a landmark or district) until you come to a tall building (landmark) on the university campus on the right (district). On your left are a cemetery and a residential area (edge and district). Proceed to the next traffic light (landmark) and turn right on 13th Street East (node and path). Proceed to South Temple Street (node and path) and turn left on it (path). You will pass a neighborhood of old homes (district) and several traffic lights (landmarks) and intersections (nodes), and you will reach the downtown area (district). Right in front of you will be a statue of Brigham Young (landmark) at the intersection of South Temple Street and State Street (node). Park wherever you can and walk to the Temple Square grounds on your right (landmark, district)."

Giving such instructions is a mundane chore, to be sure. But embedded in them is a set of cognitive orientations to places that include all of Lynch's elements, and at different levels of scale.

RESEARCH ON COGNITIONS OF CITIES

On the basis of interview and other data, Lynch described the environmental orientations of people toward Boston, Jersey City, and Los Angeles. He collected information about the symbolic meaning of each city to its residents, directions from home to work, emotional feelings that people had about such trips, and distinctive elements of the city. In addition, people were asked to draw maps and to identify the locations of various places. For a smaller group of respondents Lynch asked people to identify places from photographs, and he had them lay out photographs in a maplike fashion. People were also taken over routes they had described in the interview and were probed about locations and what they saw.

The Boston peninsula emerged as an area of *districts* (Beacon Hill shopping and theater areas), *paths* (streets), and important historical *landmarks* (old buildings and places). It was also seen as having a salient *edge*—the water surrounding the peninsula. Thus, people saw the Boston peninsula as having a strong and distinctive character, with well-defined boundaries, districts, and landmarks. Although the street system emerged as a confused maze, key paths were well known.

Jersey City, in contrast, did not have a sharp, unambiguous image. A few squares (nodes) and boulevards (paths) were salient, as were some sections of the city (districts) and landmarks (a medical center). If anything distinctive stood out in people's minds it was the edges of the city. Lynch (1960) stated:

> There is a paucity of recognizable districts and landmarks, and a lack of commonly known centers or nodal points. The city is, however, marked by the presence of several strong edges or isolating boundaries: the overhead lines of railroads and highways, the Palisades and the two waterfronts. . . . None of the respondents had anything like a comprehensive view of the city [p. 29].

In the third city, Los Angeles, the research was directed only at the central area. The most prominent feature was the civic center (district) and the strong highway boundaries (edges) surrounding it. Within this central area Pershing Square (a node or landmark) stood out clearly. Except for a few main streets (paths) near the square, the streets were vague to people. The perception of being "spread out" and "formless" characterized people's responses to the downtown area. At a larger scale, certain sections of Beverly Hills (district) were prominent, along with a series of freeways and the ocean as strong edges. But, except for these places, the downtown area of Los Angeles was not especially vivid in the minds of respondents.

Several other studies have investigated mental images of cities and places around the world. For example, Francescato and Mebane (1973) analyzed the cognitions and attitudes of residents of Rome and Milan, Italy. They interviewed males and females, people from various socioeconomic levels, and older and younger citizens of each city. Respondents were asked what they liked and disliked about their city, what they remembered about it, what they might remember about it if they moved away, what was important to them about the city, and how they would describe distinctive parts of the city to others. They were also asked to draw a map of the city. A number of results emerged that fit with Lynch's framework. For example, Milan's uniform and radial street pattern (paths) stood out clearly; streets were much more salient than landmarks or districts. The Duomo, a prominent cathedral at the center of the city, appeared in maps and other data as a landmark. Furthermore, the city center was mentioned frequently as an important district, with the Duomo as center of the district. The cathedral not only served as a landmark but also was portrayed as a node from which a variety of paths and streets emerged.

Cognitive images of Rome were quite different. The less organized, rambling, multicentered quality of Rome was evident in the respondents' reports. Few people represented Rome with a single focal point. Rather, respondents identified three main places (landmarks or nodes)—two major plazas in the city and the Vatican. Rome's central area (district) also stood out, but not to the same extent as in Milan. The most frequently mentioned elements in Rome were the Tiber River (edge), certain landmarks (the Colosseum, a park, a bridge), and the Vatican and the two plazas just mentioned. Streets (paths) were also frequently cited, but not to the same extent as in Milan. Landmarks, however, were used more often to symbolize Rome than to symbolize Milan. To put all this simply, Milan conveyed a relatively organized image based on a central city core and a neatly organized street system. Rome had a more scattered image that was anchored at its landmarks and other significant features.

This study illustrates how the five dimensions proposed by Lynch emerge as part of the cognitive orientation and attitude that people have about places. The research also suggests that these dimensions appear in the minds of people from different cultures and in images of different environments. Thus, the five dimensions may well be fundamental to many cultures. Finally, this research illustrates how different environments yield to different mental images.

DeJonge (1962) did a similar analysis of several cities in the Netherlands, using comparable research techniques. He concluded that Amsterdam conveyed a strong image that was dominated by a main street (path) along a river. In Rotterdam edges were salient, along with particular buildings and other landmarks. The cognitive image of The Hague was dominated by its landmarks of buildings, whereas Delft was represented by several residential districts. Thus, once again, Lynch's five elements were useful vehicles for describing cities, with the cognitive identities of different places reflected in the relative salience of one or more of these elements.

Milgram (1976) did a similar analysis of environmental orientations toward Paris. One consistent element in maps drawn by respondents was a boundary around the city, represented by a major highway (edge) that separated the city from the suburbs. An internal edge, the Seine River, also was salient. Next in prominence were landmarks such as the Arc de Triomphe, Notre Dame Cathedral, and the Eiffel Tower. Other key elements included well-known paths or streets such as the Champs Élysées.

Another technique Milgram used was to name a place and then ask people to associate other places with it. His results yielded networks of places that were linked together. For example, the opera house stimulated association with certain streets, places, and art galleries, yielding a network of environmental associations. Another procedure he used was to ask people to identify photographs of places and objects. Here, the result fit well with maps that respondents drew of the city.

A study of Ciudad Guyana, a city in Venezuela (Appleyard, 1970), showed that, as elsewhere, respondents' maps emphasized paths and landmarks. One facet of this study that went beyond previous research was the classification of maps in terms of types of paths. First, Appleyard distinguished between *sequential maps* and *spatial maps*. Sequential maps had paths connected in a coherent fashion, the connections (nodes) being quite important. In spatial maps, paths and sections of the maps were often unconnected and not related to one another. Second, there were varieties of each type of map. For example, some sequential maps were quite detailed and contained complete road networks, whereas others contained only main paths and branches and loops off main paths. Less sophisticated maps had the main routes laid out accurately but were incomplete in branches and paths; others were more primitive and had only fragments of sequential paths. There were also variations in spatial maps. The simplest type emphasized certain landmarks, such as buildings, with few connections between them. Others were mosaics of districts with or without connecting links; still others were more detailed and included districts, edges, and other features.

Appleyard's data also revealed that more-educated respondents drew richer and more-detailed maps. Thus, this study not only illustrates the role of Lynch's five elements in cognitive images of cities but shows that one can carry the system to a finer-grained level of analysis, to describe environmental orientations in relation to the characteristics of people and cultural groups.

Research on young Black children illustrates some of these points in a different setting. Ladd (1970) asked 12- to 17-year-old boys who lived in the Roxbury section of Boston to draw a map of their neighborhood. Four types of maps emerged: (1) *Pictorial maps,* whose main characteristics were the identification of such landmarks as buildings, trees, and mailboxes, with only a single street or part of a street drawn on the map. (2) *Schematic maps,* which were poorly organized and contained sections not clearly connected to one another. These also had an agglomeration of streets and places. (3) *Connected street maps,* which contained clear linkages between places, including streets labeled with their names. (4) *Street maps with landmarks,* which included well-organized and well-connected streets along with a number of landmarks (much like a tourist map). Landmarks included houses, gas stations, and stores. Once again, Lynch's elements and the relations that appear among elements provide a useful means for distinguishing among cognitive representations of the physical environment. At this point you might look at the map you drew of the city or town you live in, in Exercise 1 at the beginning of this chapter, and analyze it in terms of Lynch's five elements and the other ideas we discussed.

The basic features of environmental orientations—distance/location and various attributes—seem to be salient in a variety of cultures, as reflected in how people use Lynch's five elements in cognitive representations of their environments. It is too early in the history of research on this topic to draw firm conclusions, but two possibilities emerge to which future research might be directed. First, it may be that people around the world represent environments in a common cognitive and perceptual system. Lynch's framework may provide an initial basis for such cognitive representations, since cities around the world appear to be described in terms of edges, paths, landmarks, districts, and nodes to one degree or another. Furthermore, the way in which people used individual elements and combinations of elements yielded intuitively valid portrayals of different cities. One can almost profile the "personalities" of cities in terms of Lynch's five elements.

Obviously there are limitations to the idea that Lynch's elements might be culturally pervasive. They have been applied only to Western societies and urban settings; they may not apply to other cultures or to nonurban settings. And, as the work of Appleyard and Ladd suggests, future research should move to a finer-grained level of analysis and do more than merely identify the elements at a gross level.

Another serious issue concerning application of general frameworks to other cultures is the difference between an "emic" and an "etic" orientation (Price-Williams, 1975). That is, one must be careful not to impose one's own way of viewing the world on another culture (called an etic orientation) and describe that culture solely from such a perspective. Rather, one must also understand a culture in its own terms and according to its value system and its approach to organizing the world (emic orientation). Lynch's five elements derive from a Western, urban perspective on the world, and these dimensions may ignore other cultures' values and mental organization of environments. Hence, examination of similarities and differences among cultures in their cognitive organization of environments is a provocative area for future research, and it is an area that has only begun to be tapped.

KNOWLEDGE AND DIFFERENTIATION OF THE ENVIRONMENT

In the preceding chapter, we saw that people in various cultures know more about close parts of their environments and less about more remote places. We also noted that, historically, people often have had an egocentric orientation to the environment, places close at hand being "good" and successively more remote locations being increasingly "bad." Recent research has reasonably well confirmed both these ideas, as described next.

Saarinen (1973a) conducted a series of studies on geographical knowledge among college and high school students. Students from the United States, Canada, Finland, and Sierra Leone (Africa) were asked to draw maps of the world and to include places they considered important or interesting. College students in the United States also filled in the names of places on an outline map of the world.

Maps drawn by African students most often identified continents and oceans, whereas students from other countries typically had more detail on their maps. Moreover, Europeans' and Americans' maps had a greater number of small political units, such as states or provinces. Perhaps because of their travel experience, access to communication media, and educational setting, European and North American students had more specific knowledge of the world than African students did, or perhaps African students conceptualize the world on a different basis.

Students typically placed their home continents in the center of their maps, whether they were Europeans, Africans, or Americans. Just as the early European and Greek mapmakers put their homelands (or key religious places) at the center, so do modern-day students. A study by Whittaker andWhittaker (1972) elicited cognitive maps from college students in the United States, Argentina, Fiji, India, and New Zealand. There was a universal tendency to place one's home country in the center of the map and to identify those nations and regions that are in closer proximity to the homeland. Saarinen (1973a) also found a tendency to exaggerate the size of the homeland in relation to other parts of the world and to provide much more detail about places closer to home. This is even illustrated at a very local level. For example, students from western Canada drew in neighboring Canadian provinces on their maps more frequently than distant provinces (Saarinen, 1973a). The farther a province from their own, the less often it was included. Thus, home places and neighboring areas were placed in central positions, as if they were the psychological center of the artist's universe, and they were described in more detail than remote places.

A number of other factors affected student drawings of the world. For example, the unique shape of Italy as a boot and islands such as Greenland, Cuba, and Iceland were often drawn on maps, whereas landlocked cities in Africa and Europe were frequently omitted. Large countries were included more often than small ones. Current events such as the Middle East conflict or the Vietnam war resulted in the inclusion of their sites on maps. And cultural factors were evident; for instance, the British Commonwealth nations were depicted in the maps of Canadian students. In summary, the study illustrates the tendency for environmental orientations to be egocentric, to focus on the home and on that which is salient in one's immediate environment. Such results are quite compatible with the historical and anthropological analyses described in Chapter 2.

Gould and White (1974) did a series of studies on preferences for and knowledge about different parts of the United States and Europe. In one study students were asked to fill in the names of states or regions on a map of their country. The results were in line with expectations. Students all over the United States were most accurate in their knowledge of neighboring regions and increasingly less accurate the more remote the place. Naturally, there was general accuracy of knowledge about some places regardless of distance from one's home state; for example, California, Texas, and Florida were well known to everyone. Similar findings occurred among schoolchildren in Sweden, who also knew much more about their home areas and less and less about successively more remote regions. (Compare with these findings your answers to the second exercise at the beginning of this chapter.)

Orleans (1973) obtained comparable results in a study of different groups living in the Los Angeles area. Whites from upper- and middle-class areas, Spanish-speaking people from downtown areas, and Blacks from the Watts section of Los Angeles drew maps of the city and of their neighborhoods. Samples from these groups were also interviewed about their participation in various activities and organizations, locations of friends, and other topics. The results suggested that the poorer Black and Spanish-speaking groups had restricted cognitions of the city, with only sketchy knowledge of areas beyond their neighborhoods. The upper-class White groups had more elaborate cognitive representations of the city as a whole, perhaps because they traveled more and had better access to its facilities. The results also revealed the image of Los Angeles as a city with many districts and as a place where major paths (streets and freeways) predominated in people's minds.

Appleyard's (1976) study of residents' perception of a new city, Ciudad Guyana, sheds additional light in Orleans' findings and illustrates the value of the cross-cultural approach. Most studies of social class and environmental cognition done in the United States produce findings similar to Orleans'. Specifically, lower socioeconomic class is associated with restricted, less complex knowledge of the environment. Appleyard's work in Venezuela yielded the opposite results. In Ciudad Guyana, the low-income, low-education groups had a more complex and extensive knowledge of their city than the upper-class groups. This greater knowledge appears to result from the location of the low-income residential areas and the residents' greater need for extensive travel throughout the city to obtain goods and services. The upper socioeconomic groups lived in neighborhoods where more services were provided. Thus, need for and access to information can be a crucial determinant of environmental cognitions. When past experience and differences in values are added to the mix, environmental cognition reflects a dramatic cultural component.

Saarinen (1973b) conducted a related study at an even smaller level of scale—a college campus. Students at the University of Arizona sketched maps of the university and showed behavior similar to that of the participants in the preceding studies. They were more accurate about university areas and departments where they spent most of their time and which were important to them, although several well-known landmarks were present in most maps.

The studies we have cited illustrate several points. First, knowledge and cognitive representations of the environment follow an egocentric orientation, with home place as center of the cognitive world. Second, people have more knowledge about neighboring environments and successively less knowledge about more remote places. Third, these findings seem to hold at many levels of scale—the world, nations, cities, and neighborhoods. Finally, the data are congruent with those cited in the preceding chapter, suggesting the triangulation of psychological, historical, and anthropological analyses.

Another group of studies examined how people organize aspects of the large- and small-scale environment. For example, Cox and Zannaras (1973) studied the cognitive groupings of all states and various cities in the United States. College students were asked to "take each state and select the three states most similar to it." Complex statistical analyses (factor analyses) revealed several clusters of states with similar qualities. For example, one factor that distinguished states was an east-west distinction, the Mississippi River being the dividing line. Within each cluster there was also a predominant emphasis on the Northeastern states (New England and the Middle Atlantic states) and on the mountain states and plains states respectively. A second factor distinguished between the South and New England. A third factor included the Midwestern states. Other factors included Appalachian states, the Southwest, and the Pacific Northwest. Thus, people seemed to group states along several geographic dimensions.

Cox and Zannaras (1973) used a similar procedure to portray how cities in the United States and Canada were grouped in people's minds. One factor used to cluster cities was provincialism/cosmopolitanism. Cosmopolitan cities included Boston, Chicago, Los Angeles, Montreal, and San Francisco, all large cities with many cultural and other activities. Provincial cities included Fort Wayne, Little Rock, Lexington, and Macon. A second grouping included one cluster of cities in the Great Lakes urban system (Buffalo, Chicago, Cleveland, Detroit) versus those in the southwest (Albuquerque, Dallas, Denver, El Paso). A third factor involved cities from the traditional South versus the Midwest; a fourth factor included mostly Canadian cities.

This work is interesting in several respects. It shows how people cognitively group geographical locations and how there may be psychological values associated with various places, such as cosmopolitanism/provincialism, cultural values, or agriculture. In addition to understanding how physical features of the environment, such as edges and landmarks, are represented in cognitive orientations, this research suggests the existence of other psychological dimensions associated with environments.

ENVIRONMENTAL ATTITUDES

In addition to having knowledge about the environment, people have attitudes about it, including preferences or likes and dislikes for places. Research on environmental attitudes fits well with that on environmental knowledge. Gould, a geographer, has done a series of studies illustrating the point that not only do people know more about close than remote parts of the environment, but their attitudes and feelings match such knowledge; that is, near places are usually preferred over distant places (Gould, 1973a, 1973b; Gould & White, 1974). Gould worked with people from all over the United States and the world—for example, Sweden, England, Germany, Ghana, and Nigeria. In one study students from different parts of the United States ranked states from high to low on being given the following instructions: "Imagine yourself to be married and settling down. Assume that you had complete freedom to choose a state in which to live. Rank the 50 states in terms of your preferences from most to least." From complex statistical analyses, several types of results emerged. Certain regions of the United States were consistently judged positive or negative regardless of where students lived. For example, California, Colorado, and Florida were usually viewed with favor, whereas Nevada, Utah, and the Dakotas were low-preference areas for most people. The South was also rated undesirable, although Southerners made distinctions among different states in the region.

In addition, the data suggested many localized effects. For example, Californians showed greater preferences for West Coast states, including their own, than for the Northeast and for selected states here and there. They did not view the Midwest and South very favorably. Minnesotans, in contrast, not only thought highly of Minnesota and certain surrounding areas but also viewed the Northwest with favor and the South with disfavor. Alabamans perceived the United States somewhat differently, although they shared some of the general likes and dislikes noted above. Alabamans, unlike the others, made some preference distinctions within the South. Virginia, Kentucky, North Carolina, and their own Alabama were judged quite favorably, whereas Mississippi and South Carolina were not. Furthermore, they did not value the Northeast, nor were they particularly enamored of the Northwestern states of Washington and Oregon. Thus, both home place and certain selected regions were judged positively, regardless of students' location in the country.

A second group of analyses showed a general relation between distance from home and preference. The more distant a state was from one's home state, the less it was preferred. Once again, people both know and prefer certain places, and their knowledge and preference for that which is close is typically greater than for that which is distant. (Compare these data with your own answers to Exercise 3 at the beginning of this chapter. How are your results similar to and different from Gould's findings?)

Gould and his colleagues continued this line of work in Europe, Nigeria, and Ghana and found essentially the same results, although for Europe a number of cultural and political factors also emerged. Western European respondents showed general preferences for Sweden and Switzerland (neutral countries), followed by the democratic socialist nations

(United Kingdom, Norway, Denmark, France, and West Germany). At the bottom of the preference ladder were the Eastern bloc countries of Albania, Bulgaria, East Germany, and Russia.

But there were also several idiosyncratic preferences associated with cultural and political issues. For example, the Swedes not only rated their own country as most preferred but rated other Scandinavian countries and the United Kingdom quite favorably, along with other democratic nations of Western Europe (France, West Germany, Italy, Belgium, and the Netherlands). For them the dictator-controlled countries of Spain and Portugal were quite low. The English showed a similar pattern, although they were not as favorably disposed toward France as toward Sweden. Germans were similar; however, they showed strong affinities for other German-speaking countries. In an analogous way Italians preferred Catholic and Latin countries. Thus, we see once again that people show a mixture of preferences for their own country and for selected other countries and that distance, culture, and politics affect environmental attitudes.

Preference data from the African countries of Nigeria and Ghana yielded similar results. In Ghana there were generally preferences for the coastal districts and for the urban areas of the country (where there were jobs and economic opportunities), with declining attitudes for areas toward the north and interior. Birthplaces and places of residence also emerged as positive locations, as did administrative and political centers throughout the country. Similar patterns of regional and local preferences appeared for Nigerians.

Another series of studies by Gould and White (1974) tapped climatic, political, and social dimensions of environmental attitudes. An analysis of word associations to the names of various states led to several types of cognitive images. For example, places like Colorado and California were seen as highly desirable with respect to climate, whereas the Deep South, the Dakotas, Utah, and Nevada were judged unfavorable. For political values, California, Colorado, the upper Midwest, and the Northeast were rated favorably, while the Deep South was negative. On economic dimensions, California and the Northeast were judged favorably, and the South and Great Plains were considered negative.

The concept of home base as desirable even carries down to smaller-scale aspects of the environment. For example, Appleyard (1976) found that people living in different parts of a city all thought that their own neighborhoods had the best climate.

Taken together, knowledge and attitude data yield a consistent picture. Similarities exist between what people know and how they feel about their environments. There is also evidence for egocentrism, or perception of home base as "known and good." Overlying these general principles are many political, cultural, and sociological factors that affect environmental orientations, such as language affinity, cultural similarities and differences, and political values. Thus, there seems to be an orderly and pervasive human propensity to organize the geographic and physical environment cognitively, perceptually, and affectively. The data suggest that some of these modes of environmental orientation occur in a wide variety of cultures that vary in technology, history, and cultural practices.

THE DEVELOPMENT OF ENVIRONMENTAL ORIENTATIONS

How and when do environmental orientations develop? At what age do children gain the ability to understand the large-scale environment? When do egocentric orientations develop? When are environmental attitudes formed about home versus more distant places?

Stages in Piaget's Theory

The most significant work relevant to these questions is that of the Swiss psychologist Jean Piaget, who, together with his associates, has done a voluminous series of research studies and theoretical analyses of children's development. Because Piaget has been so prolific over the years, we can only touch on aspects of his work. For this discussion we will rely heavily on the excellent analysis of Piaget by Hart and Moore (1973).

A basic premise of Piaget's thinking is that the development of spatial cognition in children is "an inherent *interaction* and series of *equilibrations* between the organism and its environment" (Hart & Moore, p. 258). Thus, development combines *learning* and *maturation*, or the unfolding of genetic potentials. Also explicit in Piaget's thinking is the notion of an active organism that structures, modifies, and acts on the environment, rather than one that is merely passive and reacts to the environment. So spatial development is a transactional and reciprocal process whereby a person relates to the environment. Within these general assumptions Piaget and his associates present a rather complex approach to spatial and cognitive development that is outlined in Figure 3-2 taken from Hart and Moore (1973).

The figure first points to different chronological stages of development: infancy, preschool, middle childhood, and adolescence and beyond. We will examine each stage separately, working our way down the columns of the figure. The top half of the figure presents general cognitive and spatial capabilities at various chronological stages. The bottom section describes spatial representation systems at each developmental stage.

Infancy. From birth to about age 2, "the human child changes from an organism capable only of reflex activity to an individual capable of

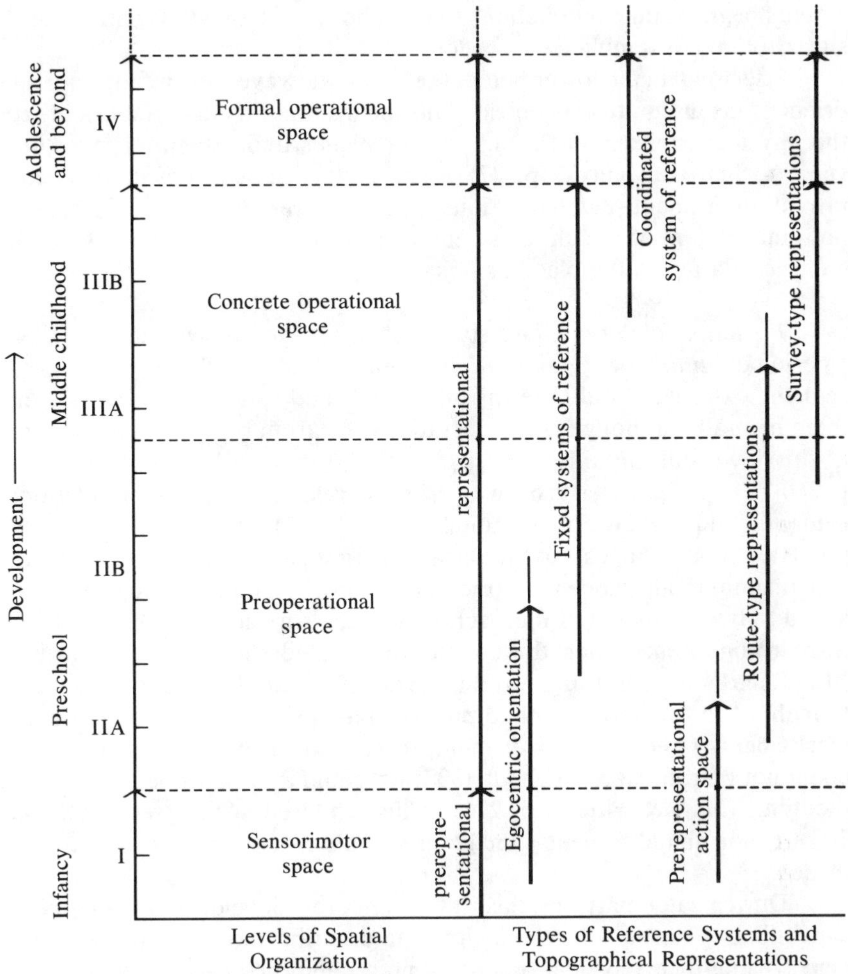

Figure 3-2. Development of spatial cognition and perception in children. Copyright © 1973 by Aldine Publishing Company. Reprinted, with permission, from *Image and Environment* (New York: Aldine Publishing Company).

coordinated action and internalized thoughts'' (Hart & Moore, p. 260).[2] During the early part of this phase, for about a year, the child is unable to evoke an image of an object when the object is not immediately present. That is, the child forgets about an absent object, as if it never existed. With development, however, the child learns that the object still exists somewhere, even if it is not present. In addition, by the end of this stage,

[2]Copyright © 1973 by Aldine Publishing Company. Reprinted with permission, from *Image and Environment* (New York: Aldine Publishing Company).

objects begin to take on relations to one another, so that the spatial world starts to have a semblance of order.

As shown in the lower half of the figure, however, the infant's spatial orientations are quite egocentric. This means that "a child first orients to the physical environment using axes or planes defined entirely with respect to his own body" (p. 275). The child's actual body movements provide cues about spatial locations, so that the representation of places is not independent of the child as center or of the actual movements of the child in relation to the place or objects.

Preschool children. This stage lasts from age 2 to age 8 and is called a period of *intuitive* or *preoperational* thought. "The child can now represent the external world in terms of symbols and can begin to operate on them mentally, although these operations, far from being systematic, are at this level only intuitive and partially coordinated" (Hart & Moore, p. 260). The stage consists of two periods in relation to spatial orientation: symbolic and preconceptual thought (ages 2 to 7) and intuitive, partially regulated thought (ages 4 to 8). During the first part of this stage, the child still maintains an egocentric orientation. For example, young children asked to build a model of their school and the surrounding area and later to rearrange items when the layout was rotated showed the following: "Landmarks were not organized in terms of a spatial whole; routes were thought of in terms of the children's own actions first, the various landmarks being fixed in terms of them, instead of vice versa, and the plan could not be rotated throughout 180°, nor could the routes be reversed in thought" (Hart & Moore, p. 276). Thus, children at the preoperational stage cannot build a mental image of complex spatial relations between places.

During later parts of this stage, children develop *route mapping* capabilities. That is, they can draw or describe the relations between places using themselves as a starting point, and they can draw a path or route to other places, but only as if they were moving toward that place. Thus, they themselves serve as basic reference points, and they have to imagine their own movement to a place in order to describe its location. During later stages, as described below, there is a shift from an egocentric orientation to a fixed system of reference in which places are anchors rather than the self being the main spatial anchor.

Middle childhood. This stage spans ages 7 to 12 and is termed the stage of *concrete operations*. According to Piaget, this is a crucial turning point, as the child breaks away from several perspectives. In addition, the child is able to deal with reversible relations in regard to an object, such as left, right, in front of, and behind.

During this stage fixed systems of reference develop. Children can now use a fixed set of geographical landmarks, such as the home and the school, not only themselves, as reference points for locating spatial objects and places; and these landmarks exist as subsets of different parts of the environment. However, these subsets of places often are separate and unrelated and do not form a well-coordinated system. At the same time the child develops "survey maps," or topographical representations that involve coordination of paths, routes, places, and objects, yielding a general conceptualization of the environment. This stage involves the child's breaking away from his or her egocentric orientation, in which the self was the center of the world. For the first time, the child begins to see objects and places as having relations between themselves that are independent of the child.

Adolescence and beyond. This stage, the stage of *formal operations*, begins at age 11 to 14 and involves extensive use of language, mathematical symbols, and complex abstractions. The child becomes able to use a coordinated reference system. The use of the cardinal directions of north, south, east, and west is an example of a coordinated reference system, in which any location in space can be determined with respect to any other location. Thus, development moves from a fixed reference system to a flexible one, in which any location can serve as an anchoring point for any other location. In addition, the child is now able to make *survey-type representations* of the environment. These involve the ability to locate paths, places, and objects in relation to one another in a unified way, not discretely or piecemeal, and to do so in terms of a variety of centers or reference points.

Other research. More recently, Siegel, Kirasic, and Kail (1978) and Siegel and White (1975) have elaborated on the basic Piagetian concepts described above. They propose a system for describing the development of children's environmental cognition and hypothesize that children first orient themselves to the environment in terms of significant *landmarks*. The next stage involves the establishment of connections between landmarks, which is essentially the development of *routes*. A final phase in the developmental sequence involves the emergence of *configurations*, much like the survey representations described earlier. Within each of these processes Siegel and his associates hypothesize two levels of spatial comprehension. Siegel et al. (1978) describe these as follows: At the lower, more primitive level is enactive, sensorimotor knowledge—knowing that one has seen a landmark, knowing that one can get from A to B, and recognizing elements within a spatial configuration. A second form of environmental knowledge involves (1) knowing not only that one has seen a landmark before but also knowing where one has seen it and knowing that this knowledge can be useful in organizing a spatial representation of the environment, (2) knowing not only that one can get from A to B but also that a number of landmarks can be placed ordinally on the line between A and B and knowing that one can start at any point on that line and with appropriate bearings can get to either terminal landmark, and (3) knowing not only that one can recognize a particular landmark in a large array but also that particular subregions can be coordinated with each other and that one will see different configurations from different vantage points.

What can be said about cultural similarities and differences in respect to these developmental stages? The answer to this question is, unfortunately, not very much. Even though the theoretical ideas presented in this section derive from an extensive body of research, little is known about children's environmental orientations in various cultures. However, some evidence exists (Dasen, 1972; Dawson, 1967; LeVine & Price-Williams, 1974) that certain stages of children's development in other than spatial areas do appear in many cultures, although the temporal sequencing may vary somewhat from culture to culture; that is, the ages at which children move from one stage to the next and the order in which children go through the stages may both vary cross-culturally. Thus, the universality of spatial developmental stages is not yet fully studied, although the principle seems plausible at present.

Studies by Stea and Blaut are somewhat related to this issue. In one investigation Blaut, McCleary, and Blaut (1970) analyzed the ability of Puerto Rican and North American 6-year-olds to interpret and make use of maps without prior formal training or experience. In a variety of tasks involving aerial photographs, they found that children with little experience and from different cultures were reasonably skilled and could make sophisticated judgments. For example, children were asked to identify various features of a small town and the surrounding countryside from low- and high-altitude photographs. Most children were able to identify transportation facilities, surface characteristics, and vegetation as well as cars, houses, and streets. In addition, children successfully solved simple navigational problems. Interestingly, there were essentially no differences between children from the United States and Puerto Rico, suggesting that the cognitive and perceptual capabilities involved in these tasks may not be culture-bound. In terms of Piaget's model, these data suggest that children had elements of fixed systems of reference and survey-type representations, in which the geographical environment was represented in other than egocentric terms and various landmarks and reference points were related to one another rather than to the self alone.

Stea and Blaut (1973) demonstrated the interplay of learning and maturation in ability to interpret complex spatial representations. Five-year-old kindergarten children from different socioeconomic levels and places in Puerto Rican society were tested on several tasks requiring interpretation of aerial photographs. The sample included urban lower- and middle-class children and those from coastal-plantation and mountain-peasant groups. All children except those from the urban lower class named an equivalent number of objects from aerial photographs, but the urban middle-class children named more objects accurately than the other groups, reflecting differential experience and learning opportunities. There were differences in what objects and places children named, in accordance with their probable learning histories: roads were most often named by urban middle-class and plantation children, and vehicles were most often mentioned by urban groups. Interestingly, children were no more accurate in describing objects in their home communities than objects in other places.

In a follow-up study designed to track the development of map-reading skills, Stea and Blaut (1973) found that mountain-peasant and urban middle-class Puerto Rican children showed the greatest increase in skill between kindergarten (age 5) and second grade (age 7 to 8) and that skill acquisition leveled out after that. Once again, however, urban middle-class children were more accurate in their photo interpretations than mountain-peasant groups. These developmental changes occurred during the late preschool and the middle-childhood stages, when, Piaget proposed, there is a shift from egocentric to fixed systems of reference.

These studies suggest the following: (1) Orientation to the large-scale environment shows a pattern of development compatible with Piaget's model. (2) The consistency among children from different cultural and different socioeconomic groups points to the possible importance of maturation and inherited dispositions, and (3) the fact of differences between urban and nonurban children, for example, also illustrates the role of experience and learning and the probable interaction of experience and maturation processes.

There is also a small amount of research on children's attitudes and preferences. How and when do such preferences develop? When do they begin to take the form of adult attitudes? Gould (1973a) studied the environmental preferences of children in the town of Jönköping, in south central Sweden. Children aged 7½ to 13½ ranked their preferences for 70 places in Sweden. The 7½-year-olds were unable to complete the task; the 9½-year-olds made a diffuse set of rankings that reflected low consensus, although the familiar pattern of preferring their own town emerged clearly. The 11½-year-olds portrayed a more expansive picture, with distinct preferences for their home town, for southern Sweden, and for the city of Stockholm. The 13½-year-olds showed a similar pattern, although they made sharper distinctions among various areas. Knowledge about places showed a comparable developmental profile. Thus, these data point to a systematic developmental progression that, among older children, leads to a set of preferences very similar to those found in the studies of high school and college students described earlier. That is, the older children showed a decided preference for home and nearby areas over distant places and selected preferences, based on factors other than proximity to home, for certain locales.

In summary, there is a gradually increasing body of knowledge about the development of environmental orientations in children within or across cultures. The studies that do exist suggest that there are basic similarities in developmental processes across cultures, but there are also differences that are due to learning and socialization. This way of thinking is compatible with Kaplan's (1973) hypothesis that our understanding of the spatial environment depends on learning capabilities, which in turn may be linked to our evolutionary history.

SUMMARY

This chapter extended the discussion of Chapter 2 to deal with how people cognitively and perceptually orient themselves to the physical environment. Emphasis was placed on empirically based approaches and dimensional aspects of environmental orientations. We subdivided environmental orientations into environmental cognitions and environmental attitudes. Environmental cognitions involve how people obtain information about the environment, how that information is processed, and the use of that information to determine locations and attributes of the environment. Environmental attitudes include feelings, preferences, and likes and dislikes for different parts of the environment.

The central sections of the chapter described research and theory on environmental cognitions and attitudes. We explored Lynch's (1960) dimensions of paths, landmarks, edges, nodes, and districts in relation to several cities in the United States and elsewhere. We also examined people's knowledge of and preferences for different parts of the environment, from such large-scale environments as nations to states, cities, and neighborhoods. Results are fairly consistent within and across cultural groups: knowledge and preference are greater for home than for distant places, although certain places are preferred regardless of distance. These results indicate the importance of cultural, political, and economic factors as determinants of environmental attitude and knowledge, along with a general relation between distance and environmental orientation. Thus, an egocentric orientation to the environment is overlaid by particular experiential factors, and these principles seem to obtain at several levels of scale.

The final section of the chapter examined the development of environmental cognitions and attitudes, particularly in light of Piaget's theory. Several stages of development are hypothesized by this theory, including an egocentric stage, in which the world is conceptualized cognitively and spatially from the perspective of self-as-center, and more advanced stages, in which the environment is conceptualized as a coordinated system of reference in which places and objects are located in a more flexible way. A facet of this theory that seems somewhat supported by research is that the development of environmental orientations involves an interaction of inborn maturational predispositions that unfold with age and cultural and social experiences.

PART TWO

BEHAVIORAL PROCESSES: PRIVACY, PERSONAL SPACE, AND TERRITORIALITY

In Part 2 we turn our attention to behavioral processes involved in people's relations to the environment. Whereas Part 1 focused on the *perceptual and cognitive* aspects of culture/environment relations, the three chapters in Part 2 emphasize *overt behaviors* in relation to the environment. We will examine the actions and behaviors that people use to regulate their relation with the social and physical world, including how they use the physical environment as a behavioral extension of themselves.

Chapter 4 deals with the topic of privacy, a concept that we use as a bridge between personal space and territorial behavior. For us the concept "privacy" addresses the means by which individuals regulate their dealings with the social world and make themselves more accessible or less accessible to others.

The concepts of personal space and territorial behavior are viewed as behavioral mechanisms by which people regulate their privacy, so that personal space and territoriality function to create a desired level of openness or closedness to others. Personal space, discussed in Chapter 5, deals with interpersonal distancing and spacing that people use in a variety of settings. Chapter 6 examines territorial behavior in humans—that is, the use and control of areas and objects in the physical environment.

Taken together, Parts 1 and 2 of the book deal with a range of human behavioral processes in relation to the physical environment. Part 1 examined cognitive and perceptual processes, which are mental and subjective; Part 2 describes overt behavioral actions in relation to the environment. Part 3 will explore how these mental and behavioral processes are reflected in environmental places, such as homes, communities, and cities.

Chapter 4

PRIVACY

There are many social behaviors that can be examined in relation to the environment. However, we will focus on behaviors related to privacy, personal space, and territory for several reasons. First, these processes have received considerable attention in the research literature, and we can draw on a fair body of knowledge about them. Second, these concepts deal with fundamental aspects of environmental behavior and bear directly on culture/environment relations. Third, Altman (1975) has already developed a framework for linking these processes that we can exploit in our quest to understand culture and environment (see Figure 4-1).

The crucial idea of Altman's framework is that privacy is a central concept that provides a bridge between personal space, territory, and other realms of social behavior. In this model privacy is an interpersonal boundary regulation process by which a person or group regulates interaction with others (Altman, 1975). Privacy regulation permits people to be open to others on some occasions and to be closed off from interaction at other times. Privacy is, therefore, a changing process whereby people attempt to regulate their openness/closedness to others.

An important feature of the framework in Figure 4-1 is that personal space and territory, along with verbal and nonverbal responses and cultural practices, operate as *behavioral mechanisms* to facilitate privacy regulation. As the framework suggests, people mentally establish a desired level of privacy—a level of interaction or openness they would like to have in a particular setting. Their desired level of privacy might involve being open and wanting to interact with another person, or it might be to avoid others and to be inaccessible to them. The framework states that people then set in motion a series of behavioral mechanisms to implement their momentary desired level of interaction. They might increase or decrease the physical distance between themselves and another person by backing away or moving quite close to that person (such behavior exemplifies the use of personal space). Alternatively, they might close their door and/or not invite someone into a territory that they occupy and control (territorial behavior). Conversely, they might indicate that an-

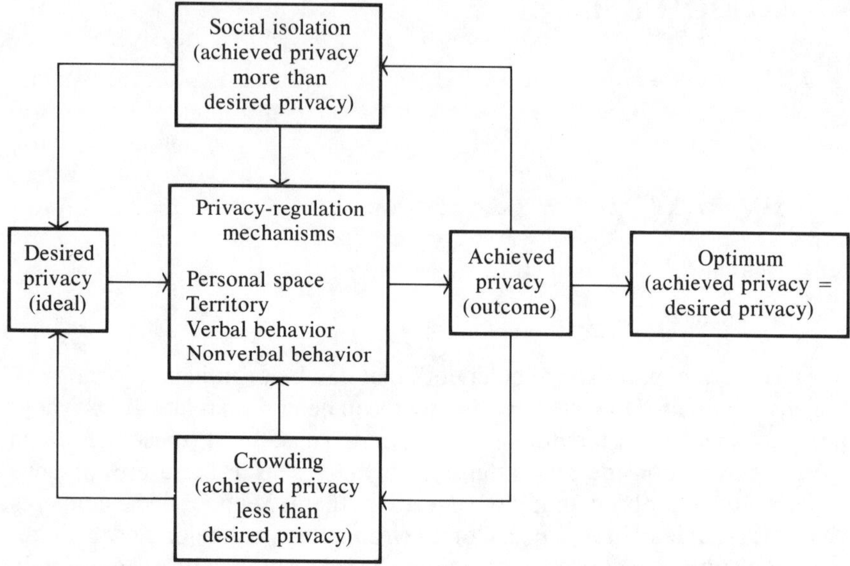

Figure 4-1. Overview of relations among privacy, personal space, territory, and crowding. From *The Environment and Social Behavior: Privacy, Personal Space, Territory, and Crowding,* by I. Altman. Copyright © 1975 by Wadsworth, Inc. Reprinted by permission of the publisher, Brooks/Cole Publishing Company, Monterey, California.

other person is welcome to visit them. Accessibility or inaccessibility might also be indicated by what people say or how they say it (verbal behavior). Or a person might reflect openness or closedness through posture, turning toward or away, looking or not looking at another person, grimacing or smiling (nonverbal behavior). Thus, people use a series of mechanisms at different times and in different patterns to implement a desired degree of contact with others.

As Figure 4-1 illustrates, sometimes things work out successfully; that is, the outcome—the achieved privacy—is equal to the desired privacy. But at other times one's level of contact is not optimal. Sometimes a person is *crowded*, as occurs when achieved privacy is less than desired privacy—that is, one ends up having more interaction than one initially wanted and tried to achieve. Crowding occurs when the behavioral mechanisms of personal space, territory, and verbal and nonverbal behaviors were not used in a successful way to protect a person or group from undesired interaction: the system undershot its mark. But sometimes privacy regulation overshoots the mark, and a person or group receives less contact than was desired (social isolation).

THE MEANING OF PRIVACY

Privacy is a widely used term, and, as with so many other terms, people often assume that there is agreement on its meaning. However, the fact is that there is not complete consensus. After an analysis of how *privacy* has been used in everyday language and in the research literature, we have decided on an approach that is, in some ways, counter to traditional usage. We will define *privacy* as "selective control of access to the self" (Altman, 1975; see Figure 4-2).

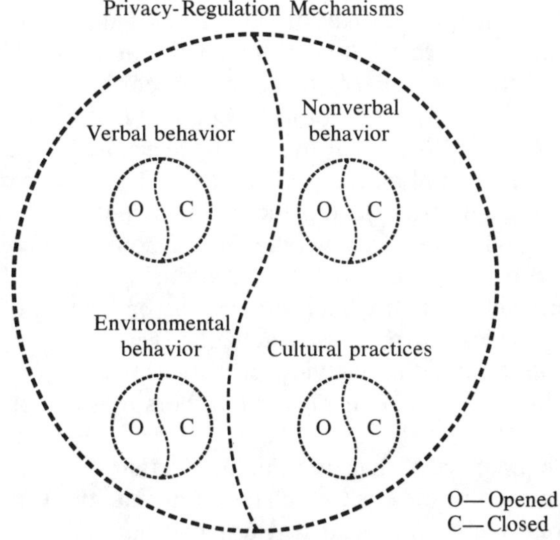

Figure 4-2. Dialectic model of privacy regulation. From "Privacy regulation: Culturally universal or culturally specific?" by I. Altman, *Journal of Social Issues,* 1977, *33,* 66–84. Reprinted by permission.

This definition highlights the idea of *selective control* as intrinsic to privacy. Selective control means that people (individuals or groups) attempt to regulate their interaction and exchange with others or with aspects of the environment. That is, people try to control their openness or closedness to others, to be sometimes open and available to others and sometimes closed and unavailable. This idea is depicted in Figure 4-2 in that the large circle, which represents a person, has a dashed boundary. Like the solid and broken lines on a highway, the boundary to the self is sometimes open and "passable" and sometimes not, depending on circumstances. People control their accessibility to others, making privacy regulation a "boundary control" process.

We depart from some traditional ways of thinking by emphasizing that privacy means *changing* boundary control, not merely "keeping out" others or shutting off stimulation. Privacy is a dynamic process whereby people vary in the degree to which they are accessible to others. Our use of the term, therefore, covers the whole gamut from extreme openness to extreme closedness.

The idea of privacy as one opening/closing process is further reflected in the small circles of the figure. Each circle has parts labeled O (open) or C (closed). This illustrates the idea that, using different behavioral mechanisms (represented by each of the small circles), people sometimes signal their openness to others and sometimes their closedness and that the open or closed part of the circle can change through time. The idea of *changing* accessibility draws on the ancient Chinese notion of yin/yang, or the concept of dialectics. According to this philosophy, which has taken on different forms throughout history, the world is made up of opposites and tensional forces that, because of their very opposition, provide unity and meaningfulness to a whole. For example, day and night, seeming opposites, lend meaning to each other. Day has no meaning without night, and vice versa. Or harmony and conflict, opposite processes, provide a unity to social relationships. Thus, for the Chinese philosophers and for many later writers, the opposition of various physical and psychological processes actually serves to provide unity to a phenomenon. So it is that we view privacy as a series of opposing forces toward being open and being closed to others, not one or the other force alone.

Another aspect of dialectic thinking is that the balance of opposing forces is in a constant state of change (indeed, the title of the ancient Chinese treatise *I Ching* means "Book of Changes"). Accordingly, one never permanently wishes to have contact (or to avoid contact) with others. Rather, the desire to be open or closed ebbs and flows over time, depending upon whom one is in contact with, the setting, and one's current internal state. Privacy regulation is an ever-changing process, the forces toward being open and being closed tipping in one or the other direction at different times.

We consider a dialectic approach to be a useful way of thinking, because it treats privacy regulation as a changing process, one that is responsive to momentary circumstances of an interpersonal, personal, or situational nature. It also fits with everyday intuitions about people's relations with others. There are times when people wish to interact with others; there are times when they wish to be alone; there are times when they have mixed feelings about being with others. But their desires and attempts to seek or avoid contact are part of a unity involving their transactions with the world about them. To be with and to be without interaction are not separate processes; they are part of the same phenomenon, "two sides of the same coin." Thus, one rarely attempts to avoid all contact with others beyond a limited period of time. And one rarely seeks to have total, unending contact. Instead, one oscillates over time, sometimes seeking interaction with others and sometimes avoiding it.

Figure 4-2 also illustrates the idea that people use a variety of behavioral mechanisms to control their openness/closedness. As discussed earlier, these mechanisms include verbal behavior whereby we let others know about our desire to interact or not interact: "Let's talk," "Can I raise an issue with you," "Sorry, I'm too busy now," "No, I can't make it this evening." Through use of a "cool" or "warm" way of speaking—so-called paraverbal communication cues—we let people know our feelings regardless of the content of what we say. We also use nonverbal modes of communication to regulate privacy. For example, we use personal space as a boundary-regulation device by moving farther from or closer to others, sometimes orienting our bodies toward them and sometimes facing away. We exhibit receptivity by nodding our heads, smiling, opening our arms, leaning forward, or using relaxed body postures. Conversely, we communicate a lack of interest by frowning, looking away, assuming rigid, symmetrical body positions, fidgeting with our clothing or rubbing our hands, and looking at our watches.

In addition to our bodies, we use objects and areas in the environment to reflect our availability to others. Sometimes we permit or even invite others into our territories; at other times we shut off personal places to access by others. We close or open doors; we use signs which say Keep Out or Welcome or which can be flipped from one side to the other to indicate our accessibility. And, once people are in our territories, we can make them feel welcome by offering them a chair (sometimes our favorite chair), providing refreshments, and inviting them to make use of the facilities. Sometimes we make people feel uncomfortable by not inviting them in, not offering them any amenities, and otherwise reflecting our displeasure, coolness, or lack of interest in having them occupy our territories.

Finally, as the fourth small circle indicates, cultures have a variety of customs, rules, and norms which communicate openness or closedness to others and which are readily understood by most people in a particular culture. For example, in present-day U.S. culture we might "drop in" to visit close friends if we are in their neighborhood, but this usually is not done at dinner time, too early in the morning, or too late in the evening. With acquaintances or strangers we typically await an invitation. We avoid coming too early to parties or staying too late; we do not usually barge through closed doors, especially bathroom doors; we are careful not to take too much of a higher-status person's time; and we are sensitive to people's looking at their watches as indications of their desire to terminate the contact. Furthermore, to avoid or terminate contact we often use a series of culturally known phrases. So Figure 4-2 reflects the idea that people have available a wide repertoire of behavioral mechanisms to make their self-boundaries permeable so that they are open and accessible to contact with others or to make the boundaries impermeable so that they are closed and inaccessible.

However, behavioral mechanisms do not operate in a rigid way, and several other features of privacy regulation need to be addressed. First, each circle in the figure encompasses a variety of behaviors that can be exhibited. More important, the various privacy mechanisms within a circle (or within different circles) work in profiles and patterns, not separately. That is, we use various combinations of behaviors to reflect our desires for interaction. Sometimes the emphasis is placed on verbal behaviors, sometimes on nonverbal behaviors, sometimes on the combination of two or three classes of mechanisms. Which combination we use may vary with the setting. In a formal situation we might select one combination of verbal expressions, tone of voice, bodily actions, and cultural practices to reflect openness or closedness. In an informal setting we might use a totally different mix of mechanisms. Furthermore, the blend of mechanisms may vary for different social relationships. With strangers we might exhibit a different pattern of behaviors to reflect accessibility than with friends or family. So the privacy framework proposed in this chapter assumes that (1) many different behavioral mechanisms are available to regulate openness or closedness to others, and (2) these mechanisms operate in myriad patterns or profiles.

This patternlike quality of privacy regulation is crucial to our understanding of other cultures. For example, in the United States, if a person closes his or her door, puts a "Do Not Disturb" sign on the door, announces beforehand that he or she wishes to be alone, and emphasizes the point by gestures, body postures, and tone of voice, then various circles in Figure 4-2 are dominated by the "closed" part of the yin/yang process. However, there are cultures in which several families live communally, no doors exist, and it is culturally inappropriate to speak loudly or to demand noncontact as people in the United States are prone to do. Yet such cultures have mechanisms to regulate contact with others that might involve different circles or different parts of the circles depicted in the figure. We will maintain that *all* cultures have evolved behavioral mechanisms that permit people to regulate their interaction with others. What differs among cultures, according to this way of thinking, is the types of mechanisms that are available to people, not their presence or absence. Some cultures, by virtue of centuries of life-style and the interaction of cultural and environmental factors, may not use doors or may not vary the content of their verbal exchange to regulate privacy. Rather, they may rely more heavily on other combinations of paraverbal and nonverbal channels of communication. By looking at only one behavior or another in isolation or by assessing privacy regulation only in terms of our own practices, we may fail to understand privacy regulation in another culture. We therefore need to understand the unique mechanisms that other cultures use to regulate privacy from an "emic" orientation, or one that attempts to view a culture from *its* frame of reference, not just from an "etic" orientation, in which we impose *our* singular perspective on a culture.

WHAT IS PRIVACY FOR?

Up to this point we have discussed how privacy works—as a dialectic boundary-regulation process whereby people control their interactions with others and as a system that involves a variety of behavioral mechanisms that operate in different profiles or patterns. But we can now ask "So what? Why is privacy so important?" Or, put another way, we can ask about the functions, or goals, that privacy serves for individuals, groups, and societies.

The goals of privacy can be examined at two levels. First, as discussed earlier, privacy regulation involves the management of social interaction. By regulating our openness/closedness, or accessibility/inaccessibility to others, we can manage our social contacts with others in accordance with our personal desires, the intimacy of our relationships, and situational circumstances. Management of interpersonal relations is an important goal of privacy regulation.

But there is more at stake in privacy regulation. We hypothesize that the psychological viability or well-being of people and groups centers on the successful management of privacy. That is, success or failure at privacy regulation may well have implications for self-identity, self-esteem, and self-worth—or the very well-being and survival capability of people and groups.

We have stated several facets of this thesis elsewhere (Altman, 1975):

> Self identity is a person['s] or group's cognitive, psychological, and emotional definitions and understanding of themselves as beings. It includes persons knowing where they begin and where they end, which aspects of the physical world are parts of the self, and which aspects are parts of others. It encompasses self understanding of one's capabilities and limitations, strengths and weaknesses, emotions and cognitions, beliefs and disbeliefs. Furthermore, self identity has a strong evaluative (positive or negative) component; that is, am I a worthwhile person to myself and others, and, if so, why? [p. 49][1]

[1]This and all other quotations from this source are from *The Environment and Social Behavior: Privacy, Personal Space, Territory, and Crowding,* by I. Altman. Copyright © 1975 by Wadsworth, Inc. Reprinted by permission of the publisher, Brooks/Cole Publishing Company, Monterey, California.

Thus, self-identity and a sense of self-worth involve the ability to control one's boundaries in relation to others. Such boundary identity and boundary control probably derive from a successful history of learning how one relates to others. It is often said in the research literature on child development that a crucial phase in socialization occurs when the child learns to distinguish between the self and the not-self in several ways. The infant learns that the mother is "different" from the self; the child learns that the world is more than where he or she happens to be at the moment; the child begins to conceptualize routes and directions in the spatial environment independently of where he or she is immediately located and independently of the home as the center of the universe: all these events reflect aspects of the learning of self/other boundaries. Thus, the development of environmental cognitions, discussed in Chapters 2 and 3, contributes to the evolution of processes concerning self/other boundaries. To a great extent, environmental cognitive processes and privacy-regulation processes are part and parcel of the more general relationship of people and culture to their environments and to one another.

Examples of unsuccessful or poor boundary definition illustrate how boundary processes are related to psychological problems. Schizophrenia, a severe psychosis involving, to one degree or another, disorientation, hallucinations, delusions, scrambled speech, confused cognitive processes, and abnormal social withdrawal and interaction, has recently been conceptualized by Blatt and Wild (1976) as a malfunction in the process of regulating the self/other boundary. They describe schizophrenics as not being able, cognitively or emotionally, to distinguish between the self and not-self, so that the world is part of them and they are part of the world, with little articulation in how they differ from events in the world. Thoughts, people, and situations exist in a jumbled confusion, without coherence or pattern, and the "psychological person" almost does not exist as an intact entity, but is an ever-changing kaleidoscope. It is as if, in our terms, the self/other boundary had an uncontrolled and inconsistent permeability, were unpredictably open or closed, and operated in a helter-skelter fashion, from the point of view of the schizophrenic and of others with whom he or she interacts. Clearly, it is hard to see how such a person can function well. And, as discussed below, our view is that an effective boundary-regulation process is crucial to individual well-being in any culture. Privacy regulation is therefore central to effective psychological functioning.

A related issue concerns a person's ability to regulate self/other boundaries in relation to environmental demands. A person who is successful at regulating openness/closedness not only comes to know where he or she begins and ends but also is able to develop a competence at controlling life events. If a person cannot achieve interaction and is consistently more lonely and isolated than is desired, or if a person cannot prevent intrusions to a reasonable extent, then it is hard to see how that person can have a clear sense of self. Hence, if someone grows up with people always intruding on his or her places, possessions, and person, and if that person is unable to prevent such boundary intrusions, then it is likely that the person will not have a favorable (or even clear-cut) sense of self or self-worth.

There is a line of research in experimental psychology termed "learned helplessness" that illustrates these ideas (Seligman, 1975). In studies in this research, animals are exposed to unpleasant stimulation, such as shock, that they cannot control. They cannot consistently respond in ways that will turn it off; it appears sporadically and without any consistency. It is as if, in our terms, they had no power to regulate their transactions with the environment. Their self/other boundary system simply does not work. In these experiments a history of failure to regulate self/other boundaries results in animals' "giving up." The animals become "helpless," cease struggling to avoid or to cope with the unpleasant circumstances, and in later situations show decreased ability to learn. They seem unable to function normally following the repeated failure of their ability to regulate their self/other boundaries. The essence of this discussion is that

> privacy mechanisms define the limits and boundaries of the self. When the permeabilities of those boundaries [are] under the control of a person, a sense of individuality develops. But it is not the inclusion or exclusion of others that is vital to self definition; it is the ability to regulate contact when desired. If I can control what is me and not me, if I can define what is me and not me, and if I can observe the limits and scope of my control, then I have taken major steps toward understanding and defining what I am. Thus privacy mechanisms serve to help me define me [Altman, 1975, p. 50].

We now come to the heart of the issue regarding privacy and culture. *The process of privacy regulation is, we believe, so central to human functioning that it is hypothesized to be present in all cultures*. People as individuals and as members of groups, we hypothesize, must be capable of regulating their interactions with others to some extent. Without such a capability, we believe that no human being can survive psychologically or perhaps physically, whether he or she is an urban dweller in a technologically complex society or a rural villager in an isolated society. The ability to control, manage, and pace interactions is hypothesized to be culturally universal.

But how is it, one might ask, that people in some cultures do not seem to be able to avoid social contacts? They live in crowded dwellings, often several families to a residence, there may be no walls or doors to separate people from one another, everyone seems to know everyone else's business, and so on. The answer lies in our theoretical framework, described earlier, which stated that privacy is a multimodal process and involves a variety of regulatory mechanisms—some environmental, some verbal, some nonverbal. A society's lack of effective environmental privacy mechanisms, for example, should not lead to the conclusion that people in that society have no privacy whatsoever. The thrust of our position is that, if one looked "properly" at a given culture, one would uncover *some* set of mechanisms that people use to make themselves more or less accessible to others. Examining a culture only in regard to environmental mechanisms (or any other single mechanism alone) is apt to give a distorted picture of how that culture regulates privacy.

To put all this in a nutshell, we hypothesize that *all* cultures have mechanisms that permit their members to regulate privacy. Some cultures emphasize one set of mechanisms, whereas other cultures emphasize another set. What differs among cultures is *how* they regulate privacy, not whether or not they have a basic capability for self/other boundary control.

PRIVACY AS A CULTURAL UNIVERSAL

The remainder of the chapter examines the hypothesis of the cultural universality of privacy. At the outset it is important to realize that there are many difficulties with such an analysis, and there is considerable controversy among anthropologists and cross-cultural psychologists concerning the question of cultural universals (see Lonner, 1979, for a detailed treatment of this issue).

One problem is related to the "emic/etic" matter that we raised in Chapter 2. There is a point of view, termed "cultural relativism," that holds that cultures are unique and must be understood in their own right, not just by imposing the values or way of thinking of the observer's culture. That is, one must adopt an "emic" perspective to understand a given culture. According to such thinking, the search for cultural universals may lead to an "etic" flaw. That is, one might misperceive how a culture "really works" if one approaches it only from the vantage of one's own culture. This, incidentally, is a complaint often raised by representatives of minority cultures in the United States, who state that the imposition of White middle-class values on their activities is inappropriate and that minorities must be understood in light of their own values.

A purely relativistic approach, however, may ignore similarities among people, and some believe that there is utility in searching for communalities across cultures while still maintaining sensitivity to cultural uniqueness. The latter view fits our perspective with regard to privacy. We are willing to explore the hypothesis that certain aspects of privacy regulation are culturally universal but that regulation is achieved differently in different cultures.

Another tricky issue concerns the level of abstraction at which cultural universals are described. Surely, people everywhere eat, sleep, and procreate, and most cultures have some form of religious or cosmological views, family structure, and social organization. But we must do more than merely assert the universal presence of such activities, or else we will be guilty of stating what Walter Lonner, a prominent cross-cultural psychologist, described as "yawning truisms"—obviously correct statements, but so what! Knowing that people eat and sleep says little about their culture. So we must go beyond such superficial statements. But what does "going beyond" yawning truisms mean? Lonner (1979) suggests that an analysis of cultural universals should do one of several things: examine how a universal fits into a society's institutions, see how it functions and examine its behavioral dynamics, or explore its relation to a theoretical system. We intend to do all three with privacy regulation—to examine privacy in relation to different aspects of a culture's institutions and practices, to explore how various privacy mechanisms work within and across cultures, and to study privacy within the conceptual framework proposed earlier.

There are other problems with the study of cultural universals, and we will address them next as part of our plan of attack.

A STRATEGY FOR EXAMINING PRIVACY IN DIFFERENT CULTURES

We will examine privacy regulation in different cultures from two perspectives:

1. *Case examples of cultures that appear to have either very little privacy or a great deal of privacy.* People in some cultures have been described in the anthropological literature and elsewhere as seemingly unable to avoid or shut off interaction with others. Other cultures have been portrayed as just the opposite—people hardly interact with one another, and they seem to be quite isolated socially. If our hypothesis is plausible, then we should find that each type of culture does, in fact, have available to its members compensatory privacy-regulation mechanisms. Such mechanisms might not be environmental ones, but could involve cultural customs and verbal and nonverbal behaviors that people use in a compensatory way. Identifying such mechanisms requires, of course, that we look at cultures in light of the theory of privacy outlined above—namely, that privacy is a dialectic, multimodal boundary-regulation system.

2. *Case examples of social relationships.* A second aspect of our strategy involves the analysis of various social relationships. For example, we will examine how people in different cultures manage relationships with strangers and casual acquaintances, spouses, mothers- and fathers-in-law, and children. Here again we expect to discover that people

in all types of social relationships have behavioral mechanisms that permit them to regulate their accessibility and inaccessibility. Although there may be differences in *how* privacy is regulated across cultures and relationships, we still hypothesize *some* pattern of behavioral mechanisms that allows people to maintain successfully a desired level of self/other openness and closedness.

Before we examine different cultures according to this strategy, you should be aware of some problems with such an analysis, in addition to those raised earlier. First, it is not easy to use anthropological materials to explore privacy. Many cultural descriptions are not explicit about privacy regulation, either because the ethnographer was not interested in privacy or because privacy was not analyzed within our perspective. Hence, there may be cases in which privacy was not even described or a culture may have been depicted, for example, as having "no privacy" or "total privacy." In such instances, are we to conclude that our approach is invalid—or that the ethnography was incomplete according to our theoretical approach? In any event, there will be cases in which we may not be able to test out our ideas.

A second problem concerns the meaning of a particular behavior. Suppose that we describe a behavior as a privacy-regulation mechanism—for example, a use of the environment, a cultural practice, or a nonverbal behavior. How can we know that the behavior is "truly" related to privacy regulation? Perhaps it really concerns religious issues or political or economic aspects of the culture. So there is a potential problem in assigning behavioral events to the domain of privacy rather than to other facets of a culture's life.

These problems are not easily solved, and you must be sensitive to them. Naturally, we will try to avoid these traps, although traps make the test of our ideas very difficult. However, our goal is not to "prove" the point, but to examine the plausibility of the idea of privacy as a cultural universal. It will take much more systematic analysis of cultures across the world, with attention to good sampling and selection, careful ethnographic analyses, and solutions to the problems raised above, before we can come close to "proof." For the present we only wish to demonstrate a way of thinking; future research is necessary to determine the validity of our approach. With these advance warnings in mind, let us now consider case studies of (1) cultures with apparently maximum or minimum social contact and (2) various social relationships in other cultures.

Cultures with Apparently Maximum Social Contact

Mehinacu culture. The anthropologists Gregor and Roberts provided an excellent example of a dialectic, multimodal analysis of privacy regulation in the Mehinacu Indians, a small tribal group in the jungles of central Brazil (Gregor, 1970, 1974; Roberts & Gregor, 1971). On the face of it, the Mehinacu have little power to avoid contact with others. In one village, five houses were located around a small plaza, so that all residents who were outside could see and be seen by others as they moved about. In each building several families lived communally, sharing the general space, although each family had its own area for sleeping and eating. People could easily see and hear what was happening in other parts of the dwelling unit; they entered the residence without announcing themselves; the thatched walls of the buildings were not very effective sound reducers. Furthermore, paths leading into the plaza were long and straight, so that people could be observed at great distances. Villagers were also able to recognize one another's footprints in the sandy paths around the village; agricultural fields outside the village were right next to one another, so that everyone knew a great deal about others' whereabouts.

Considering all these features of life among the Mehinacu, people seemed to have very little capability for closing themselves off from others. But Roberts and Gregor had a dialectic, multimodal approach to privacy regulation very much like ours, and they stated that one must look at other facets of Mehinacu life to understand privacy regulation. Furthermore, they indicated that these people in fact did have a variety of means for regulating their openness/accessibility to others. For example, there was a maze of twisting and winding paths beyond the village, and there were a number of secret clearings that people used to avoid others. There was also a practice for people to leave the village for lengthy periods, and some even had houses and gardens miles away, to which they retreated with their families for extended stays. Furthermore, there were several cultural practices that helped people control interaction. For example, men had a house that they used for social and religious purposes; women were not permitted access. People did not enter others' dwelling units without permission, and even those who lived in the same building were careful not to intrude on another family's space. The Mehinacu also avoided exposing others' misconduct, and they did not ask one another embarrassing questions. If such information was revealed, then the Mehinacu deliberately lied about themselves. So, side by side, in a dialectic sense, we see privacy mechanisms that the Mehinacu used to make themselves accessible and inaccessible to one another.

A vivid feature of Mehinacu life that also fits our analysis concerns the practices of seclusion and isolation, which spanned many years of a person's life. One period of seclusion occurred when a couple had its first child. At this time the mother, father, and child lived behind a wooden partition erected in their living space, and they were isolated from others for several weeks, especially when there were no other children in the family. After this period the child continued to be isolated and was rarely taken outside until the age of 1 or 1½ years.

Another period of seclusion often lasted for 2 years and occurred when boys reached 9 or 10 years of age. At this time a boy remained inside his home behind a wooden partition and rarely had contact with others, although he was able to leave the house after sundown. Even food and bathing water were brought to him, and he urinated through a wooden tube that was pushed through the thatched wall of the dwelling. During this period the boy was taught to speak quietly, to refrain from play, and to avoid emotional displays. Girls were also isolated following their first menstruation. Other instances of isolation occurred on the death of a spouse or when men learned to become religious leaders. It was possible, theoretically, for a Mehinacu villager to spend up to 8 years of life in seclusion.

Roberts and Gregor interpreted the simultaneous seclusion and openness in Mehinacu culture in a dialectic fashion, to the effect that the culture had evolved mechanisms that permitted a shifting balance of openness and closedness. This ethnographic analysis is a good illustration of the need to examine privacy as a multimodal process, involving a mixture of environmental, verbal, nonverbal, and cultural practices. By focusing only on one aspect of life, such as environmental factors, one would have obtained a distorted view of the Mehinacu privacy-regulation system. Gregor (1974) said:

> Information on rules of privacy . . . may be buried in descriptions of etiquette, or must be inferred from the characteristic house type and settlement pattern. . . . The diffuse definition of relationships and the exposed settings characteristic of many primitive communities demands a different kind of ethnography; an ethnography sensitive to the delicate interplay of privacy and publicity that emerges from social conduct [p. 348].

This analysis fits our approach quite well. Roberts and Gregor's work was done with a framework like ours to begin with, so that the notion of privacy as a dialectic, multimechanism process is very evident. Furthermore, although many of the behaviors they described might have other functions (for example, child seclusion may serve to protect an infant from disease), it also is plausible that the pattern of behaviors they identified is linked to regulation of social interaction.

Javanese culture. Another anthropologist, Geertz (cited in Westin, 1970), described certain groups in Javanese culture whose members also had apparently little ability to avoid others. Homes were of bamboo, had thin walls, and were not tightly built, so that sounds could be heard easily and there was some visual access. Furthermore, many homes did not have doors or fences or other barriers around them. It was also a custom, Geertz reported, for friends and acquaintances to wander freely in and out of houses. Inside, people went from room to room without announcing themselves. So, once again, people seemed to have no vehicles to make themselves inaccessible to others—at least in physical terms. But Geertz observed that the Javanese did, in fact, have a variety of means for regulating their contacts with others that were not strictly environmental mechanisms. For example, people were very restrained in their interactions, decorum was elaborate, politeness was a rigidly practiced habit, people spoke very softly, and, as Geertz stated, "Javanese shut people out with a wall of etiquette" (Westin, 1970, p. 160).

Pygmies of Zaire (the Congo). Turnbull (1961) wrote a rich ethnography about the Pygmies of Zaire, who live in the northeast corner of the Ituri Forest, a heavily vegetated rain forest in the Congo. The Pygmies, also known as the BaMbuti, are a hunting-and-gathering people who live in temporary camps. They live in huts very close to one another and share resources, so that everyone can see and hear what others are doing. Again, individual Pygmies seemingly have no way to shut out social contacts. Yet these people also reflect the principles we enunciated previously. For example, huts, which are made of large leaves, are repaired and rearranged frequently. Turnbull noted that the arrival of a new family or person in a camp might result in a door being moved from one side of the hut to the other, especially if the new arrival is disliked by the older resident. One can almost keep track of arguments, jealousies, and conflicts from the location and changes in location of doorways. The Pygmies also sometimes build "spite fences" between huts during serious disagreements. This constant shifting and modifying of the environment serves as a symbol of changing self/other boundaries and reflects how a particular behavioral mechanism is used effectively to regulate social interaction. Though largely environmental, these practices demonstrate the dynamic quality of privacy regulation among people who live in close contact and who otherwise seem to have no way to reduce or avoid contacts with others.

The Pygmies also exhibit a long-term dialectic quality of privacy regulation—sometimes joining and sometimes withdrawing from larger groups. Periodically the Pygmies separate into small family units and live apart from others for up to 2 months at a time. However, Turnbull observed that they begin to long for communal life after a while and seek out larger encampments. It is as if the Pygmies oscillate between periods of separateness and togetherness, a cycle that they follow year after year.

Thus, a society with apparently little ability to regulate privacy because of a communal life-style actually does have behavioral mechanisms—some environmental, some involving long-term withdrawal—to regulate social interaction. What is especially interesting about this example is a dialectic process that not only involves the simultaneous presence of openness and closedness but also includes oscillating cycles of accessibility over long periods of time.

Woleia Atoll. Another example comes from a completely different part of the world—a South Pacific atoll called Woleia, a 5-mile by 2½-mile island in the western Caroline Islands (Alkire, 1968). The 600 people who live on this atoll engage in agriculture and fishing and live in a communal setting with extensive face-to-face contacts. Again we see a situation that seemingly involves very little ability to avoid social interaction. However, Alkire observed a number of elaborate rules governing male/female relations which he believed served as vehicles to compensate for the extensive contact among people (and which might also operate to lessen heterosexual competition or jealousy). For example, male/female contacts are minimized or heavily ritualized in a variety of ways: Women are responsible for agriculture, men for fishing. In cleaning, village areas are separately assigned to men and women, and they never work together. Men and women do not dance with each other, nor are men with religious training allowed to eat with women. Furthermore, areas near canoes and the beach are off limits to women, whereas interior paths are considered women's areas; when a woman has to pass near a canoe house, she takes as wide a detour as possible. Men must not bring religious items into homes, which are women's domains, and a man is prohibited from spending time at home during the day. And people walking alone do not stop to talk with members of the opposite sex. Thus, it appears that the Woleia culture has a variety of practices to control interaction between men and women, perhaps because of the extensive contact that might otherwise occur in such a small physical environment. Once again, we see side by side, in a dialectic relation, factors producing openness and closedness and specific cultural mechanisms for regulating social interaction.

Other examples. The Ngadju Dayak of Borneo, Indonesia, live in villages and farm hamlets along a river (Miles, 1970). Some people reside in long houses that sometimes have 20 to 30 families; but most live in smaller dwellings with 2 to 3 families. This culture does not consider houses to be permanent residences, and they last for only a few years. Living arrangements are quite flexible, and people come and go at will, joining new communities without entering into long-term residential commitments. So, although people live communally and seemingly cannot avoid social contact, it is easy to regulate interaction simply by coming or going, staying or leaving. Moreover, families that live together are explicitly territorial. For example, everyone has his or her own sleeping mat and sleeping area, families have separate storage areas and eat at different times, people leave if a husband and wife are arguing, and it is customary not to interfere in other families' child rearing and discipline. Thus, there is a series of cultural practices to control excessive interaction.

A similar life-style characterizes the Choco Indians, who live in tropical forests in Panama (Faron, 1962). The Choco are a horticultural, hunting-and-fishing people and live in communal residences with no partitions and little evident means for shutting off interaction. People do chores in the home with few strict role assignments; whoever is available does things and everyone shares resources. Sleeping, eating, and relaxing also occur visibly, and, with the exception of sexual activity, life is quite public. Yet Miles (1970) observed an easy exit and entry system from communal residences, with people coming and going without elaborate rituals. Group composition changes often, so that withdrawal may serve as a compensatory system for regulating interaction, much as it does for the Ngaḍju Dayak of Borneo.

Similar practices were reported by Draper (1973), who studied the !Kung Bushmen of southwestern Africa. Members of this hunting-and-gathering society live in encampments of 15 to 40 people. According to Draper, the !Kung live in very close quarters and seem to enjoy intense interaction. Yet they have a norm of easy entry and withdrawal from encampments, like the cultures just described, so that people have a readily available mechanism to shut off interaction and to avoid conflict whenever they desire.

Summary. In exploring the hypothesis of privacy regulation as a cultural universal, we described cultures in which people have little chance to make themselves inaccessible to others or to avoid or shut off social contacts. Yet, in all cases, we were able to uncover behavioral mechanisms that enable people to regulate their interaction with others. These include cultural practices, space use and space allocation, physical withdrawal, distancing, and the like. Thus, opportunities and forces for people to be open to one another exist side by side with opportunities to be inaccessible, fitting our dialectic theme of privacy regulation. Furthermore, these examples illustrate the second aspect of our thesis—namely, the existence of culturally specific behavioral mechanisms to regulate privacy. What differs among these cultures is not the capability to regulate interaction but the particular ways in which this regulation occurs.

Cultures with Apparently Minimum Social Contact

In this section we examine cultures on the opposite side of the coin—those in which social contact is apparently minimal. Frankly, our examples are not completely satisfying; we had a great deal of difficulty locating cultures that, on the surface, were portrayed by anthropologists as involving little contact among people. Whether this is due to the rarity of such cultures, to anthropologists' neglect of such societies, or to their lack of interest in such processes is unknown. Nevertheless, here are instances we located.

Geertz, the anthropologist who described the Javanese culture cited earlier, also studied a neighboring society, the Balinese (Geertz, cited in Westin, 1970). At first glance people appear to have little accessibility to one another. Balinese families live in homes surrounded by high walls, entranceways to the yards of houses are through narrow doorways that are often locked, and it is customary only for family and friends to enter houseyards without invitation. On the face of it, this is an isolated, private existence. Yet Geertz pointed out that there was "a tremendous warmth, humor, [and] openness" among the Balinese, suggesting the presence of behavioral mechanisms to permit both accessibility and inaccessibility of people to one another (p. 17).

Another example comes from the Tuareg, a Moslem people living in the North African countries of Mali, Niger, and the Sudan (Murphy, 1964). The Tuareg, a camel-, goat-, and sheepherding people, are organized into tribal and subtribal groups of 50–200 people. Murphy's description of the male Tuareg dress customs is most relevant to our analysis. Adult males are seemingly inaccessible. They wear a sleeveless underrobe and a long, flowing outer garment that reaches from the shoulder to the ankle. In addition, they wear a turban and a veil that covers the face except for a narrow slit around the eyes. The veil is worn at all times once a male reaches adulthood—when he eats, sleeps, travels, and the like. Maximum inaccessibility? No, says Murphy, a dialectically oriented anthropologist. Openness and closedness is a dynamic, changing, multimodal process among the Tuareg, just as in other cultures. For example, the veil does not remain in one position but is ever so slightly raised and lowered to fit various social relationships. Higher-status males lower the veil and expose more of their faces when interacting with lower-status people, as if to signal their lack of psychological vulnerability. Moreover, the Tuareg are very sensitive to slight eye movements and to shifts of body posture as interaction progresses. So the veil serves as a kind of literal boundary-regulation mechanism, and the Tuareg achieve varying levels of accessibility and inaccessibility through several behavioral mechanisms that are played out in different combinations.

Another example comes from Galt's (1973) description of the inhabitants of Pantelleria, a town of 3000 people in Sicily, Italy. Life in this town seems to involve rigid separation of people from one another and even animosity. Families mistrust one another, people are uncooperative and jealous, there is a strong norm of individuality and little seeming warmth or extensive contact among people. A closed, isolated, and inaccessible life-style seems prevalent. But Galt also observed that the Pantellerians have an annual, week-long carnival that serves to bind the people together and operates as a counterforce to the noncooperative life-style that prevails most of the year. For example, a few months before the carnival week, people are pressured into planning the event. As planning progresses, group cohesion mounts and is accentuated by competition with other towns that are also planning carnivals. Everyone wants to have the best carnival, and the once hostile and uncooperative townspeople of Pantelleria gradually develop a sense of unity. In addition, during the carnival itself people behave quite differently than during the rest of the year, as a spirit of warmth, openness, and good will prevails. People wear costumes, they dance with one another even if they are strangers, joking and teasing are done good-naturedly, and people are encouraged to drink. Moreover, men may ask women to dance without first obtaining permission from their husbands, and, in a symbolic sense, women become communal in a way not at all characteristic of the society (this is a society with rigid norms about male/female relationships, and extramarital contacts, especially for women, are severely frowned on). Carnival week produces relaxation and good-spirited contacts between people, even between those who normally were suspicious, competitive, and hostile during the year. So in spite of an ordinarily closed life-style, Pantellerian culture uses the ritualized activity of the carnival as a vehicle for people to interact in a positive and open way.

Another example of a society with apparently maximum privacy is not an anthropological case (or even a real one at all), but comes from a science-fiction story by Isaac Asimov (1972), the physicist and writer. Although one cannot use such an example as scientific documentation, Asimov's description of life on another planet illustrates our hypothesis. On this planet, colonized by earth people many generations before, people lived alone and were totally served by computerized robots that looked like people and were programmed to speak and to respond to questions. A value emerged over the centuries in this culture to the effect that people were repelled at the idea of face-to-face contact with other humans. Personal contact, touching, and being in the mere presence of others were extremely aversive and upsetting. This value was experienced vividly by an earth detective, who was brought to the planet to help solve a crime, as he tried unsuccessfully to interview inhabitants face to face. Although direct social contacts never occurred, people interacted by means of an elaborate video system whereby the "image" of another person could be brought into one's home, and one could literally have dinner and conversation without that person's being there. To the outsider people appeared to be in one another's presence, but they actually were not. Thus inhabitants of this planet had worked out a system for achieving contact along with preserving their cultural values about noncontact. But, as Asimov suggested in his story, this was not sufficient. One member of the culture came to realize her need for "real" human contacts, and the story ended with (along with successful resolution of the murder) her plan to migrate to another planet where she could have actual face-to-face interaction with others. Although this mythical culture had presumably evolved in a way to provide a sufficient balance of contact and noncontact, the story implies that it actually had not done so and that it would eventually topple as a viable society.

Among the Balinese, Tuareg, and Pantellerians (and in a science-fiction society), we see examples of cultures that seem to have little openness and accessibility. But a somewhat different look at these cultures, through the window of a longer time period or through other aspects of their lives, suggests differential accessibility, achieved through a variety of privacy-regulation mechanisms. Again, what differs among cultures is not the presence or absence of privacy-regulation capabilities but the particular mechanisms that cultures use to achieve different degrees of contact among their members.

Social Relationships and Social Processes

Our strategy for considering privacy a cultural universal also involves examining types of social relationships that differ in closeness. We will examine (1) peripheral relationships, in which people are relative strangers or are casual acquaintances, (2) closer social relationships, such as those between in-laws, and (3) relatively intimate relationships—for example, between husbands and wives or parents and children. We will explore the idea that such relationships exhibit a dialectic quality of privacy and behavioral mechanisms that enable people to manage their social bonds.

Relationships with strangers, acquaintances, and neighbors. The Pygmies of Zaire, described earlier as living in a tropical forest (Turnbull, 1961), have a relationship with Bantu Negroes, an agricultural people who live in villages at the edge of the forest and with whom the Pygmies sometimes work and trade. Contacts between these cultures are intermittent and friendly, and the two cultures often share resources to which one of them has unique access. For example, whenever the Pygmies make a major meat kill, such as an elephant, the villagers are invited into the forest to join in the feast. Because their customs demand courtesy and sharing, the Pygmies permit the villagers to stay as long as they desire, although after a time the visitors become an irritant. It is as if there had been too much contact between them, at least from the point of view of the Pygmies. To rid themselves of their now unwanted guests without violating their norms of hospitality and courtesy, the Pygmies engage the villagers in a gambling game, much like dice, at which the Pygmies are particularly skilled. Within a short time the villagers are stripped of all they possessed, and they soon leave the camp and return to their village. Thus there exist, side by side, cultural practices that facilitate social contacts and mechanisms to reduce contact.

Another example appears in a description of the Lapps of northern Europe, a reindeer-herding people (Paine, 1970). The Lapps live in a harsh environment, and people are very dependent on and helpful toward one another, even strangers and slight acquaintances. There is a norm that any visitor to a camp may enter a tent without an invitation, sit down, and take part in the ongoing activities. The occupant cannot refuse entry to the visitor, but has to accept the newcomer's presence. Although this might appear to reflect a lack of control over privacy, mechanisms do exist to close off undesired contact when the occupant of the tent desires to do so. If one feels negative toward a visitor or desires not to interact, one simply feigns falling asleep right in the visitor's presence. For us this would be impolite; to the Lapps it serves as a perfectly acceptable signal that it is time for the visitor to leave (perhaps analogous to our looking at our watch to signal the desire to end a conversation). Although the Lapps' environmental circumstances may have required certain practices of openness, they also have mechanisms to close themselves off from others—yielding a kind of dialectic unity.

Consider still another type of relationship, in which pairs of unrelated Chinese families in Malaysia live together in the same residence, in some respects as neighbors sharing facilities (Anderson, 1972). There is considerable contact, and families are highly accessible to each other, but Anderson noted that family groups use several cultural practices to maintain a degree of separation. For example, there are strong taboos about entering or even looking into the other family's sleeping area. Each family has its own storage areas and stoves and uses different parts of the communal kitchen. In addition, there are clear status relationships between the elderly and the young, and between men and women, that serve to regulate contacts. Moreover, anyone in either family may discipline children, and particular punishment is levied on children who "invade" other people's areas. Anderson also observed that people in different families maintain neutral and unemotional relationships with one another. Once again, we see openness and closedness existing together in a dialectical system, along with a rich repertoire of behaviors and cultural practices that serve to regulate interaction.

Relationships between in-laws. In American culture the relationship between sons-in-law and mothers-in-law has been a traditional source of comedians' jokes and novelists' and playwrights' themes and a well-known problem (at least in folklore) faced by many husbands and wives. Is this a myth? Is it unique to American society? How, if at all, does it relate to our analysis of privacy?

To the first two questions, the answer is that distant, cool, or hostile relationships between children-in-law and parents-in-law are present in many cultures. Sometimes strained or formal relations occur between a mother-in-law and son-in-law, sometimes between a daughter-in-law and mother-in-law, sometimes between a father-in-law and a new child-in-law. All combinations of parent- and child-in-law relationships have been portrayed in one or another culture as hostile, aloof, formal, or strained (not that this occurs all the time in all cultures, but it seems to be a frequent phenomenon). For example, Murdock (1971) examined "in-law avoidance" in 89 cultures, selected to be representative of societies around the world. He found widespread occurrence of respect, formality, absence of joking, and avoidance between different combinations of children-in-law and parents-in-law.

How might this phenomenon be accounted for in our framework? In many cultures the usual practice is for a newly married couple to live in close proximity to the husband's or wife's parents—in the same village or community and sometimes even in the same dwelling. Hence, there is often forced proximity and contact between people who previously may have been strangers or at least have not lived together on a day-to-day basis. In sociological terms, it is as if a new person entered headlong into the middle of a primary family group. Not only might this disrupt a family's prior life-style: new interaction patterns, new modes of family organization, and new ways of getting things done are probably necessary. A radically new level of contact and life-style might be forced on people. We hypothesize, according to a dialectic framework, that compensatory mechanisms would operate to reduce contact between people to an acceptable level. Respect, detachment, and hostile and aloof dealings between in-laws might function as such mechanisms. Which in-laws are involved will depend on whether a new couple lives with the wife's or husband's parents and what role either parent has in the home and family structure. In our own culture, living with in-laws is not common. However, many of the jokes, cartoons, and comments about mothers-in-law in our society revolve around "your mother coming to visit us," or vice versa, the implication being that forced proximity and contact will create problems of one sort or another. Thus, in-law avoidance may function as a dialectic counterforce to the close contact that often occurs between a child-in-law and parent-in-law.

Naturally, there may be other reasons for in-law avoidance, such as competition involving jealousy, helping, love, and other social relations between a child-in-law and parent-in-law or economic and social factors. So what is proposed here can only be viewed as a possibility, although it seems plausible in relation to the other analyses discussed in the chapter.

A second facet of in-law avoidance that bears on privacy regulation involves the variety of behavioral mechanisms by which avoidance is expressed in different cultures. Some practices involve formality and respect; others involve the absence of positive emotional behaviors such as joking, hugging, and kissing; others involve polite forms of address; and some go so far as to minimize conversation between in-laws. Still others involve distinct and prescribed seating and sleeping arrangements. Thus, there is evidence for both a regulation of the balance between contact and noncontact according to our dialectic framework and the use of a variety of behavioral mechanisms that differ among cultures.

Consider examples of in-law avoidance in different parts of the world. Among the Yuma Indians of southeastern California, a man and his mother-in-law traditionally maintained detachment and aloofness. They did not joke, they avoided expressing positive feelings, they rarely kissed or embraced each other. A somewhat different way of relating to in-laws occurs among certain groups in Thailand (Tambiah,1969). Here, newly married couples live with the wife's parents, and a rigid physical arrangement regulates contact between a man and his mother-in-law. For example, a son-in-law is not allowed to enter the dwelling through a certain doorway near his parents-in-laws' part of the house. And, once in the dwelling, he is forbidden to enter their sleeping area. The son-in-law also sleeps in a remote corner, his wife and father-in-law separating him from his mother-in-law. In this society, in-law separation is reflected in environmental arrangements and spatial practices, whereas in some other cultures avoidance is displayed in verbal and other modes of behavior.

Among the Mehinacu (Gregor, 1974), the tribal group in Brazil described earlier, it is taboo for in-laws to touch each other's sleeping hammocks or to have face-to-face encounters in the entranceways to their home or if they happen to meet on a path. When in-laws interact, they avert their eyes and do not look directly at each other. Furthermore, at meals they never pass food directly, but place an item on the ground near the other person. Mehinacu in-laws never mention each other's names. They speak only briefly to each other, about important issues, and a new son-in-law speaks to his father-in-law through his wife. Among members of this close-living society, then, as with other cultures, there are a series of mechanisms for regulating contact between in-laws that may have developed to compensate for their physical and psychological proximity.

LeVine (1962) described still another type of avoidance phenomenon—between cowives (women having the same husband) in three polygamous societies in Kenya, the Gusii, the Kipsigi, and the Luo. These cultures have different living arrangements among cowives, from close proximity to considerable separation. Among the Luo, wives' homes are quite close, and the women share a common yard. Gusii wives live in adjacent dwellings, but they often have fences separating their huts, and they have their own gardens and cattle pens. Kipsigi women live at a distance from one another and have little day-to-day contact. LeVine noted that the often jealous and hostile relationship between cowives is reflected in mutual accusations of witchcraft and sorcery. He tested and confirmed the hypothesis that the closer cowives live to each other, the greater the accusations they make about each other's sorcery and witchcraft powers—an avoidance process that lessens contact between them. Once again, the greater the forced contact or physical proximity between in-laws or between those in similar relationships, the greater their hostility or avoidance, and the more prevalent the use of a variety of mechanisms to create a psychological separation between them.

Relationships within families. As with strangers and those in close relationships, we expect to find that members of families exhibit dialectic openness and closedness toward one another, with privacy achieved through a variety of culturally specific behavioral mechanisms.

Among the Mehinacu, the Amazon culture described earlier, husbands and wives have a set of mechanisms to regulate their contacts with each other. For example, a couple generally bathe together publicly several times a day, walk side by side, and eat from a common bowl—all reflecting considerable mutual openness and accessibility. When they have disagreements, they specifically avoid doing these things and thereby signal to each other that their relationship is strained and that they are no longer as accessible to each other. Another mechanism involves the position of their sleeping hammocks. Typically, a husband and wife hang their hammocks from the same pole, with the husband's hammock slightly higher and with their heads only a few inches apart. But if they are angry with each other, hammocks might be mounted on different poles, several feet apart.

An example of a long-term dialectic appears in certain parent/child relationships. In many societies there is a practice of initiating males into manhood when they reach adolescence. The initiation rituals sometimes involve severe experiences—isolation, circumcision, tests of courage and strength, painful ceremonies of one sort or another. Whiting, Kluckhohn, and Anthony (1958) hypothesized that initiation rites were more frequent in societies in which boys had been especially close to their mothers in childhood and that one goal of these rituals was to break the maternal bond and to ensure that a boy would begin identifying with the male role. In an analysis of 50 societies they found this hypothesis to be supported. Adolescent male initiation rites were most prevalent in societies in which a young boy slept with his mother for at least a year, to the exclusion of the father. In the logic of our framework, cultures with high social contact between a mother and son had developed mechanisms to alter and break off that contact in later years, yielding a long-term dialectic balance of mother/son interaction. As one example, among the Kwoma of New Guinea, a child remained close to the mother, slept in the mother's arms, and was nursed for 2 to 3 years. The child was held by the mother all day, the father slept separately on his own bed, and the parents did not engage in sexual intercourse during the period before weaning. But this changed abruptly at the time of weaning, when the child was put in his own bed, the parents slept together and engaged in intercourse in the same room as the child, and the mother no longer held the child. Thus, in a longitudinal way, we see a cycle of high contact followed by low contact.

These examples of various types of social relationships provide evidence compatible with our framework of privacy regulation as a cultural universal. However, cultures are unique in that they have a variety of mechanisms for regulating interaction between strangers, acquaintances, in-laws, and family members. These mechanisms enable people to shut themselves off from others or to be open to others. In general, then, our analysis has attempted to document the central role of privacy in culture/environment relations, including its presence as a dialectic, multimodal process.

SUMMARY

This chapter examined the concept of privacy. We first described privacy as a central construct around which other processes, such as personal space and territory, can be anchored. Some salient features of privacy regulation include these: (1) Privacy is a dialectic, boundary-control process, not a one-way, "keep out" process. People change in their desires to be in or out of contact with others, and they are sometimes accessible and sometimes inaccessible to others. Hence, privacy regulation involves management, pacing, and regulation of exchange with the world. (2) Privacy regulation involves more than environmental mechanisms alone: verbal behavior, nonverbal behavior, environmentally oriented behavior, and cultural practices. All these levels of behavior function as a coherent unity, various behaviors substituting for, compensating for, and amplifying one another. A central thesis was that privacy regulation is a multimodal process involving many levels of behavior and that it operates as a "social system," not merely an environmental one.

The chapter then considered the functions that privacy regulation serves for individuals and groups, including management and pacing of social interaction. More important, we hypothesized that the ability to regulate and control privacy is essential to people's well-being, viability, and self-identity. We therefore examined privacy regulation as a culturally pervasive process. The thesis was explored that the capability of people to regulate privacy is a cultural universal. We posited that what differs among cultures is the particular set of behavioral mechanisms used to regulate privacy. For a host of reasons—environmental, cultural, political, economic—cultures differ in how their members regulate contacts with one another. Some rely heavily on environmental mechanisms, others do not. Some use mixes of verbal and nonverbal behaviors, others use these plus environmental mechanisms, and so on.

We attempted to explore the idea that privacy regulation is a cultural universal by looking at two kinds of evidence. First, we examined cultures in which people seem to have little opportunity to be alone and out of contact with one another and cultures in which people seem to have little contact. We illustrated that such cultures have, in fact, a repertoire of alternative mechanisms that enable people to regulate and pace their openness/closedness toward one another. Second, we examined privacy in various types of social relationships: (1) between strangers and casual acquaintances; (2) in closer social bonds, such as those between in-laws; and (3) in very intimate social relationships, such as those between husbands and wives and between parents and children. Once again, we illustrated that people in such relationships have ways of making themselves more or less accessible to each other.

In completing this analysis, however, we feel obligated to remind you that there are many complexities and difficulties in making inferences from anthropological data about privacy regulation. Accordingly, you should consider our discussion of privacy as a cultural universal to be a preliminary one and one which offers a hypothesis that needs to be examined in more detail in future research.

Chapter 5

PERSONAL SPACE

A fundamental way in which we use the environment in social interaction is to distance ourselves from other people. By moving closer to or farther away from others, we make ourselves physically and socially more accessible or less accessible to them. To get a better feeling for spatial distancing as a social process, consider a few experiences that you may have had or that you might try out yourself:

1. You are on a large, empty elevator. Someone gets on and stands directly next to you. Or you are on an empty bus and someone gets on and sits down right beside you. How would you feel if someone acted in these ways? What would you do? How do people normally position themselves in such situations?

2. Your girlfriend or boyfriend is very close to you in an intimate setting. How would she or he respond if you moved back a couple of feet? Or, conversely, you and a casual acquaintance whom you meet on the street probably use a certain distance from each other while talking. What would happen if you moved closer, perhaps to 6 inches away?

3. Next time you are at an airport, observe how people select seats in a boarding area. If plenty of seats are available, do they sit right next to one another or not? Do they sit in the same row or area of the lounge? What happens as more and more people arrive; how does the seating pattern change?

4. Think of as many "distance phrases" as you can that people use to refer to their relationships with others, such as "I keep her at arm's length," "I wouldn't touch him with a 10-foot pole," "She was breathing down my neck." What does each phrase imply about the social relationship?

These examples illustrate the simple but often unverbalized fact that we actively use distance between ourselves and others in everyday social relationships. This chapter examines such "personal spacing" as one of the several environmental mechanisms that people use to regulate their privacy, or accessibility to others.

Students of animal behavior, called ethologists, have long observed that animals actively use distance in their dealings with one another. We have all observed that birds sitting on a telephone wire seem to be spaced at equal distances, as if the birds had laid out the distances between themselves with a tape measure. Or you may recall how a pair of strange dogs will approach to a given distance, stop, size each other up, and then either move closer or flee. And sometimes when an animal is approached too rapidly, it will attack or otherwise signal displeasure.

Hediger (1950), a well-known ethologist, described several distance zones that animals maintain from one another. He used the term *personal distance* to refer to the normal spacing that animals in a group usually adopt, as in the example of birds on a telephone wire. He also identified a related distance, "social distance," or the maximum distance that animals in a social group use; beyond this distance group members are unable to maintain satisfactory contact. Thus, social distance is an "envelope" that contains the group. Other distances include "flight distance" and "fight distance." Flight distance, Hediger stated, is that band of space within which an animal will permit another to approach. If a stranger approaches within the boundary of the flight zone, the animal will flee. If a stranger approaches too rapidly beyond that zone and/or if flight is impossible, the stranger will have entered a fight-distance zone, and conflict may occur.

Do people also use space as a vehicle of communication and as a means for regulating their contacts with one another? Most present-day environmental researchers would probably say "Yes, indeed." Sommer (1969) vividly described human spacing as follows:

> Personal space refers to an area with an invisible boundary surrounding the person's body into which intruders may not come. Like the porcupines in Schopenhauer's fable, people like to be close enough to obtain warmth and comradeship but far enough away to avoid pricking one another. Personal space is not necessarily spherical in shape, nor does it extend equally in all directions. . . . It has been likened to a snail shell, a soap bubble, an aura, and "breathing room" [p. 26].

Thus, personal space is the space within an invisible boundary around people that is with them everywhere they go. However, as we shall show in this chapter, personal spacing is not fixed and unchangeable. Just as privacy is a dynamic, changing boundary-regulation phenomenon, so personal distance, one of several privacy-regulation mechanisms, shifts with circumstances. Sometimes we move closer to others and sometimes we move away, as we attempt to maintain an "appropriate" or "desired" level of contact with them.

HALL'S STUDY OF HUMAN SPACING

Edward T. Hall, an anthropologist, sensitized social and behavioral scientists to human spacing in a book titled *The Hidden Dimension* (1966). Hall posited two central ideas. First, he stated that North

Americans systematically use four spatial zones in their dealings with others in everyday situations. These zones, termed the intimate, personal, social, and public zones, represent levels of interpersonal contact that are used to reflect closeness or intimacy. Furthermore, use of these zones varies with the settings within which people find themselves—for example, public versus private. The second facet of Hall's thinking is crucial to our interest in culture and environment. Using anthropological observations, Hall hypothesized that different cultures use space as a communication vehicle in rather distinctive ways. Some cultures have customs whereby people maintain close distances, even among strangers; other cultures do just the opposite. Hall stated that analysis of spatial practices can provide important clues about a culture. Therefore, as in earlier chapters, we see the linkage of culture to environmental phenomena, this time involving the simple use of distance. Let us now examine Hall's ideas in more detail.

Use of Spatial Zones

Hall hypothesized that people in American society typically interact with others in one of four spatial zones: intimate, personal, social, and public.

Intimate zone. This zone spans 0 to 18 inches and includes a close phase (0 to 6 inches) and a far phase (6 to 18 inches). Hall (1966) described the intimate zone as follows:

> At intimate distance, the presence of the other person is unmistakable and may at times be overwhelming because of the greatly stepped-up sensory inputs. Sight (often distorted), olfaction, heat from the other person's body, sound, smell, and feel of the breath all combine to signal unmistakable involvement with another body [p. 110].

For a sense of what it means to relate to another person in the intimate zone, especially in the close phase, adopt a distance of 0 to 6 inches with a friend (or even look at yourself in a mirror). Note, however, that certain visual cues are not easily seen at very close distances. For example, you cannot see a person's body, arms, or legs very well. You will observe how visual cues are salient at this distance. You can see fine details of the face, such as skin texture, blemishes, slight muscle twitches around the eyes, nose, and mouth, eye color, pupil dilation, hair roots. You will also easily notice auditory cues at the intimate distance, such as breathing, sighing, moaning, whispering, and rustling of clothing. And you may be able to feel the heat of the other person's body, depending on his or her arousal level. Furthermore, in most cases you will be able to pick up even the slightest olfactory cues—shaving lotion or perfume, deodorant (or lack thereof), the person's breath (sometimes including parts of a recent meal). Finally, it is possible to touch almost any part of the other person's body at this distance; in fact, at the close phase of this zone your bodies may be touching.

The opportunities for rich and detailed communication are extraordinary in the intimate zone. It is perhaps for this reason that Hall (1966) stated "The use of intimate distance in public is not considered proper by adult, middle class Americans" (p. 111). This statement reflects the idea that the use of spatial zones varies with settings and with culture. In public, formal situations it is inappropriate in our culture to enter the intimate zone of another person. When circumstances force us into that zone, as in a crowded elevator or bus, we often hold our bodies rigid, avoid touching others, and look in one direction in a blank and unemotional way. We act as if to say "I know this closeness is not appropriate, and I will reduce all communications to ensure that our relationship is not misinterpreted."

Another aspect of spatial zones is that distance in and of itself is not the crucial factor. Rather, distance provides a *medium* within which a number of communication channels operate. Thus, at the intimate distance, visual, auditory, olfactory, and other channels of communication can operate in a particular way. As discussed later, the operation of such channels alters dramatically in other zones. So, when you think about distance or spatial zones, remember that what is important is not merely the use of space, but that different distances provide the opportunity for various communication cues to be used and detected.

Finally, Hall observed that spatial zones are differentially appropriate for various social relationships. The intimate zone is ordinarily reserved for people in an intimate relationship, such as close friends or lovers. Strangers or acquaintances typically do not use this zone in our culture. If you move into the intimate zone of a stranger or acquaintance, you are likely to observe any of a variety of reactions. People might move back with or without a comment. They might giggle or have a strange look in their eyes. Sometimes they might even move closer and act in a romantic way, if they interpret your behavior to mean a desire for more intimacy. In any case, they are unlikely to continue a casual conversation in the intimate zone. Instead, they will readjust their distancing to suit the setting and/or their interpretation of your relationship to them, or they may change the definition of the relationship to a more intimate one. (If you try this experiment, do so carefully and at your own risk!)

Personal zone. This zone ranges from 1.5 to 4 feet, with a close phase up to 2.5 feet and a far phase spanning the interval 2.5 to 4 feet. This is the zone that is commonly called "personal space," and it is hypothesized that movement closer than this zone, into the intimate area, will produce tension, anxiety, and stress, especially in public or between strangers. Hall (1966) referred to this zone as analogous to "the distance [identified by Hediger as] consistently separating the members of noncontact species. It might be thought of as a small protective sphere or bubble that an organism maintains between itself and others" (p. 112).

Communication possibilities continue to be rich in the personal zone, although less so than in the intimate zone. One can still easily touch another person in the close phase of the zone. In the far phase, people can touch hands if they extend their arms, so that the phrase "keeping someone at arm's length" applies to this zone. Heat cues and body odors are not very evident in the personal zone, although strong odors may be noticed. Odors of perfumes, deodorants, and other substances may be communicable, especially if the substances are used heavily or are coupled with unusual body heat. Visual detail is still rich in both the near and far phases of the personal zone, and one can see the fine details of another's face as well as other parts of the body.

The personal zone permits a range of contact between people, from relatively intimate to more formal. It is a zone that people commonly use in public, and it seems to be a "normal" contact distance in our culture. Furthermore, the personal zone enables people to remain in reasonable proximity or to move toward more intimate or less intimate communication.

Social zone. This zone spans the interval 4 to 12 feet, with a close phase of 4 to 7 feet and a far phase of 7 to 12 feet. Hall stated that this zone is acceptable for a range of contacts in our culture but that beyond this distance people lose the ability to communicate easily with one another. Social distance appears in business settings, among coworkers, and in some social situations. For example, the typical office desk is about 30 inches wide, so that people sitting in chairs on opposite sides of the desk are located somewhere in the middle of the zone. Even for executives who have wider desks, it is likely that interaction will be somewhere in the social zone.

Touching is not possible at this distance, except with extreme effort; and most olfactory and heat cues are also absent. Visual and auditory cues serve as the main vehicle of communication in the social zone, although they operate quite differently than in the intimate and personal zones. It is still easy to see a person's face and body clearly, and a range of information can be observed visually, from reasonably fine details to gross body movements and postures. However, the rich visual detail that was observable in the intimate and personal zones is no longer as clear. Auditory cues are also important at the social distance, and voice volume can remain at a "normal" level, although Hall observed that speaking levels in the far phase of the social zone tend to be louder than normal. In summary, the social zone is used in public, business, and social settings, when people need or want to be in contact with others but not in an overly intimate or intense way.

Public zone. This zone extends beyond 12 feet, with a close phase of 12 to 25 feet and a far phase beyond 25 feet. This is a formal distance used on public occasions and is usually reserved for high-status figures. Public speakers are typically located in the public zone in relation to the nearest member of the audience. Another example occurred in the Arab/Israeli peace negotiations following the Yom Kippur war, when the two sides sat at tables positioned across from each other at a distance of 25 feet.

Obviously, touch, thermal, and olfactory cues do not operate in this zone. Gross gestures, general body postures, and relatively holistic impressions about a person can be obtained visually, whereas fine details such as eye color and skin texture are not available. In addition, speech becomes more formal at this distance, enunciation and phrases are more formalized, and emotional expression is exaggerated in order to be understood. Hall noted that actors and actresses learn to accentuate their movements, vocal expressions, and mannerisms in order to compensate for these distances and to achieve psychological closeness or contact with their audience.

In addition to looking in a mirror or positioning a friend at these various distances, you can find many places in the everyday environment where people use these spatial zones. Public distance and its associated cues are easily perceived in a theater or in a lecture hall, where the instructor is usually at least 12 to 25 feet away from people. Observe how teachers and actors behave at these distances and note the kinds of cues they convey as they communicate. To see intimate, personal, and social distances, visit a public place like an airport and watch people in different relationships—lovers, family members, strangers asking for information. You are apt to see in such settings the range of distances that Hall wrote about.

Culture and Use of Space

Central in Hall's theorizing was that people from different social and cultural backgrounds have different practices regarding distancing, arrangements of furniture, home layouts, and angles of orientation and facing. Throughout *The Hidden Dimension* and elsewhere, Hall described how different cultures use space in different or unique ways. For example, he observed that Germans are extremely sensitive to spatial invasion and achieve physical privacy in the form of private rooms, fences, closed doors, and heavy walls. For Germans, Hall said, the physical environment is an important aspect of the self, and it provides a literal boundary that people use to separate themselves from others. For the English, things are somewhat different. The English too are a private people, but the physical environment is not as important a vehicle to regulate contact with others as it is for the Germans. Hall suggested that the English maintain psychological distance from others by verbal and nonverbal means, such as voice characteristics and eye contact, and by cultural practices and etiquette, as reflected in the well-known English reserve, reticence, and politeness. He attributed this style of maintaining psychological distance to the fact that the English are not accustomed to private or personal places, including offices, so that psychological mechanisms are more important in privacy regulation.

Hall described Middle Eastern, Mediterranean, and Latin cultures as highly sensory, with people interacting very closely—nose to nose, breathing in one another's faces, and touching. He hypothesized that these cultures are more contact-oriented than northern European and North American cultures—at least in public settings and with strangers. Close distances and associated cues of touch, smell, and body heat are more prevalent in contact cultures (and this closeness often creates difficulties for those not accustomed to having someone breathe in their faces, touch them, or emit a variety of odors normally hidden in Western cultures by soaps, deodorants, sprays, and perfumes).

Hall's analysis of the use of spatial zones in different cultures was based on observational anthropological evidence. His work was a major stimulus to subsequent research on personal space, and beginning in the 1960s social scientists, primarily psychologists, took up the challenge and began researching personal space within and across cultures.

RESEARCH ON PERSONAL SPACE

The study of interpersonal distancing, or personal space, has been of considerable interest to researchers. As of 1975, Altman reported the existence of about 200 empirical, quantitative studies of personal space. Since interest in the area continues, it is likely that there are at least 300 studies now in the literature. We cannot hope to review all research on this topic; instead we will focus on studies that bear most directly on the relation between culture and the environment. For more thorough coverage of this topic, see Altman (1975), Altman and Vinsel (1977), and Evans and Howard (1973).

How have researchers studied personal space? A little knowledge of research methods will help you appreciate the studies discussed later. Altman (1975) identified three types of personal-space research methods: simulation studies, laboratory studies, and field and naturalistic studies.

Simulations use figures or symbols representing people. Participants are asked to arrange, place, or make judgments about them in relation to the use of space. A variety of simulation techniques have been used over the years, involving dolls, silhouettes of humans, line drawings, and abstract symbols. Simulation techniques have been the most popular procedure and account for almost half the studies in the literature, perhaps because they are easy to administer and permit experimental control over situations.

A second method, laboratory research, asks people to approach others to some point, usually of discomfort, or to respond to the approach of others toward them. In laboratory studies, people are observed in artificially created settings that are not part of their everyday environments, and some control over conditions is exerted by the researcher. About one third of the studies reported by Altman (1975) were laboratory studies.

The third type of personal-space research method, used in about one fifth of the studies in the sample described by Altman (1975), involves field and naturalistic techniques. Here personal space is studied in everyday settings such as classrooms, libraries, and playgrounds. Typically, measures of spatial distancing in natural settings are done unobtrusively, without people knowing that they are being observed. For example, children might be photographed by means of long-distance telephoto cameras as they play in schoolyards.

Research on Spatial Zones

The first aspect of Hall's thinking concerned the use of intimate, personal, social, and public zones. To what extent does research substantiate his ideas? What zones do people use in various circumstances?

To answer these questions, Altman and Vinsel (1977) examined over 100 empirical, quantitative studies of personal space, restricting themselves to those investigations that provided actual distance measurements between people. Some studies were done in the laboratory, others in the field. Some used males, others females, and others mixed-sex groups. A number of studies focused on intrusion into personal space. Other studies dealt with people in intimate relationships, others examined the behavior of strangers. Some reports focused on people with different personality characteristics, and others dealt with people from different cultural and ethnic groups. Thus, the studies reviewed included a broad spectrum of variables and situations.

Figure 5-1 summarizes the results of Altman and Vinsel's analysis. The data are shown separately for people who were standing (open circles) and people who were seated (solid circles). It makes sense to distinguish between these conditions because seating arrangements are likely to

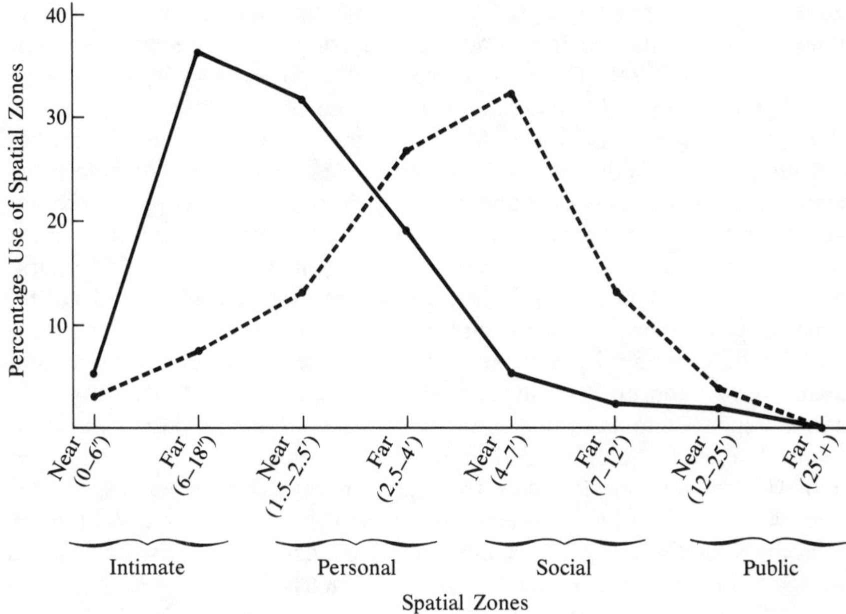

Figure 5-1. Distribution of use of near and far phases of spatial zones. ○——○ = standing relationships (n = 59), ●——● = seated relationships (n = 30). From "Personal Space: An Analysis of E. T. Hall's Proxemics Framework," by I. Altman and A. M. Vinsel. In I. Altman and J. F. Wohlhill (Eds.), *Human Behavior and Environment: Advances in Theory and Research,* Volume 1. Copyright 1977 by Plenum Publishing Corporation. Reprinted by permission.

involve somewhat greater distances between people than standing arrangements—that is, when distance is measured from body to body or chair to chair.

Consider first the data for people who were standing. Here the most frequently used distances were in the far phase of the intimate zone and the near phase of the personal zone, averaging in the neighborhood of 18 inches. This is pretty much what Hall hypothesized for public, everyday contacts. Since these data came from many types of people—friends and strangers, males and females, people with different personality characteristics—the results are actually quite impressive. Notice also that very few people stood in the close phase of the intimate zone (0–6 inches) and very few people used the social or public zone. Thus, Hall's ideas are pretty well confirmed for ordinary day-to-day use of standing distances.

The second curve of Figure 5-1 shows comparable information for people who were seated. Here we see a shift in distances: people tended to use the far phase of the personal zone and the near phase of the social zone. When people interacted in seated arrangements, the distance between them (measured from body to body or chair center to chair center) was about 4 feet. This is an increase of about 1½ feet from the usual standing distance. This increase is accounted for by the length of one's thighs in the seated position. Again, there is remarkable consistency in seating distances, quite in line with Hall's ideas that spatial distances are fairly uniform across people and settings. Furthermore, people seat themselves neither very close to others nor very far away. It is as if they knew and chose a normative and "acceptable" physical relationship to others. So, for the most part, Hall's ideas regarding the use of spatial zones, especially the personal and social zones in everyday contacts, are substantiated. The stability of these findings reinforces the idea that personal space is an important mechanism used to regulate social interaction. In some respects one can think of the space around one's body as an "ultimate" barrier that can be used to make oneself more or less accessible to another human being. It is therefore not surprising that personal space is a pervasive and reliable phenomenon. Now the question is "What other factors make a difference in spatial practices, especially those of concern in this book—namely, cultural and ethnic factors?"

Personal, Interpersonal, and Situational Determinants of Personal Space

Many of the 300 empirical studies of personal space have examined the effect of personal characteristics of people, intimacy of social relationships, and numerous other variables on distancing behavior. Our goal is not to review this research in detail, since it is not always directly germane to culture/environment issues. Following is a brief summary of some of the better-known relations between personal space and other variables.

Intrusion. A popular area of research concerns reactions to intrusive approaches by others. The usual procedure in such studies is to have an experimenter's confederate approach an unsuspecting person at a distance likely to be perceived as inappropriate and intrusive. Usually the subject does not know the intruder, the invasion is unexpected, and it is intended to violate social norms. Observations are made of reactions to invasions—for example, flight, leaning or turning away, fidgeting, and verbal comments. From an analysis of about two dozen invasion studies, Altman and Vinsel (1977) found that people typically reacted negatively to close approaches by others. They exhibited such behaviors as moving away, turning, looking away, and fidgeting, all of which reflect attempts to increase the psychological distance between themselves and the intruder. In other studies people were also very reluctant to intrude on others or to get too close to them. And, when forced to intrude, they exhibited discomfort, lowered their gaze, and acted nervous. The results of both kinds of studies are so clear-cut and consistent that we can infer the existence of strong cultural norms in the United States regarding appropriate distances and spatial relationships between people. These intrusion studies, coupled with the data presented earlier about freely selected interaction distances, strengthen the plausibility of Hall's ideas about how people in the United States use space in their day-to-day dealings with one another.

At this point you might review the first two exercises at the beginning of the chapter and see how your own experiences fit with the research findings on intrusion and reactions to intrusion.

Interpersonal relationships. An early and popular area of research examined distancing behavior and interpersonal relationships, especially degree of acquaintance and attraction as a determinant of spatial proximity. A large number of studies showed that people use less space and approach others more closely when they like them or are friendly with them, compared with those they know less well or with whom their experiences have been less positive. Altman and Vinsel (1977) noted that there was a trend for close friends to use the far edge of Hall's intimate zone and for acquaintances and others in less intimate relationships to use the close phase of the personal zone. This not only lends support to Hall's basic ideas about use of spatial zones, it shows that the degree of intimacy of an interpersonal relationship plays a role in spatial distancing.

Individual factors. Although Hall did not emphasize individual differences in relation to spatial behavior, this has been a popular topic of study. Individual factors include personality, biographical or demographic variables such as age, sex, and height, and social roles such as status or position in an organization. One consistent finding is that people maintain larger distances from those labeled as deviants or those having some kind of personal or physical stigma. For example, people position themselves farther away from others labeled as epileptics, homosexuals, drug addicts, or criminals than they do from "normal" people. Like the intrusion and attraction research described earlier, these studies illustrate the changing accessibility of the self to others, manifested in physical distance and its associated channels of communication.

Relations between distancing and other behaviors. Our analysis of privacy in Chapter 4 described the use of a series of behavioral mechanisms to regulate level of contact between a person and others. These mechanisms include use of personal space, territorial behavior, verbal behavior, nonverbal behavior, and cultural practices. We also stated that these mechanisms operate as a coherent system, in profiles or patterns. That is, different behaviors sometimes substitute for one another, sometimes operate additively, and sometimes compensate for one another.

A number of studies have examined this systems idea, specifically in relation to how distance works in combination with other behaviors, such as eye contact, smiling, and body postures. Much of this work was stimulated by the theorizing of Argyle and Dean (1965), who proposed an "equilibrium theory" compatible with our approach to privacy regulation. Their idea was that people define an acceptable or appropriate level of intimacy they wish to have with another person (much like our idea of a desired level of privacy). People then use a blend of behaviors to achieve a state of "equilibrium" that reflects the desired level of intimacy. However, in the course of interaction sometimes one behavior will change and thereby alter the intimacy level, so that people become more or less intimate than appropriate. In such instances, Argyle and Dean hypothesized, other behaviors would operate in a compensatory fashion. For example, if people approach too closely, one might adjust looking behavior, body position, and so on to restore a desired level of intimacy. Patterson (1973) reviewed a large number of studies and found reasonable support for the operation of compensatory processes: for example, the greater the distance between people, the more eye contact they had, the more directly they oriented their bodies to face each other, and the more they leaned toward each other. One can see how these findings relate to our discussion of privacy in Chapter 4, where we emphasized the mix of behaviors, including use of personal space, that people use to regulate interaction. Thus, the Japanese, who live in relatively high-density situations, compensate by reserve and politeness to regulate their self/other boundaries. The contact cultures of the Mediterranean and Middle East, however, use physical features, such as walls around houses, to limit interpersonal access to a select few, with whom they then interact at high levels of intimacy and physical closeness. Thus, compensation processes not only operate in regard to personal spacing but are reflected in the general process of privacy regulation.

But do not conclude from the intrusion studies or those examining the equilibrium theory of Argyle and Dean (1965) that *compensation*, or an attempt to restore a given level of psychological closeness, always occurs. There is also evidence that *reciprocity* is often exhibited in social interaction. That is, sometimes people will act in a tit-for-tat way. For example, when you move closer to someone, the person may not move back or show other forms of withdrawal. He or she may actually reciprocate and come even closer to you. To account for this, Firestone (1977) suggested, as one of several possibilities, that reciprocity may operate in a developing or close social relationship in which one party likes the other, (and vice versa) whereas compensation may occur more frequently in an invasion situation with a stranger. Patterson (1976) proposed a general theoretical model to predict when compensation or reciprocity might occur. He hypothesized that a change in someone's intimacy behavior (for example, coming closer, touching, and other forms of psychological closeness) creates a state of arousal (physiological and/or psychological changes of heightened sensitivity). This arousal state is then labeled as either positive (liking, love, or good feelings) or negative (anxiety, tension, or discomfort). If the aroused state induced by the psychological closeness of the other person is labeled as positive, Patterson's theory is that a person will reciprocate the closeness. If it is labeled as negative, as in an intrusion, the person will exhibit compensatory behavior, or some form of withdrawal.

The ideas of compensation and reciprocity in relation to personal space and culture are potentially very important. Different cultures are likely to exhibit compensation and reciprocity in different circumstances and in different ways. Because most of the research on these processes has not examined their operation in different cultures, this would be an extremely illuminating program of research to pursue.

Group space boundaries. Most of our knowledge of personal space focuses on individuals. Groups, however, also often behave as if there were various spatial boundaries around them. For example, Knowles (1972) tried to intrude on pairs of males, females, or males and females as they walked down the street. They were approached head on by a confederate, who acted as if he were going to bisect the pair and walk between them. Most pairs, especially male/female ones, avoided the intruder and swung off to the side as a group, suggesting their attempt to maintain the pair intact. In other studies Knowles (1973) and Cheyne and Efran (1972, 1973) showed that people avoided intruding on groups and were reluctant to pass through conversing pairs or larger groups. Thus, not only do individuals act as if they had boundaries, but so do groups. Here again, it would be interesting to see how group boundaries operate in different cultures.

In summary, a number of studies support the idea that spatial behaviors operate in concert with many other levels of behavior, including verbal and nonverbal responses. These findings also fit well with Hall's ideas, since he suggested that spatial distances are important in permitting the operation of various channels of communication.

Although most of the work reviewed thus far did not address relations between culture and spacing, these studies bear indirectly on our interests. For example, the data show that people in a variety of situations and social relationships use systematic spacing practices. As Hall implied, the far edge of the intimate zone and the near edge of the personal zone (18–24 inches) are rather common for standing relationships. People in face-to-face contact rarely come closer or stand farther away. Seating distances are a bit greater, hovering around the far boundary of the personal zone and the close edge of the social zone (about 4 feet). The consistency of this behavior across a wide range of situations and social relationships is impressive and suggests that the use of spatial zones may be a pervasive practice in our culture. Whether or not such stability applies to other cultures or to subcultural groups within the United States is a question to be addressed in the next section of the chapter.

The data also show that personal space is not static, but is responsive to a range of interpersonal and situational factors, such as friendship and personality. Once again we can ask how personal space operates in response to such factors in different cultural settings.

Personal Space and Culture

As discussed earlier, a major feature of Hall's analysis concerns cultural differences in use of space. Hall observed that furniture arrangements, home design, distances, and angles of orientation between people varied across cultures. A deduction from Hall's analysis deals with spatial practices of "contact" and "noncontact" cultures. For example, Hall depicted Middle Eastern and Mediterranean societies as highly sensory, with people interacting at very close distances. Such contact cultures contrast with northern European ones, where people tend to be more reserved and use much less physical touching and sensory contact in their social interaction.

Hall's thinking has stimulated a small amount of research on how people from different cultures or subcultures orient themselves spatially in social situations. The data base is rather slim: only about a dozen empirical cross-cultural studies have been conducted. There are probably several reasons. For one, it is not easy to do cross-cultural analyses. One needs access to different cultures, and the work is expensive and time-consuming. For another, relatively little research on personal space has been done in naturalistic settings; most studies have involved simulations or laboratory analyses. Such procedures are not always portable to other cultures, and the procedures themselves may be strange and not easily understood by anyone other than American college sophomores. Another reason is that psychologists who have done research on personal space are simply not tuned in to the need for cross-cultural research. Their focus has been on the basic dynamics of personal space in relation to such variables as attraction, intrusion, and personality, and their training and orientation have predisposed them to put cultural factors in a secondary place.

Another general issue concerns the populations that have been investigated. Only a handful of cross-cultural studies have examined different nationality groups—for example, people from the United States compared with people from Middle Eastern, Latin American, or European cultures. Another batch of studies, the majority of the presently available pool, analyzed differences and similarities in personal spacing among ethnic groups in the United States—Black, Hispanic, Chinese, Hawaiian.

All this is to say that, while Hall's hypotheses about cultural differences in spatial practices are provocative, the present body of empirical knowledge is quite skimpy and needs to be buttressed by additional data. Given these qualifications, what do we know about culture and personal spacing?

Cross-national analyses. Cross-national studies provide some support for the idea that people from contact cultures use closer personal spacing than those from noncontact cultures. In an early study, Watson and Graves (1966) compared American students with students from Arab countries who were studying at U.S. universities. Observation of group discussions showed that Arabs positioned themselves closer to one another, faced more directly toward one another, had more eye contact, touched one another more, and spoke more loudly than Americans. A recent study conducted in the waiting rooms of doctors' offices in Australia and Indonesia lends further support to cultural differences in spacing (Noesjirwan, 1977). Indonesians, more contact-oriented than Australians, tended to choose seats closer to strangers and talked more with them than Australians did. These findings are what Hall would have predicted.

Other evidence comes from studies by Little (1968) and Sommer (1968), both of whom used simulation techniques. For example, Little (1968) asked people from five countries to position doll figures in relation to one another. His results also supported Hall's ideas. People from the contact cultures of southern Italy and Greece placed figures closer together than people from the noncontact cultures of Sweden and Scotland; people from the United States used intermediate distances.

In a different type of study, Sommer (1968) asked college students from different countries to rate the intimacy of various seating arrangements. American, English, Swedish, Dutch, and Pakistani students all judged side-by-side seating to be the most intimate, followed by corner-to-corner and opposite seating arrangements, respectively. The more physically distant the seating locations, the less intimate everyone judged them to be. Although there were some differences among nationalities, the general similarity among them suggests potential cross-cultural uniformities, at least among educated members of different societies.

Other cross-national studies have been less successful in showing spatial differences. For example, Forston and Larson (1968) found no differences between Latin American and North American college students, and Engebretson and Fullmer (1970) reported few differences in the spacing of Japanese Americans, Hawaiian-born Japanese Americans, and Caucasian Americans.

In summary, existing research lends some, but not overwhelming, support to Hall's ideas about personal spacing in contact and noncontact cultures. Because there are many factors to consider, such as the setting and characteristics of the people with regard to status, education, and assimilation to one another's cultures, a great deal of additional research is required.

Personal spacing in U.S. ethnic groups. A number of studies have examined personal spacing among various ethnic groups in the United States. Most of these studies compared Blacks and Whites, although a few looked at Hispanic Americans (Mexican and Puerto Rican Americans). Only occasionally have other groups, such as Asian Americans, been researched.

Unfortunately, these studies do not provide very clear results, and there appear to be factors other than ethnicity that may affect personal spacing among people from these groups. For example, sex, socioeconomic factors, age, and other variables discussed earlier probably interact with cultural background to affect distancing behavior. Such variables have not always been dealt with systematically in existing studies, and we are therefore able to draw only weak conclusions. Here again we can say in advance that much more research is needed.

Two early studies found that Blacks maintained greater spacing from each other than Whites. Willis (1966) found weak evidence that Black students stood farther apart than White students as they met and conversed on a college campus. Baxter (1970) did an ingenious study at the Houston zoo, where observers judged the distance between people in pairs who were looking at animals in an exhibit. Mexican Americans, members of a contact culture, generally stood closest together, Blacks stood farthest apart, and Whites stood at intermediate distances. But the results were actually quite complex, and there were several factors that made simple interpretations inappropriate. For example, among Whites and Blacks mixed-sex pairs stood closest, whereas all-female Mexican American pairs were closest. So it is difficult to draw any general conclusions from this research.

The two studies reported above that showed Blacks using greater distances than Whites are contradicted by investigations in other settings. For example, Jones (1971) took photographs of Black, Puerto Rican, Italian, and Chinese people on New York streets and found no differences among groups in distance or angle of orientation. Later, Aiello and Jones (1971) showed that middle-class White children stood farther apart than lower-class Black and Puerto Rican children, with no differences between the latter groups. Black and Puerto Rican children also showed less-direct body orientations (facing versus not facing).

These results are indeed confusing, and there are many other variables to consider beyond ethnic background. Two such factors, age and socioeconomic status, have received some attention in the literature. For example, Jones and Aiello (1973) compared the spatial behavior of upper-lower-class Black and middle-lower-class White children in different school grades. They found that in the first grade Black children stood closer together than White children, but this difference disappeared by the third grade and even reversed itself by the fifth grade. Furthermore, there were complicated sex effects such that Black girls stood closer together than Black boys and White girls stood farthest apart. And Black children of all ages faced each other less directly than White children did. This study suggests the importance of age and developmental differences coupled with sex and cultural differences.

The role of socioeconomic status was examined by Scherer (1974) in a very clever pair of studies. Scherer observed Black and White children in school playgrounds, using long-distance photography. Observers were located at a distance from schoolyards, unbeknownst to the children, who were systematically photographed as they interacted during recess. Scherer's first study compared Black and White children in Grades 1 to 4. No differences in personal spacing were found for these children, all of whom were from lower socioeconomic backgrounds. In a second study, Black and White children from both middle and lower socioeconomic levels were compared. There still were no differences between poorer Black and poorer White children, and there were no differences between middle-class Black and middle-class White children. However, *both* middle-class groups used larger distances than their socioeconomically lower counterparts; the differences were stronger for Whites. Scherer's studies are the first to separate ethnic and socioeconomic factors and the first to suggest that the previously obtained differences between Blacks and Whites may be related to socioeconomic factors: differences in personal spacing between ethnic groups may be attributable to socioeconomic, age, sex, and other factors as much as (or more than) to ethnic differences. Another possibility is that the absence of differences between subcultural groups within a society may be due to the very pervasiveness of personal-spacing behavior within the culture at large. That is, within a culture, subgroups may all use relatively consistent spacing, or members of different groups may learn early the spacing practices appropriate with other groups and settings and adjust their behavior accordingly.

In summary, a modest amount of research suggests that people from so-called contact cultures use closer interaction distances than those from less contact-oriented cultures, in line with Hall's ideas. However, much more research needs to be done on this topic. The number of available studies is small, they are based on just a few cultures, and they do not systematically take into account sex (or, for groups, sex composition), socioeconomic status, and other variables in interaction with ethnic background. This is a potentially ripe field for investigation, but it is only at its beginning.

SUMMARY

This chapter examined personal space, or interpersonal distance, as one of several privacy-regulation mechanisms. The concept of personal space, quite prevalent in animal-behavior studies, was initially applied to human social functioning by Hall, who proposed two general ideas: (1) people use any of four spatial zones when interacting, depending on the setting and the intimacy of the social relationship; (2) some cultures use closer interaction distances than others.

In his first hypothesis, Hall proposed the existence of four spatial zones of interaction: the *intimate zone* (0–18 inches) is usually adopted by people in close personal relationships, typically in private situations; the *personal zone* (1.5–4 feet) is the normal spacing that people maintain in day-to-day interaction; the *social zone* (4–12 feet) is commonly used in public and is the distance of ordinary business and impersonal contacts between people; and the *public zone* (12–25 feet and beyond) is a distance usually reserved for high-status people and/or public and formal settings.

An analysis of over 100 studies indicated general support for Hall's spatial zone hypothesis (Altman & Vinsel, 1977). People who interacted while standing typically used the far edge of the intimate zone (about 18 inches) or the near end of the personal zone (18–30 inches). People who were seated were typically separated by about 2.5–4 feet, the upper boundary of the personal zone, or they used the lower boundary of the social zone (4–7 feet). These findings were quite stable across a range of conditions, such as sex differences, personal factors, and attraction between people. Thus, Hall's ideas about spatial zones are well supported by empirical data.

We also briefly reviewed research on factors found to affect personal space. For example, people who know or like each other position themselves closer than strangers or acquaintances. The idea of acceptable zones of spacing is confirmed in studies in which people are approached too closely by others, usually by strangers. Such intrusions often lead to withdrawal and behaviors reflecting discomfort, as people attempt to re-establish appropriate distances from others. Other research shows that personal space is one of a series of behavioral mechanisms that operate to facilitate a desired level of intimacy. Thus, as people move closer to or away from each other, there are compensatory responses involving changes in eye contact, body postures, leaning, and other behaviors.

We also examined research on the second aspect of Hall's theorizing—namely, cultural differences in use of space. Here the data somewhat supported the idea that people from contact cultures (Latin American, Mediterranean, Middle Eastern) maintain closer personal distances when interacting than those from noncontact cultures (northern European and related cultures). However, research data comparing spacing of ethnic groups in the United States are complex and do not allow a clear interpretation about the role of cultural factors in personal spacing. Rather, variables such as age, sex, and socioeconomic status seem to be more important than ethnicity, or at least to interact with cultural factors in as yet undetermined ways.

Much more research is needed on personal space, especially in relation to cultural factors. There is a sufficient body of knowledge to indicate that the simple use of environmental spacing is an important means of privacy regulation and that it may well be culture-specific in some respects and universal in others. Given the promising data now available, future research concerned with culture and environment must understand better how this fundamental privacy-regulation mechanism operates across a range of social systems.

Chapter 6

TERRITORIAL BEHAVIOR

The idea of territory is everywhere in our lives:

1. A dog viciously attacks another animal that comes into its yard. The invader meekly retreats. However, the situation is reversed in the invader's yard.
2. A child quickly learns the term *mine* to refer to his or her toys and is terribly upset when someone else uses them.
3. Members of the neighborhood gang refer to the street they live on as their "turf," and they defend it vigorously against trespassers.
4. The homeowner puts up signs, fences, and shrubbery around the yard and is furious at people who pass through without permission.
5. The faculty member who is fed up with parking difficulties rents a private parking space for $300 a year.
6. The tennis courts of a country club have a sign that says "Members Only—Outsiders Not Permitted."
7. A nation carefully demarcates its boundaries and guards against any trespassers—individuals or armed forces—from a neighboring nation.
8. A student places his or her books and jacket on a table in the library or cafeteria to "save" the seat.

These are just a few examples of how people ordinarily use the term *territory*. There are a number of issues about territory in these examples that we will address in this chapter. For example, the concept of territory is applicable to both humans and animals in relation to the objects and places they possess or control. It applies to ownership and control by individuals, small groups, larger organizations, and even countries. Furthermore, the concept sometimes involves "defense" of a place, ranging from threats to actual aggression against a potential invader. Territories also vary in scale, from objects to rooms, homes, small-scale geographical areas, and whole nations. Finally territories are often marked or personalized and display the presence of an owner or occupant. Thus, "territory" is a complex concept that has a number of properties.

The present chapter will examine various facets of territorial behavior described above, especially in relation to culture and environment. First, we propose a definitional and conceptual framework for the analysis of human territorial behavior. This is followed by a description of territoriality over the course of human history. In keeping with the general theme of the book, the remaining parts of the chapter consider the functions of territorial behavior in relation to personal identity and regulation of social systems and how territoriality has operated in different cultures and periods of history.

A DEFINITIONAL ANALYSIS OF TERRITORIAL BEHAVIOR

The concept of territory is not new; it has been applied to animal behavior for centuries. For those interested in animal territoriality, extensive analyses appear in Carpenter (1958), Eibl-Eibesfeldt (1970), Moyer (1976), Nice (1941), Wilson (1975), and Wynne-Edwards (1962).

There are many definitions of animal and human territorial behavior, several of which were integrated by Altman (1975), whose examination of these definitions suggested several central themes. First, *territory* refers to objects, places, or geographical areas that can vary in size from small to large and can have any shape, such as toys, seats at a table, rooms, homes, and nations. Second, most definitions include the idea of ownership or control over use of a place or object. Control can cover the range from others not being permitted entry or use to others being permitted in limited ways. Third, many definitions suggest that occupants personalize places in some way—for example, animals by secretions, excretions, and noises and humans by use of symbols and artifacts such as fences and signs. Fourth, various definitions suggest that territories can be controlled by individuals, small groups, or large groups. Fifth, some definitions suggest that occupants often resort to defense and protection of territories in the face of actual or potential invasion by others. Sixth, many definitions, especially those dealing with animal behavior, refer to the functions of territories, such as mating, population control, rearing of young, and protection of resources (Carpenter, 1958, referred to about 30 functions of territorial behavior). If we pull together some of these ideas, human territoriality can be defined as including these features:

1. There is control and ownership of a place or object on a temporary or permanent basis.
2. The place or object may be small or large.
3. Ownership may be by a person or group.
4. Territoriality can serve any of several functions, including social functions (status, identity, family stability) and physical functions (child rearing, food regulation, food storage).

5. Territories are often personalized or marked.
6. Defense may occur when territorial boundaries are violated.

From this definitional analysis, it should be evident that territoriality is very complex. In fact, the term *territoriality* has so many properties and dimensions that we probably should not use a single word to cover all the things to which it refers: different types of territoriality may operate according to different rules. So keep in mind the complexity of human territorial behavior and try to avoid the trap of assuming that all territorial phenomena are identical.

A HISTORICAL PERSPECTIVE ON HUMAN TERRITORIALITY

A question of continuing interest concerns the existence of territoriality in the history of mankind. Has territorial behavior been part and parcel of our evolutionary past? Does evidence of territoriality appear among early peoples, before the time of fixed communities? What do archeological and anthropological analyses of earlier periods of history tell us about territoriality?

One controversial issue that is rooted in these questions concerns the biological and evolutionary basis of human territoriality. Is territorial behavior learned, or is it inborn and inherited? This is an extremely complex issue and is not yet resolved. All we can do is introduce you to the problem and give you a sense of its dimensions (for more comprehensive discussions see Altman, 1975; Moyer, 1976; Suttles, 1972; Wilson, 1975). In the past two decades social scientists, ethologists, and others have explored the genetic and evolutionary bases of various aspects of human behavior, including aggression (Lorenz, 1966), altruism, or helping behavior (Campbell, 1975; Wilson, 1975), social processes (Tiger, 1969), and territorial behavior (Ardrey, 1966; Wynne-Edwards, 1962). American psychology has long been dominated by an environmental-determinist philosophy that considers most human behavior to be primarily a result of learning and environmental factors. Consequently, the possibility that some important human processes might have a biological and evolutionary basis created much controversy and furor. We will not resolve the question here because the matter is very complex and is not yet settled. But it is something to be thought about and discussed. In the long run, as with so many other aspects of human behavior, it is probable that both environmental and biological and genetic factors operate in an interactive fashion, although we do not yet know the nature of the interaction. However, we can proceed reasonably well with our analysis of territorial behavior without being obligated to answer the "learned versus innate" question.

Biologically oriented scholars state that humans are part of a long evolutionary process that has affected many facets of their behavior. Since territorial behavior is so widespread in animals and humans, it is probable that, like animals, people have an evolutionary history that involves territorial functions associated with biological survival. Several writers, however, note that not all animals are territorial, that to postulate a gene—or even a propensity—for inheritance of territoriality is to oversimplify, and that the tremendous variability in animal and human use of space makes the assumption of simple genetic underpinnings remote.

We have obviously oversimplified this complex issue, and those who wish to examine the matter further are referred to the sources cited above. It is sufficient for our purposes to state that the "biological versus learned" aspect of territorial behavior is a popular and controversial issue these days, and it is likely to occupy the attention of scholars for years to come.

Another interesting question concerns the existence of territorial behavior in humans over the course of history. Some writers believe that early people exhibited territorial behaviors even in prehistoric times; others believe not. Here again, this is a complex question, and you should not expect absolute closure; rather, think about the historical pervasiveness of territoriality in terms of the complexity and varieties of territorial behavior, discussed in this chapter. Instead of reaching a simple "yes" or "no" conclusion, one might be more analytical and ask about what types of territory, what types of people and groups, and what types of functions existed in different periods of history and in different cultures. At present, the historical pervasiveness of human territoriality has not been addressed in a systematic and analytic framework. Instead, the question has been treated as if all territories were alike, whether they belonged to individuals, groups, or large collectives and regardless of the functions they served. The issue is further clouded by the fact that most anthropological and historical treatments examine territoriality as if it were a separate process, independent of privacy. On the contrary, we described territoriality as one of a series of privacy-regulation mechanisms and suggested that it be examined in relation to privacy and other boundary mechanisms, not as a separate process. As you read about the historical background of territoriality, attend to the following issues: (1) the dimensions and varieties of territoriality in humans and (2) territoriality in relation to the process of privacy regulation.

Lee and DeVore (1968) provide some facts that place the historical basis of human territoriality in perspective. They indicate that people, in one form or another, have existed on earth for some 2 million years and have lived as hunter-gatherers without permanent, settled communities for over 99% of this time. Only in the last 10,000 years have people farmed, domesticated animals, used metal, and learned how to harness energy beyond that of their own bodies. Furthermore, of the estimated 8 billion people who have ever lived on earth (as of 1968), only about 6% have become agriculturalists, about 4% have lived in industrialized societies, and the rest have been hunter-gatherers. However, one must also realize that only a small proportion of the present-day world population live as hunter-gatherers. Because of the absence of written records and the problem of inferring what life was like so many thousands and hundreds of thousands of years ago, it is hard to answer questions about the presence and form of human territoriality in preagricultural times.

One school of thought states that territoriality in humans is a long-standing historical process that extends back to periods when people (and even ancestors of present-day *Homo sapiens*) lived a nomadic life with no permanent settlements, no herding or animal-husbandry practices, and no agriculture or farming. Such people simply lived off the land. They ate fruits, berries, roots, and other naturally growing food, sometimes supplemented with meat from animals or insects they killed or found dead. Since food could not always be stored for long periods, people often spent many hours of their daily lives foraging. Some writers hypothesize that groups in such subsistence circumstances had territories which they used on a regular basis and over which they had some control.

Some writers also believe that territorial behavior is deeply rooted in our evolutionary history. According to Malmberg (1977), protohominids (precursors of *Homo sapiens*) may have had territories, partly for self-protection and partly to permit them to function in environments that contained food (Clark, 1960). Hockett and Archer (1964) theorized that such territories consisted of core areas that were defended against intruders, even though they might not have been well marked. Bates (1953) reasoned that the widespread occurrence of territoriality among mammals, our closest animal relatives, makes it likely that territoriality is also central to human functioning. In general, such theorizing about the pervasiveness of territoriality in human history centers on the following ideas: territoriality is a widespread phenomenon among mammals and in our evolutionary ancestors; protohominids required known places for food, security, child rearing, and other reasons; territories may not have been completely fixed or stable, but they probably existed among our ancestors.

But several writers question whether early people had territories that were stable or defended. Lee and DeVore (1968) noted that ownership of territories varies tremendously among present-day hunter-gatherer groups. For example, they observed that Hadza and !Kung Bushmen of Africa, nomadic hunter-gatherer peoples, do not engage in conflict over space with neighboring groups. When there is the possibility of conflict, one or the other group will simply withdraw and leave an area. Furthermore, Lee and DeVore stated, marginal and unpredictable food supplies in many parts of the world result in flexibility of group organization, with people coming and going, producing rather changeable social systems. This makes is difficult, they believe, for strong territorial identities to arise. Besides, the absence of very much personal property and the need to be flexible regarding location of food result in weak attachments to and feelings of ownership about places. Although particular individuals or groups might be drawn to certain locales for kinship or ritual reasons, not all groups seem to show active defense of places or attachment of strong values of ownership to places. Other writers have adopted a similar position (Reynolds, 1966, 1972). For example, certain Australian aborigines (Barnes, 1970) have a number of areas where they forage over the course of the year, moving from place to place, but they do not defend such places or prevent others from using them. Still other writers (Tringham, 1972) theorize that territoriality in earlier peoples was probably variable, depending on the availability of food, water, and other resources.

Other writers state that one needs to be careful about how a social group is defined and what criteria are imposed on the concept of territory. For example, Godelier (1977) argued that, although some groups exhibit considerable exchange of members, there still are territorial processes operating. For example, among the Australian aborigines, people are free to use their relatives' land. And among the Pygmies, people may move from band to band, and they have access to the resources of the group with which they are affiliated at a given time. However, they cannot use the territories of groups with which they have no relationship.

Basehart (1967), an anthropologist, worked from records of the movements and behavior of prereservation Mescalero Apache American Indians. He argued that the most fruitful way to think about the Mescalero Apache is as a "resource-holding corporation" in which a geographical territory with fairly specific boundaries is held in common as a food-gathering resource by all individuals defined as Mescalero Apache. Even though there is no political unit corresponding to this definition, since the Mescalero are a loose agglomeration of small bands organized around individual leaders, the resource-holding corporation serves to maintain a food supply for all group members. Basehart (1967) wrote:

> The key notion defining the resource holding corporation is the rule providing freedom of access for all Mescalero to any resources in Mescalero territory. No Mescalero had exclusive right to any resource by virtue of discovery or prior exploitation. . . . Mescalero viewed territory primarily in terms of the resources offered for their pattern of exploitation rather than in relation to geographical boundaries. . . . Mescalero, then, thought of themselves as free to roam on extensive territory utilizing without hindrance whatever resources were available [pp. 285–286].

Citing work by Lapovsky (1962), Basehart maintained that a similar pattern of territoriality was found among many hunting-and-gathering societies having high mobility and weak political structure, including the Konkoma Lapp, Iban, Plateau Tonga, and Turkana. This pattern ensures societal subsistence in areas where the amount and geographical distribution of food fluctuate considerably.

Determining the presence or absence of territories requires careful analysis of the relationship between various groups. In addition, overly literal application of ownership and defense criteria as aspects of territoriality can lead to erroneous conclusions. In a scholarly analysis of food production and distribution systems cross-culturally, Lenski (1966) makes the point that our European definition of ownership is too narrow and restricts our understanding of land use among other cultures. We tend to think in terms of single ownership and exclusive use, while in other cultures, including many in Africa, land is conceived of as a resource in which many parties—for example, farmer, king, village—might have an interest.

Although some groups, as noted above, may not have a sense of ownership, they sometimes show strong psychological attachments to places. For example, Tuan (1977) stated that Australian aborigines exhibit a distinction between "estates" and "ranges." Ranges are the regions used to hunt and gather food, and they are associated with physical survival, but estates are the spiritual homes, or "dreaming places," of kinship groups and their ancestors. It is with such ancestral homes that the aborigines feel deep emotional ties, and it is there that particular rocks, hills, and streams have important personal meaning. A similar analysis of Australian aborigine orientations to the land has been offered by Rapoport (1977). And Basehart (1967) reported that the Mescalero Apache home "range" included several sacred mountains that were important in the spiritual life of the society. In the same way, immigrants to a new land may always cherish and revere their homeland as a central place in their lives, even though they no longer control it or use it regularly; spiritually it is "theirs." So the concept of territory exists at many levels of meaning, and we must be careful about simplistic, sweeping statements. Furthermore, you can see how the concept of territoriality is related to environmental cognitions and perceptions discussed in Chapters 2 and 3, through the images we have about territories and the way they fit into our beliefs and feelings about our environment.

Part of the disagreement about the historical basis of territoriality may very well stem from differences among definitions. If by *territoriality* one means "frequent and regular use of an area," then many early people certainly exhibited territorial behavior, since they were generally restricted in their movements. If one insists that strictly nonoverlapping and exclusive use of places is a critical component of territoriality, then the evidence is less clear, since there often has been simultaneous and overlapping use by different groups with easy movement in and out of bands and geographical areas. And if one insists that human territoriality always demands defense against use by outsiders, then territoriality was probably not always evident in early people. Much of the issue, then, depends on the definition that one wishes to use.

In spite of disagreements about the presence of territoriality in earlier times in human history, most writers agree that, with the rise of agriculture some 10,000 years ago and, to some extent, with the development of practices of herding and animal husbandry, humans became quite territorial. Once people settled down to become farmers or to raise animals, territorial behavior became quite prevalent (Barnes, 1970; Martin, 1972; Reynolds, 1966, 1972; and others). People became attached to their land and resented its use by others, they became sensitive about where their land began and ended, and they resisted free and uncontrolled access by others. Lenski (1966) argues that the emphasis on land ownership probably arose during the shift from simple horticultural technologies, in which the amount of land available far exceeded that which could be cultivated, to more intensive agricultural technologies, which placed a premium on all available land. In addition, agriculturists often cooperated with one another, practiced division of labor, shared crops, and engaged in mutual protection. This cooperation probably contributed to the formation of stable communities and the need to define boundaries, to establish governance structures, and to develop mechanisms for resolving land conflicts. Thus, within the past 10,000 years a large portion of the world's population has settled down and exhibited increased territoriality, involving ownership and defense. Even among people practicing animal husbandry and herding, who did not always live in a fixed place, territorial behavior probably became quite strong in relation to grazing areas and protection of livestock from raids. We can, of course, expect territoriality and defense to be more salient where overlapping land use occurs. For example, the range wars of the American West in the 1800s were partly caused by the cattle ranchers' conviction that sheep grazing is deleterious to grasslands used by bovines.

Thus, whether or not one wishes to argue about the long-term underpinnings of human territoriality, the fact is that among modern people, who are more or less settled down, territorial behavior is widespread. Among hunter-gatherer people, who at one time were the most prevalent group and who nowadays are diminishing, the situation was probably more variable. Some exhibited all the behaviors included in the concept of territoriality, such as defense; others seemed to confine their activities to particular geographic regions; others exhibited such fluidity with respect to group membership and land use that it is hard to answer the historical questions about territoriality one way or the other. But, with the advent of agricultural and pastoral life, it is clear that territoriality among humans became widespread.

A FRAMEWORK FOR VIEWING HUMAN TERRITORIALITY

Table 6-1 summarizes how we will deal with human territoriality in the remainder of this chapter. A key idea is that territorial behavior is one of several mechanisms used to regulate privacy and self/other accessibility. Along with personal space and verbal and nonverbal behavior, territoriality permits people to make themselves more and less accessible to others.

Table 6-1. Aspects of territorial behavior.

Actors	*Scale of Territories*	*Types of Territories*	*Functions of Territories*
Individuals	Objects	Primary	Personal Identity
Small Groups	Rooms	Secondary	Regulation of Social Systems
Large Collectives	Homes Communities Nations	Public	

The first two columns in Table 6-1 indicate that territories can be occupied and controlled by a variety of actors (individuals, small groups, communities, and larger collectives) and that territories vary in scale, from small to large. The third column points to three types of territories: primary, secondary, and public. This important distinction, described in detail below, refers to the idea that human territories vary in their importance in the lives of the occupants. Some territories, such as homes, are primary territories and are extremely important to the well-being and lives of their occupants. Public territories, such as seats on a bus or places in line, are generally not very important: they do not occupy a central role in the lives of their users.

The right side of the table lists functions, or goals, served by territoriality. Personalizing a place permits a person to be distinguished from others and contributes to a sense of uniqueness and identity. Regulation of relations within and between groups is an important goal served by territorial behavior, and it contributes to the smooth functioning of social systems.

The discussion to follow is organized around (1) the distinction among primary, secondary, and public territories and (2) the functional qualities of territories. The roles of actors and scale are incorporated throughout the analysis.

PRIMARY, SECONDARY, AND PUBLIC TERRITORIES

The third column in Table 6-1 points to one major facet of human territorial behavior—the types of territories in the everyday lives of people. The terms *primary, secondary,* and *public,* applied to territories, parallel in some ways the sociological classification of social groups. Primary groups include husband/wife pairs and families and are usually very central to a person's life. Secondary groups are associations that may be important but involve only part of a person's life, such as work groups, athletic teams, and social clubs. A public, or reference, group is more diffuse, like a professional association or the citizenry of a nation. Our classification of territories partly, but not completely, reflects this continuum of closeness of affiliation and involvement with different kinds of groups and places.

Another aspect of our classification of territories is more psychological and relates to individuals' feelings of involvement with and control over a place. Some territories are long-term and are strongly controlled by occupants, such as a bedroom or a family home (primary territory). In addition, such territories are often personally very important to people and play a crucial role in their lives. Other places are short-term, are not as extensively controlled by occupants, and are less important to their lives in general, such as a bus seat, a restaurant table, or a tennis court in a local park (public territory).

Primary Territories

"Primary territories are owned and used exclusively by individuals or groups, are clearly identified as theirs by others, are controlled on a relatively permanent basis and are central to the day-to-day lives of the occupants" (Altman, 1975, p. 112).

Examples of primary territories are easy to specify: a person's bedroom, a family home, a family farm, a company's offices, a community's property, a nation's land. Each of these places is psychologically important to its occupants and is something with which they identify strongly and which they occupy on a relatively long-term basis. Furthermore, primary territories are usually under the complete and unambiguous control of their members. In our society, one rarely enters someone's home without explicit permission, and the home is a place over which occupants generally have complete control.

Unexpected or uninvited intrusions into primary territories are a serious matter and can lead to strong defensive actions. For example, it is permissible and legal in our society to protect one's home against intruders, and it is permissible under world law to defend one's nation against undesired entry or invasion. Perhaps the protection of primary territories is allowed because such territories are so important to a person's or group's well-being and viability. It may also be, as our privacy framework suggests, that inability to control a primary territory successfully may be a serious affront to the psychological well-being of a person or group. Since such territories are so crucial and so much identified with a person's or group's life, inability to control access on a regular or predictable basis may have implications for self-esteem, self-identity, and the ability to function well. Furthermore, in our culture we look very unfavorably on people who do not have regular and stable primary territories. We call them "vagrants" and consider them to be marginal and undesirable people, subject to arrest and to fines. Thus, it is believed to be important for people to have homes (and places within homes, such as bedrooms) where they can retreat, where they can assume a certain image and status within a family and within society, and over which they have relatively complete control. So, in a variety of ways, primary territories are crucial to the lives of people and groups in our society.

Primary territories are also widespread across cultures. Most people, families, and kinship groups seem to have places or things which are identified with them and over which they have control—an area of land; a tent, hut, or other form of dwelling; a bed, a sleeping mat, certain objects. And rules of entry to places or use of items that are under the control of an owner or occupant are evident in most cultures. Even those in communal living arrangements often possess primary territories, such as the Mehinacu (Gregor, 1970, 1974; Roberts & Gregor, 1971) and the Ngadju Dayak of Borneo (Miles, 1970), described in Chapter 4. In these cases a family may live in one section of a communal dwelling but still have control over a primary territory; for example, others do not enter a family's area without permission, people have their own sleeping areas and mats, families eat separately and have their own cooking utensils and storage areas. As another example, Lewis (1959, 1961) observed that very crowded families in tenements in Mexico have strict norms about not entering others' homes without an invitation.

The concept of primary territory applies to individuals as well as to larger social units. In Western society a person's bedroom and many items in it are primary territories over which the occupant has complete control. Among the Fulani people of West Africa, Prussin (1974) observed that the wife is owner of the interior furnishings of a hut, including decorations and utensils, whereas the husband is responsible for the outside walls and the hut itself. In earlier times, when these people were nomadic, the woman was owner of the whole tent and everything in it. Similarly, in the homes and communities of Pueblo Indians, to be described in Chapters 7 and 8, the woman controls and owns everything within the home, whereas the man owns the gardens and livestock.

The concept of territory can also be applied to larger groups. For example, Peterson (1975) cites an 1878 account of the rituals followed by strangers and messengers who approached an encampment of Australian aborigines:

> The messenger, on approaching the camp of the tribe to which he has to deliver a message, does not at once break in on their privacy. He sits down at a considerable distance from the camp, but usually within sight of it, and makes a very small fire of bark and twigs for the purpose of indicating his presence by the smoke. After the lapse of a quarter of an hour, one of the aged blacks approaches him, carrying in his hand a fire stick, or piece of thick bark ignited at one end. The messenger presents his token to the old man, who scans it and orders his conduct accordingly [p. 60].[1]

In a similar vein, Parker (1968) noted that messengers or visitors approaching an Iroquois Indian village were required by law to give a warning call at specified intervals during the approach.

Failure to engage in these or other rituals, symbolizing respect for the group and its boundaries, could lead to overt hostility and aggression. Note that respect for a physical place occupied by a group may be less important than the respect shown for the boundaries and rights of the social group itself. One might argue in the same way that, while the physical structure of the home or of any primary territory is essential, it might be better said that the physical place is only a symbol or representation of the sanctity of the person or group that occupies the place. According to this line of reasoning, primary territories serve as symbols of the importance of control over a person's or a group's own self/other boundaries, both spatial and psychological boundaries. For Australian aborigines, the geographical locale is important only because a group happens to be there. What is crucial is the regulation of access to the social group and the geographical resources that it happens to control. Peterson (1975, p. 60) made this point in discussing the fact that it is impossible for aborigine groups to defend large geographic areas: "An alternative strategy for defending the land is to make acceptance into the local land-using group a preliminary requirement for using the resources in its territory; that is, by defending the boundaries of the social group rather than the perimeter of the territory itself."

Secondary Territories

Secondary territories are less exclusive, less psychologically central, and less under the control of their occupants than primary territories. Secondary territories are exemplified by the neighborhood bar, the private country club or social club, and the neighborhood street. They have a

[1]This and all other quotations from this source are from "Hunter-Gatherer Territoriality: The Perspective from Australia," by N. Peterson, *American Anthropologist*, 1975, *77*, 53–67. Copyright 1975 by the American Anthropological Association. Reproduced by permission of the American Anthropological Association.

blend of public availability and some control over their use by occupants. They are a bridge between primary territories, which are owned by occupants and where occupants maintain strict control over use, and public territories, which can be used on a temporary basis by almost anyone who follows basic social rules. An example is a private country club, which is limited to members and their guests. As a secondary territory, the club may be quite important to its members, although probably less so than their homes. Furthermore, its membership can consist of large numbers of people. It has, therefore, elements of both private and relatively public access.

Another example, studied in detail by Cavan (1963, 1966), is the neighborhood bar. Cavan observed that, although bars are theoretically open to any member of the public past the minimum age requirement, a particular bar was, in fact, a secondary territory, and its users exhibited some control, albeit informal, over its use by outsiders. At different times of the day, different groups "owned" the bar. People had their favorite seating locations, and the bar served as an important part of the social life of its regulars. Outsiders who happened to wander in were often treated abusively. They were stared at, questioned and mocked in a hostile way, and often made to feel unwelcome. Thus, there was a group that exhibited some control over the place, in spite of the fact that the bar was theoretically public and available to everyone. Yet, while the place was important to the regular users, their control was not as long-lasting or as pervasive as it is in a primary territory.

Secondary territories are evident in many cultures. For example, urban sociologists beginning in the 1920s observed that many neighborhoods and streets were more or less controlled by gangs. Sommer (1969) reported a journalistic account of a neighborhood in Chicago where one street was populated solely by Blacks and the neighboring street was used primarily by Irish Whites. Each street was rarely used by the other group, and each was self-contained, with its own services and shops (from one perspective these streets may actually have been primary territories, since access by different ethnic groups was almost totally restricted). A similar situation was reported by Boal (1969) in an analysis of territoriality in Belfast, Ireland. Here the separation between hostile Roman Catholics and Protestants was crystallized along a particular street that separated these two groups. On the two sides of the street, extending into areas beyond the street, one might as well have been in two different worlds. There were different shops, different newspapers, and different value systems that were visibly evident. People from either side of the street could theoretically use the facilities of the other side, but it simply was not done very often.

The idea of secondary territory does not necessarily involve continuous use and control of a place; use and control can be intermittent, as

Cavan's (1963, 1966) analysis of bars indicated. A similar example was offered by Suttles (1968), who described how different ethnic groups in Chicago used a short-order restaurant on a time-sharing basis. Italian, Puerto Rican, Mexican American, and Black groups literally took turns using a particular restaurant and avoided the place when others were there. Thus, although each group theoretically had access to the place and it was important to all groups on a long-term basis, the restaurant was controlled by each group in turn, according to an implicit and mutually agreed-on set of principles. At San Quentin State Prison, use of the inmates' canteen was similarly restricted. Black, Chicano, and White prisoners had their own hours for using the canteen. The schedule was official and was published in the prison newspaper. One of us recalls a small restaurant, The Green Grill, that served an ethnically mixed high school in Chicago. There was an invisible line down the middle of the restaurant, with "Jewish tables" and "Italian tables" on opposite sides of the line and practically no crossing over into each other's territories.

An important aspect of secondary territories is their potential for misunderstanding and conflict. Because they involve a blend of public accessibility and private use, it is easy for people to misread and even be unaware of the existence of secondary territories. Thus, one might easily wander into a neighborhood and not know that it was regarded as a secondary territory by the residents. Newman (1972), an architect, theorized that a considerable amount of crime in urban low-cost housing projects may be due to the lack of "defensible space" in such places. He theorized that, because of their design features, certain semipublic areas—hallways, stairways, entranceways to buildings, paths and walkways—(1) are not easily kept under surveillance by occupants and (2) do not give the appearance of being "owned" by anyone and are therefore easily accessible to potential criminals.

Although some people question Newman's data (see Altman, 1975), his theory fits well with our description of secondary territories as susceptible to conflict and misinterpretation. Newman's solution to the problem is to clearly design semipublic areas with some of the characteristics that we have attributed to secondary territories. For example, he proposed the use of fences and symbolic barriers such as hedges, the clustering of entranceways to serve a few apartments, and the creation of enclosed minipark areas. As a result of these and other means, Newman hypothesized, (1) residents will have a greater sense of identity with a place, (2) it will be easier to see and question intruders, and (3) outsiders will perceive such areas as secondary territories under the control of occupants.

Thus, clearly defining secondary territories through markings and other environmental messages may make conflict less likely. This is illustrated in a variety of examples: the street in Belfast, the use of graffiti on walls by an urban gang whereby a street is labeled as its turf (Ley & Cybriwsky, 1974), the architectural design solutions of Newman, the use of symbols and signs such as "Do Not Enter: Members Only," and a variety of other techniques.

Conflict and misinterpretation about secondary territories can also occur at a societal level. A case in point is the recent conflict over fishing limits in international waters. For example, a few years ago conflict between American fishermen and Venezuelan officials followed Venezuela's declaration of a 200-mile extension of the legal coastline into previously international waters.

Social roles can also serve to demarcate secondary territories. For example, in many cultures there are clear norms about who can use what places. As described in Chapters 4, 7, and 8, many cultures practice forms of sex segregation in use of places. For example, the Pueblo Indians have a religious and social building reserved for use by males; the Dogon culture of Africa has separate men's and women's ritual buildings. Such places function as secondary territories and probably serve to minimize male/female conflict.

Public Territories

Almost anyone has the right to use public territories on a temporary, short-term basis as long as he or she observes certain minimal social rules. Parks, public beaches, seats on a bus or train, restaurant tables, and seats in a theater all are examples of public territories.

Goffman (1971) identified several types of public territories: *Stalls* are public spaces to which people can lay temporary claims, such as tennis courts and telephone booths. In such places control is largely restricted to the time of occupancy. *Turns* involve order of access to some source and are illustrated by places in line at movies, supermarkets, or refreshment stands. *Use space* refers to the area around a person that is temporarily recognized as being under that person's control. For example, the area in front of a person viewing an art exhibit or looking in a store window is usually not intruded on by others; passersby tend to go around and behind the viewer. Public territories are temporary, and they usually are not central to the lives of their occupants. Furthermore, almost any member of a society or subgroup is permitted access to public territories as long as the person observes some general social rules; for example, one must wear clothing on most beaches, one must not litter public parks or remove natural material from preserved areas.

Public territories appear in all cultures. No matter how small a community, one usually finds areas that most members of the culture can use. For example, a central marketplace or plaza, a street, shopping areas, and public thoroughfares exist in almost any community in the world.

This is not to say that public territories are available to *all* members of a culture, for that is certainly not so. Until the civil-rights movement and subsequent legislation in the United States, Black Americans were not permitted access to certain public restaurants, public restroom facilities, or front areas of buses in certain regions of the country. And in countries like South Africa there presently are severe restrictions on the use of public facilities by nonwhites. Similarly, in many other parts of the world certain groups within cultures are denied access to public facilities on the basis of their ethnicity, nationality, religion, or social class.

Variation in Scale

One can view primary, secondary, and public territories as a series of psychological boundaries that vary in their closeness, centrality, and importance to the person or group that owns and occupies them. One also sees evidence of such boundaries at many levels of scale and in many cultures around the world. For example, in New Guinea, Fraser (1968) reported that some communities are organized around a central street to which everyone in the community has free access. Yet, on closer examination, one observes that different clans have their homes clustered together on certain parts of the street and that these areas serve as secondary territories within the community. In addition, individual homes or clusters of homes are organized around a particular kinship line, and these essentially function as primary territories. An analogous arrangement occurred when various subtribes of the Cheyenne Indians came together for political or religious activities (Fraser, 1968). There was a systematic placement of tipis around a central gathering area, a public territory that was available to everyone. There also were clusterings of tipis according to clan and kinship lines that reflected secondary territories. Finally, there were smaller groupings of tipis of families that served as primary territories.

One can even carry the successive arrangement of territories down to areas within individual homes (see also Chapters 7 and 8). For example, Alexander (1969) found that certain low-income families in Peru arranged their homes to regulate access to different parts of the residence. The front porch was reserved for strangers; casual acquaintances were permitted entry into the formal parlor, which was just inside the home. Closer friends could go farther, into the informal living room and kitchen, which were located deeper in the house. And Zeisel (1973) described how certain spiritualist Puerto Rican families treated their living rooms as sacred places, with entry restricted to close friends and family. Thus, at several levels of scale and in a variety of cultures and settings, one sees the systematic arrangement of primary, secondary, and public territories.

THE ACTORS AND SCALE OF TERRITORIES

In Table 6-1 we pointed out that an analysis of territorial behavior requires attention to the actors and to the scale of territories. In some respects we have already addressed these topics in our discussion of primary, secondary, and public territories. That is, we noted that territories exist for individuals, as in the examples of bedrooms and seats on a bus, for small groups such as families and teams, for moderate-sized groups such as clubs and fraternities, and for large collectives such as residents of a city or a nation. There is little systematic research on how different actor/territory combinations work. At this stage in the history of research, all we can do is point to the potential importance of actors in relation to different types of territories and ask you to be alert to possible similarities and differences.

The situation becomes even more complicated if one changes frames of reference in relation to actors. For example, from the perspective of an outsider, the whole interior of a family home is a primary territory. It is a place the family occupies and controls on an enduring basis, and the family has complete freedom to determine how and when visitors may use its home. However, from the perspective of family members themselves, the home can be depicted as involving primary, secondary, and public territories in relation to the family as users. Parental bedrooms and older children's bedrooms usually function as primary territories, the occupants having considerable control over access and use. Other areas of the home might function as secondary territories, with access limited to subgroups of the family, such as a suite of rooms and bathroom shared by a subset of children. Still other places in the home may serve as public territories, such as the kitchen or family room, where everyone in the family has control on a temporary basis. Hence, we need to examine territories within and across cultures from the perspective of different users, recognizing that what is primary, secondary, or public territory may vary with actors, settings, and level of analysis.

FUNCTIONS OF TERRITORIAL BEHAVIOR: PERSONAL IDENTITY AND REGULATION OF SOCIAL SYSTEMS

In our brief discussion of animal behavior at the beginning of this chapter, we stated that territorial behavior serves a variety of functions, many of which are associated with basic life processes, such as rearing of young, mating, and ensuring a food supply. Although some of these functions apply to biological aspects of human behavior, our analysis will be directed primarily at social and psychological aspects of human territoriality.

Edney (1976) emphasized the theme that territoriality is an important organizer of human life at the level of communities and large groups, small groups, and individuals. Edney stated that territoriality functions to facilitate social processes such as planning, anticipating others' behavior, engaging in uninterrupted activities, and having security. Furthermore, territories permit the performance of functions such as child rearing and food management in a regularized routine and in a predictable place. So, Edney stated, life would be chaotic without territories. In line with these themes, we will emphasize two general functions of human territoriality: (1) management of personal identity and (2) regulation of social systems.

How do territories manage personal identity? They serve to articulate the boundary between the self and others, whether the self is an individual or a group. By personalizing a room with decorations, an individual puts a personal stamp on the environment, informs others where his or her place begins and ends, and also portrays to the world the values and beliefs that he or she holds. In a similar way, clan members of the Haida Indians of the northwestern United States and Canada display their collective identity through totem-pole decorations. Communities and nations adopt symbols and slogans that are displayed to reflect their self-images and to mark their territorial boundaries. Personalization serves to portray simultaneously one's distinctiveness from others and one's common ties with a community. Personalization can help, therefore, to organize life and facilitate social relationships. In our terminology, identity management facilitates the regulation of self/other boundaries between a person or group and the social environment.

The second function of human territoriality is regulation of social processes, including control over various resources. Here we refer to the pacing of human interaction in respect to important resources or activities—food, sleeping, elimination, child rearing (Edney, 1976). Primary, secondary, and public territories permit people to survive physically and psychologically and to conduct life's functions in an orderly and systematic way. It would be hard to function well without any territories at all, whether they be a portable tent or permanent home, a temporary encampment of a nomadic group, or a nation that has stable borders. This is not to say that it is the territories themselves that are important; rather, what is crucial is access to the resources they contain.

These two general functions—identity management and regulation of social systems—are related, since they both deal with control of access to the self and to things related to the self. And they both deal with processes involving the relation of individuals and groups to the social world. At the most general level, therefore, territorial behavior in humans functions as a boundary- or privacy-regulation mechanism in accord with the ideas expressed in Chapter 4. Before considering each of these functions in detail, however, we will discuss the generic process of boundary regulation in relation to human territoriality.

Territorial Behavior and Boundary Regulation

Marking of territorial boundaries. Among animals and people a hallmark of territories is boundaries that are marked or personalized. Animals delineate their territories by excretions, secretions, noise, and other means, as signals to potential intruders and perhaps as reminders to themselves where their places begin and end. When people mark territories, however, they usually employ natural geographic indicators or artifacts and symbols; they rarely use secretions or excretions.

Stilgoe (1976) did a fascinating analysis of the history of territorial boundaries and their marking in Western society. He traced the history of land-boundary delineations from the ancient Greeks and Romans through the English and French of the 15th to 17th centuries to the early settlers of the United States. According to Stilgoe, the ancient Greeks and Romans were extremely sensitive about boundaries that separated people's land. In fact, the Romans had a deity, Terminus, who was the god of land boundaries. One could find everywhere in the Roman Empire so-called Termini stones, which had the likeness of the god carved on them. These stones were used to separate fields and to define ownership boundaries. Those who moved or overturned these stones were subject to extreme penalty under both religious and civil law, and some violators were burned alive. Furthermore, to avoid confusion, homes in classical Greek and Roman cities were separated by at least 2½ feet, with the intervening space not owned by either party but consecrated to the boundary god.

Eventually, in later Western history, annual ceremonies were held as reminders of boundaries around agricultural fields and community property. For example, in 15th and 16th century England, annual Rogationtide ceremonies (later called perambulation ceremonies) involved a careful review of a village's boundaries. The local priest led a lengthy procession around the village and pointed out the boundaries of the community. The ceremonies included appropriate prayers, religious utterances, and statements from the Bible such as "Cursed be he that removes his neighbor's landmark," Deuteronomy 27:17 (Stilgoe, 1976). At times children's heads were deliberately bumped against landmark trees or other markers to ensure that they remembered important boundary distinctions. These ceremonies focused on village boundaries, and each person had to define his or her own property. In cases of conflict about individual property lines, village elders settled disputes until surveying became a practice in the 17th and 18th centuries.

Attention to boundaries carried over into the New England settlements of the United States. Town borders were perambulated annually, and negotiations were frequent among neighboring towns. Individual ownership was initially defined by natural indicators, such as streams and rows of trees. Later, people erected wooden and stone fences, used lines of burned trees, and eventually relied on surveys and formal land filings. With the development of surveying, maps, and legal filing codes, the annual process of perambulation faded. However, Stilgoe noted that our annual Halloween ceremonies, including the jack-o'-lantern, are remnants of early pagan and later medieval religious boundary customs and that "the jack-o'-lantern is the ghost of a long ago remover of landmarks forever doomed to haunt boundary lines" (Stilgoe, 1976, p. 14).

Boundary definitions appear in a variety of forms. For example, many cities throughout history have had walls surrounding them, to control access to their interior. Obviously, defense was a major function of such walls, but other goals were served as well (see Chapter 9). For example, many medieval cities in Europe had walls not only for military defense but to control the economic operation of the city. And in ancient China parts of cities were walled off because of their religious significance (Tuan, 1974). We see that many functions can be served by boundary definitions.

Groups smaller than communities or cities also use a variety of boundary-regulation and marking mechanisms. For example, Ley and Cybriwsky (1974) found that urban gangs in Philadelphia used graffiti on walls to mark their neighborhood territories. The researchers were able to plot the location of gang territories in relation to where and how graffiti were painted on building walls. The content of the graffiti included the names of members of gangs, gang names, threats to other groups, and slogans. Through these markings, groups attempted to define their territories and to regulate access of outsiders to their places.

Finally, we can move to the scale of individuals or small groups. They define their boundaries in a variety of ways. As discussed in Chapters 7 and 8, family homes around the world are marked by a variety of boundary devices—fences, hedges, and signs. In some cases territorial markers can carry the force of law. The Iroquois Indians, who live in New York State and eastern Canada, have a written political constitution and code of personal behavior called the Great Peace and Law of the Longhouse (Parker, 1968). The law is composed of 117 paragraphs, or wampum. Parker (1968) reports the 107th wampum as follows:

> A certain sign shall be known to all people of the Five Nations which shall denote that the owner or occupant of a house is absent. A stick or pole in a slanting or leaning position shall indicate this and be the sign. Every person not entitled to enter the house by right of living within upon seeing such a

> sign shall not enter the house either by day or by night, but shall keep as far away as his business will permit [p. 57].

Recent research also indicates that boundary definition occurs quite frequently in public settings. For example, Sommer and Becker (1969) found that such markers as sweaters, sandwiches, and books served as protectors of territories in cafeterias and libraries. Similar results have been obtained by Shaffer and Sadowski (1975) in a bar, where personal materials such as sweaters and book bags served as territorial protectors of tables. Thus, boundary regulation occurs in a variety of forms and for a variety of actors, from individuals to communities to nations.

Occupancy and use as territorial indicators. Territorial control is often symbolized by markers or other indicators of ownership, but boundary definition is often evident from mere occupancy of a place. For example, Sommer and Becker (1969) and Becker (1973) found that occupied rooms or tables were avoided by others, suggesting that occupancy itself is a symbol of territorial control. In an analysis of city life in Chicago, Suttles (1968, 1972) observed how different neighborhoods took on unified characters as a function of the activities and visibility of their residents, such as gangs, vigilante groups, and conservation groups. The character of a neighborhood often was defined simply by the presence of its occupants and the use of facilities by children, mothers, old people, and others who sat on stoops and at storefronts and who engaged in a series of regular and visible activities. The ethnicity of a neighborhood also contributed to its sense of territoriality. Although boundaries may have existed in the form of major highways and streets, the sheer presence of people and their unique and evident characteristics contributed strongly to a sense of territory.

Ley (1972) observed a similar phenomenon in urban ghettos of Philadelphia. Gangs often marked their turfs with slogans painted on the walls of buildings, as described earlier, but simple occupancy and use of neighborhood facilities also conveyed their territorial control.

> In the daytime, but more particularly on summer evenings, whole families empty onto their porches, their stoops, and the sidewalk itself. Particularly in white ethnic neighborhoods, it is not uncommon to see members of a family and their friends sitting on chairs around the television set, perhaps eating, drinking or smoking, so that essential characteristics of the dining room are being reenacted on the sidewalk. In this manner surveillance and social control passes beyond the household and onto the street [p. 6].

Similar practices were common in our own childhoods in New York and Chicago. Here, young people who were part of a large social group could always be found at a particular candy store (a combination newsstand and telephone center, soda fountain, and candy dispenser). Anywhere from 15 to 30 young people gathered daily at "their" candy store and simply "hung around" or planned social activities. Hours would be spent there (to the dismay or pleasure of the store owner, depending on how much money the group spent), and the group members felt considerable identity and esprit with one another and with the place. Scattered throughout a neighborhood were many such stores, which essentially functioned as community centers, with little overlap of occupants. Yet there was no articulate boundary definition or markings; people simply knew who belonged to which place and where different group territories were located.

Similar practices occurred among both old and younger people in local parks. We recall older people spending hot summer evenings sitting in a local park with their friends, socializing, debating, and escaping the heat of their apartments. Groups typically had their own "spots" in the park, usually no more than a couple of adjacent benches where they sat, along with their own chairs or blankets. Such places were not marked in advance, nor did the occupants have any legal or other rights to the area. Yet it was known as their "spot," and others rarely intruded. This pattern also occurred for young people, who had their own "spots" (as far from the adults as possible, of course). Once again, there was little confusion about which group owned which "spot." Yet in all these instances there was no explicit boundary condition or marking to signify ownership. Use patterns were sufficient to define group territories.

As another example, Suttles (1968) observed how groups of different ethnic compositions vied for space in a local public park. Even within a single ethnic group, such as Italians, different parts of the park were occupied by different groups. Occupancy of the most- and least-desired places was directly related to the power of the group. Such practices are also evident in other cultures, as noted by Malmberg (1977). For example, Malmberg cited a study by Lerup (1972) of a park in Stockholm, Sweden, that had territories occupied by different groups—southern Europeans, students, and others. And numerous examples of such practices appear in the urban sociological writings of Suttles (1968, 1972), Thrasher (1927), Whyte (1943), and others.

A similar process occurred among Protestants and Catholics in Belfast, Ireland, described earlier (Boal, 1969). Although we have emphasized the role of the single street as an explicit boundary between neighborhoods, it was far more than that boundary itself that defined the territories of the two groups. Within each neighborhood, the occupancy by Catholics or Protestants was evident in a variety of ways—different kinds of churches, different newspapers, political advertising, wall markings of various kinds that reflected political and religious views. Similarly, as noted earlier, Peterson (1975) described the customs among Australian aborigines in respect to strangers or messengers who visited another group's encampment. The visitor waited at the fringe of the encampment for someone to recognize him and to admit him to the territory occupied by the group. Although one might view the group's space as a territory, with a firm boundary around it, Peterson observed that among these nomadic people it was not the space or locale per se that was important. Rather, the crucial thing was admittance to the social group, wherever it was located. Thus, occupancy of a place, almost any place, reflected territorial ownership.

A related practice occurred among certain American Indians of the 1800s (Fraser, 1968). As described in detail in Chapter 9, when different Cheyenne Indian bands came together for religious and/or ritual groupings, their tipis were arranged in an encampment in a particular way, with different tribal groups located in particular places around a large, open circle. Each band had a fixed and known place in the assemblage. Furthermore, aside from visible markings on tipis, there were no group boundary designations, nor was the particular piece of land important. Rather, the occupancy and massing of people defined the territory, and access to and membership in a particular group were central, not the particular piece of land on which the group was located.

Another series of examples concerns squatter settlements around the world (Malmberg, 1977). These settlements are quite common in cities in Central and South America, Africa, Asia, and elsewhere. Squatters are groups of people, often families and extended kin groups, who simply stake out a piece of unclaimed ground and move in. Their homes are typically shacks built of scrap material, often without plumbing or electricity, and they have no legal rights to the place. Eventually, occupancy determines ownership, although it is often supplemented by articulated boundaries around houses, which can include fences and walls, stone boundaries, and the like. For example, Malmberg (1977) cited from Martin (1969), who commented on the squatter settlements of Lousaka, Africa:

> Although none of the property legally belongs to the residents, there is no doubt in anybody's mind about the *de facto* ownership of each piece of ground. Ask a householder where his ground ends and his neighbour's begins and he will be able to show you. With a stick he will delineate exactly the boundary line in a flat dusty piece of ground. There is neither post nor stones nor hedge since there is no need of them; the forces of nature have arrived at a state of equilibrium. A challenge of the neighbour's property has been made, discussion and even argument have been held and the matter settled [Martin, p. 213].

In some settlements occupancy was often supplemented by various rules and practices. For example, although squatter families in Colombia and Peru did not have community service facilities or formal civic organizations, these small communities quickly developed their own social norms (Rogler, 1967). One powerful norm concerned intrusion. Intrusive people were reacted to very negatively, and families within a community sometimes secluded themselves from others.

Occupancy indicators of territory can occur at the level of individuals, families, and larger social groups. For example, among the Pueblo Indians, who live in communities of terraced dwellings surrounding a central plaza (see Chapter 7), control over space is quite different than in Western culture. Dwellings look alike, status is not confirmed by amount of space that one possesses, and exteriors are not uniquely labeled. Yet cultural practices and occupancy patterns reflect territories very clearly. Members of extended families live in close proximity, resulting in areas of the pueblo that are known to be theirs. Furthermore, cultural norms give ownership to different classes of people. The women own and manage the home and its interior (this was also the practice of the Fulani of Africa, Prussin, 1974). The men own the livestock, tools, religious objects, and fruit trees, and the clan or extended family owns the garden and land. All this occurs without visible boundaries or markings, suggesting that role occupancy can define territories.

Identity and Self-Definition

We now examine a major function of personalizing and marking places that one occupies or owns: expressing, establishing, and maintaining self-identity. Our thesis is that territories permit people and groups to display their personalities and values through the vehicle of the physical environment. People put their personal stamp on places not only to regulate access to others but simultaneously to present themselves to others, to express what they are and what they believe, and, thereby, to establish their distinctiveness and uniqueness. Thus, personalization of an environment not only involves control of access to places but serves that aspect of privacy concerned with establishing self/other distinctiveness.

Personalization in relation to identity expression occurs in a variety of places—bedrooms, offices, homes, and public displays. Primary territories such as homes are excellent examples of how we use territories to portray ourselves to others. The American home often displays openly the personality and values of its occupants—the elegant decor that people present in their formal living rooms; poster-covered rooms of teenagers that display athletic heroes, rock bands, and the latest obscenities; family rooms and their collections of trophies and family mementos; landscaping, Christmas light displays, decorated entranceways and doorways of suburban homes. As discussed in Chapters 7 and 8, not only does the home serve as a primary territory that family members control, but considerable effort is directed toward using the home to display the individuality of its occupants, as if to establish their psychological identity and separateness from others.

Hansen and Altman (1976) analyzed the decorations placed on dormitory-room walls by freshmen during their first quarter at the University of Utah. They found that about 90% of the new students decorated within 2 weeks of coming to the university and that almost 100% had decorated by the end of the first quarter. Frequently used decorations included reference items (maps and calendars), abstract items (landscapes, graphic art, and so on), personal-interest items (sports pictures, rock-band pictures, and so on), entertainment items (radios and sports equipment), and personal-value items (religious and political displays). Although many of these items were commercially produced, examination of a particular student's room was quite revealing of his or her interests, likes and dislikes, and related aspects of personality. We suspect that many students displayed themselves through decorations as a way to inform others of who they were and what they wished to convey by way of self-image.

Personalization not only occurs in primary territories, such as dormitory rooms, but often appears in public places, frequently in the form of graffiti. Ley and Cybriwsky (1974) examined graffiti as an expression of individuality, specifically distinguishing them from graffiti used to claim territory, as in the gang behavior described earlier. They observed that in Philadelphia and New York there were individuals who were self-proclaimed "Kings of the Wall" (p. 492). Many of these were young Blacks who roamed the cities widely along main transportation lines, leaving their spray-painted "signatures" in a variety of places, often in large letters. Signatures included such names as Cool Earl, Cornbread, Bobby Cool, and Sir Smooth. The signatures, often artistically and neatly accomplished, appeared on bridges and overpasses, on walls and streets, and in such exotic places as on airplanes that were secretly decorated and even on an elephant at the zoo.

Interviews with graffiti kings indicated that they (and those who used their names) were not interested in claiming territories but were concerned more with self-expression and display of their uniqueness and identity:

> I started writing . . . to prove to people where I was. You go somewhere and get your name up there and people know you were there, that you weren't afraid. . . .
>
> I don't feel like a celebrity normally. . . but the guys make me feel like one when they introduce me to someone. "This is him" they say. The guys knows who the first one was [Ley & Cybriwsky, 1974, p. 494].

Personalization also occurs on a group scale, as in the recent rise of "folk art" practices in ghetto communities. As described by Sommer (1971), whole communities organized projects whereby giant murals were painted on the sides of buildings, sometimes several stories high. These murals contained a variety of themes, often had bright and multicolored designs, and can be interpreted as communities displaying themselves and their values through the use of the physical environment. The muralists' goal in many cases was not to claim and demarcate territories but to express themselves as intact and cohesive groups.

The expression of self-identity through personalization takes a variety of forms and can involve individuals, families, groups, and nations. Furthermore, personalization seems to occur on all types of territories—primary, secondary, and public. Consider the following examples:

1. The decorative totem poles of the Indians of the northwestern American continent reflect lineage and clan affiliations.

2. The homes of chiefs and religious leaders in numerous cultures are larger and more elaborately decorated than those of ordinary people, reflecting their status.

3. Churches of all denominations and throughout history are usually beautifully decorated, partly to symbolize community identity with certain practices and beliefs.

4. Entrances to cities in ancient China and in the Middle East were often ornately decorated with gods, mythological figures, and animals, all reflecting the beliefs and cosmology of the inhabitants.

5. Façades of many government buildings and institutional places in modern society are decorated in such a way as to enhance people's identification with the institution.

6. Offices often contain expressions of the user's values and personality, in the form of flowers and plants, photographs, and mementos.

7. In many cultures allocation of space to males or females is accompanied by differential decoration. Among many groups females not only "own" the interior of the dwelling but often display their identification with the place through decorations.

8. The Plains Indians of the United States often decorated their tipis, expressing not only tribal values but also individual, clan, and family qualities.

We have emphasized how personalizing and decorating territories can reflect the identity of the occupant. Very often, of course, personalization serves both to signal that the territory is controlled by the occupant and to depict self-identity. And sometimes it is not easy to distinguish between these two processes. Nevertheless, we wish to sensitize you to the idea that territorial personalization may not always (or only) serve to regulate other people's access to a place and to the resources of the place: it may also permit expression of one's identity and uniqueness.

Regulation of Social Systems

The framework of this chapter states that a second major function of territoriality is regulation of social systems. Edney's (1976) analysis of territoriality as crucial to the organization of social life for individuals, groups, and communities states the point well. His theme is that, without ownership, occupancy, and control of various spaces, human interaction would be chaotic; this idea is evident in the historical and cultural examples presented throughout this chapter. For example, the perambulation ceremonies in medieval England (Stilgoe, 1976) illustrate the regulatory function of territoriality at individual, group, and community levels. The march through and around the village, where the priest identified the boundaries of the community's property, emphasized to everyone where land ownership began and ended, thereby preventing conflict. A council of elders also adjudicated disagreements between individuals in a peaceful fashion. Thus, making territories salient served a regulatory function at the level of individual, group, and community.

A great variety of studies show how territoriality contributes to the effective regulation and viability of social systems: gang graffiti in urban settings (Ley & Cybriwsky, 1974), demarcation of Irish Protestant and Catholic neighborhoods (Boal, 1969), establishment of firm boundaries in the form of walls and defense structures around communities and cities (Saalman, 1968), allocation of space in communal dwellings, cultural practices about ownership of dwellings, animals, gardens, and lands by males and females, families, clans, and tribes (Prussin, 1974; Rapoport, 1969a, 1969b), and practices for entering social groups and gaining access to their resources (Peterson, 1975). You need only reread many of the examples of boundary establishment presented earlier; they can be reinterpreted to reflect their role in regulating social interaction in a variety of settings.

We can also see how territories help maintain the well-being of social systems by examining *failures* of territorial control. That is, poorly functioning social systems may occur when territorial regulation is not operating effectively. Or, conversely, systems in a state of disruption may subsequently show breakdowns in territorial functioning. (Note that we are avoiding any statement about which comes first—disruption of the system or breakdown of territoriality. Either sequence may happen.) Several examples in the literature from historical, anthropological, and psychological research depict the linkage of poorly functioning social systems and ineffective territoriality.

Consider two studies that examined the behavior of pairs of U.S. Navy sailors who volunteered to live and work in social isolation for periods ranging from 4 to 10 days as part of a Navy research program on team functioning (Altman & Haythorn, 1967; Altman, Taylor, &

Wheeler, 1971). This research examined a number of aspects of behavior, including performance, stress, social interaction, and territorial behavior. Of particular interest here is the relation between territorial behavior (defined as exclusive use of beds and areas of a 12 × 12 cubicle by individual team members) and social viability. Both studies showed that pairs of men who established territories during the first day or two developed more-viable and better-functioning groups. They performed better on work, showed fewer stress symptoms, and were able to stay in the isolated environments longer. Groups that did not establish territories early exhibited conflict and poor functioning. They appeared to be disorganized, did not go about the job of group formation in a systematic way, and apparently had not prepared themselves for the isolation experience or for the difficulties of living with just one other person for a long period. The epitome of an organized and successful group was one pair of men who decided early on the first day where they would keep their clothing, who would have what space for storage, and what their eating schedule would be. Through this territorial behavior and a variety of other means, they organized their environment to produce a coherent life-style that permitted them to function in a viable way.

Further evidence for a relation between territoriality and group stability appears in studies of unusual populations. For example, O'Neill and Paluck (1973) found that the introduction of territories among a group of retarded boys led to a decline in aggressive behavior. Another illustration comes from research conducted in a rehabilitation center cottage that housed 17 boys (Sundstrom & Altman, 1974). The researchers studied the relation between the dominance of members of the cottage group—as measured by how influential they were judged to be by their peers—and their control of space. Territorial behavior was determined by daily mappings over a 10-week period of the location of the boys in bedrooms, a dormitory area, a lounge and TV area, bathrooms, or elsewhere in the cottage. The results showed a variety of relations between dominance and territorial behavior.

During the first 5 weeks of observation, the influential boys were more territorial and spent large amounts of time in particular areas in the cottage. The less powerful boys distributed themselves throughout the cottage. During a second period of observation the situation changed dramatically, perhaps because of the removal of two dominant boys from the group and the admission of two subsequently dominant newcomers. Territorial behavior dropped sharply, and there was no longer a relation with dominance. That is, all boys tended to be everywhere in the cottage, with almost no one having a frequently used location. Furthermore, fights, teasing, and misbehavior rose sharply, suggesting that the group was in turmoil. Thus, when group composition changed, the social system was upset, and this was reflected in disrupted territorial behavior. During a third period there were fewer extreme changes in group composition. Less dominant boys now tended to be more territorial than highly dominant boys, and there was a partial return to a stable social structure. However, the fact that highly dominant boys still exhibited considerable disruptive behavior suggested that the group had not yet returned to a stable system. Thus, territoriality is closely linked with social dynamics and mirrors the degree to which groups are effectively or ineffectively functioning.

Another idea implicit in the preceding studies is that social change of one kind or another may manifest itself in a variety of ways—disrupted social and cultural customs, malfunctioning group operation, and the like. What is interesting to us is that social change may also show its disruptive effects on established territorial practices. This is clearly illustrated in the study of the boys' cottage, where the social system and the territorial system were upset when new boys were introduced into the cottage. Let us now examine some culturally based examples of social systems in the process of change and experiencing disturbances in territorial practices.

Social change is an inevitable process, as cultures are exposed to new technology and to one another, as populations and resource needs rise and fall, as external and internal political events intrude on social systems. A major form of social change that is presently occurring on a worldwide scale concerns the "sedentarization" of nomads. Many nomadic societies around the world are settling down at a rapid rate. Peoples who at one time moved from place to place over the course of seasons, months, or years to hunt and gather food, to herd animals, and to grow crops in different places are in the process of settling down for a variety of reasons. Some nomadic peoples have discovered Western technology, such as trucks and farm equipment, and adapted it to their way of life. They can now herd livestock and undertake agriculture more efficiently. In other instances, governmental negotiations with adjacent nations about boundaries have resulted in nomadic sedentarization. Still other nomads are often fiercely independent and create problems for modern bureaucratic governments, which often wish to contain nomadic peoples so as to stabilize the internal politics of their countries.

One example of territorial problems associated with the settlement of nomads occurred in connection with the development of the Aswan Dam along the Nile River in Egypt and Sudan (Fahim, 1974). Because of the project, the Sudanese government decided to resettle a group of agricultural people, the Halfan, in a series of small villages. Although the Halfan were able to continue their agricultural ways and style of life, they found the situation stressful for several reasons. For example, they had to adjust to a new land and new requirements for agriculture. In addition, there were other people in the area—Butana nomads, a sheep- and cattle-herding people, who were required by the government to settle down near the villages of the newly settled Halfan. Conflict between the groups arose quickly and centered on a number of issues. One serious source of disagreement involved the Butana practice of grazing sheep and cattle on the land occupied by the Halfan, who were rather sensitive to territorial boundaries. The Halfan viewed the nomads as violating their territories, whereas the nomads viewed all the land as accessible to them for grazing. Conflicts also centered on work and social relationships, and there was increasing contact between the groups as they used the public facilities of the village. Thus, with resettlement, sedentarization, and massive social change, old territorial concepts no longer applied and conflicts mounted. This example from Sudanese Africa seems reminiscent of the conflicts that occurred in the frontier days of the western United States, particularly among sheepherders, cattlemen, and farmers. Each group viewed use of the land in a different way, territorial issues at the time had not always been completely resolved, and negotiated agreements sometimes took years to achieve and often required the intervention of local and national governments.

Breakdowns in territorial and social systems also occur in modern urban settings, where social change is often rapid and dramatic. For example, Ley and Cybriwsky (1974) found that the graffiti painted on walls by gangs in Philadelphia depicted stable and unstable aspects of the social structure of the community, including territorial boundaries. Established and powerful gangs clearly marked their areas of control, and as one moved closer to the core area of a group's territory, markings were even more frequent. And these markings typically conveyed feelings of group identity and cohesion. Areas of conflict in borderline sections often contained the graffiti of several groups, including threats and taunts to others. These transition zones were also frequently the sites of group conflict and fighting. In certain neighborhoods, where people feared encroachment by other groups, graffiti reflected both group identity and feelings of hostility toward outsiders. A longitudinal analysis of the graffiti used by people and groups in various sections of neighborhoods could well document the history of social changes that inevitably seem to occur in such settings. So Ley and Cybriwsky's analyses depict how territorial behavior reflects the stability of groups and their attempts to regulate social interaction, coupled with instability and the breakdown of territorial behavior. Again, this is not to say that territorial behavior necessarily causes social stability; rather, it may only be an indicator of the state of a social system.

Another demonstration of the role of territoriality in stable and unstable social systems appears in the research and theorizing of Newman (1972). Newman compared crime rates in low-cost urban housing developments and concluded that the designs of public and semipublic spaces were related to crime. In general, his hypothesis was that certain design features permitted occupants to maintain surveillance over public areas, with the result that these places became psychologically defensible and crime rates were lower. In our framework, Newman's ideas point to the need for greater clarity of public, secondary, and primary territories and for clearer articulation of territorial boundaries, thereby permitting greater regulation and control by occupants. Places in which territorial transitions and ownership were least clear existed in developments where anyone could gain access to an apartment unit through a single entrance serving a large number of families, where access to semipublic areas was easy, and where surveillance by occupants was not possible. In addition, Newman hypothesized poor defensible space in buildings where there were many occupants to a floor, where stairways were not easily surveyed, and where indications of psychological ownership were ambiguous. He claimed that crime rates were lower in clustered dwelling units that contained fences, landscaping, and other means of distinguishing between public and group areas. Crime was also reported to be less frequent in designs where entrances served small clusters of families and where windows and paths were positioned to permit surveillance. Although there is controversy about the accuracy of Newman's data (see Altman, 1975), his ideas are compatible with our distinctions among primary, secondary, and public territories as serving to help regulate social systems. In particular, secondary territories seem especially conducive to conflict and to social-system instability.

Thus, among the Halfan and nomadic people of the Sudan, among the gangs of Philadelphia, and in an analysis of crime in urban housing developments, disruption and conflict seem to be focused around secondary territories, where people and groups have overlapping access and control. It would be interesting to analyze other forms of social disruption, especially within and across cultural and ethnic groups, to locate examples of successful and unsuccessful establishment and management of secondary territories. In summary, there is reasonable evidence that territorial behavior not only functions to establish and maintain personal identity but also plays a central role in the viability of social systems.

SUMMARY

This chapter analyzed territorial behavior within the framework of privacy presented in Chapter 4. Territorial behavior was depicted as one of several behavioral mechanisms that operate in the service of privacy, helping regulate access to the self.

We first undertook a definitional analysis of the concept of territoriality to illustrate that territorial behavior is complex and has several dimensions and properties. For our purposes, territorial behavior involved the following characteristics: (1) ownership or control over access to places, (2) variation in scale from small to large, (3) service for a variety of functions, including social and biological needs, (4) personalization or marking, and (5) possible defense against intrusion by outsiders. We also examined the question whether human territoriality is learned or innate and the history of human territoriality.

The major emphasis of the chapter was on a framework of territoriality that analyzed types of territories, actors, and functions of territorial behavior. Three types of territory were described: primary, secondary, and public. Primary territories are exclusively owned, occupied, and controlled by individuals and groups on a long-term basis, and they are quite important to the lives of their users. A person's bedroom and a family home are examples. Secondary territories are somewhat less important to occupants and are often controlled in a limited way on a long-term basis. Country clubs, team workspaces, and the like are secondary territories. Secondary territories are available to a greater range of people and are less exclusively controlled by occupants than primary territories. Thus, secondary territories have a mixture of public and private accessibility. Territories of the third type, public, are available to most members of a society, usually on a short-term basis; occupancy and control are temporary. Seats on buses, places on benches, and tables in a restaurant are examples.

We discussed major functions of human territoriality, including self/other boundary regulation, personal-identity management, and regulation of social systems. We traced the central role of boundary regulation from ancient times to the present and noted the variety of ways in which historical and contemporary cultures mark boundaries—through religious ceremonies and activities, decorations, and graffiti. Occupancy of territories without markings is a frequent practice, and the presence of users alone is often sufficient to indicate ownership and control.

The function of personal-identity management is evident in individual and group personalizing and decorating of territories. The graffiti in certain urban settings, dormitory and home decorations, and group and community displays that appear in many cultures attest to the thesis that human territoriality is a vehicle by which people extend their personalities and values onto the physical environment and thereby achieve a sense of self-identity.

Finally, we examined the important function of territoriality concerned with regulating and managing social processes within and between groups. As noted by Edney (1976) and others, territoriality serves to smooth out the functioning of social groups. It permits people to know where their own and others' places begin and end and where and how they control access to various resources. This regulatory role of territoriality is especially salient when social processes are in a state of disruption and change. Using several research examples, we showed that breakdowns in territoriality may be associated with social disruption.

A theme of the chapter was that territoriality in humans is a pervasive quality and appears in many forms and for many different actors but that it is a complex phenomenon. Accordingly, one should not use the concept in a simplistic fashion. Rather, one should try to specify carefully its dimensions, functions, and actors and to examine its operation carefully and systematically.

PART THREE

PLACES IN THE ENVIRONMENT

This part of the book strikes out in a new direction and focuses on environmental places. Recall that our overall framework (Figure 1-1) described the relation among people, culture, and the environment as involving psychological processes, such as world views and environmental orientations, discussed in Part 1, and behavioral and social processes, such as privacy, personal space, and territory, discussed in Part 2. We now consider a third set of factors—namely, the places that people create, such as homes, neighborhoods, and communities.

Before beginning the discussion, we believe it is important to repeat our overarching theme concerning the relation among psychological processes, behavioral processes, and places—each is dependent on the others, each can be a "cause" of any other, each can be affected by any other. For example, the design of a home or community is affected by the cultural values, privacy-regulation practices, and perceptions and cognitions of members of a society. But the design of a home or city in turn can affect perceptions and cognitions and privacy-regulation practices.

Accordingly, to search for "the" particular and universal chain of causation between variables is a mistaken effort; multiple directions of influence are probably the rule. Try to keep this theme in mind as you read the remaining chapters of the book, because it is easy and tempting to search for simple causes and effects when considering complex places like homes and cities.

There are many environmental places that can be examined from a cultural perspective—homes, communities, cities, schools, playgrounds, hospitals, prisons. By considering the design, location, and use of such places, one can learn a great deal about how cultures are similar and different in their relation to the physical environment. Obviously we cannot consider all environmental places in a single volume. Therefore, we will analyze homes, small communities, and large environmental units such as cities. These places were chosen for several reasons. First, homes and communities are important to people, and a great deal of their attachments and emotions are associated with these places. Hence, homes and communities provide a rich vehicle for understanding culture/environment relations. Furthermore, the availability of considerable anthropological and historical data makes the analysis of homes and communities quite feasible. Finally, all cultures have homes and communities of one sort or another, and it is possible, therefore, to do a better comparative analysis of these places than of prisons, hospitals, or other settings.

Chapter 7 focuses on the design and history of homes and on cultural differences among them. Chapter 8 examines the American home as a culturally distinct place.

Chapters 9–11 examine larger-scale communities, cities, and urban regions. The emphasis in Chapter 9 is on cultural and historical differences in community and city designs. Chapter 10 examines psychological and social aspects of life in cities. Chapter 11 considers some proposals for ideal communities and cities of the future.

As you read these chapters, be sensitive to the idea that the perceptual and cognitive aspects of human/environment relations (discussed in Part 1) and the behavioral processes of privacy, personal space, and territory (discussed in Part 2) affect, are affected by, and are embedded in places like homes, communities, and cities.

Chapter 7

HOMES AROUND THE WORLD

In examining a place like the home it is tempting to try to answer such questions as "What role do climate and the physical environment play in home design? What is the contribution of cultural factors, such as religion, world view, and family structure, to home design?" For several reasons, posing questions in these ways may not be fruitful. First, home designs are probably a result of many factors, not one or two alone. Such factors include climate, natural resources, social studies, religion to name just a few. It is highly improbable that any one of these alone "caused" homes to have one or another set of characteristics. Second, the contribution of even a single factor, such as climate, may vary from locale to locale. A factor may be important in one place but not at all important in another one. Thus, in extreme climates—for example, in the Arctic or in equatorial jungles—climate may play an important part in home design, whereas in temperate regions, climate may be less influential. Third, because of the complex interplay of many factors over hundreds and even thousands of years, it is often not possible to do more than say that factors *X, Y,* and *Z* may be important: one may not be able to separate out their exact or unique contributions.

We prefer to deal with the issue from a different perspective—namely, *the home as a reflection of culture/environment relations*. Rather than ask what "caused" various home designs, we prefer to ask what the home reveals about culture/environment relations. In a sense, we are interested in using the home as a "window" to see how different cultures relate to their physical environments.

This is not to say that we will ignore how climate, resources, technology, and other factors are related to home design. However, we will consider such factors within the guiding perspective of homes as reflections of culture/environment linkages and without an ax to grind about how particular variables lead to certain design characteristics of homes. Perhaps this is a less rigorous approach than is common in modern-day social and behavioral sciences, in which the attempt is to "nail down" causal factors and to identify the exact magnitude of their contributions. But the issues associated with home designs across cultures and historical periods are too complex and too interwoven to isolate variables one at a time.

Figure 7-1 summarizes our approach. It portrays the home as a reflection of several facets of a culture and as a place that has many "windows" through which one can see how a culture relates to its environment. Home design can reveal many things: climatological and environmental factors; the level of technological resources available to a society; family structure and role relationships; the religion, cosmology, and world views of a society. As with the parable of the blind men touching different parts of an elephant, each proclaiming that the part he experienced was the "true" elephant, so it is that there is no "correct" way to understand homes in relation to culture/environment issues. The home reflects, simultaneously, many facets of culture/environment links, each of which is correct at some level of analysis, but each of which is also incomplete if viewed by itself.

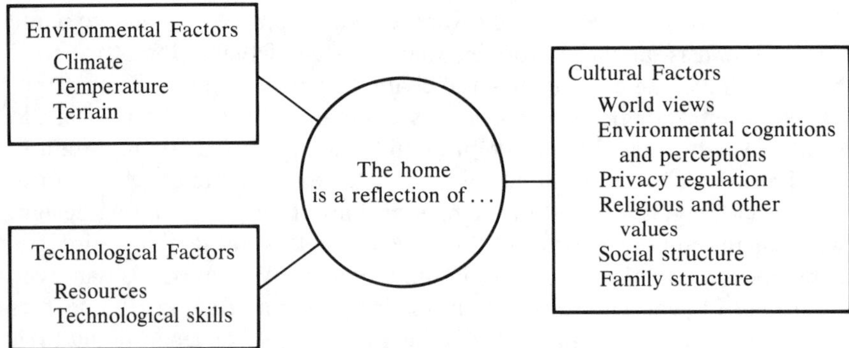

Figure 7-1. The home in relation to other factors.

A HISTORICAL/CULTURAL PERSPECTIVE ON HOUSING

Before examining the home as a reflection of technological, climatic, cultural, and other aspects of a society, it may be useful to identify different types of housing, the evolution of house forms, and the general cultural contexts within which house forms exist.

Diversity is the key term to describe homes around the world and throughout history. From the elaborate palaces of the French kings of the Renaissance to the tents of the nomadic tribespeople of northern Africa; from the mansions of the motor and mining barons of industrialized Western society to the squatter shacks of Central and South America; from the plush condominiums of New York and Chicago to the small houseboats of Hong Kong Bay; from the tract homes of middle-class American families to the grass huts of African tribal groups; from the modern home equipped with family room, patio, bedrooms, living room, kitchen, and laundry room to the one-room temporary huts of African Pygmies—diversity and variation in home design seem to be the rule.

There are many ways to classify homes, but the following dimensions seem especially appropriate for our purposes: permanent/temporary, differentiated/homogeneous, and communal/noncommunal.

Permanent/Temporary

In many parts of the world, especially in Western society, multiple- and single-family homes are relatively permanent structures, are located on particular sites, and are designed to last for many years. Homes are rarely moved about, and when they are, it is the occasion for a newspaper photograph showing someone's home being transferred down the highway to a new location. When a family moves, it usually leaves its residence behind and rents or buys a new one that is equally permanent. The exception, especially in the United States, is the increasingly popular "mobile home." Although these structures are theoretically movable, the fact is that they are not really very mobile and they require special hoisting and transport facilities when moved. And more and more mobile-home communities have a permanent quality about them, as residents erect fences around their little patches of land, plant grass and shrubbery, install patios, and adopt many of the trappings of homes on fixed sites.

However, permanent homes are not universal. Some portion of the world's population still consists of nomads, who do not settle in a particular place but who move about with their homes or construct new homes at each site. For example, certain Mongol people, the Plains Indians of an earlier period in the United States, the Tuareg tribespeople of northern Africa, the Bedouins of Asia Minor, and the nomads of Iraq and Iran live in tentlike structures made of a variety of materials, often animal skins. All or part of their homes is carried with them and is assembled and disassembled as they move about. Other nomadic people—for example, the Pygmies of equatorial Africa and the Bushmen of South Africa—do not carry their homes with them but build them anew out of available materials, such as wood, leaves, thatch, and brush.

Whether homes are permanent or temporary fits in with other aspects of a culture. For example, permanent structures typically appear in agricultural, urban, or technological societies, and temporary structures are characteristic of hunter-gatherer and some herding cultures. Moreover, nomadic societies are likely to have simpler community and governance structures, whereas permanent communities, because of stable resources and facilities and because of continuous personal, social, economic, and political relations among people, often have more-elaborate political and governance structures.

Differentiated/Homogeneous

House forms also vary a great deal in the complexity of their designs. For example, in modern Western society, there is considerable internal differentiation of places within homes. Even in modest homes and apartments we see specialization of rooms—the kitchen, bathroom, bedrooms, living room. The more well-to-do also have breakfast nooks, dining rooms, guest rooms, powder rooms, and family rooms. But differentiated dwelling spaces are not universal. For villagers in Nigeria, Ethiopia, and elsewhere in Africa, among many Asian and Polynesian cultures, for people in various parts of the Middle East, among the Navajo Indians of the southwestern United States, and in many other cultures, there is little internal differentiation of space. All rooms are alike, and families often live in a single area—eating, sleeping, working, and playing in the same space. Very often, however, the single room itself is differentially used. For example, as described later, in the one-room Navajo hogan, family heads, guests, and important people sit along the west wall facing the sacred east, and women sit on the south side. Thus, although the Navajo dwelling itself does not have separate rooms for different activities, the space is used in a differentiated fashion.

The differentiation of space often conveys something about cultural values and practices. Cultures with undifferentiated residential space tend to be technologically less complex and very often in marginal socioeconomic straits. Furthermore, it is likely that privacy regulation is achieved by physical withdrawal from the dwelling or by a variety of nonverbal and psychological practices, rather than by environmental mechanisms. And nomadic peoples often have undifferentiated space, since such homes are simpler to move and easier to construct, whereas settled people are likely to exhibit a range of house forms from undifferentiated to elaborate and diverse living spaces.

Another dimension of diversity relates to similarities and differences among *dwellings* within a society. In Western cultures, especially in the United States, homes vary considerably from one another in design, size, and layout. In fact, diversity and individuality are sought in American homes. Even in tract developments, where houses are often very similar, people invest enormous amounts of time, energy, and money to make their homes look different from their neighbors'. But this is not a universal practice. Among the Pueblo and Navajo Indians, homes are identical, as they are among various tribal groups of Africa, South America, the Pacific, and elsewhere. Furthermore, the diversity of home structures is independent of the nomadic or settled character of a culture. Some nomadic groups, such as the earlier Plains Indians of the United States, used tipi dwellings that, though basically alike, were often uniquely decorated. And many permanent homes in European farm communities are essentially identical. For example, Atkinson (1969) observed that traditional Swiss Bernese farmhouses of the 18th and 19th centuries often differed in size and other features, but they nevertheless had common façades, similar roofs and structural designs, and relatively comparable interiors.

One major basis for differentiation of homes is status. In some cultures most people have similar residences, whereas chiefs, religious leaders, and the wealthy have larger and more elaborate homes. Rapoport (1969a) stated:

> Many societies display some differentiation in house form based on stratification in that society, whether by military prowess, wealth, or age. In parts of Africa the compound may be larger and have more retainers, wives, or cattle; the house may be more decorated, as in Southeast Asia; the roof may have more bands of thatching, as among the Peul of Africa. The skulls or scalps of enemies may be displayed as symbols, or the wealth and prestige of the owner may be expressed through size and number of retainers or elaboration of the carved columns, as among the Kwakiutl [p. 11].[1]

Rapoport observed that differentiation of house form is strongly linked to the technological and industrial development of a society. In technologically complex societies, house forms are more diverse. In addition, differentiation of homes often appears in cultures with greater stratification among members, based on economic, political, religious, and social status.

Another aspect of the differentiation of house form involves the home-construction process (Rapoport, 1969a). Rapoport used the term *primitive* to denote the most basic level of home design and construction. At this level there is little role specialization. Expertise about home design and responsibility for construction are shared by everyone. Examples are the Eskimo igloo, the Navajo hogan, the African hut, and the Indian tipi. "Any member of the culture can build the buildings which the groups needs, although in many cases . . . this is done cooperatively by a larger group" (Rapoport, 1969a, p. 3). Typically, homes all look alike, and there is a strong unverbalized tradition about design qualities. People build their homes without considering alternative designs, and if you

[1]From Amos Rapoport, *House Form and Culture,* © 1969, p. 3, 8, 11, 21, 55, 94. Reprinted by permission of Prentice-Hall, Inc., Englewood Cliffs, New Jersey.

asked why homes are built in a particular way, the answer would probably be "Because they have always been built that way; that is the way it is done." Similarity in form and absence of specialized building skills and construction roles among people probably go along with a technologically simple and socially undifferentiated society.

Rapoport's (1969a) second category of home design and construction is *preindustrial vernacular,* which involves "a greater, though still limited, number of building types, more individual variation of the model, *built by tradesmen*" (p. 8). Here there are specialists who, to varying degrees, are experts in house construction. However, Rapoport stated, tradition still dominates, and homes are not so much uniquely designed as they are variations on a traditional model. Both tradesmen and the owner "know" what the basic style of house will be: it will be what it always has been. Its variations, if any, are not based on a desire to be unique or on esthetic criteria, but are related more to functional matters such as terrain, wind, and sun. Furthermore, preindustrial vernacular buildings have what Rapoport called an "additive" quality. That is, they are open-ended and can be added onto as needed. For example, Amish farmhouses of central Pennsylvania often take on a unique appearance as families grow, with additional rooms simply appended to the main building. Although construction in the preindustrial vernacular process is the responsibility of a specialist, the consumer often participates in the building process, client and builder differing only in skill. Thus, this style of housing involves a traditional design, with variations dictated by functional demands, and with unstated cultural values guiding the characteristics of homes.

Rapoport called the third level of home design *modern vernacular*. In modern, technologically advanced societies there are "many specialized building types, each building being an original creation . . . *designed and built by teams of specialists*" (Rapoport, 1969a, p. 8). Home designs range from simple to complex and large to small, with esthetics, image, and originality, rather than tradition, playing central roles. This is not to say that tradition is absent or that there are no similarities among homes. After all, most American homes have bedrooms, bathrooms, kitchens, and living rooms. However, there is, relatively speaking, diversity in home styles. Furthermore, in the modern vernacular system there is considerable differentiation of functions associated with cultural values and traditions: for example, there are rooms for eating, sleeping, and toilet functions. In addition, the consumer plays little part in the construction of modern vernacular homes. Specialists do the work and include carpenters, landscapers, electricians, and plumbers. This increased specialization of function usually goes along with differentiation of roles and technological development of a culture, as in industrialized societies.

Communal/Noncommunal

Most of us who live in the Western world of Europe and North America automatically think that it is universal for families or individuals to have their own residences, be they detached dwellings, apartments, or mobile homes. And we think of the occupants of dwellings as typically being parents and children or singles who live alone or who share living space with others. But the fact is that these arrangements have not always been present in contemporary or earlier cultures. For example, from the 1600s through the 1800s, poor people in England lived in one- or two-room hovels that were airless and windowless, and children left the home as early as possible, often to live in "big houses" of well-to-do people, where they served as apprentices and servants (Earle, 1935). These larger houses often had many residents, sometimes up to 25 people, not all of whom were related. In addition to the primary family of a mother, father, and children, there often were servants, apprentices, and clerks who worked for the family, not to mention visiting business acquaintances and friends. Thus, certain homes during this period were both communal living places and places of business.

Communal living takes many forms and is the rule in a number of cultures. For example, the Iroquois Indians of the northeastern United States traditionally lived in multifamily "long houses," 80 to 100 feet in length (Morgan, 1965); the Mehinacu of Brazil, described in Chapter 4, also lived in large communal dwellings (Gregor, 1970, 1974; Roberts & Gregor, 1971). In most cases, however, families had their own spaces in these communal dwellings, and there often were partitions that separated families. Nevertheless, there still were considerable visual and auditory contact and easy access to all areas in the residence.

Undoubtedly there are many other dimensions that can be used to distinguish housing characteristics, such as technological practices, styles of construction, and spatial arrangements and layouts. Some of these issues will be discussed later. Our intent here is not to provide an exhaustive list of dimensions, but only to suggest a few features of homes that bear on culture/environment relations.

There also appear to be some correlates of permanent/temporary, differential/homogeneous and communal/noncommunal homes. For example, to the extent that homes are permanent, we might expect to see a more complex social system involving land-use rules, complex governance systems, and the like. Or the greater the degree of home differentiation, the more likely it is that people will use environmental mechanisms to regulate privacy, such as doors and private rooms. In communal living arrangements, one might not see typical environmental privacy mechanisms; instead various cultural practices and norms probably enable people to regulate their dealing with one another. Thus, a glimpse into homes from the perspective of the few dimensions proposed here may reveal a great deal about social relationships and practices in a given culture.

THE HOME IN RELATION TO ENVIRONMENT, TECHNOLOGY, AND CULTURE

In accord with Figure 7-1, we will now examine the home as a "window" to many facets of a society—technology, physical environment (climate, terrain), and culture (family structure, social system, religion and cosmology). The home is "affected" by such factors and in turn "affects" many of these factors in a complex interplay of variables.

Climate

An obvious way in which homes reflect their surroundings is in relation to climate, which includes temperature, humidity, wind, rain, radiation, and light (Rapoport, 1969a). While one might debate whether or not climate generally affects home design, there seems to be little doubt about the issue in extreme climates, as among the Eskimos of the Arctic, the herders of Siberia, and people in Middle Eastern countries and tropical climates.

The Eskimo igloo has often been described as the ideal and elegant solution to the harsh, cold, and windy climate of the Arctic (Cranstone, 1972; Rapoport, 1969a). For example, the hemispheric shape provides the least wind resistance, and the igloo is often situated parallel to the wind (there is a tunnel entrance) to avoid its full force. In addition, a small wall is constructed at the tunnel entrance to keep the wind from blowing in. Eskimo encampments are also positioned so as to avoid undue exposure to the severe elements of the Arctic. An igloo village is often located near the sea in a place sheltered by adjacent mountains, so as to avoid severe wind as much as possible (Rapoport, 1969a).

Several other design features of the igloo reflect responsiveness to the climate. For example, the tunnel entrance into the igloo is curved to prevent cold air from flowing into the dwelling. There are often additional, separate sections within the tunnel to facilitate heat retention. One tunnel entrance may serve several dwellings that are connected by interior passages. This helps retain heat and avoids exposure to the outside. The interior of the igloo is elevated above the level of the tunnel. Because heat rises, this design feature preserves heat. Interior heating is partly accomplished by seal-oil lamps; these operate quite well in the hemispheric shape of the interior, which is more efficient than a rectangular surface in preserving heat. In addition, the interior walls partly melt and then freeze, making for a strong seal. It is said that the igloo becomes so strong because of this melting and freezing that a polar bear could walk across the top and not damage the dwelling (Cranstone, 1972). By hanging animal skins on the inside walls and ceiling to create an air space, the occupants achieve additional warmth by means of a storm-window effect. Because of all these heating techniques, Eskimos are often portrayed as wearing very little clothing while in the igloo. In fact, one observer noted, "Living in one is like having your head in the tropics and your feet in the Arctic" (Cranstone, 1972, p. 488).

Rapoport (1969a) described several other examples of a direct relation between home design and climate. For example, Mongol Yurt people of Central Asia use several layers of felt material on their tents to create insulating air spaces. They vary the number and nature of layers with seasonal changes. The stone houses of Ireland are built low in cold and windswept areas; people in several parts of the world keep animals in their houses to provide heat; barn and home designs often reflect attempts to capitalize on prevailing sun and to avoid severe winds.

Dwellings in very hot tropical or dry places are also often responsive to climate. For example, Pueblo Indian dwellings in the hot, dry areas of the southwestern United States reflect, in part, an adaptation to the climate. Pueblo communities are multistoried, rectangular, terraced dwellings that are stacked on one another in a steplike fashion, with ladders and inside passages used to connect units. The dwelling units are made of clay, mud, and stone and have thick walls. The steplike stacking of dwellings minimizes surface exposure to the hot sun and maximizes cooling, especially in the lower inside rooms. Moreover, the flat roofs can be used for sleeping on hot nights.

Rapoport (1969a) also describes how some homes in hot Middle Eastern countries are built with thick outside walls and high ceilings. This not only keeps out the heat but allows the heat to rise to the top of the dwelling during the day. Such a configuration also permits retention of some heat during the cold evenings. Many Middle Eastern homes also have an inner courtyard that contains shrubbery, foliage, water pools, and ponds. These design features, Rapoport states, may lower ground temperatures and facilitate the flow of cool air.

One dramatic residential building style appears in the Matma culture of the Sahara Desert, Africa (Rapoport, 1969a). Homes are built some 30 feet underground. There is a central court with a roof, and additional rooms and storage areas are simply tunneled out as needed. Such an arrangement is cool indeed and allows for efficient temperature control in a climate noted for its extreme heat. As Rapoport notes, underground living in such climates is not unusual and appears in many parts of the world—Egypt, China, Israel, Australia.

In tropical climates temperatures are high and there is considerable humidity and rainfall. Here dwellings are needed to provide shade and protection from rain, and they should have little heat-retaining quality. The solution? In such climates one sees dwelling designs that have several common features: (1) no walls or very thin walls and screening to capture prevailing breezes and to facilitate heat loss, (2) raised dwellings to facilitate air flow underneath (and to keep out insects and animals), (3) roof designs that protect the dwelling from torrential rains but also avoid heat buildup. As Rapoport (1969a) states:

> The roof becomes the dominant element on these houses and is, in effect, a huge, waterproof parasol, sloping steeply to shed torrential rains, opaque to solar radiation, and of minimum mass to avoid heat build-up and subsequent re-radiation. It also avoids condensation problems by being able to "breathe." Deep overhangs are protection against both sun and rain, and also allow ventilation during rain [p. 94].

In such homes, there are often no walls separating areas, windows have open-vented screens, and people sleep in hammocks that facilitate air flow and minimize the buildup of body heat. So in extreme climates most dwellings are responsive to environmental demands. But not all are:

> The Boro of the Western Amazon, and a number of other tribes in the Amazon area, live in large communal houses with thickly thatched roofs and walls. There is no provision at all for cross-ventilation, an essential in the hot, humid climate. It would be difficult to find a worse solution in terms of climatic comfort, although it may be good protection against insects. One assumption might be that these houses were introduced from elsewhere, and are the status symbol of some more powerful group [Rapoport, 1969a, p. 21].

There are many other anomalous examples (Rapoport, 1969a): The rubber barons of South America who built thick-walled dwellings in the Amazon jungles, the replacement of thatched roofs with tin ones in parts of Japan and elsewhere (tin is noisy in the rain, produces condensation, and rusts; however, it has considerable status value). Or we can point to the example of our own dwellings, especially those in the moderate climates of parts of the United States. Here there are enormous variations in home design, and many designs almost ignore climate. Although it is true that homes in northern New England and in the northern Midwest are constructed differently than homes in southern California and Florida, generally Americans do not worry a great deal about design in relation to climate. Central heating and air-conditioning systems, thermopane windows, insulation, and storm doors have permitted us to be less attentive to climatic conditions. The siting of homes in relation to the sun, roof configurations, and food-storage systems are all relatively unimportant, as we merely turn up the heat or air conditioning, put food in our freezers, or shop for supplies only as we need them. Until the last few years, climate has been relatively unimportant in American home design. But who knows what will happen after the newly discovered energy crisis becomes more evident—with shortages of oil and gas and with rising heat, electricity, and water bills? Will the design of homes become more responsive to climatic conditions? Will people in cold and windy places begin to use different designs and insulation techniques? Will those in the hot, dry climates of the Southwest or the humid climates of the southeastern United States evolve home designs along the lines of the cultures described above?

A potentially knotty issue is that changes in the design of homes may not be so easy to produce. First, we live in a society with permanent homes, where a large proportion of the dwellings have already been built, and they cannot be redesigned very drastically. Second, the ability to virtually ignore environmental conditions has existed for at least 100 years in the United States, and it is not likely that Americans will be receptive to dramatic change all at once. However, if the energy crisis is real and comes down on us hard (and it does appear to be real), the last third of the 20th century may show radical social changes and crises in relation to dwelling forms and their link to cultural/environmental issues.

Technology and Resources

Knowledge, wisdom, and available resources are simultaneously reflected in a culture's house forms. The presence or absence of complicated design and construction features such as arches, angles, electricity, and plumbing tells us something about the technological stage of development of a culture. The availability of natural resources also is evident in house forms. For example, homes on the Adriatic coast of Yugoslavia are built largely of stone, which is abundant there; they are not built of scarce wood. Eskimos use snow, a vast supply of which is readily at hand, and Pygmies use large leaves and wood from nearby trees.

Rapoport (1969a) described several facets of home construction in relation to technology and resources—the construction process, materials, portability of the home, and ability of structures to withstand lateral forces, weathering, and gravity. Our discussion will not address all these factors but will only touch on some general issues of home design in relation to technology and resources.

The earliest known human homes were natural caves, a good reflection of the limited technology available to early people (Alexander, 1976; Earle, 1935; Raglan, 1964). In fact, Earle (1935) observed that the first settlers in the United States, faced with limited technology and resources when they arrived, dug caves into the sides of hills, shored them up with logs, covered them with sod and earth, and lived in these part caves, part constructed homes until they were able to build more permanent dwellings. As another early house form, Alexander (1976) and Raglan (1964) speculated that early hunting-and-gathering people probably built simple lean-tos and windbreaks, sometimes freestanding and sometimes built by bending and lashing tree limbs to create a partly circular arrangement.

Raglan (1964) proposed three stages in the technology of housing beyond the use of caves and simple lean-tos. The first stage was construction of so-called beehive huts. These were circular dwellings, sometimes with a pit dug inside, that had a symmetrical dome and sides built of the same material from top to bottom. Because such structures have roofs close to the ground, the technology required to support the structure is simple. Furthermore, dugout arrangements also can be quite functional in certain climates.

Another feature of dwellings of early people was their circular shape, as seen in the homes of various tribal groups in Africa, as well as the Eskimo igloo. Why was and is circularity so prevalent? Raglan suggested that one reason for the construction of circular homes rather than rectangular ones is that squares, rectangles, and their underlying basis, the right angle, simply do not appear very often in nature. The circle and its elements, in contrast, are everywhere in nature. The sun and moon are ever-present symbols of circularity; fruits, berries, and eggs reflect circularity; the winding of streams and the shape of many leaves and flowers make salient the idea of curves and circles as intrinsic to nature. Animal dwellings reflect circularity in one form or another—beehives, anthills, openings to tunnels and winding tunnel arrangements, birdnests. Even the shape of the human body and its parts reflects roundness and curves—the head, the eyes, the nostrils, the mouth and tongue, breasts, buttocks. So the idea of roundness is a common and familiar one. And, as discussed in Chapter 2, many cultural world views emphasize roundness and circularity. For the ancient Chinese, heaven was symbolized as circular; for the Oglala Sioux, the purest form was the circle. Consider the following passage from a tenth-century Irish text:

> Though you do not see it, it is in roundness that each element has been appointed, and it is in roundness that the stars circle about the wheel of the earth; and it is in roundness of form that the souls are seen after going forth from their bodies; and in roundness the circle of the noble heavens is seen, and in roundness is seen the circuit of the sun and moon. All that is fitting, for roundness without beginning or end is the Lord, Who always was and always shall be and made all these things. That is why the world has been embodied in a round form [Dillon, cited in Raglan, 1964, p. 150].[2]

[2] This and all other quotations from this source are from *The Temple and the House*, by L. Raglan. Copyright 1964 by Routledge & Kegan Paul Ltd. Reprinted by permission.

The design of homes and views about the nature of the universe are an interesting example of how environmental cognitions and perceptions, discussed in Chapters 2 and 3, fit with environmental products to form a coherent unity. In line with the general theme of this volume, the preceding examples illustrate how culture/environment relations are exhibited in a united way in many facets of human functioning—from perceptions and cognitions to the places in which people live.

In addition to the presence of the circle in nature and in the cosmology of many cultures, circular construction is much simpler and requires less technology than construction involving right angles. To build rectangular structures, one must understand—perhaps only implicitly—physics, geometry, and structural stresses and forces. But the simple beehive structure can be easily grasped in a trial-and-error arrangement—laying poles on the ground around a central point, then raising and leaning them against one another, lashing them together at the center, and then covering them with bark, reeds, or leaves. If the inside area has been dug out, the task is that much easier, since supports can be shorter. If one uses branches that bend easily, then the shape of the dwelling is also likely to be circular or domelike.

Raglan (1964) hypothesized that the next stage of dwelling construction involved the *rondavel,* which he described as follows:

> This, like the beehive-shaped hut, starts with a circle on the ground, but the principle of its construction is quite different. A wall, about five feet high or sometimes less, is made, often of forked posts interlaced with strips of bamboo or bark. The conical roof, which is made of light but stiff poles, their tops tied together and their bottoms inserted into a circular bundle of flexible twigs, is lifted onto the wall and then thatched. This radical departure from the principle of the beehive-shaped hut was a brilliant invention which deserved to, and did, spread over most of the world [p. 194].

Such a shape has several architectural advantages over the beehive hut—more interior room for people to stand or sit, greater vertical storage, and perhaps better climate control. The rondavel structure also involves specialized construction in that the building requirements and techniques for the vertical walls are different than for the roof, the latter sometimes having its frame built on the structure and at other times being built elsewhere and then placed on the walls.

The last stage in the history of home design, and the most sophisticated technologically, is the rectangular house, "a complete break from all that had gone before, involving not only a knowledge of how to lay out a right angle but ability to make some form of framed truss" (Raglan, 1964, p. 194).

Rectangular and angular buildings appear throughout the world in a variety of forms. Such construction requires technical knowledge of bracing concepts to handle lateral forces of wind, forces associated with gravity, relations between structures and spans of support, and comparative knowledge of materials in relation to weight and load characteristics (Rapoport, 1969a).

Rectangular designs have many practical advantages. First, they provide efficient use of interior space, and they permit easier separation of functions than circular arrangements do. This is also true for use and allocation of land; most farm plots are rectangular, not circular, and thereby permit use of every piece of land, whereas curvilinear arrangements could not be easily used to allocate land. Second, rectangular arrangements are easier to expand than circular ones. One can add on to a rectangular dwelling and still make use of an existing wall, whereas additions to circular dwellings generally require more new construction. Third, a large dwelling is easier to build if rectangular, since it can be constructed in semi-independent sections in respect to forces, loads, and design characteristics. Increasing the size of a circular dwelling beyond some point changes the technological requirements enormously in terms of supports and structural design requirements.

Another aspect of the technology of home construction involves use of local natural resources. In North America, people generally pay little attention to the local availability of wood, brick, or other materials when considering home design. Materials can be shipped great distances, technology permits use of synthetic materials, and we assume implicitly that we can build a home from almost any material that we want and can afford. On an upper-middle-class street, one might find homes built of pine or redwood, brick or fieldstone, stucco or aluminum siding. Roofs may be constructed of tar, wood shingles, stone coverings, or almost any other imaginable material. Glass appears in a variety of forms—thermopane, plain, tinted, opaque, and for some with affluence or a flair for the unique, stained or colored glass.

Our lack of concern with the availability of building materials in the immediate geographic area is probably atypical. In many places around the world people are quite responsive to available resources. As mentioned earlier, the Adriatic coast of Yugoslavia is well known for its abundance of rocks and its scarcity of wood, and one finds homes in villages and towns built almost completely of rock, including walls and roofs. The pueblos of the southwestern United States are built largely of sand and mud; Eskimo igloos are built of snow; palm leaves are used in the South Pacific; reeds are used in marsh-dwelling communities of Iraq and Peru; bamboo is used in many parts of Asia, where it grows plentifully.

An example of relatively rapid change in reliance on local materials occurred in the development of colonial homes in the United States (Earle, 1935). The early New England settlers lived in part-cave, part-built structures; Southerners first copied the tipis and wigwams of local Indians and built their dwellings of deerskin, grass mats, and palmetto leaves. In both instances, there was initially almost total reliance on available resources. Later, the colonists built one-room log cabins from the readily available timber of forests and covered the roofs with bark and thatch. Still later, the northern English settlers added a sleeping loft in the upper part of the cabin and eventually added extra rooms. In the South, homes also gradually became larger and larger, rooms and outbuildings were added, and homes eventually came to be constructed of stone, mortar, and finished wood. Thus, the trend was to rely at first on local resources and eventually use a combination of local and remote resources. Gradually home design became a blend of the parent European culture and local needs and conditions. This trend was also evident in the Dutch colonial settlements of New York (Earle, 1935). Over time Dutch dwellings came to be set close to one another in rows and to have gabled roofs and a front roof façade that had a steplike design. The homes also had small windows and decorative weather vanes and door knockers, and doors were divided horizontally at the middle, as in Dutch homes in Europe. So the early and later colonial periods of the United States reflect almost a recapitulation of the history of homes—initial dependence on available resources and simple technology, with eventual incorporation of cultural values and advanced technology into the design of homes.

Culture

The role of culture in house form is most evident in certain of its facets: cosmology, religion, and family and social structure. In reading the material that follows, think back to our discussion in Chapters 2 to 5, and you will see how various aspects of environmental cognition and perception, as well as ideas of privacy and other behavioral processes, blend in with certain features of home design.

Cosmology. Chapter 2 described cultural differences in "world views": perceptions and cognitions about human relationships to nature, the wilderness, and cities; conceptions of vertical and horizontal dimensions; perceptions and attitudes about near and far places. Here we will examine how such world views are associated with house forms in various cultures and throughout history.

One aspect of cosmology that appeared early in relation to house form concerned horizontal and vertical dimensions of the universe. The horizontal nature of the universe, especially the cardinal directions of north, south, east, and west, has been pervasive across cultures, historically and presently, as discussed in Chapters 2 and 3. From the ancient Egyptians and Sumerians to the Pueblo Indians, and from the Western world with its complex technology to traditional societies, the idea of cardinal directions or some variant is prevalent. For example:

> The four corners or quarters are often mentioned in the Bible. Isaiah speaks of the "four quarters of the land" and of bringing the wind from "the four ends of the earth" (VII, 2 and XXXVII, 9); Jeremiah of the "four winds of the world" (XLIX, 36). . . . And St. John "saw four angels standing at the four corners of the earth and holding back the four winds. . . ."
>
> The legendary emperors of China were said to have controlled the four quarters of the heavens. They were sometimes paired with four spirits symbolized by the White Tiger of the West, the Green Dragon of the East, the Red Bird of the South, and the Dark Warrior of the North. During the Han dynasty the ruling classes decorated their coffins with the four animals denoting the four quarters, with a golden sun and a silver moon on the top [Raglan, 1964, p. 163].

Such world views, in a variety of forms, have occurred throughout history and found their way into religious buildings, palaces, and homes. Several such examples are provided by Rapoport (1969a):

> The prevalence of sacred or privileged corners or sides is almost universal. In Fiji the east wall is for the chiefs. In China, although the whole house is sacred, the northwest corner is the most sacred. The Mongol yurt is divided into four parts: to the right of the door the husband and wife, facing them the guest of honor, and to the left the other guests in descending order of importance. The altar is always on the left of the bed as one enters. In the Arab tent there is also a ritual space which differs among tribes; as one example, the entry in the Tuareg tent is always on the south, with the men on the east side and the women on the west. This ritual space distribution is found in houses in India, in Lapland, and among the Northwest Indians. The most complex is the Madagascar house. . . .
>
> The internal division in this house is according to the stars, with 12 divisions corresponding to the 12 lunar months. Each division has a different use, such as rice or water jar storage, according to religious prescriptions which also affect the furniture arrangements; the bed, for example, is always in the east, with its head to the north. The main facade with the door and windows faces west, since west is the principal direction, the people call themselves "those who face the West," and the house is closely related to the religious plan of the universe. The north is the entry for notable visitors, the northeast corner is the most sacred, and the north wall is the place for ancestor cult. If someone is to be honored he is invited to take the north place [p. 55].

Or consider Raglan's (1964) description of the Oglala Sioux sweat lodge:

> The *onikare* (sweat lodge) of the Oglala is a hemispherical building of young willows. "It utilizes all the powers of the universe; earth and the things

> which grow from the earth, water, fire, and air. The willows which make the frame of the sweat lodge are set in such a way that they mark the four corners of the universe; thus the whole lodge is the universe in image, and the two-legged, four-legged, and winged people are contained within it. The round fireplace in the center of the sweat lodge is the center of the universe." The leader of the ritual "makes an altar of the center pole by placing tobacco at the four corners" [p. 157].

Vertical dimensions are also sometimes reflected in home design. As discussed in Chapter 2, many cultures have focused on the vertical dimension of the universe and the earth, as exemplified in heaven, earth, and hell. For example, among central Asian nomad groups described in Chapter 2, the sky is viewed as a tent or roof over the earth, and heaven consists of hemispheres stacked above the sky. The tent itself is considered to be a small-scale version of the whole universe. The opening in the roof of the tent, where the central supporting pole is located, is believed to be an access that leads up to the sky and to heaven.

The home as psychological "center" of the earth and universe is also a concept that has appeared in various cultures. For example, the multidwelling community of the Pueblo Indians and the home itself are the psychological center of their earthly world view, as are the homes of the Navajo Indians. Even in the present-day United States, people often allude to a childhood or parental home as if it were the psychological and historical center of their world view.

Religion. For many people in present-day Western societies the idea of the home as a religious place may seem strange. To be sure, some Jewish families attach a mezuzah (a capsule containing a small prayer scroll) to the door jambs of their homes, or they may conduct certain religious services in their homes (the lighting of Sabbath candles, Passover services). And Catholic homes may contain religious pictures, crucifixes, and other items. But people in the Western world do not, for the most part, view the home as a place that regularly and systematically has religious significance. For most religious activities, we generally use churches or synagogues rather than homes. But this is not true for all cultures; many societies attach considerable religious meaning to the home. For example, among certain Mongolian groups "the family altar is on the left of the bed as one enters. There are offertory dishes, prayer wheels, censers, and vessels for holy water, and a lighted oil lamp is placed on the shrine every evening" (Raglan, 1964, p. 9).

In certain parts of traditional China, Raglan observed that paper symbols of gods were pasted on doors to protect the home, altars of various gods appeared throughout the house, and the main room had an ancestral altar at which various ceremonies were practiced. Describing the Ainu of Japan, Raglan (1964) quoted from Munroe, who stated:

> The Ainu seem never to have had temples. The nearest thing to such was the house of the village chief. This was much larger than ordinary houses and was often resorted to on great occasions such as the Bear Festival. . . . In times of emergency or communal anxiety special services of supplication might be held there, but as a rule every man's house was his temple, enshrining the hearthfire sacred to Kami Fuchi [p. 10].

Many other examples could be cited, but suffice it to say that, to one degree or another, the house can be an important religious place, although this is by no means a universal practice.

Family and social structure. Family and social structure are also often evident in homes. The role of parents *vis-à-vis* each other, parent/child relationships, the presence or absence of an extended family structure, and numerous other features of family life are easily visible in dwellings. Bochner (1975) illustrated these ideas in an analysis of the interior spatial arrangements of homes in several Asian cultures. He discovered that the layout of traditional Chinese homes reveals several aspects of family structure and cultural values. Religion is quite important, as evidenced by the central location of religious shrines near the sleeping place of the parents and the grown children. Living arrangements also reflect an extended family, with married sons and their wives living with the male's parents. The home also illustrates the dominant role of parents, with their sleeping quarters centrally located near the religious shrine. Sex segregation of children is also practiced, with girls located in the center of the dwelling and boys located in a far corner. Girls' sleeping areas are also near the kitchen and eating area, perhaps reflecting their responsibilities for preparing meals.

The traditional Thai home reflects similar values. Again, parental sleeping quarters are centrally located, boys and girls are segregated, married children live on the premises, and a religious shrine is ever-present. Sex segregation also occurs, although the boys sleep in a semipublic area, suggesting the cultural value of privacy for girls. The home is also a food-storage area, and the very important basic food, rice, is kept close at hand.

According to Bochner (1975), the traditional Japanese plan is somewhat similar, with the parental sleeping area in a central place near the dining area and the fireplace (where the family spends a great deal of time eating, conversing, and engaging in group activities). Once again there is sex segregation of children, and married children are present in the home.

The Sarawak house plan of Java illustrates a very different arrangement. It is a communal home for a number of families, some of whom are unrelated. The residence is divided into sleeping areas, storage areas for food and animals, and a common living area. The sleeping areas are occupied by separate families, with the headman, or community leader, in a central location. Rice, an important food commodity, is stored in the building, and chickens and small animals roam freely in the main corridor of the structure. There is a common living area, available to everyone, that extends the length of the building. The communal living arrangement and the use of semipublic space undoubtedly reflect a rather different lifestyle than any of the other examples mentioned thus far.

The traditional long house of the Iroquois Indians also reveals the blend of a communal life-style and individual family arrangements (Morgan, 1965; Rapoport, 1969a). These houses were 60 to 80 feet long, with some up to 100 feet. Compartments of 6 to 8 feet in width were arranged on both sides of a central hallway, and Morgan (1965) described the living arrangements as follows:

> At each end of the dwelling was a doorway covered by suspended skins. Between each four apartments, two on a side, was a fire pit in the center of the hall, used in common by their occupants. Thus a house with five fires would contain 20 apartments and accommodate 20 families, unless some apartments were reserved for storage. They were warm, roomy, and tidily kept habitations. Raised bunks were constructed around the walls of each apartment for beds. From the roof poles were suspended their strings of corn on the ear, braided by the husks, also strings of dried squashes and pumpkins. Spaces were contrived here and there to store away their accumulations of provisions. Each house, as a rule, was occupied by related families, the mothers and their children belonging to the same gens [clan] while the husbands and the fathers of these children belong to other gentes; consequently the gens or clan of the mother largely predominated in the household. Whatever was taken in the hunt or raised by cultivation by any member of the household, as has elsewhere been stated, was for the common benefit. Provisions were made a common stock within the household [p. 127].[3]

Several features of the Iroquois life-style are worth noting: the communal living in some respects but privacy and family separateness in other respects; the extended kinship arrangement with related people living together, maternal lines determining the arrangement. The importance of women in the Iroquois culture is also indicated by the fact that each long house had a "matron," a senior women who was responsible for managing and allocating food supplies in the whole dwelling. Furthermore, the senior Iroquois women, clan mothers, appointed chiefs and could remove them if necessary. Thus, the design of the traditional Iroquois long house tells us a great deal about the culture's life-style and its familial and social structure.

[3]From *Houses and House-Life of American Aborigines,* by L. H. Morgan. © 1965 by The University of Chicago. Reprinted by permission.

Still another form of residence—the African compound—speaks to the relation between social structure and home design. Rapoport (1969a) described several compound arrangements in polygamous cultures in Africa. For example, among the Moundang of the Cameroons, the walled compound of a man and his several wives contains separate huts for the man and for each wife; the hut of the main wife is located near the entry to the compound. The all-important food granaries are located at the center of the compound, where they can be protected and managed.

INTERPLAY OF ENVIRONMENTAL AND CULTURAL FACTORS IN HOME DESIGN

Thus far we have examined factors one at a time in relation to home design—climate, technology, available resources, religion, and family and social structure. Examples were given of each factor separately, as if it operated independently. However, the central theme of this chapter is that it is impossible to say "Home design is primarily a result of factor *X*," whether *X* be climate, terrain, or religion. Rather, the design, use, and characteristics of homes are a complex interplay of many factors taken together, and the contribution of separate factors is often impossible to ascertain. The matter is further complicated by the fact that a given variable, such as climate, may be important in one setting and culture but may play hardly any role in another place. Our approach has therefore been to focus on the interplay of variables in a fashion analogous to that seen in an impressionist painting, where fine details are absent but where the interaction of color, composition, tones, and brightness yields a coherent unity. To illustrate this theme we next examine two cultures that illustrate the blend of many factors in relation to home design.

There have been many anthropological analyses of the Pueblo and Navajo Indians of the southwestern United States. There is, however, considerable variation within each of these cultures, so that any single statement is apt to be somewhat incorrect. For this discussion we will draw heavily on Rapoport (1969b) and on earlier reports by Morgan (1965). These two analyses are particularly useful because they provide a good blend of anthropological and architecturally relevant observations.

The Pueblo Indians

The Pueblo Indians live in the high desert country of the southwestern United States. They are a diverse group of people affiliated with Hopi, Zuñi, and other tribal cultures. As Rapoport (1969b) noted, the term *pueblo* is the Spanish word meaning "town" and refers to the culture's practice of living in terraced, apartment-house-like dwellings that are clustered together in a community arrangement.

Pueblo settlements dating back to 1100 A.D. have been discovered in the southwestern United States, although it is not certain that the people who constructed them were direct forebears of present-day Pueblo Indians. Many of the early settlements were built into massive caves, about 100 feet high, that were formed by erosion. These communities often had upwards of 100 rooms and faced out onto large canyons, as at Mesa Verde, Colorado. Other communities built pueblo structures on mesas and in more open settings.

Architecturally, the typical pueblo is a several-story structure of rectangular dwellings, arranged in a steplike terraced fashion from front to rear. The dwellings are clustered together. They have flat roofs and internal passages between rooms. The pueblo structure faces a central plaza in which a variety of activities take place, such as community cooking and dances. The different levels of the structure are reached by ladders. The doors and windows to dwellings face the plaza, and the rear wall typically has no openings.

The design and construction of the pueblo reveal its responsiveness to environmental circumstances. For example, Rapoport (1969b) observed that pueblos often appeared to be part of the flat, mesa-dotted landscape of the Southwest. In addition, they were colored the same as the natural terrain and were often hard to pick out from a distance. The walls were thick, producing a cooling effect, and were made of stone and mud. Roofs and floors were made of clay, brush, and grass and were supported by beams extending through the walls. The terracelike construction was also effective in temperature control, since a minimum of surface was exposed to the sun and heat. The terracing and irregular staggering of rooms created a maximum of shade surface. In addition, the interior rooms received no direct sun and could be used for storage. Thus, the general structure of the pueblo communities fit well with environmental circumstances of climate and available resources.

The design of the pueblo may also have been effective for defense. The lower floors often had no openings to the outside, and in case of attack, the ladders could be withdrawn and the whole pueblo could become a rather difficult place to attack successfully. Some observers believe that active defense was not the primary basis of the design; rather "symbolic defense" of the sacred center of the pueblo may have contributed to this unique configuration.

But the pueblo and its apartments also had religious and practical significance. For example, the sun and its solstices are important parts of the Pueblo religion and are associated with periodic ceremonies during the year. The whole pueblo is oriented systematically to the sun, to the sacred directions of east and north, and in relation to the cardinal points and the mountains. A recent analysis (Reyman, 1976) indicates that the positioning of the pueblo itself or certain apartments and windows may also have had more than symbolic value; it may have served for accurate identification of seasons of the year using the sun's angles and the shadows it cast.

Details of pueblo construction and room arrangements were provided in an early account by Morgan (1965), who used his own observations as well as records provided by explorers, soldiers, and others who had contact with Pueblo groups during the 1800s and as early as the 1600s. The internal arrangements of traditional family living varied from pueblo to pueblo. In some pueblos, rooms were 6 to 8 feet by 8 to 12 feet; in other places Morgan noted somewhat larger rooms. A family might occupy a few or several rooms, depending on the pueblo; the largest room was a gathering place where the family worked, ate, cooked, and so on. In some instances other rooms were used for storage, cooking, or sleeping. The women were usually responsible for finishing the interior, which involved plastering the walls with watered earth or white clay. The interiors contained hooks, shelves, and storage places for skins, food, personal effects, and tools.

Rapoport's (1969b) central theme was that the architectural design of the pueblo meshed well with the cultural values of the residents. A central ingredient of Pueblo life, particularly for Hopi groups, is the harmony between people and nature. The sun has a central role in relation to the harmony, balance, and renewal of life. Various rituals throughout the year celebrate this harmonious relationship of people, animals, and nature, as do Hopi art, mythology, and community design. Prayer sticks are placed over key beams in the structure, new houses are consecrated and blessed, the home and community are considered holy places, and the community as a whole is treated as an intrinsic part of the landscape. The central plaza serves many religious and cultural functions, as well as being a general gathering and work place. In addition, the religious kivas, or sacred rooms used by men, are located in the plazas of the older pueblos. They are carefully sited and their interiors are arranged so that the men sit on the south side facing north toward the fire pit and the Sipapu hole (the mythical place where people were thought to have emerged from the bowels of the earth—see Chapter 2). Here again we see how world views, cosmology, and different aspects of environmental cognition and perception, discussed in Chapters 2 and 3, are reflected in the characteristics of homes and places.

Rapoport (1969b) stated that the pueblo not only is compatible with the religious values of its inhabitants but also reflects the community and social organization of the culture. Among the Pueblo Indians social organization is based on a tightly knit community in which community success rather than individual prominence or feats is important. Furthermore, this culture holds a strong norm of egalitarianism. Accordingly, all people have similar apartments, and personal prestige is not manifested in visible differences in dwellings or possessions. In addition, the culture is organized around female kinship lines and a clan system, with a family unit consisting of parents, unmarried children, married daughters and sons-in-law, and grandchildren. Apartments for extended families are all grouped together in traditional pueblos, where one house is the "traditional, permanent ancestral clan house, where sacred property is kept; the leaders are the clan mother and her brother" (Rapoport, 1969b, p. 71).

The value of community identity and various territorial relationships among people are also reflected in the distribution of ownership and responsibility. The clan owns the gardens and land; women own the house and its stores; men own the livestock, tools, fruit trees, and religious objects. The central plaza also provides a community focus where important political, religious, and ceremonial events take place. With all the dwellings facing the plaza, the idea of unity and the commitments of people to one another and to the whole pueblo are subtly reinforced. Here we see how concepts of privacy regulation and territoriality, discussed in Chapters 4 and 6, are manifested in the Pueblo home and community.

In summary, we have illustrated how the traditional Pueblo Indian community, including home design and internal arrangements of space, reflects many influences—climate, resources, and technology, as well as world views and religious values, family and community structure, and other facets of culture. All these factors are present in the homes of the Pueblo Indians, and their intermeshing is so complete that it is impossible to say "what caused what" or to weight precisely the importance of one factor with the others. They simply all fit together as a unity. In addition, the Pueblo culture shows how various cognitive, perceptual, and behavioral processes discussed in Parts 1 and 2 are evident in environmental places such as homes and communities.

The Navajo Indians

The Navajo Indians, the largest Indian group in the United States, also live in the hot, dry southwestern states of Colorado, New Mexico, Arizona, and Utah. Anthropological data suggest that the Navajo were originally a northern group who migrated south over the course of centuries. They came into contact with other Indian cultures, including the Pueblo people, and eventually became an agricultural and herding society. In spite of their contacts with the Pueblo Indians, and in spite of similarities in climate, resources, and technology, the Navajo retained their characteristic house form, the hogan (Rapoport, 1969b). The preservation of this dwelling form in a totally new environment speaks to the power of cultural factors as determinants of house design.

Rapoport (1969b) provided an excellent description of the design features of the hogan, and we will rely on his analysis. Although there are several types of hogan, the basic shape is circular. The so-called forked-stick hogan is apparently the oldest and most basic form. It is about 20 feet in diameter and has a support structure consisting of five logs, each of which is 10–12 feet long. One log each is placed at the north, south, and west directions. The remaining two logs are used to form a doorway on the east side of the structure. These five logs form a frame, which is covered with branches and is held together with mud plaster. Other forms of hogans are the stone hogan and the larger earth-covered hogan (whose support structure consists of four upright logs and beams used as a frame). Another variety, the six-sided hogan, is the most common form nowadays; it starts with a four-pole frame, around which is built a six-sided log cabin topped by a domelike roof. In many respects the earlier forked-stick hogan is a basic circular structure, whereas the other forms are of the rondavel variety (Raglan, 1964), with vertical walls and separate domed roofs.

The siting, design, and internal space arrangements of the hogan are closely linked with religious, social, and family values. With respect to religion and mythology, the hogan is a sacred place:

> The hogan . . . has a mythological base. The prototype was believed to have been built by the Holy People out of turquoise, white shell, abalone shell and jet, corresponding to the four principal sacred colors—turquoise, white, yellow and black—while the hogan of the first man was built of sheets of sunbeam and rainbow. The hogan is always consecrated to insure long life and happiness to the occupants, the main ceremony being the House Blessing Way. This speaks of beauty radiating from the hogan in all directions and also refers to the supremacy of the women in the hogan, reflected in the symbolism of the structure: The east pole is the Earth Woman, the west the Water Woman, the south the Mountain Woman and the north the Corn Woman. The principal deity is also female: Changing Woman [Rapoport, 1969b, p.75].[4]

The door of the hogan faces east, in the direction of the rising sun. In Navajo mythology the sun is the husband of the deity Changing Woman, and it is important for the home to receive "the first blessing of the rising sun" (Rapoport, 1969b, p.74). Furthermore, religious rituals take place daily and throughout the year in the hogan, so that it has an important symbolic and sacred role in the life of the Navajo people:

> The position of objects and people in the hogan, and all seating arrangements are strictly laid down. . . . The hogan is divided into spheres reflecting the important directions of east, south, west, north, zenith and nadir which are associated with sacred colors. Each part of the hogan is sacred and the House Blessing Way names many parts: the rear corner, center, fireside, side corners, doorway and surroundings of the hogan. The all

[4]This and all other quotations from this source are from "The Pueblo and the Hogan: A Cross-Cultural Comparison of Two Responses to an Environment," by A. Rapoport. In P. Oliver (Ed.), *Shelter and Society*. Copyright 1969 by Barrie & Jenkins, London. Reprinted by permission.

> pervasive sun symbolism is seen in the "sunrise path" inside the hogan along which people must move. Women are always on the south side, men on the north. The male head of the family and important visitors, such as the officiating medicine man, face the doorway. The bodies of the dead must be removed through a hole in the north wall. It is significant that all forms of the hogan have this identical arrangement [Rapoport, 1969b, p. 74].

In addition to internal arrangements, the siting of hogans is in accord with cultural values. The Navajo, an agricultural and sheepherding people, consider the nuclear family and clan to be important in their day-to-day lives. Their hogans reflect these kinship bonds and tend to be arranged in small clusters around maternal lineage lines, with two or more related families in proximity to one another. However, because of their herding occupation and the need for grazing space, hogans are usually spread across the terrain—an arrangement that is totally different from the Pueblo practice of concentrating homes in small communities. Furthermore, a Navajo family may own more than one hogan in distant places and may move to one or the other home to graze its sheep.

In some respects the focus of the Pueblo Indians around the clan and the larger community contrasts with the Navajo, who, while emphasizing the importance of the clan, hold to a very strong norm of individuality. These differences seem to be reflected in different residential arrangements—the Pueblo live in homes located around a community plaza, whereas the Navajo have dispersed dwellings.

Rapoport (1969b) also observed that hogans are positioned in accordance with Navajo values about the need to be in harmony with and respectful of nature. Thus, ideally, hogans were not located too close to water, perhaps because of sanitation or to avoid intruding on others' water rights.

From the examples of the Pueblo and Navajo Indians, and from many other examples presented in this chapter, we see how the dwelling reflects a variety of aspects of a society's existence—its environment, technology, religion, family structure, social organization, and so on—not one factor alone, and not one factor necessarily or universally more than other factors. Furthermore, the Pueblo and Navajo homes illustrate the interplay of environmental cognitions and perceptions with behavioral processes in relation to tangible places in the environment of different cultures.

SUMMARY

The present chapter focused on a most important environmental place—the home. The initial part of the chapter identified several dimensions for classifying homes in different cultures. In some cultures homes are permanent, whereas in other cultures homes are temporary, either built anew from available materials as families move about or transported from place to place and made of portable structures and materials. Homes also vary in differentiation/homogeneity; that is, they may or may not have separate rooms for separate functions, and they may differ from one another very much or hardly at all. Another facet of differentiation relates to the construction process, and here we used Rapoport's (1969a) classification of home construction processes as *primitive* (people build their own homes, and all homes are alike), *preindustrial vernacular* (homes are built by tradesmen, but there is still considerable homogeneity of forms), and *modern vernacular* (there are both specialized building types and specialized builders). Another dimension relates to living style and addresses whether people live communally with more than one nuclear family in a dwelling or in separate homes. These dimensions depict, in part, how homes mirror many cultural and environmental variables. For example, in communal living arrangements one might expect different modes of privacy regulation and territorial practices than in noncommunal arrangements; for nomadic cultures one might expect the home to reflect different cosmologies, attitudes toward territory, and family structures than for cultures with permanent homes.

The chapter also examined the design and use of homes in relation to variables such as climate and available resources. In extreme environmental conditions, homes are very responsive to environmental demands, as in the Eskimo igloo, the thick-walled and high-ceilinged homes of the Middle East, and the open-sided, heavily roofed homes of the tropics. The resources and technology of a culture are also related to home design; homes vary from simple circular designs to complex rectangular arrangements in technologically advanced Western societies. Homes also reflect a variety of cultural values: world views and mythology, religion, and family and social structure. Such factors are evident in many societies regardless of the level of their technological development; the home often serves as a psychological and cosmological center, a religious or sacred place, or a reflection of family structure.

The last section of the chapter analyzed Pueblo and Navajo Indian dwellings and illustrated our basic theme that a variety of environmental and cultural variables are evident in home design and use and that it is extremely difficult to single out which factor or factors are most important in a particular case. Rather, our conceptual orientation is to view the home as a window through which one can simultaneously see a culture's social structure, religion, world views, and relationship to the physical environment. The next chapter continues our analysis of the home but focuses on the present-day American home as a reflection of environmental and cultural variables.

Chapter 8

THE AMERICAN HOME

Chapter 7 dealt with homes around the world in relation to environmental factors such as climate, technological factors, and cultural factors such as religion, social structure, and societal values. This chapter presents a "case study" of the American home in terms of environmental and cultural variables, something similar to what an anthropologist studying American culture might do.

Although it is fascinating to analyze homes in one's own culture, there are some real dangers in so doing. For example, there is no homogeneous "American society," and one must be careful not to make overly sweeping statements. The United States has many subcultures based on ethnic, regional, and socioeconomic dimensions. Furthermore, there are many types of residential dwellings in American society, and the cultures and life-styles associated with them are diverse. Apartments, condominiums, mobile homes, single-family dwellings, duplex and triplex homes, rented and owned residences, apartments for singles, families, and the elderly are just some of the residential arrangements in the present-day United States. However, there may be some common qualities in American homes that are found across ethnic, regional, and socioeconomic groups. So, in spite of the difficulties of doing an "anthropological" analysis of American homes, we shall proceed.

The first part of the chapter describes some general characteristics of American homes: who lives in them, their permanent/temporary qualities, and their degree of differentiation/homogeneity. The second part describes American homes in terms of two dialectic processes: individuality/community and public/private. The third part examines particular places in homes from a cultural perspective, such as patios, living rooms, kitchens, bedrooms, and bathrooms.

SOME GENERAL CHARACTERISTICS OF AMERICAN HOMES

Communal/Noncommunal

The preceding chapter pointed out that there is considerable variation around the world in regard to the occupants of homes. In some cultures, such as traditional Japanese and Chinese societies, an extended kinship arrangement prevails, in which married children live with their parents. In other cases, such as the Iroquois long house, whole clans resided in the same dwelling. In still other cases unrelated people share a home. The model in present-day middle-class America is quite different. For the most part, a home is occupied by a single nuclear family, consisting of parents and children; one does not typically find more than one family, even relatives, occupying the same dwelling. Of course, a grandparent may live with a family, especially after a spouse has died. But it is probably rare for married grandparents to live with a family, and it is very unusual for a modern nuclear family to live in the grandparents' home.

In present-day middle-class American society, even the elderly typically live separately from their children. They maintain their independence as long as they can, and they obtain necessary services and companionship in planned (and sometimes unplanned) communities for the elderly, many of which are located in warm climates, as in Arizona, California and Florida. Even the disabled or poor sometimes live in "nursing homes," not with their children or other relatives. Analogous practices hold for young adults. Although we do not cast out our children at an early age, there is a norm in middle-class American society for young adults to leave the family home before they are married and to live alone or with friends, sometimes in so-called singles communities.

There are many reasons that the nuclear family is the typical residential group, not the least of which is that the tremendous mobility in American society means that extended-family members often do not live near one another. But this living style may have deeper roots in the American value system. Thus, having one's own home and maintaining one's independence and individuality are central American values that might also have contributed to the practice of having single-family residences.

Permanent/Temporary

There is considerable variability in American society with respect to the temporary or permanent quality of homes. For several decades the technical and professional middle-class stratum of American society has been very mobile. With the economic and population growth of the last 30 years, many families have moved every 3 to 5 years to distant locations, new communities, and new climates and environments. (In fact, it is estimated that one of five families moves every year.) For many people the idea of children being raised in the same community or a family settling into its "dream house" has not materialized. Instead the expectation has been that a better job, a promotion, or a productive career depended on one's willingness to move to new locations. Thus, the upper-middle-class American family lives in a house for a few years and then packs up its possessions and moves on. The home itself is occupied by another equally mobile family, which lives there for a few years and then itself moves on. Obviously, this extraordinary mobility does not apply to all segments of American society. Many families live in the same dwelling for many years and raise their children in the same community. So *diversity* with respect to the permanent/temporary character of homes is probably characteristic of American life.

Differentiated/Homogeneous

Using Rapoport's (1969a) classification, there is no question that the American home is of the modern vernacular form. Homes are usually built not by the occupants but by skilled specialists—plumbers, carpenters, electricians. The occupants often have little to do with the basic construction process, although after occupying the dwelling they may modify the basic structure according to a "do it yourself" norm. Furthermore, very few American homes are designed by architects who work with individual clients. Rather, most houses and apartments are designed in advance, and potential occupants choose from alternative plans that often permit only slight modifications.

Most American dwellings are similar. They have kitchens, living rooms, bedrooms, and bathrooms, although there is some variability among homes with respect to the presence of other rooms, such as dining rooms, studies and dens, guest rooms, and family and recreation rooms. So, although tradition strongly governs the presence of certain rooms, the types of rooms within homes vary somewhat.

The American home is also characterized by considerable diversity of design. Number and size of rooms and the relation of rooms to one another vary considerably, and the configuration of internal space often differs from one dwelling to another. In addition, American homes have considerable specialization of function. There are separate rooms for cooking, bathing and elimination, sleeping, and recreation. This is certainly in contrast to many other cultures, where the same interior space is used for many functions.

Diversity also applies to the exteriors of homes. People go to great lengths to create different exteriors for their homes, by landscaping, painting, or using different types of brick and wood. Unlike people in many traditional societies, where all homes look alike, the American family takes pride in and seeks variation in its home.

A Conceptual Framework for Viewing American Homes

Given the general features just described, a central theme of our analysis is that the American home represents two dialectic interplays: (1) between individuality and community and (2) between open and closed, or public and private, characteristics.

Individuality/community. One side of this dialectic states that American homes reflect attempts by occupants to be singular or unique and to achieve a certain amount of distinction through the vehicle of their homes. The other side of the dialectic states that people also use their homes to reflect their ties and identification with the larger community in which they reside.

The idea of the American home as a symbol of individuality was articulated by Cooper (1976), an environmental designer. Using the psychoanalytic ideas of Carl Jung, Cooper explored the idea that homes in modern America are symbols of the self. She said:

> As we become accustomed to, and lay claim to, this little niche in the world, we project something of ourselves onto its physical fabric. The furniture we install, the way we arrange it, the pictures we hang, the plants we buy and tend, all are expressions of our images of ourselves, all are messages about ourselves that we want to convey back to ourselves, and to the few intimates that we invite into this, our house.
>
> In the contemporary English speaking world, a premium is put on originality, on having a house that is unique and somewhat different from others on the street, for the inhabitants who identify with these houses are themselves struggling to maintain some sense of personal uniqueness in an increasingly conformist world. On the other hand, one's house must not be too way-out, for that would label the inhabitant as a nonconformist, and that, for many Americans, is a label to be avoided [p. 437].[1]

In American society the essential worth of the individual is a deeply rooted value. We speak of the rights and freedom of the individual, the opportunity to pursue one's own direction and to achieve whatever potential one possesses. We espouse the idea that people are unique and have the right to "do their own thing." While these values are not always subscribed to or afforded all segments of society, they are traditional ideals that have existed in the American culture for many years. In this chapter we will explore the idea that individuality is also evident in the design and use of American homes.

Side by side with individuality, American homes portray the value of community ties. The home not only displays the uniqueness of individuals, it also reflects linkages with neighbors and the community. Such bonds are associated with traditional American values of duty, responsibility, and loyalty to the community and to the society as a whole. Traditionally, Americans have believed in the "destiny" of their nation as the protector of democratic principles and as the upholder of important religious principles. Americans have also believed in their ability to work

[1]From "The House as Symbol of the Self," by C. Cooper. In H. Proshansky, W. H. Ittelson, and L. G. Rivlin (Eds.), *Environmental Psychology*. Copyright © 1976 by Holt, Rinehart & Winston, Inc. Reprinted by permission of Holt, Rinehart & Winston.

together and, where necessary, to subordinate individual needs to the good of the community and the nation. Americans are also "joiners" of organizations—clubs, churches, community organizations, and causes of various kinds. Thus, duty and responsibility to others and to one's community are traditional American values, and we will illustrate how such values are also reflected in home design and use.

Public/private. A second dialectic of American life that is reflected in homes concerns openness, or accessibility, and closedness, or inaccessibility, to others. The American value system calls for people to be friendly, available, open, and honest with one another, to "have their cards on the table," and to render help when needed. But there is a coexisting opposite norm in American society—namely, to be private and to respect the privacy of others. We espouse such values as "minding one's own business," maintaining family secrets, not forcing oneself on others, not displaying fears, exhibiting strength even when one feels anxious, and not being overly expressive. Thus, values about the inaccessibility of people to one another exist alongside those emphasizing openness. As we shall see, these dialectically opposite values are, to one degree or another, also evident in American homes.

Before beginning our analysis of the American home, there are some qualifications to our approach that you should keep in mind. First, there is tremendous variability in American homes and in adherence to the values described above, and to speak in universal terms is simply not appropriate. Therefore, we will restrict the analysis to one segment of American society and to one type of American home—middle-class suburban residents and their dwellings. These families typically live in detached single-family dwellings, although more and more people reside in townhouses, duplexes, and condominiums. They are middle- to upper-middle-class, and their occupations include office worker, skilled technician, and professional and managerial positions. This stratum of American society probably reflects most strongly the values of individuality/community and openness/closedness described above. Obviously other groups need to be analyzed as well, but for illustrative purposes we will focus on the middle-class levels of American society. This is clearly a limitation of which you should be aware.

A second issue, related to the theme of Chapter 7, is that the design and use of the American home probably reflect a complex interplay of a variety of environmental and cultural factors. It is therefore important that we not seek the simple "cause" of home design and use, but that we be sensitive to the range of variables that might be involved. With these issues in mind, let us now play the role of "visiting anthropologist," to see how the American home reflects a variety of cultural and environmental variables. Our plan is to examine different parts of the American home, outside and inside, in terms of the dialectic polarities described above and the cultural and environmental factors that the home reflects.

DIALECTIC INTERPLAYS IN THE AMERICAN HOME

Location and Orientation of Homes

Is there any logic to the location and positioning of American homes? Do they face in certain directions for climatic reasons, for religious reasons, or at particular distances from public paths or in relation to neighboring homes?

From our perspective it seems that the siting of the American home almost totally ignores environmental factors such as climate. Eskimo igloos are often positioned parallel to the wind to minimize wind/chill effects; homes in the Middle East often have an inner courtyard that contains trees and water to create a cool place. American homes, on the contrary, seem to be positioned in almost every conceivable relation to wind, sun, and weather, and little attention seems to be paid to climatic or environmental conditions. Perhaps the reason is modern technology. We have storm windows and thermopane glass to retain heat and to eliminate drafts; if it is too hot, we turn on air conditioners and do not worry about locating homes near shady trees. With few exceptions, American home builders and users virtually ignore climate and related factors in positioning homes on sites.

Is there concern with religion or cosmology when siting homes? Recall that the Navajo hogan is positioned according to the cardinal directions, with the east side reserved for the entranceway. The emperors' palaces of ancient China faced south, a holy direction (Tuan, 1974); the homes of Wichita Indians had four entrances in relation to the cardinal directions (Raglan, 1964); in certain parts of India houses faced east (a holy direction) regardless of topography, so that doors and entranceways often faced uphill in an awkward arrangement (Rapoport, 1969a). To our knowledge such religious and cosmological factors rarely enter into decisions about how to site American homes.

But how *is* the siting of houses determined in middle-class America? One set of determinants probably results from building codes concerning lot size, minimum distance between adjacent homes and between street and home, sewage and utility capacities, and so on. In line with our general theme, however, is the idea that the siting of homes may also be related to American cultural values of individuality/community and public/private relations between people. American homes are usually located at the middle or rear part of a lot, with a visible expanse of land separating the home from public thoroughfares. The most decorative parts of the home—its facade, brickwork, and major entrances—all face toward public streets and thoroughfares. One might speculate that this siting arrangement is related to the home as a reflection of the individuality/community dialectic. On the individuality side of the dialectic, the front of the home is designed and located to exhibit to others the unique and idiosyncratic characteristics of its residents. The front yard is planted with grass and shrubbery, Christmas lights are displayed in the front, the upkeep and personalization of the front are carefully done (we bet that the front lawn receives more fertilizer and more care than the back lawn), trash, debris, and garden equipment are usually kept in the rear, vegetable gardens are rarely grown in the front yard, and so forth.

The individuality theme is well reflected in new communities where houses are often similar in design initially. Very quickly one sees repainting of homes in different colors, addition of decorations and facings that have no functional value, unique landscaping, addition of carports and garages, all of which serve to individualize homes. Is as much effort devoted to rear areas of homes? We think not, except for the tendency to demarcate boundaries with fences and shrubbery.

Landscaping is a traditional American vehicle for achieving individuality and uniqueness. Consider the enormous amounts of time, energy, and funds that people invest in their lawns, as they meticulously cultivate the weed called "grass." In a never-ending cycle, they keep it manicured well below its normal growing length, they feed it fertilizer to keep it green and growing, they water it profusely, and then they cut it down. They revel in the thick growth of the grass weed, become upset when other weeds invade their lawn, and feel a sense of accomplishment when their grass is equal to or better than that of their neighbors. The ultimate compliment occurs when one neighbor says to another "Your grass looks great; how do you do it?" Yet grass and some shrubbery serve little functional purpose—they cannot be eaten, and they barely affect cooling or heating. Sometimes lawn care is carried to an extreme, as in places like Salt Lake City, where people take great pride in their landscaping. They grow grass and shrubbery that are often unsuited to the high desert climate and terrain, they invest a substantial part of their fragile water supply in watering lawns by means of elaborate sprinkling systems, and in the midst of periodic droughts, they worry about what will happen if their lawns do not receive enough water.

The siting of houses and activities associated with the yard and exterior not only serve to express individuality but simultaneously reflect identification with the community. That is, the motivation to present the best house front possible and to have an attractive front yard and lawn may be not only to appear unique but also to reflect involvement with one's community and neighbors. This is evident in the projects that often capture whole streets and communities. Some neighborhoods are lawn-

and shrubbery-oriented and engage in cooperative planting projects, sharing of tools, and garden and lawn contests. Others get caught up in redecorating the outsides of homes, Christmas lighting contests, and construction of carports.

The front area of homes as a simultaneous indicator of individuality and community was vividly demonstrated by a friend who used his front yard to display his uniqueness. However, he did so in a way that temporarily alienated his neighbors, because his acts went beyond the limits of community acceptance. As we see in this example, he failed to keep the poles of the individuality/community dialectic in an appropriate relationship. At Christmas one year he chose not to decorate his home with exterior lights, a custom that was particularly strong in his neighborhood. Such decorating not only allows people to express their individuality through unique lighting arrangements but simultaneously creates neighborhood unity. Our friend's home, without any decorative lights, stood out rather dramatically. Eventually he was approached by some neighbors and was reminded of the community norms. His response, obviously passively resistant and an assertion of his individuality, was to toss out a single string of Christmas lights on his front lawn. Needless to say, his response did not endear him to his neighbors. While his actions reflected individuality, they also violated community norms beyond informally permissible limits.

At another time, this same friend demonstrated the same point. He bought two sheep and allowed them to graze on his front lawn, the idea being that the sheep would keep the grass trimmed and would also contribute eventually to the family food supply—all this in a conservative, suburban community of upper-middle-class homes! The neighbors rallied to this issue and discovered an ordinance that forced him to remove the sheep. In both incidents this man had used his front yard to reflect his individuality, but he had done so in a manner that conflicted with the role of the front part of American homes as a symbol of community bonds.

The other dialectic—namely, openness/closedness, or public/private—also appears in the siting of American homes. The readily visible front yard and home reflect an open display of the family to outsiders, such that everyone can see an important part of the American family's life and values in its yard, lawn, shrubbery, landscaping, and decorations. It is a common practice for passers-by to look at one another's yards and homes, and they probably make inferences about a family and its values. In this way the front of the home and lot is a public display area of a family to outsiders. Yet the home is also located toward the middle or rear of the lot, somewhat separate and private from the public thoroughfare. Furthermore, there are strong norms not to walk across or even to enter yards without permission. So, simultaneous with the openness and accessibility of family homes is a strong element of separation and nonaccessibility. In parts of Canada and England (Cooper, 1976), by contrast, many homes are blocked from view by high shrubbery, trees, and fences in the front yard, and there is a sharp demarcation between public thoroughfares and private property. Similarly, homes in the Middle East and parts of India present a blank wall to public thoroughfares, and information about family life is almost totally inaccessible to passers-by. Thus, the siting and front-yard practices of American homes convey a simultaneous blend of individuality/community and openness/closedness.

Thresholds and Entrances to Homes

The entrance into the American home, the doorway area, is something people take for granted and hardly notice. Is the threshold, like other parts of the home, a reflection of environmental and cultural factors? To what extent does it reflect individuality/community and open/closed dialectics?

To provide some perspective on these questions, we will first examine other cultures and historical periods, in which it is clear that thresholds to homes have had mythological and religious significance. Our discussion will rely on Raglan (1964), who provides a vivid analysis of this facet of homes.

In earlier times gateways and entrances to the palaces of rulers and to religious places were holy and sanctified. The entrances to such places were literal boundaries between the secular, profane world and the sacred, holy world. In many religious places statues of deities, monsters, and other figures protected entrances, and symbols of various kinds signified the sacred quality of thresholds and helped ward off evil. According to Raglan (1964), entrances to homes also have had a sacred quality, as if they too were a separation between the "cold, cruel world" and the warm, protective haven of the home.

In what ways, if at all, does the typical American home reflect such values? In general, we do not seem to attach strong religious or cosmological values to entranceways. To be sure, one can point to the Jewish custom of affixing a mezuzah (prayer scroll) to the doorposts of a home. A pious Jew will touch this mezuzah when entering or leaving his or her home, in recognition of the sacred quality of the place. But, for the most part, the threshold of the American home rarely has religious meaning. There are, however, other practices that may relate indirectly to mythological or religious values. For example, at Halloween the front doors and entrances to many American homes are decorated with jack-o-lanterns, witches, and other symbols of the holiday. At Thanksgiving, a quasireligious holiday in the United States, it is customary to decorate the front door with harvest and agricultural symbols, such as wheat and corn, to symbolize gratitude for the fruits of the soil. Analogous practices occur at Christmas, when such symbols of the season as evergreen and holly wreaths are placed in windows and doorways. Why are such symbols placed on doors? Perhaps they hark back to religious and mythological festivals; perhaps they help symbolize the sacred quality of homes; perhaps they reinforce the idea of the threshold as an important transition boundary between the world and the private domain of the residents.

The design of thresholds and entranceways to homes may also be understood in terms of the individuality/community and accessibility/inaccessibility dialectics. Shrubbery and landscaping leading up to doorways frequently display symbols of a family's uniqueness. A finely landscaped pathway may lead to the door, and a lamppost or marker set in the ground with a family name is often located at the beginning of an entrance path. Such markers may take the form of "The Smiths," "The Charles Smiths," "Jane and Charles Smith," or the like. (Note that the content of the marker also tells us something about the family's and culture's view of male/female roles.) Other decorative markers at entranceways can include a family's initial on a storm door or the family name on a welcome mat or nameplate.

At the same time, however, thresholds and entranceways reflect a sense of community and bonding of a family with neighbors and friends. The care with which entranceways are treated symbolizes respect for visitors, who are presented with "the best" the family can offer as they approach the home. Visitors are also expected (and themselves expect) to approach and enter the home through the most important entrance, the front door, whereas family and close friends in American homes often use side and back doors (Altman, Nelson, & Lett, 1972). At night the entranceway may be lighted, there is often a "welcome mat" at the doorway, and sometimes there are special decorations to symbolize the hospitality of the family toward friends and community. Thus, the threshold of the American home simultaneously reflects individuality and community bonds.

The thresholds of homes also convey openness/accessibility and closedness/inaccessibility of families to outsiders. Visitors rarely cross the threshold of a home unless invited to do so. And inviting or not inviting someone to enter a home is a clear signal of the occupant's desire for more or less contact. One can keep visitors "at bay" by not inviting them to cross the threshold, and this is a powerful device in American society to regulate interaction, especially with salespersons. In fact, door-to-door salespersons are often trained to "get a foot in the door" quickly, to keep the threshold and communication process permeable and open. As soon as feasible, the strategy is to cross the threshold and get inside the house, making oneself a form of guest and obligating the occupant to be polite and listen to one's sales pitch. Thus, door-to-door sales training is designed to shift the dialectic balance from closedness and inaccessibility when salespersons are outside the home to openness when they are inside.

Raglan (1964) observes that the threshold itself is often treated as a sacred part of entranceways to homes. He notes that Teutons, Finns, Syrians, Egyptians, Persians, and other peoples hold the belief that one must never step on the threshold of a home, but must step over it. In both historical and contemporary cultures people also have believed that one must step over the threshold with the right foot first. (The mother of one of the authors always instructed him to step out of the house on the right foot on the first day of school.) The reasons for such practices are numerous and include beliefs that spirits, souls, fairies, and deities or mysterious beings live under thresholds. Other people simply believe that it is "bad luck" to step directly on a threshold. Carrying a bride across the threshold to a new home, rather than allowing her to walk over it, also relates to the importance of the threshold. While there are many facets to this custom, including the traditional dominance of the male (perhaps even a symbol of earlier practices of capturing brides forcibly), Raglan (1964) believes the custom is related to the sacred quality of the threshold and the desire to avoid "bad luck" and evil spirits as one moves from the profane and secular world to the sacred residence. For example, in Morocco the rationale for this custom is that the threshold is haunted by dangerous spirits. And among Yemenite Jews the bride is prohibited from stepping over the threshold for 30 days lest demons attack.

In general, then, there are relatively few religious or cosmological beliefs and customs in American culture regarding entranceways or thresholds. To our way of thinking, the threshold of the American home, like the siting of the home, is not strongly affected by environmental factors or religious and cosmological values. Rather, it seems more to reflect the dialectic interplay of individuality/community and accessibility/inaccessibility processes.

The Interior of American Homes

Individuality is a pervasive feature of the interior of American homes. Americans try to create unique interior spatial arrangements which are unusual compared with those of neighbors and which suit their individual needs. In renting or buying an apartment or house, they ask a variety of questions: "Where is the kitchen in relation to the dining room and living room? Are the children's bedrooms accessible yet separate from the parents' bedroom? Are there enough bathrooms, and are they in the right places? Is it easy to get to the backyard or patio?" How different this is from many traditional cultures where arrangements of space are dictated by customs, each home essentially a carbon copy of all others! The Iroquois long house, the Navajo hogan, the Pueblo apartments, and the simple dwellings of many African societies were all designed in the same way, with relatively little attention to individual preferences. How would Americans react if every home had a similar interior configuration? Surely this would be repulsive, even though modern homes have many common features. "Meeting a family's unique needs," "having something special and different," are the phrases that Americans use in conversation and advertising when referring to their ideal residence.

Uniqueness is also reflected in the specialization of room functions in American homes. There are special rooms for cooking, eating, sleeping, entertaining, and relaxing. In fact, individuality is often symbolized by the sheer number and variety of rooms in a home. Americans also believe that parents and children should sleep apart and that parents should have a larger and more elaborate sleeping room. The parental bedroom often has better exposure to sun, shade, and views, a separate bathroom, and other conveniences. It is often called the "master bedroom," connoting both the general status and individuality of parents and the symbolic role of the father as head of the family.

Another middle-class American family goal is to have a home where each child has a separate bedroom or, at least, shares a room with no more than one other child. Children who share rooms are usually same-sex pairs, especially as they approach the teenage years. There is usually no rule about which sex has a separate bedroom, although females or oldest children are often given their own bedrooms. No general cultural rules operate in this area; room assignments are more a function of individual family traditions and pragmatic considerations.

Individuality also holds for other rooms in the home. Very often American fathers have special rooms such as a study or workshop that they control and often decorate and personalize (Altman et al., 1972). Mothers also sometimes have special rooms, such as a sewing room, although Altman et al. (1972) found that mother's special room often was a totally public place, such as the kitchen or family room.

A widely accepted value in American culture is that the mother is responsible for and controls many facets of the home. She controls activities in the kitchen (perhaps not so enviable a function, since she usually shops, prepares meals, and cleans the kitchen and the rest of the home). In addition, most areas in the home are the responsibility of mothers, including interior design and furniture selection and arrangement. As noted in Chapter 7, this is a common practice in many societies. Thus, much of the home in middle-class American society has the stamp of the female's personality. In fact, visitors usually discuss the qualities of the home with the woman and compliment her on them, since it is known that her energies, imagination, and uniqueness are displayed in the interior decor and design. The converse seems to be true for the outside of the American home, which is generally recognized as the domain of the senior male, the father. This practice also appears in many other cultures, where the outsides of homes, agricultural fields, and animals are the responsibility of the male.

The decor of homes also symbolizes the desire of American families to be unique. Unlike many other cultures, Americans endeavor to have different decor and furniture than their neighbors. To be like others is not desirable; it makes one appear "ordinary." For those who can afford it, professional interior designers are paid to help decorate and personalize homes. For others, individual tastes, home-decorating magazines, and furniture displays in department stores are used. Many people also seek a theme to their furnishings, often of an ethnic or national character. They may decide on a Japanese, Chinese, Swedish, French Provincial, or even Early American style. Sometimes one theme will be carried throughout a home, sometimes different rooms have unique themes.

The idea of individuality and uniqueness of homes is also evident in how spaces are used and displayed to visitors. Consider the following vignette (a bit overdone, we must admit) of how middle-class Americans entertain first-time guests in their home. In preparation for the visit, considerable time and energy will be spent cleaning the home so as to display the image of order, friendliness, and interest in the guests. The visitors will be greeted at the formal front entrance to the home and then ushered into a "public" room, such as the living room. Very often a tour of the home will follow, with special features of areas and rooms pointed out, especially those that the occupants themselves uniquely introduced. Males will often go along on the tour, but they generally remain in the background, the discussion centering on the females. It is customary in American culture for the female visitor to be especially attentive to various features of the home and to compliment the hostess on unique and clever aspects of the spatial arrangements and decor. If the male is complimented at all, it is usually because of some technical skills he displayed, such as wallpapering or carpentry, but everyone acknowledges that such skills were exercised under the guidance and control of the female.

The focus on individuality and specialization of function is also reflected in the entertaining pattern that follows the tour. Cocktails are served in one place, the living room; dinner is served in another place, the dining room; postdinner activities take place in still another place, the family room. Depending on the weather, people may visit the "patio," an outside place for cooking, eating, and relaxing during summer. Visitors may also use a bathroom called "the powder room" to eliminate or to freshen themselves up. Obviously, this is a somewhat stereotyped description of how homes are used, but it illustrates how individuality is characteristic of middle-class American homes.

Thus far we have stressed the individuality of the interior of American homes. But the other side of the dialectic, community, is simultaneously present in homes—in relation to family members themselves and to the family with respect to outsiders. Considering the family itself, not only are there primary territories that reflect the individuality of family members, but there are also public territories where people come together and exhibit family unity. Family members typically eat together in a kitchen or dining area, they jointly use a patio, family room, or living room, or subsets of a family might share common facilities, such as bathrooms or other secondary territories. These community areas may be decorated to display the whole family as a unit. In living or family rooms one might see photographs of family members and ancestors, trophies and mementos depicting the achievements and history of family members, the best furnishings and dishes. Although such places illustrate the uniqueness of the family to outsiders, they also serve to reinforce the community and bonds of family members with one another.

Family identity is also manifested in rituals and practices that occur in various places in the home. For example, the Jewish Passover meal is a symbol of family unity. Special dishes are used; family and friends gather in the dining area for prayer, storytelling, eating, and singing. The practices of observing Christmas around a carefully located Christmas tree, celebrating birthdays in particular places, and watching football games in a particular room all serve to highlight the common bonds that family members share. The fact that there are particular rooms where people gather for routine and special events testifies to the idea of the home as a place for family members to express both individuality and community with one another.

The community feature of the home also involves the family in relation to the larger social system. Through the home a family expresses its ties with outsiders and the community at large. For example, the use of rooms in culturally acceptable ways confirms the family's acceptance of societal norms. We do not sleep in kitchens or dining rooms, we do not have too many people sleep in one room, we do not keep the "wrong" kinds of animals in our homes, and we more or less adhere to basic social practices. Furthermore, most American homes are personalized and decorated within the "normal" constraints of American society. Thus, although there is considerable variation in decor, most middle-class homes have similar types of furnishings and arrangements. For example, Altman et al. (1972) found that not only did the typical middle-class American living room contain chairs, lamps, and sofas, but it was quite common to have a grouping composed of a sofa, coffee table, and one or more end tables and lamps all arranged as a central unit. People also use certain places for particular functions when dealing with outsiders. The living room is used for entertaining special guests, the dining room or area is used for eating, front doors are used for admitting visitors. Not only do these practices allow the family to present itself as a unique entity; they inform the guests that they are special to the family and that the residents extend to them a special bond of affiliation. These practices also convey to outsiders that the family follows accepted social customs and that it adheres to some general norms about how to deal with and relate to others in a community. So an examination of the middle-class American family reflects a dialectic interplay of individuality and community in how the home is used, its decor, and its layout. This theme will be illustrated in more detail when we consider particular places in the home later in this chapter.

In addition to the individuality/community dialectic, the interior of American homes involves an interplay of openness, or accessibility, and closedness, or inaccessibility. The inaccessibility side of the dialectic is readily evident in most homes. Family members have primary territories, such as bedrooms, over which they have considerable control and which they use to regulate interaction. Doors may be closed to avoid contact, family members typically do not intrude into others' spaces or violate closed doors, and there often are strong norms about ownership and privacy (Altman et al., 1972). Special rooms within the home, such as a study, den, or workshop, often function as primary territories and can be used to minimize contact with others when desired. Even when there are no specially "owned" places, families frequently have rules about interaction. That is, the home may contain public places that are available to everyone, but if these places are occupied by one member of the family, the others stay away; an example is a family room used to entertain anyone's guests.

The home is also used to facilitate contact and accessibility between family members. The door to a room conveys accessibility by being open; there are a variety of public places in the home that are specifically used for interaction between family members, such as kitchens, family rooms, and dining areas.

The home is also used to regulate contacts with outsiders. Not only do fences, gates, entranceways, and other features of the exterior convey accessibility/inaccessibility, but this also occurs inside homes. Certain areas are available to visitors, and other places are usually inaccessible to them. In an analogy with the theater, Goffman (1959) used the idea of "front regions" and "back regions" in homes. Front regions are like the stage in a theater, where actors present certain images they wish to convey to an audience. Self-presentations are carefully managed and conveyed through speech, dress, and the stage setting itself. So it is in homes, as visitors are presented with certain styles of behavior by their hosts and as they are restricted to certain parts of the home—for example, living rooms, guest bathrooms, or family rooms. Back regions of the home are often unavailable to outsiders. Like dressing rooms or off-stage areas in the theater, back regions are places where actors have their props and makeup and put themselves together for their performances.

In the home, back regions include kitchens and bedrooms. In bedrooms, people dress and groom in order to present themselves in accord with some appropriate role, perhaps as neat and impeccably dressed actors. The back region itself, hidden from guests, may be a shambles and not at all congruent with the actor's self-presentation, with clothing and accessories strewn all over, beds unmade, and disorder reigning. Similarly, kitchens often function as back regions. A meal may be presented to guests in a gracious, neat, elaborate, and organized fashion, the host and hostess displaying a demeanor of serenity and organization, as if the whole process were something they engaged in daily. However, peeking into the kitchen often provides a rather different picture. The kitchen may be in a state of disarray and confusion, with food and utensils scattered about; the hosts might be irritated and confused, as they try to manage the situation. Yet, when they cross the barrier between the front and the back region, in either direction, their demeanor may change to fit the setting—appearing calm, organized, pleasant, and gracious as they go on-stage, and confused, informal, and flustered as they go off-stage, much as actors and actresses do in the theater.

Places in the home do not serve solely as either front or back regions. The same area may be open or closed to visitors, depending on the purpose of the visit, the relationship of the outsiders to the family, and a number of other factors. The point is that the interior of the family home simultaneously has features that permit openness/accessibility or closedness/inaccessibility. And, as with all dialectic processes, the degree of openness or closedness varies from time to time and circumstance to circumstance.

In American society there are no completely rigid rules about which parts of the home are to be open and which are to be closed, so that there will be family differences in this process. For some families the kitchen or family room is a readily accessible front region, while for other families such places are back regions.

Comment and Clarification

A few clarifications need to be made about the preceding dialectic analysis. First, the individuality/community and accessibility/inaccessibility dialectics are only two of a large number of dimensions that might be used to describe homes. We emphasized these two pairs because they seem to capture well the main sources of similarity and variation in the particular subset of American homes that we examined. It may well be that additional dialectic dimensions will round out this analysis, and you may wish to explore that possibility on your own.

A second issue is that our analysis of homes was directed at a broad cultural level, not at the homes of particular families or individuals. That is, we portrayed the typical American suburban home as having the *potential* for openness or closedness and for the expression of individuality or community. Although such potential exists, it does not necessarily follow that all individuals in that subculture will use their homes on a daily or even longer-term basis to express equally both sides of these dialectics. Thus, a particular individual or family may use the home primarily to reflect individuality and not community or may emphasize the inaccessibility of the home to others. Or individuals and families may emphasize one or the other facet of each of these dialectics at different times in their life histories. For example, a family with young children in a suburban development might exhibit more concern with accessibility and community in its home as it shares problems of child rearing, young adulthood, community, and development with its neighbors.

A related point is that individual and family changes in dialectic balances are apt to be more rapid than broad cultural shifts. That is, an individual's needs for individuality or community (or accessibility or inaccessibility) might vary from day to day or even hour to hour. Consequently, the home might be used at one time to express openness to others and shortly thereafter be used to express closedness. Broad cultural values about the use of homes, such as norms for visiting or entertaining others in one's home, are apt to be less changeable than individual behavior. Thus, the American home is a *dynamic* place, and one must be careful when trying to understand the behavior of a particular person or family and not assume that a momentary analysis of events according to these dialectic dimensions captures the permanent state of affairs.

One must also be cautious in applying these two dialectic dimensions in other cultures. Just as with individuals and families, there is no reason to expect that the homes of all cultures will reflect both poles of each dialectic in an equivalent way. There are cultures—for instance, among certain poor families in Mexico—where people simply do not entertain or even permit others into their homes (Lewis, 1959, 1961). Socializing is done in restaurants or in other places outside the home. And, as noted in Chapter 7, homes in many cultures are not decorated or personalized to the extent that they are in suburban American society.

The fact that other cultures may emphasize one or the other pole of our twofold dialectic analysis does not mean that these dimensions are useless. On the contrary, they permit one to compare different cultures along a common set of characteristics. However, such variation does mean that one must be sensitive to the application of these dimensions outside the American subcultural group that we have investigated. Furthermore, because the home is a dynamic and changing place, on both a long-term and short-term basis, one should apply these and other dialectic dimensions over relatively long periods of time, to see how individuals, families, and different cultural groups exhibit different degrees of the individuality/community and openness/closedness dialectic dimensions.

PLACES IN THE AMERICAN HOME

The Living Room

We have examined general features of the middle-class American home in relation to the dialectic interplay of individuality/community and openness/closedness. We now focus on particular rooms in homes, largely in terms of their general characteristics and cultural underpinnings.

The American living room might well be described as the most important room in the home but also the one least used by a family. This room is decorated and personalized with the greatest care and has the most expensive furnishings in the entire home. It is an important display area for visitors and outsiders but, in many homes, is used only infrequently by family members. To call it a "living room" is sometimes an anomaly indeed, since so little actual living takes place in it. For many American families the living room is as close to being a sacred place as any area in the home, although it rarely contains altars, religious objects, or shrines. Rather, it is sacred in a psychological sense and serves as a symbol of the family's status and values. The living room is a prime example of Goffman's (1959) front region, for it is in this room that guests are often entertained. (It is also a room that children and pets often may not use except when guests are present.)

The living room is also usually located centrally, readily accessible from the front door of the home, and it often faces out toward the public street. Congruent with the stereotype of "suburbia USA," the living room sometimes has a large "picture window," which permits the family to have a view and, perhaps, to incorporate the outside environment into the home. The location of the living room and its windows also permits passers-by and neighbors to gain a glimpse into the best room in the house. Thus, this room serves a two-way communication function, perhaps a reflection of the individuality/community and public/private dialectics.

Some cultural and historical trends about the living room are worth noting. As described in Chapter 7, ordinary homes were originally simple structures, often consisting of only a single room where all activities took place—eating, cooking, sleeping, and working. Truly, the whole dwelling was a "living room." Eventually, separate areas and rooms were used for different activities, although the center of day-to-day activities, including work, still took place in the largest room, called the "living room." Aries

(1962) observed that as late as the 16th and 17th centuries in Western Europe well-to-do families lived in large houses with many residents—the nuclear family, servants, visitors, apprentices. The center of the house was often a large room where people ate, conducted business, and sometimes even slept. This was an all-purpose room, with tables and chairs set up for meals as needed, and with beds put up and down daily. This arrangement even occurred in the castles of royalty, where the focus of activity was in a "great hall" in the center of the castle. Here eating, sleeping, meetings, and entertainment all took place (Alexander, 1976). (Even royalty sometimes slept in the corner of the great hall, in a curtained-off area.) This pattern of residential design and life-style also appeared in ancient Egypt and Greece (Alexander, 1976). Naturally, among the wealthy there also were separate rooms for a variety of activities; however, centralized, all-purpose rooms seem to have been prevalent in homes throughout the world and over the course of history.

In the United States, the early pilgrims in New England had rather simple homes that eventually became more elaborate over the years (Alexander, 1976). Sleeping quarters were on the second floor, and the first level contained two large rooms separated by an entranceway. One room, the living room, was used by the family for day-to-day activities such as eating, cooking, and working. The other room, the parlor, was reserved for important events such as weddings, funerals, and entertaining important visitors. It is in the parlor that one sees the roots of the modern-day American living room. That is, the present-day formal, well-decorated, and almost "off-limits" living room is really a modern version of the earlier "parlor." The present-day "family room," described next, is analogous to the living room of earlier times.

The Family Room

The family room in middle-class American homes has several popularized names that may be associated with differences in function, such as *recreation room, rumpus room, all-purpose room,* and *TV room*. Although we sometimes think of the family room as a modern concept, it is really a throwback to the living room of earlier periods, as described above. The family room is, theoretically, a central place in the home where family members come together to read, converse, watch TV, and engage in recreational activities. The label *all-purpose room* conveys the intended concept in its most general form. In some cases, however, the room is designed and used mainly for recreation and leisure, as evidenced by the terms *recreation room* and *rumpus room*. In some families this room serves as a playroom for young children. Toys may be stored there, children may have free use of the room, a stereo system or TV set may be available. Even though the family room is a revival of the earlier living-room concept, in modern American homes it is used in fewer ways. For example, people do not usually work or conduct business in the family room, nor do they usually prepare food or eat in it on a regular basis. It is more of a gathering place and recreational area, or a general-purpose room for activities not undertaken in other parts of the home.

Obviously, not all homes have a family room, and it is less often present in apartment dwellings, especially lower-middle-class and lower-class dwellings. In such houses everyday activities often take place either in the living room itself or, depending on size, location, and family customs, in the kitchen. As children in apartment residences, we recall that the kitchen was "the living room," where we listened to the radio and later watched TV, held family conversations, and engaged in various activities, including schoolwork. For us the living room was a formal place. Yet, in other families the living room was used for day-to-day activities and to entertain guests, although children's recreation often occurred in bedrooms, hallways of apartment buildings, or the streets. However, in modern suburban America such day-to-day activities frequently take place in the family room.

The Kitchen

The kitchen is a place that Americans take for granted as a separate room in homes. The fact is that many cultures do not have separate kitchens as we know them, and the kitchen is even sometimes used as a place for sleeping, working, and other activities.

The American kitchen usually has some quite standard items (Altman et al., 1972)—stove, sink, refrigerator, cabinets, and drawers. The kitchen is the center of activity for preparation, cooking, and sometimes eating of meals, and it is generally the domain of the mother and daughters (Altman et al., 1972). The kitchen is also a back region (Goffman, 1959), a place where the family is off-stage and relaxed and where outsiders normally do not spend much time.

Kitchens are frequently used for eating and other activities, depending on their size, their location, and other facilities in the home. In some homes the kitchen is very small and adjacent to a dining area or a separate dining room. In others the kitchen itself contains dining space, ranging from an area in which a table and chairs can be located to a small "breakfast nook" or a place where people sit on stools at a built-in counter (much like those in public diners). When the kitchen includes dining facilities, it may be used for some recreational activities, such as television watching. There may also be a separate dining room that is reserved for guests.

As noted earlier, families in many cultures live in a single room or in just a few rooms, and food preparation and dining may take place in a main living room, in a kitchen, or in other places. For example, the Iroquois Indians who lived in long houses cooked in central areas that served several room units (Morgan, 1965); in Western Europe of the 17th and 18th centuries, people often used the same room for cooking, eating, sleeping, and work. Among poor people of Mexico, a separate area of the room was set aside for cooking and eating, but all living took place in a single room (Lewis, 1959, 1961). And in colonial New England food preparation, eating, and work often were done in a single room on the main floor of homes (Alexander, 1976).

Smith (1976), a newspaper reporter, wrote an account of the use of kitchens in the present-day Soviet Union that well illustrates differences in cultural practices:

> We found . . . that visitors who are truly welcome in Russian homes are usually ushered immediately to that most humble and yet most homey of places—the kitchen table, if the kitchen is large enough to accommodate more than a couple of people. The table, whether in kitchen or sitting room, has a central place in the Russian home, a tradition carried on from country life. . . . Russians go right to the table when friends call. It is usually a small table, overcrowded but in that way more intimate, since Russians, living close to one another all the time, like the physical proximity.
>
> One Sunday lunch at the Pasternak's we were ten around a table no larger than one in an American breakfast nook, children mixed in with adults and a grandfather in no particular order. Knees bumped unselfconsciously all during the meal as Russians bump each other while shopping or standing pressed together at church.
>
> The table, however, functions as much more than a place where Russians take their meals. The table is a meeting ground. For hours, Ann and I have sat with Russians around a table drinking strong tea . . . and talking all afternoon, evening and into the night about practically anything. In the Russian home, the table takes the place of the American den, family room and fireplace. It is the center of social life, a bridge between humans, a place for communion [p. 108].[2]

Contrast Russian use of kitchens with the practice of Ludwig II, king of Bavaria in the late 1800s, who had a special elevator built into his castle so that a whole dining table could be lowered from his private chambers into the kitchen, where it was set with food, and then returned to him. This enabled the shy and reclusive monarch to avoid the anxiety-provoking company of even his own servants.

All this speaks to the point that the way modern middle-class suburban Americans use their kitchens is not universal. Rather, the relatively

[2]Copyright © 1976 by Hedrick Smith. Reprinted by permission of TIMES BOOKS, a division of Quadrangle/The New York Times Book Co., Inc. from *The Russians* by Hedrick Smith.

specific use of kitchens in American society attests to the norm that rooms are specialized places, each having its own function.

The Patio

A relatively recent feature of American homes is an outdoor patio area, typically located in the backyard. This area varies in size from a small slab of concrete to a large area that may be enclosed by a roof, a fence, and shrubbery. The patio has emerged as a central focus of suburban American life. It is typically used in warm weather for a variety of activities—reading, sitting, recreation, entertainment, sunbathing, and eating. The patio often has its own distinctive furniture and may contain plants and flowers. Cooking facilities are usually available on patios and vary from portable charcoal-burning grills to permanent gas stoves.

Use of patios often involves a rather interesting role reversal by American men and women concerning meal preparation. Although women continue to be responsible for shopping, designing meals, and doing much of the preparation, men often assume responsibility for cooking on the outdoor facilities of the patio. Why this happens is hard to say. It might simply be that parts of meal preparation still occur in the kitchen and a woman cannot be in two places at once. Or one might like to speculate about "deeper" sociological or cultural evolutionary processes associated with the male cooking role on the patio and the ancient male role as "keeper of the fire."

In some respects the frequent use of patios by Americans is strange, since the inside areas of modern homes are often more comfortable in temperature and more free of insects and smoke from cooking. Furthermore, one is often in a very public setting, visible to neighbors and subject to the intrusions of young children, cats and dogs, wind and dust. How is it, therefore, that there is such a strong affinity for outdoor living in modern America? This desire for the outdoors is also evident in the recent trend for American families to camp out and to live in tents and recreational vehicles. People seem to delight in cooking over fires, chopping wood, lugging water from communal taps, washing dishes in primitive conditions, not showering or shaving for days at a time, and living in crowded tents or campers. Alexander (1976) summarized this whole matter by saying:

> One of the most remarkable phenomena of the twentieth-century culture is the desire to be outdoors. Throughout history man has endeavored to create shelters that protected him from the elements and to find better methods with which to cook his food. However, now that sturdy, air-conditioned and centrally heated structures are common and cooking facilities are efficient, man increasingly turns toward the outdoors to spend his time and to cook his food over open fires [p. 133].

Some outdoor living has been historically prevalent in American society. Alexander (1976) observed that, in turn-of-the-century America and before, single-family dwellings often had a front porch that faced onto the street. Porches served several functions—family gatherings, escape from the heat of the interior in the summer, entertaining neighbors and friends. With the advent of the automobile and its noise, fumes, and generally disturbing character, Alexander (1976) hypothesized, outdoor activities shifted to a patio at the rear of the home, and they eventually expanded into activities such as cooking.

Outdoor living is obviously not unique to American society, as illustrated in this and the preceding chapter. For example, ancient Egyptian and Greek homes had interior landscaped gardens and courtyards that were used for living, entertaining, and recreation. Courtyards and gardens are also common today in the Middle East and in Mediterranean cultures. So the combination of indoor and outdoor areas of homes is a long-standing tradition in many cultures.

Bedrooms and Beds

In Goffman's (1959) terms the American bedroom is a back region that is usually not accessible to visitors. In our framework bedrooms are also primary territories and are psychologically important to their occupants. Bedrooms are typically remote from public areas and in multistory homes are most often located on the upper levels. The American bedroom typically contains a bed, a closet for clothing, one or more bureaus, and sometimes tables and lamps, bookshelves, desks, and chairs (Altman et al., 1972).

As mentioned earlier, the custom in middle-class American homes is for parents to share a bedroom, usually the largest and most elaborately furnished one, and for children to occupy other bedrooms. But separate bedrooms for family members have not been the custom historically or in other cultures. Except for the very wealthy or royalty of earlier times, the separate bedroom is relatively recent in Western society and appeared around the 15th century (Laird, 1935; Luce & Segal, 1966). In the dwellings of earlier times, families slept in a single room in which they ate and lived. Even if dwellings had more than one room, separate sleeping places were not always available. During the biblical period, sleeping spaces often involved little more than a cluster of pillows in a corner of the dwelling. As described earlier, larger houses during the Middle Ages had main rooms where most day-to-day activities took place (Aries, 1962). Very often collapsible beds were simply set up in a corner of these rooms. Similarly, among the 17th-century French Renaissance kings, sleeping areas with beds were also used to entertain guests and to conduct royal business during waking hours (Aries, 1962; Luce & Segal, 1966).

In Europe, Laird (1935) observed that beds first appeared in the corners of living areas. Later they were built into the walls of houses and sometimes were covered with protective curtains and shutters. Gradually, sleeping alcoves appeared, and only much later were there separate bedrooms. So the idea of separate bedrooms and fixed sleeping areas has not, historically, been a common facet of home design.

American bedrooms generally function as primary territories and involve long-term use and control by occupants. Hence, it is customary for people not to intrude on others' bedroom spaces, although this restraint is by no means a universal practice in American families. For example, Altman et al. (1972) found that male children rarely entered their parents' bedroom without knocking on a closed door; they were also careful to knock on the closed doors of their sisters' bedrooms. However, they more frequently intruded into their brothers' rooms. In addition, free access to others' bedrooms varies with role in the family and with age of children. For example, in American families, the mother who remains at home to manage day-to-day affairs has considerable access to bedrooms and any room in the house, although even she might not have free entry to all places, especially as children become older.

Even when people share bedrooms, they exhibit primary territoriality. For example, Rosenblatt and Budd (1975) found that husbands and wives usually had their own sides of a bed, separate bureaus or bureau drawers, and their own sides of closets. Altman et al. (1972) reported similar practices among children who shared a bedroom.

Bedrooms in American families are also important vehicles for expressing individuality through decorating and personalizing. In traditional middle-class homes the parents, especially the mother, play a central role in decorating a child's room. Sex-role typing is evident in how parents decorate and furnish children's bedrooms. Girls' rooms are made "feminine" through the use of the traditional color pink, frilly draperies and bedspreads, delicate furniture, and soft colors and in a myriad of other ways. Boys' rooms are "masculinized" with larger, heavier, and more angular furniture. Draperies and bedspreads are bolder, and such toys as soldiers, trucks, guns, and sports equipment are in contrast to the dolls, cookware, and "feminine" play materials given to girls (Parke & Sawin, in press).

It has been our observation that, as children approach the teen years, they begin to express their own individuality through personalization. Posters and pictures of sports heroes, music groups, TV and film personalities, and scenery, along with personal mementos and obscenities, begin to appear in their rooms. Sometimes this is a matter of considerable dismay to parents and may contribute to the interpersonal crises frequent between parents and teenage children in American society.

However, gender-linked practices still dominate. In a recent study of the decorations of college dormitory rooms, Vinsel, Wilson, Brown, and Altman (1977) found that males used larger decorations, especially those containing sports and other personal-interest themes, whereas females used smaller decorations that reflected personal relationships, such as pictures of family and friends. Females also displayed more handmade and noncommercial decorations—macramé, collages, and so on. Almost all students in this and an earlier study (Hansen & Altman, 1976) decorated their dormitory rooms, indicating a norm in American society to individualize one's living space, regardless of its size or permanency of ownership.

Along with the American custom of separate bedrooms is the practice for people to sleep in different beds—except for married couples (Altman et al., 1972; Parsons, 1972). It is rare indeed for children in American middle-class society to sleep in the same bed with their parents or siblings on a regular basis. But, here again, sleeping alone is not always the rule in other cultures. For example, Murray (1965) reported that family members sleep in the same bed or in close proximity to one another in a number of other cultures. And who sleeps with whom varies. Among certain Australian Bushman groups, a girl sleeps with her grandmother or with another female relative, while boys sleep together (Murray, 1965). Caudill and Plath (1966) surveyed 300 Japanese families and found different combinations of family members sleeping together at different stages of a child's life. Young children slept with their parents or with extended kin, such as grandparents; older children slept with siblings.

The evolution of sleeping practices is also apparent in one or two generations of American immigrants. The family of a parent of one of the authors migrated to the United States in the late 1800s and initially lived in a crowded tenement in New York City. In this family the three young sons slept in one bed, and the only daughter slept in her own bed in her parents' bedroom. Eventually, when the boys were older, their bedroom was given to the girl, and they slept in the living room and kitchen. When the family could afford a larger home, the girl was given her own bedroom, the two younger boys shared one bedroom, and the older boy had his own room. Thus, in a single family we see the evolution of sleeping practices from communal arrangements to increasingly separate ones.

Another aspect of bedrooms concerns the location of furniture. For Americans the arrangement of furniture is usually based on esthetics, available wall space, window and closet locations, and door positions. Americans do not position beds according to religious, cosmological, or mythological prescriptions. Elsewhere in the world, people do. For example, Easter Islanders in the South Pacific sleep parallel to the long axis of their homes, facing the door; some American Indian groups in the Southwest do not sleep in the direction of the sacred east; certain Indian

Brahmin groups believe that sleeping places are sacred and need to be periodically purified with cow dung (Murray, 1965).

The bed itself is usually the most prominent piece of furniture in the bedroom. The following remark by Guy de Maupassant, the French author, captures much of the feeling that people have about their beds: "The bed comprehends our whole life, for we were born in it, we live in it, and we shall die in it" (cited in Parsons, 1972, p. 421). Parsons (1972) also reported that by the time the average person in Western society reaches age 65, he or she may well have spent close to 40% of his or her lifetime in bed. An important object of furniture indeed!

There are a great variety of American bed forms. For example, couples often use a standard "double bed," a 54-inch by 74-inch bed. Variants include the "king size" and "queen size" beds, which are larger than the usual double bed. The "Hollywood bed" consists of two single beds located side by side with a single headboard—a kind of together-but-apart arrangement. Other bed forms include the standard single, or twin, bed and a variety of folding beds that can be stored when not in use, "Murphy beds" and sofa beds. A more exotic form of bed is the "water bed," a water-filled plastic case that does not have a mattress or spring. Actually, this form of bed is not so innovative; the Romans used cradlelike beds filled with warm water some 2000 years ago (Luce & Segal, 1966). There are also a variety of esoteric beds, such as the "Playboy" bed of Hugh Hefner, reported to be circular and capable of being rotated 360°.

The history of beds in other cultures is no less diverse than that of bedrooms or other parts of the home. In many present-day cultures, as in earlier cultures, beds do not exist, and people sleep on a variety of things—mats, skins, pillows, grass or leaves, platforms made of bamboo or other materials (Laird, 1935). In biblical times sleeping places varied from pillows temporarily arranged on the floor to elaborately decorated beds fashioned from wood, ivory, bronze, gold, or silver. Egyptian, Greek, and Roman beds generally were low, narrow tables that were used for both sleeping and daytime sitting (Luce & Segal, 1966). During the Middle Ages, most poor people did not use beds; they slept on benches, storage cabinets, or the floor (Laird, 1935). However, over time beds appeared and became larger and bulkier and were finally located in separate bedrooms.

With the Renaissance and the 16th- and 17th-century French kings, beds became ornate and decorative (Laird, 1935; Luce & Segal, 1966; Wright, 1962). Louis XIV was said to have had over 400 beds (Laird, 1935), many of which were decorated with gold, silver, inlaid wood, and elaborate carvings. Guests, diplomats, and courtiers were received in these ornate royal bedrooms for business and entertainment. It was also said that Louis XI had an elaborate bed permanently located in the

French Parliament building, where he listened to debates as he reclined in bed. Another elaborate bed was the famous bed of Ware of England (Laird, 1935), immortalized in Shakespeare's *Twelfth Night*. It was built by Jonas Fosbrooke, who spent 30 years carving and constructing it. The bed was 11 feet square, and 68 people could sleep in the main area. A trundle arrangement, whereby another bed was pulled out from the bottom, slept 34 people. It is said that Edward IV, king of England, liked the bed so much that he gave Fosbrooke a pension for life.

Another exotic bed was owned by an Indian maharajah (Wright, 1960). This bed, weighing over a ton, had a life-size female nude figure at each corner of the bed. When the maharajah lay down, a music box was tripped off, two of the figures automatically fanned the area around his face, and the figures at his feet brushed away the flies.

Bathrooms

The typical middle-class American bathroom has been described by Kira (1976) as a three-fixture, 5-foot by 7-foot room, with tile walls and a tile floor. The three fixtures are a bathtub (often combined with a shower), one or two sinks, and a toilet. These pieces of equipment speak directly to the functions of this room for Americans. First, the bathroom is used in accordance with its name—to bathe, shower, wash one's hands and face, and perform other activities associated with personal hygiene. A second set of functions of the bathroom concerns urination and defecation. A third function of this room involves personal grooming—combing hair, applying makeup, and so on. Most American bathrooms are equipped with mirrors and storage areas for grooming supplies. A fourth function of bathrooms is related to health and illness. The American bathroom typically contains a "medicine cabinet" affixed to the wall and drawers that are used to store medicine and first-aid equipment. Thus, the bathroom has some of the elements of a dispensary or hospital emergency room.

The four functions of bathrooms are all related to body and health maintenance, and the appearance of the bathroom suits the image well. It usually contains tiled floors and walls and has an aura of hospital-like cleanliness. The tile and decor are often rather stark, the color scheme is dominated by white or slightly tinted tiles, and decorations usually consist only of shower curtains, window curtains (often on a very small window), and occasionally scatter rugs. One rarely finds extensive personalization of bathrooms, except perhaps for initialed towels. Thus, the atmosphere in many traditional American bathrooms is that of a nonpersonalized, hygienic, pristine, austere place. Even when guests are shown through the home, bathrooms are not displayed with the same enthusiasm as other parts of the home. Touring guests often only glance into the room and do not enter it, and the discussion about the bathroom is usually muted and brief. Bathrooms do not rank high as places where Americans display their values or personality to others, nor do Americans invest themselves in bathrooms to the same extent as in other parts of the home. Popular magazines on interior design, however, are beginning to suggest that bathrooms be given more attention in regard to personalization. Perhaps the values of the next generation of Americans will result in the bathroom's being a less austere place.

Still another function of bathrooms, quite unrelated to hygiene, health, elimination, and grooming, is to avoid others and to be alone. Many people report that the bathroom is one of the few places in the home where they can think and meditate, read, or just be alone. Yet the typical American bathroom is quite ill suited for such activities. There is usually no place to sit, except on the commode or on the hard tile floor, and neither place is very comfortable for very long. Most bathrooms lack other amenities for relaxation, such as proper lighting for reading, book racks, or snacks. Hence, using the bathroom for relaxation or to avoid others is quite incongruous with its design. Furthermore, access to the bathroom for long-term relaxation or privacy is not always possible, since the typical lower-middle-class American home has only one or one and a half bathrooms to serve all family members (Altman et al., 1972).

If one were to characterize the cultural qualities of the American bathroom, what might they consist of? We propose the following: *solitude, antisepsis, modesty*.

The bathroom: a place for solitary activities. Bathroom activities, especially bathing and elimination, are usually done alone in American culture, often behind closed doors. Altman et al. (1972) found that the more intimate the activity (for example, bathing or elimination rather than dressing or washing), the greater the likelihood that a bathroom door was kept closed. However, the custom of being alone for such functions is not universal in other cultures, nor has it prevailed throughout history.

In ancient Rome bathing was typically done in public baths (Wright, 1960). The Baths of Caracalla were 1100 square feet in area, some six times the size of St. Paul's Cathedral in London, and could accommodate several hundred bathers. In the fourth century A.D., Rome had 11 public baths that were available to the general populace, and there often were public toilets associated with these bathing facilities. The Emperor Vespasian, in the first century A.D., had public urinals installed in Rome so that people would not freely urinate wherever they happened to be, suggesting the rather public quality of elimination during this period of history. In the Middle Ages in Europe, bathing continued to be a communal affair, with public baths quite common. In addition, family members often bathed together at home, perhaps one or two at a time in a common tub, often because of a shortage of hot water.

Toilet functions in medieval Europe were rather haphazard. Toilet activities were practiced casually, using buckets, corners of rooms, or public streets (Wright, 1960). Thus, the American custom of being alone for hygiene and elimination may well be unique to present-day American culture.

During the Renaissance and up to the 18th century, bathing (and even elimination) continued to be somewhat communal. The French Renaissance kings often entertained and conducted business while in the bathtub or on the toilet (the term *throne* for the toilet derives from the elaborate design of their toilets and from their custom of holding court while seated thereon—Wright, 1960).

In the 1800s and thereafter, bathing and toilet functions became more solitary. Some people in the United States continued to use public facilities—for example, certain immigrant groups who did not have adequate facilities at home—but people began to use solitary facilities more and more, even in public restrooms. The exception is, of course, the male public urinal, which is generally a communal arrangement, whereas toilet commodes are usually located in separate stalls.

The propensity for Americans to bathe and eliminate alone is not, of course, universal in other present-day cultures. In Japan, for example, bathing is often a family or public affair, and it serves social as well as hygienic functions. And in many parts of Europe toilet facilities are rather open and are located in public areas. There are, of course, exceptions to the American practice of solitary hygiene and elimination—in schools and gymnasiums, for example. But, for the most part, Americans consider bathing and toilet functions to be best accomplished alone.

The bathroom: an antiseptic place. For most Americans the bathroom symbolizes cleanliness and hygiene (Kira, 1976). Americans attribute good physical health (and even mental health) to bathing and washing, and to be clean is a virtue in and of itself, as evidenced in the phrase "Cleanliness is next to godliness." Similarly, toilet functions are often linked to hygiene and health. To be healthy, TV advertisements say, is to be clean, to have bright and shining hair, to have unblemished skin, and to eliminate on a regular basis—all in an antiseptic, sweet-smelling, germfree environment. Thus, bathing, elimination, and grooming are almost strictly hygienic activities—for their own sake or to receive praise and recognition from others for being clean. Only rarely do we engage in these activities for fun or for relaxation (except for an occasional bath); and rarely do these activities serve a social or religious function.

The physical design of American bathrooms matches well the emphasis on the hygienic and antiseptic qualities of bathrooms. As noted earlier, the modern bathroom is the storehouse of hygienic supplies and equipment—the bathtub and shower, sinks, towels, hair dryer, grooming equipment, and medical supplies. The physical design of the bathroom also conveys its antiseptic, germfree qualities—white tile, straight-line designs, few decorations or other displays, a place that is easy to clean, few nooks and crannies that harbor germs or dirt, hard, shiny porcelain surfaces—all hygienic and antiseptic, just like the doctor's office or hospital.

Once again, such values are not historically or culturally universal. For example, Kira (1976) and Wright (1960) noted that, for ancient Greeks and Romans, bathing was not for hygiene only; it also served a variety of social and relaxation functions. In Rome, bathing was a multistage affair involving entry into a warm room, being rubbed with oil, rinsed, scraped, and reanointed with oil, and entering a cold bath. Bathing served the goals of relaxation and socialization and reflected the Romans' high regard for the human body. Similarly, in many Middle Eastern cultures the public baths and steam rooms are places for relaxation and socializing, not just hygiene.

During the Dark Ages and the medieval period, hygiene and toilet facilities were treated rather casually. People were physically quite unclean, royalty included, at least by present-day standards. Bathing was infrequent, and dirt became a badge of holiness, as shown in the following examples paraphrased from Wright (1960):

- Saint Agnes was said to have died unwashed at the age of 13 (and this was considered to be quite noble and holy).
- Saint Benedict was reported to have said "To those that are well, especially to the young, bathing shall seldom be permitted."
- Monks practiced taking cold baths "to cool their passions," and some, it is said, sat up to their necks in cold water whenever they had "worldly thoughts" [p. 24].

Thus, cleanliness was not considered a virtue, hygienically or otherwise, except in certain circumstances, for it interfered with religious values of penance and guilt. Rather, dirt personified the inherent evil and sinful nature of people and almost served as a symbol of one's piety.

Hygiene associated with elimination was also rather lax during this period. Common people used slop buckets, which were often emptied into open street sewers or dumped out of windows. Cesspits were dug wherever convenient. Toilets in castles were often built in the towers, at the bottom of which might be a barrel (or nothing). Some toilets even emptied into moats surrounding castles, producing a twofold danger to invaders—the water, and what was in the water. In medieval London, the Thames River became totally polluted, and many believe that the lack of sanitation contributed enormously to plagues and epidemics during the Middle Ages.

During the Renaissance attitudes toward bathing and toilet functions were more positive, at least among royalty and the upper classes of England and France. The French kings of the period had elaborate bathrooms and sophisticated plumbing systems. For example, Louis XIV had an octagonal, rose-pink marble bathtub 10 feet wide and 3 feet deep. When Louis XV decided to use it as a garden fountain, 22 men were needed to lift it (Wright, 1960). Bathrooms, including toilets, were also elaborately decorated, and as noted earlier, royalty often bathed and eliminated while entertaining guests or conducting court business. Although bathing and toilet use were still rather primitive among the common people, the Renaissance period shows shifting values toward these activities, at least among the social elite.

Beginning in the 1800s and up to the present time, values changed in the direction of hygiene and cleanliness. In the middle and late 1800s bathing became very much associated with health. A variety of bathtub designs appeared—sitz baths, hip baths, foot baths, sponge baths, and the like (Wright, 1960). Bathing was claimed to cure diarrhea, dyspepsia, colic, gout, and a variety of other ailments. While cleanliness was upheld as one outcome of bathing, so was health maintenance and cure of diseases. Because of the epidemics and plagues that had swept Europe during the preceding years, toilet facilities were also geared toward health and hygiene. Water- and earth-closet toilets, the latter containing chemicals, charcoal, and dirt, were designed to minimize the health hazards of human waste. The invention of the flush toilet in the late 1800s by Thomas Crapper, an Englishman, was hailed as a great advance. By the 1920s, the ideology of bathrooms in relation to hygiene and health was strongly entrenched in American society. Gradually, the American bathroom reflected more and more the virtues of health and hygiene in its design and use, and reached the point where it is today—an austere, clean, sanitary, efficient, simple place where cleanliness and health maintenance are evident in every facet of its facilities, design, and activities.

The bathroom: a place of modesty. Bathrooms are not usually located in prominent places in American homes, nor are they made especially visible. They are small rooms, rather austere in design and decor, and Americans do not seem to worry about their design to the same extent that they do for other parts of the home.

Kira (1976) observed that bathtubs, sinks, and toilets are usually poorly designed from a human-factors and safety point of view, again reflecting the lack of attention Americans devote to this part of the home. For example, bathtubs and showers are notoriously slippery and dangerous, and they have little storage space and are too small; sinks are usually too low, faucets are poorly placed, and other aspects of design are less than desirable. In addition, toilets are too high off the floor, controls are not easily accessible, and body support is poor.

Kira (1976) also described the rather negative, modesty-laden attitudes that Americans have toward bathrooms, especially in regard to toilet functions. In addition, bathing is typically viewed by Americans as solely in the service of hygiene, and the act of bathing itself may reflect American attitudes about the importance of cleanliness. People use all manner of sprays, deodorants, and chemicals to remove dirt and to hide body odors. The bathroom itself is kept clean with sterilizing agents, germ killers, and deodorizers. Thus, it appears that anything associated with natural bodily processes and odors is viewed negatively. Although bathing is treated as a virtue by Americans, it is done mainly to eliminate negative odors and body dirt and is not typically viewed as a pleasurable event in its own right. Accordingly, it must be done in private, in a sterile and austere place.

American attitudes regarding toilet functions are somewhat modest and perhaps even ashamed. Such attitudes are manifested in a variety of ways—for example, in the names Americans attach to the place: *bathroom, little girls' room* or *little boys' room, powder room, john, restroom,* and *comfort station*. Americans rarely use the term *elimination room* or *urination and defecation room*. Furthermore, the acts of elimination themselves are labeled in language that is designed to conceal. Thus, Americans assign the numbers "one" and "two" to urination and defecation, respectively; they use such expressions as "I have to see a man about a dog" or "I have to make a deposit in the bank" to refer to elimination. American children are taught to use such words as *wee-wee, poo-poo,* and *doody*. In addition, American culture has strong taboos about discussing elimination in public, except in derogatory or humorous ways. Acts of elimination cannot be shown in the mass media, people do their best to prevent others from hearing the noises made during elimination, and they are ashamed of the odors they create while eliminating. So, in a variety of ways, American attitudes about elimination and bathing are reflected in the design of the typical American bathroom—a small, austere, minimally decorated place that is subordinated to the rest of the home. It is as if Americans avoided putting their personal stamp on the bathroom or making the place too pleasant, perhaps as a way to downplay its functions.

Here again, other cultures do not view things exactly as Americans do. Kira (1976) and Wright (1960) provide several examples showing that elimination and its products are not viewed so negatively: Eskimos store urine to wash cooking utensils; men from certain North American Indian groups urinated on one another before entering a sweat lodge; ancient Romans used urine in the process of dyeing fabrics; in traditional Tibet, people kept samples of the feces of the Dalai Lama, the religious and political leader, in lockets as a religious and good-luck symbol. Americans, in contrast, flush away waste products.

So the basic theme of this and the preceding chapter prevails again—namely, that aspects of the home and its use have varied considerably throughout history and across cultures. The home and its places reflect well the values, norms, and attitudes of a society. So it is with that simplest and smallest of all places in American homes—the bathroom.

SUMMARY

This chapter adopted an anthropological perspective as it explored the present-day single-family dwelling of American middle-class society.

A central theme of the chapter was that the American home can be described in terms of two dialectic processes: individuality/community and accessibility/inaccessibility. With respect to the individuality/community dialectic, some authors have focused on the American home as a vehicle used to express the individuality and uniqueness of its users. While we agreed with this analysis and provided instances to support this theme, we also showed how the American home simultaneously portrays the other side of a dialectic polarity—namely, a family's ties with the larger social community.

A second dialectic dimension concerns openness and closedness. American homes are vehicles by which a family reaches out and makes itself accessible to others. Through design, decoration, and use of homes, people disclose who they are, their values, and their likely orientations to others. But home design and use also permit people to minimize their accessibility to others.

The chapter then analyzed various aspects of the American home in terms of these dialectic processes—exterior locations and orientations, thresholds and entrances, and general interior arrangements. The location of homes on lots, landscaping, and outdoor decorations reveal well the dialectic interplay of individuality and community. Siting of homes not only contributes to a sense of family uniqueness but also displays to others an interest in the community and neighbors and reflects support for community expectations. Similarly, the exterior of the home expresses the accessibility of the family to others by displaying the family's values, interests, and life-style. Yet the use of shrubs and fences and the concealment of certain facets of the home also control access by others to the family, reflecting the accessibility/inaccessibility dialectic.

The threshold and entranceway to American homes also reveal the two dialectic processes. Uniqueness is represented by decorations, nameplates, landscaping of entryways, and the like, whereas community ties are evident in various symbols of welcome, in the care given to the main entrance used by guests, and in related ways. Openness and closedness of homes are also evident in thresholds and doorways, which can be used to indicate accessibility or inaccessibility of a family to outsiders.

The interior of the American home also reflects these two dialectic processes. People seek out interior designs appropriate to individual needs, but they concurrently develop or choose arrangements that permit communal ties within the family and between the family and outsiders. Separate rooms for individuals and common rooms for the family go hand in hand. Unique decor portrays a family's individuality, yet personalizing often ties in with community and subgroup values. Openness and closedness are simultaneously evident in that the home is divided into front and back regions that are differentially available to outsiders.

The last section of the chapter examined particular places in American homes and contrasted their design and use with what has been found in other cultures and periods in history. A major theme of this analysis was that present-day design and use of places in American homes are not universal and that the attitudes and practices that prevail regarding various places clearly signal cultural values.

The living room is the most sacred and formal room in the American home and is an elaborately decorated and furnished place whose use is often restricted to guests. Its historical roots go back to the time when it was the main room and was used for most day-to-day activities. The American family room, a relatively recent part of homes, seems to have emerged as an all-purpose room for everyday living and, in many respects, is analogous to the living room of earlier historical periods. The kitchen is also a very central part of American homes and is often the center of family activities such as eating and conversing. The patio is also a feature of many American homes; it is an all-purpose area often used for cooking and eating, recreation, and entertaining. Bedrooms and beds are also central aspects of American homes. They serve as important primary territories, usually under the control of their occupants, and they strongly reflect individuality.

The last place we examined was the bathroom. Present-day American values consider this room to be a place where people are generally alone and where they engage in hygiene, elimination, grooming, and health activities. The bathroom is designed and treated as an antiseptic and austere place, it is very small and contains few decorations, and it is not enthusiastically displayed to outsiders. American uses of and attitudes about bathrooms contrast with those of other cultures and periods in history, in which the bathroom has often been publicly displayed and richly personalized and in which its functions have not been as taboo as they are in American society.

The central theme of this chapter was that the American home, like homes around the world, reflects a variety of environmental and cultural influences and, as such, serves as a window to understanding a social system.

Chapter 9

COMMUNITIES AND CITIES

The next three chapters examine larger-scale settings: communities and cities. The present chapter analyzes the design characteristics of cities and communities in a historical and cultural perspective; Chapter 10 explores psychological and cultural dynamics of adjustment to, and stresses and strains of, city life; Chapter 11 considers idealized cities of the future, new towns, and other "utopian" concepts of community design. In some ways, therefore, the three chapters focus on cities and city life of the past, the present, and the future, respectively.

Cities have always been controversial places. During some periods of history cities were viewed in very negative ways; at other times people considered them ideal places. But regardless of how people presently feel about urban settings, there is a simple and inviolable fact that we must face: cities are here to stay. People have lived in cities for centuries, and much of the world's population presently does. Extrapolations suggest that this pattern will continue far into the future. So the issue is not whether people will or should live in cities but what can be done to make cities and communities better places.

Consider a few facts. People have lived in settlements, some relatively small, for about 10,000 years; the first large cities appeared in Mesopotamia around 5500 B.C. (Fischer, 1976). Somewhat later, great urban centers appeared in China, in Central and South America among the Aztec, Inca, and Maya cultures, in Egypt, and in Europe (Rome and Athens). So cities have existed for thousands of years in a variety of cultures around the world. However, the *proportion* of people who live in urban areas has shifted over the course of history. In earlier times most of the world's population did not live in cities. For example, as late as 1850, only 2% of the people in the world lived in urban areas (Fischer, 1976). Today, about 25% do. And it is estimated that, by the year 2000, 40% of the world's population will live in large cities.

Within the present-day United States, the population of cities and the surrounding metropolitan areas has been steadily rising. When the nation was founded, in the late 1700s, less than 3% of its 3 million people lived in urban areas (Campbell, 1976). In 1970, Campbell (1976) estimates, 70% of the people in the United States lived in urban settings. This figure is far above the worldwide estimate of 25%. Furthermore, the United States presently has 250 metropolitan areas with populations greater than 50,000. And 33 of these contain over 1,000,000 people each (Campbell, 1976). The rapid growth of the urban and metropolitan population in the United States is vividly portrayed by Alexander (1976, p. 73): "It has been estimated that urban space equivalent to the size of Hartford, Connecticut, must be constructed *each* week of *every* year until the year 2000 to house and serve the 100 million additional Americans expected to be born during this period."

The situation is the same in many other parts of the world. For example, in 1944 the population of Seoul, Korea, was 940,000; today it is over 6 million. Like it or not, therefore, urbanization is part and parcel of life; it has been so for thousands of years, and it is likely to be so in the future.

Another set of facts you should know concerns the size of cities throughout history. It is well known that modern cities and urban communities vary tremendously in size. Some cities are small, numbering in the thousands of people; other cities, like New York, Chicago, Hong Kong, and Tokyo, number in the millions. Such variations in size have occurred throughout history, although not to the same degree as now. Some ancient Chinese cities had over a million people, as did Rome around the second century A.D. But these were exceptions; most earlier cities were relatively small. For example, in the Middle Ages, what is now Germany had several thousand cities, but few of them had populations greater than 10,000 (Saalman, 1968). Cologne, one of the largest cities in Germany during the Middle Ages, achieved a population of only 30,000 at its peak. During this same period, London, England, had about 50,000 residents—rather small in comparison with the ancient cities of China and the Middle East or modern cities.

There are several messages that we wish to convey through these historical and contemporary facts. First, urban living is in a period of accelerating growth everywhere in the world, and there is no reason to believe that it will be otherwise in the coming decades. Second, human experience in cities is not new. Cities have existed for thousands of years and in a variety of cultures. Third, there is value in trying to understand cities and communities in terms of culture/environment relations, not only for its sake but perhaps to see ways urban life can be enhanced. Given these facts and themes, we are now ready to explore urban settings.

CONFLICTING VIEWS ABOUT CITIES AND THE "GOOD LIFE"

We live in a historical period when cities and urban life are considered bad. Our images of large cities like New York, Chicago, and Detroit are of crowded, crime-ridden places which are undergoing severe financial problems and which have multitudes of poor people who are dirty, unhealthy, and unemployed. Furthermore, we often perceive urban residents as discourteous, pushy, selfish, and unsympathetic. Of course, we sometimes have positive feelings about cities: we value their unique cultural opportunities, excitement, high-style clothing and fashions, cosmopolitan people, and good restaurants. But on a net balance, it is probably fair to say that cities in the present-day United States are viewed rather unfavorably and probably fit the cliché "a nice place to visit, but I wouldn't want to live there."

Negative images of urban life are not unique to our society or to the present historical period. Similarly, positive feelings about cities have appeared at different times in history, sometimes to the point of idealization and reverence. Recall from Chapter 2 that Tuan (1974) provided a framework to describe historical views of the wilderness, rural life, and cities. One set of attitudes, appearing in the late 18th century, held cities in relative disfavor. Thomas Jefferson's statement cited in Fischer (1976, p. 16) captures the feelings that many people held at the time: "I view great American cities as pestilential to the morals, health, and the liberties of man." This theme carried into the 19th and 20th centuries in America, where the "middle landscape" of rural areas, small towns, and villages was idealized by the romantic writers of the period. Even today in America we see the stereotype of the "good life" as involving small communities that have plenty of green space, adequate cultural opportunities, and a systematic design that avoids the chaotic sprawl of suburbs and the assortment of evils found in cities. Fischer (1976) summarized present-day values when he said that people nowadays believe that modern cities emphasize new and unfamiliar cultures, strangeness among people, individualism, and social change, whereas farm, rural, and some suburban settings convey the image of nature, familiarity and friendliness of people, community bonds, and traditions, all of which lend psychological security to our lives.

But lest we forget, similar attitudes have existed at other times in history. Many cities in medieval and Renaissance Europe were places to be feared, with their high crime rates, minimal sanitation, dense population, cramped living conditions, and squalor. And we all know about Sodom and Gomorrah, the biblical cities which epitomized the evils of urban settings and which God destroyed because of the immoral behavior of their residents. So throughout history there have been times when cities and city life were viewed with disfavor and urban settings were perceived as a negative force in the lives of people.

But there also have been times when cities were treated as ideal and perfect places. According to Tuan (1974) and Wheatley (1971), many ancient Chinese and Middle Eastern cities were the symbols of religious and cosmological values, with kings, emperors, and priests at the center, along with important shrines and religious symbols. Furthermore, many of these cities were designed in a systematic way, incorporating cosmic and religious ideals into their designs. Similarly, in ancient Greece, the philosopher Plato described the "perfect" city as being located in the center of the nation, with religious temples at its center and with the rest of society radiating around it. As another example, the Bible portrayed Jerusalem as the religious center of the world and as a very positive place. Furthermore, in spite of their many problems, the medieval cities of Europe were also undoubtedly viewed with respect and loyalty. They were the seats of government and religion, they served as marketplaces for the distribution of goods, they were the places where people could go for protection and for carnivals and festivals, and they often functioned as the lifeblood of a region.

In modern times, although cities have a generally negative image, people also hold positive feelings about them. As we saw, Thomas Jefferson was a severe critic of urban life; yet he was simultaneously responsible for fostering the growth of Washington, D.C. He wished it to be a magnificent city, a symbol of American values, and it was to be built in the tradition of the grand cities of Renaissance Europe. The U.S. Capitol Building at the center of the city, surrounded by other important buildings, was intended to portray Washington, D.C., as the symbol of America and as an "ideal" city.

In summary, this brief historical sweep suggests that cities were sometimes viewed as negative places and sometimes as positive places. Actually, it may be that a dialectic analysis best fits attitudes toward cities. Thus, at any point in history, it is possible that *both* positive and negative attitudes existed simultaneously about urban life, although one attitude or the other may have prevailed at a given time. For example, New York City can be depicted at present as a dirty, crime-ridden, financially stricken, and decaying place. But one can still find descriptions of New York as the most stimulating city in the world, as having a unique charisma, and as a place of opportunity. (Needless to say, different segments of a city's population—rich or poor, one ethnic or religious group or another, individuals with varying preferences—may have different feelings about the city, so that we cannot speak of a singular view of an urban area that is held by all its residents.)

A central theme of this chapter is that cities, like homes (see Chapter 7), involve a complex interplay of many forces—religion, politics, economics, culture. These factors are reflected in the physical design of cities, the life-style of their residents, and urban institutions and dynamics. Cities, therefore, are not simple places. They are not the result of singular factors, and they do not affect people in a singular way. The goal of this chapter is to unravel some general qualities of urban and community settings, especially in relation to cultural and environmental variables.

OUR GENERAL ORIENTATION

There are many perspectives that one can adopt to understand urban and community settings. Ittelson, Proshansky, Rivlin, and Winkel (1974) describe six alternative perspectives that are linked to various disciplines. First, one can focus on architectural or design features of cities—the style of architecture, construction characteristics, traffic flow, and the like. Second, one can emphasize geographic factors, such as a city's relation to the terrain and the geographic distribution of people. A third perspective is sociological and addresses political, religious, and other institutions or such social problems as crime and mental illness. Still another perspective is historical: one can trace the long-term development of cities, changes in life-style, and other related processes. An anthropological perspective can deal with cultural groups and cultural processes. Finally, a psychological perspective operates on the level of the individual and examines stress, coping mechanisms, imageability, and behavior in communities and cities.

Each of these perspectives is legitimate and, indeed, quite necessary for a complete understanding of urban life. Our approach to understanding community and urban life has several elements, partly described in previous chapters. First, although our orientation is social-psychological, the goal will be to examine communities and urban settings using all the orientations described above, at least to some extent. Second, as described in Chapter 1, our framework is a "systems oriented" one that will treat cities and communities as both a "result of" and a "cause of" other factors. That is, we will try to describe the functions that cities and communities play in people's lives, contemporaneously, cross-culturally, and historically, and not always try to uncover specific causal links between variables. Communities and cities evolve and operate as a result of a multiplicity of variables, such as religion, economics, politics, and physical environment, and it is not easy to single out the separate roles of such variables. So, just as with homes, our focus will be on the role of communities and cities in the lives of people and, simultaneously, how these places reflect the qualities of a culture within which they are embedded.

Another feature of our approach will be to examine a range of community settings from small-scale villages and temporary encampments to large urban settings, on the grounds that there are potential similarities as well as differences associated with variations in scale.

The organization of the discussion to follow pretty well matches that in Chapter 7, where we examined homes. The next section of the chapter emphasizes the physical design features of communities. Subsequent sections address the relation of physical environment, political factors, economic factors, and religious and other cultural factors to community and city designs.

PHYSICAL DESIGN FEATURES OF COMMUNITIES AND CITIES

A salient characteristic of communities—small and large—is their variation in physical design. Present-day communities and cities in the Western world, Asia, and the Middle East, ancient cities of China, South America, and elsewhere, and small villages in Africa and the South Pacific have a variety of configurations and layouts. Consider a few examples, beginning with relatively small communities.

Small Communities

Near one end of the scale of planning and permanence are the communities of the Mbuti Pygmies of Zaire (Fraser, 1968). The Pygmies are a hunting-and-gathering people who do not live in permanent communities; rather, they roam in small bands and camp temporarily in different parts of the forest. Women construct simple huts of branches and leaves and arrange them in a clearing without any preestablished or rigid planning process. The huts do not face in particular directions with respect to cardinal directions, the sun, or other factors, and there are no particularly favored arrangements with respect to status or other variables. However, some elements of community planning are reflected in site selection and layout of the camp. For example, sites are generally located near streams and in shaded areas. In addition, Fraser (1968) observed that huts faced more or less toward the center of the clearing rather than toward the forest, and many group activities took place in the central area. Hence, even this very elemental layout shows that a community plan mirrors some aspects of the culture—response to water, the nonhierarchical status system, arrangement around a center to reflect group cohesion.

One can literally see certain cultural values of the Pygmies in the physical arrangement of their camps.

Another example comes from the Cheyenne Indians of the 1800s (Fraser, 1968). The Cheyenne were a nomadic people who were divided into separate kinship bands that lived and hunted separately during most of the year. Periodically, however, bands came together for rituals and ceremonies. One important gathering took place at the summer solstice and was called the Renewal of Sacred Arrows. This event symbolized tribal cohesion and usually involved the whole Cheyenne people, who came dressed in their finest to celebrate with songs and dances. Another ceremony, related to the renewal of the world and water, was called the Sun Dance. When the Cheyenne assembled for these rituals, the community was laid out according to a traditional plan that involved a C-shaped ring of tipis, the opening facing the rising sun in the east. At times there were as many as 1000 tipis in this formation, three and four deep, with the diameter extending to a mile. Not only did the camp circle face northeast, so that the first rays of the holy sun would shine on the camp, but the entrance to each individual tipi faced in the same direction. Custom also governed the location of various bands around the circle, and there were privileged locations—for example, near the south side of the eastern opening. Moreover, special community lodges were located in certain places in the community. When the encampment was concerned with the election of chiefs, the leaders of all the bands met in the Great Council Tipi, at the center of the circle. Although the arrangement varied from time to time, the eastern orientation of the community, the concept of center, and the location of family bands in their own areas all reflect the role of cultural values in community planning. This is a particularly vivid illustration of how world views and environmental cognitions and perceptions, discussed in Chapters 2 and 3, are reflected in environmental places, such as communities.

Not all traditional communities used a circular community design. For example, the Haida Indians of the northwestern American continent lived in linearly arranged winter villages (Fraser, 1968). These fishing-and-hunting people lived in large, wooden, rectangular houses that were lined up in a straight row parallel to the sea. All dwellings were built alike, and there were no salient status differentials among houses. Houses often were separated by only 2 to 7 feet. Fraser noted that the extraordinary wind velocities and extensive rainfall in the area may have resulted in these close living arrangements.

Another example of a linear community, the Mailu people of New Guinea, an agricultural and fishing society, lived in villages of up to 500 people. Each village consisted of two rows of houses facing each other across a street 30 to 50 feet wide. The whole community paralleled the seashore. Houses were all alike except that men's club buildings were located directly in the middle of the street between the rows of houses, and members of an extended family lived in close proximity to one another.

The traditional community designs described thus far were relatively undifferentiated with respect to layout and types of housing. But even in traditional societies, there is considerable variation. For example, the Trobriand Islanders of New Guinea have village arrangements that reflect differentiation according to function, status, and role relationships, especially leadership (Fraser, 1968). One such village plan was generally circular, with two concentric rings of houses facing toward the center. The outer circle housed married people, widows, and widowers and also had some storage buildings. The inner ring contained more solidly built ceremonial huts, food storage structures, some bachelors' houses, and the homes of the chief's kin. The chief's hut and his ceremonial yam house, the latter an elaborately decorated building, were at the very center of the village. The village burial and dance grounds were also in the center of the village. Buildings in the inner ring were systematically arranged, with the wives of the chief in one section and his clansmen in another section. The yam (a basic food source), the chief, and the social structure of the community are all, therefore, visibly evident in the relatively differentiated design of Trobriand villages.

In summary, there is considerable variety in the design of even the simplest communities. Moreover, these small, sometimes temporary communities reflect important aspects of a culture's life and values—physical environment, economics, status, social structure, world view, and cosmology. And there are various degrees of differentiation in community design, with some communities composed of similar houses in uniform layouts and others having variations in homes and other structures. Finally, there are differences in community planning and construction processes. In many societies there is little detailed planning or decision making about the design of communities. People simply follow and repeat designs that everyone knows to be "the way" for laying out things, just as they did for home designs in certain cultures described in Chapter 7. Contrast this with current Western practices, in which city and regional planners and other specialists develop new designs for communities, consciously attempt to provide certain functions, and have considerable opportunity for innovation and variation in design.

Moderate-Sized Communities

As described earlier, medieval Europe was dotted with thousands of small towns and cities whose populations often numbered only a few thousand people. Although these cities varied in physical design, many of them reflected common elements associated with cultural, economic, political, and environmental factors. For example, medieval cities were located near rivers and bodies of water whenever possible, for a water supply and transportation. They were also often positioned on hills, overlooking valleys and broad expanses, partly for defense and perhaps for symbolic and esthetic reasons. In addition, many towns were enclosed within walls. The medieval period was one of political instability in Europe, with local kings, dukes, and barons controlling their own neighborhoods and competing with one another. Often individual towns were largely on their own in terms of economics, politics, and self-protection. As a result, it was common for cities to have protective walls surrounding them (Saalman, 1968). These walls were often 25 to 35 feet high and 3 to 6 feet thick and had a series of watchtowers along their length.

The design of towns was quite similar from locale to locale, with limited variations within a few general themes. For example, because of economic and terrain considerations, the protective walls were often built around as small an area as possible. For example, the wall of the medieval town of Rothenburg, Germany, was about two miles in circumference. The eventual result was crowded conditions, narrow streets, and tall buildings, as more and more people moved into the towns. Buildings were constructed of locally available wood and stone and varied in size and elaborateness, depending on the wealth and status of the occupants.

Because of the central role of religion and politics, government houses and churches were usually located at or near the center of medieval towns, with an adjacent open plaza used as a marketplace and ceremonial center. Major business shops and wealthy people lived near the town center, and the main streets of the city often led from the central square to the city gates. The more remote from the center of the town, the poorer the homes and the people, and the narrower and more irregular the streets. As a city grew, new outer walls were constructed, and sections of the town developed their own squares and marketplaces, leading to a more complex design arrangement.

One facet of the design process that sharply distinguishes these larger-scale cities from the traditional small communities described previously is that most medieval towns were planned, designed, and built by specialists. Many German cities of this period had a *Baumeister*, a building master, whose job was to design and supervise the construction and later modifications of a city. Although the *Baumeister* was undoubtedly restricted by political, religious, and other factors, he nevertheless could express individual creativity in town planning. In addition, skilled artisans did the construction, each a specialist in his own area. Thus, in these European cultures and, indeed, in most larger-scale communities throughout the world, planning, design, and construction were at a "modern vernacular'' level, to use Rapoport's (1969a) terminology, wherein specialists were involved and variations in design were permissible. As a result, walls, towers, and entrance gates took on their own distinctive qualities from city to city, as did buildings, homes, and sections of towns.

Three themes that we applied to small communities in traditional societies also fit larger towns and cities. First, a variety of factors are reflected in community design—physical, economic, political, religious, and social. Second, although design in moderate-sized communities within a culture often shows considerable uniformity, variation also occurs as a function of local factors. Finally, the array of variables associated with town design operates in a complex network, and it is difficult to cleanly separate their contributions.

Large Communities and Cities

Large communities and cities of the past and present, and in a variety of cultures, show many of the same qualities described above. For example, many great ancient cities of China, the Middle East, and elsewhere were designed partly in accordance with religious values and world views of the time (Tuan, 1974). The circle and, later, the rectangle, as well as dominating the design of homes and other structures in many parts of the world, were involved in the plans of many ancient cities. In Egypt, Iran, and other parts of the Middle East, cities were designed in circular arrangements, often with a series of concentric walls. For example, Tuan (1974) described Baghdad, whose construction began in 762 A.D., as a city whose original plan called for three concentric walls, with entrance gates located at the four cardinal positions. Many ancient Chinese cities used a combination of rectangular and circular designs, with heaven and the universe represented by the circle and the here-and-now of earth symbolized by a square. The combination of circle and square was also portrayed in Plato's description of the mythical city on the lost island of Atlantis. The rectangular shape also appeared in biblical cities of ancient times. Tuan (1974) states:

> In the Old Testament, for example, we find the Lord telling the prophet Ezekiel, "You shall set apart the whole reserve, twenty-five thousand cubits square, as sacred, as far as the holding of the city." The four sides of the city—northern, eastern, southern, and western—were each named after the tribes of Israel. . . . In *Revelations* the isometric and orthogonal character of the heavenly Jerusalem was emphasized. It "was built as a square, and was as wide as it was long. It measured by his rod twelve thousand furlongs, its length and breadth and height being equal" [p. 161].

The physical characteristics of many early city designs were closely tied to the religious, political, and commercial life of their residents. For example, an emperor's palace, a religious shrine, or a monument to a deity was often located at the physical center of a city. Thus, the ancient city of Ecbatana in Iran had seven concentric walls, and the king and his nobles lived at the center in an area on higher ground, overlooking the rest of the city (Tuan, 1974). Describing the original city of Baghdad, Tuan (1974) states:

> At the center of the round city stood the great palace. Its area covered a space measuring 200 yards square, and its central structure was crowned by a great green dome, the summit of which, topped with a figure of a horseman, reached a height of 120 feet above the ground and could be seen from all corners of Baghdad. Next to the palace stood the Great Mosque. Other buildings in the Round City included various public offices such as the treasury, armory, chancery, the land tax office, the chamberlain's office, and the palaces of the younger sons of the caliph [p. 156].

These examples illustrate, once again, how the world view and cosmology of a culture, which include orientations to vertical and horizontal dimensions as well as attitudes about the universe and the world, are manifested in one form or another in the places that people create. Thus, culture and environment, as well as having mutual impact, have a unity and coherence that exist at many levels of functioning—perceptions and cognitions, behaviors, and environmental places.

Variability in the physical design of cities is as evident in modern cities as it is in ancient communities. Grid patterns, spoke patterns, circular arrangements appear in a bewildering variety in many modern cities. For example, Washington, D.C., was designed in the 18th century by the Frenchman Pierre L'Enfant, under the sponsorship of Thomas Jefferson. The city, planned as a symbol of the newly founded republic, had the Capitol Building at the center, diagonal avenues radiating from the Capitol, streets arranged in a grid system, and numerous circles and squares. As described in earlier chapters, Salt Lake City, Utah, the original Western settlement of the Mormon pioneers, was laid out according to a perfect grid system, with street designations specified precisely by east-west and north-south directions, all oriented around the Mormon Temple at the center of the grid. Here we see, then, two radically different city designs, each symbolic of and representing in concrete form a different value system.

Of course, modern cities are not always so carefully planned. Many, such as Los Angeles, have simply grown helter-skelter with little, if any organization or preconceived sense of design. In Los Angeles, tract after tract of homes has appeared in response to population pressures; they extend toward the north, south, and east, one basis for their location being the elaborate freeway system that envelops and crisscrosses the region. There is also little sense of a psychological "center" or unity to

Los Angeles and little evidence of religious, political, or other symbolism (Lynch, 1960). In other cities, such as New York, Philadelphia, and Baltimore, the original designs were markedly affected by the bodies of water and rivers near which these cities were founded. They were initially located adjacent to water transportation routes and gradually spread inland, often in a piecemeal fashion. Such cities were shaped largely by land configurations and commercial convenience. Even recently the mountainous palisades on the New Jersey side of the Hudson River in New York have limited urban development along the shoreline. On the New York side, however, accessibility to the river permitted the early development of the city adjacent to the river.

In spite of the frequent lack of planning, cities sometimes exhibit orderliness at another level of analysis. In Los Angeles identifiable sections and local communities emerge and establish their own organization in the form of shopping malls, churches, parks. Even in seemingly confusing cities like Rome, one finds focal points and sections that have physical and psychological coherence. Or in a city like New York, especially Manhattan, physical design beyond the original city at the foot of Manhattan Island is organized on a reasonably systematic grid pattern. In addition, one finds identifiable sections of the city, each with its own physical and psychological unity. There are the Wall Street area, the West Side area along the Hudson River, the East Side area along the East River, the Midtown area with its centers of Times Square and Columbus Circle, the Central Park area, the uptown areas of Harlem, Washington Heights, and others. Thus, though not wholly planned (except for the grid arrangement of streets), Manhattan has several sections that have distinct qualities along both cultural and physical dimensions.

In summary, small and large and ancient and modern communities exhibit a variety of physical forms. Physical factors such as proximity to water affected the design of some; for others, population pressures were important. For still others, commercial, political, religious, and other cultural factors influenced the design.

A point to keep in mind is that we cannot assume that the physical layout used for cities evolved over history in a linear, step-by-step fashion, from one physical arrangement to another. There does not seem to be any orderly progression of city plans, nor do there appear to be increasingly "better" designs over history. Present-day cities are not "better" than ancient ones in beauty or social effectiveness. Although there certainly have been marked technological changes in city design and planning, there is no evidence that communities of the present or communities from our own culture are "better" or "more advanced" than those of other cultures or earlier historical periods. We prefer the perspective that, historically and contemporaneously, one can examine city designs as a reflection of a series of factors and processes that operate within cultures, including physical, environmental, economic, political, religious, and social variables.

CITIES AS REFLECTIONS OF A VARIETY OF FACTORS

In this section we will examine how cities, like houses and other places, mirror aspects of the life of their inhabitants. Specifically, we will analyze city design and functioning in relation to the following: (1) physical environment, including terrain, resources, and climate; (2) political and economic factors, such as defense and commerce; and (3) sociocultural factors, including religion, cosmology and world views, and social structure.

Physical Environment

In Chapter 7 we described how homes reflect (among other things) environmental factors such as climate, terrain, and physical resources. Similarly, communities and cities sometimes exhibit the influence of the natural environment. Even the simple temporary encampments of the Mbuti Pygmies reflect such factors. The selection of sites in naturally open clearings large enough to house a band and the positioning of hut openings toward the center may, in part, be attributed to the heavily vegetated forest; that is, the Pygmies must rely on natural clearings and on the protective value of facing their huts inward. And, as already noted, Eskimos' selection of village sites in the protective cover of mountains and near the sea that provides their food supply represents a simple adaptation to environmental factors. We also described the Cheyenne Indian encampments as being in a C-shaped arrangement, with the camp and tipi openings facing the east and the rising sun. While this arrangement fits well with Cheyenne religious values and cosmology, environmental factors may also be involved. For example, the sun striking the opening of a tipi provides a bit of early-morning warmth in the chilly western plains of the United States. And, since the wind blows from west to east in that part of the United States, having tipi openings face east is responsive to a second aspect of the physical environment. Fraser (1968) observed that certain groups of African Bushmen, a nomadic people who live in desert and swamp regions in southern Africa, have simple encampments arranged in a semicircle around the headman's hut. The headman usually locates his hut near a shade-providing tree, and this site serves as a meeting place for the men. Given the hot regions in which the Bushmen live, selection of a meeting site near a shady tree is an obvious adaptation to the physical environment. Among the Haida Indians of the Pacific Northwest, described earlier, houses were arranged in a line, often no more than 2 to 7 feet apart. Although this arrangement may reflect the strong social cohesion of these people, it is also possible that the tremendous wind velocities and rainfall in this region contributed to the massing of houses close together (Fraser, 1968).

Comparable examples also appear in more technologically complex societies. For example, many cities of medieval Europe and the New World of the 1700s and later were located near rivers and bodies of water for transportation and human use. This same environmental responsiveness appears in the history of many towns and cities in the United States. Salt Lake City and many others in the southwestern United States clearly illustrate responses to environmental conditions. With water crucial for farming and survival, the site chosen by the Mormon pioneers for Salt Lake City was close to a canyon that had a plentiful water supply. And the growth of the Salt Lake area was also undoubtedly based on five such canyon water supplies within relatively close proximity. In other parts of this region, one will invariably find towns and communities located near mountain canyons from which water flows. However, one must be careful not to attribute city and community locations and designs to environmental factors alone, a theme emphasized throughout this book. The design configurations of communities like Salt Lake City, for example, are partly independent of environmental factors and may be due as much to religious and cultural values as to anything else. Thus, the grid and coordinate system of Mormon communities in the Southwest is almost identical from town to town, regardless of their size and the particular terrain or environment in which they are located.

Similar practices exist in many large modern cities. London, New York, Philadelphia, Washington, D.C., and Tokyo were all founded near water—a key environmental factor necessary for transportation and survival. New York was first located at the tip of Manhattan Island with access to two rivers and the bay of New York. Baltimore and Philadelphia were founded near rivers and protected port areas. Many of these and other cities grew inland, often in a helter-skelter fashion, each new growth phase taking on the configuration of the surrounding water and land, much like contour lines on maps.

City designs have also been responsive to climate. For example, Montreal, Quebec, located in a region of severe winters, has begun to develop underground facilities. Malls, shopping areas, connections between various streets in the city are underground and have controlled climates and easy transportation access to outlying areas of the city. Minneapolis, Minnesota, and other cities in severe winter climates have built sheltered pedestrian passageways across streets from shopping area to shopping area.

In summary, communities and cities of all sizes reflect the physical environments in which they are located. Yet, as we have suggested repeatedly throughout this book, simplistic cause/effect statements are not sufficient. Cities, like homes, are complex places and are responsive to a variety of factors and forces, none of which acts alone.

Politics and Economics

Economic and political considerations undoubtedly contributed to the origin and design of cities, as people in agricultural societies organized to distribute crops, to gain protection, and to enter into mutually beneficial arrangements. Many communities, from small-scale traditional ones to larger cities, were located on higher ground, overlooking valleys and the surrounding terrain. The political implications of this practice are clear—for example, in medieval Europe. During this period instability and political upheaval were prevalent, with many regions carved up into small areas controlled by local kings or minor royalty. Defense was facilitated by having communities on higher terrain.

The cliff dwellings of the American Indians at Mesa Verde, Colorado, and elsewhere in the Southwest also reflect political factors in community siting. These communities of the 9th to 11th centuries often housed several hundred people and were located in openings formed by erosion in the walls of giant gorges and canyons. The openings were 60 to 100 feet high and hundreds of feet long and deep. Farming was done on a plateau far above the community and reached by steps carved into the rock walls. A unique protective system was designed into the series of steps. By beginning on the wrong foot, one would eventually get trapped in the middle of the climb, with feet tangled. Therefore, a stranger had a good chance of getting into trouble high above the canyon floor and on rather sheer walls.

Walls or other physical boundaries are vivid symbols of political and economic factors in relation to community design. In community after community in Africa one finds "compounds," or clusters of huts and storage buildings surrounded by a stockade wall or connected by fences or barriers. For example, in the Cameroons, Africa, several families will form a circular community with men's and women's huts on the outer perimeter interspersed with smaller huts that serve as kitchens. Protective fencing, scrub growth, and thickets are also located between huts. The headman's hut and granaries are located in the center of the community, and there is usually only a single entry to the compound (Fraser, 1968). In other communities walls are built of wood, stone, dirt, or other materials. Some traditional communities, such as those of the Gbande in Liberia, Africa, have both a wall and a ditch surrounding towns (Fraser, 1968). As another example, villages of certain American Indian cultures in the southeastern United States were surrounded by stockades built of upright logs or thin tree trunks. And, of course, there are the well-known stockade forts built by White settlers during the westward expansion of the 1800s in the United States.

In medieval Europe many towns were encircled by high walls and towers, with ramparts and walkways located along the wall for surveillance and defense against invasion. An interesting illustration of the interplay of political, technological, and economic factors in community design is the switch from fortified hilltop castles to walled cities as a defensive strategy in Europe. The development of the cannon made the hilltop fortress less defensible. As a result, many ruling noblemen moved to residences in the center of protected or walled cities. Walls also played a role in the economic life of a community, since taxes and regulation of market activities could be managed by controlling access to the city. Similarly, walls and stockades in many traditional societies served the function of housing livestock, grain, and other goods.

Walled cities have existed throughout history. Early Egyptian settlements were fortified with walls, as were the great cities of ancient China, the Middle East, and elsewhere. Tuan (1974) quoted from Herodotus, who described the ancient city of Babylon:

> [It] stands on a broad plain and is an exact square. In magnificence, no other city approaches it. It is surrounded, in the first place, by a broad and deep moat, full of water, behind which rises the wall. In the circuit of the wall are a hundred gates, all of brass [p. 163].

An extraordinary wall also surrounded Ch'ang-an, a Chinese city of the Han period (200 B.C.–220 A.D.). The city wall enclosed an area of about 30 square miles and housed within it nearly 1 million people (Tuan, 1974).

The internal design of communities also reflects economic and political factors. For example, in many traditional communities, ancient cities, and even some modern cities, political power is associated with "center." Among the Bushmen of Africa, the Yoruba of Nigeria, the South Nias people of Indonesia, and others, it is common for a chief, headman, or village ruler to live in the center of the community (Fraser, 1968). A similar practice existed in ancient China: the emperor was located at the center of a city. A somewhat different arrangement exists in Washington, D.C. Here, the Capitol Building, the home of Congress, is located at the center of the city, with streets and avenues radiating from it, as if to symbolize the central role of the people's representatives in the nation's affairs. Although the president is important, his residence is not at the center of the city.

Washington, D.C., also has a combination of diagonal and grid streets, along with squares, plazas, and circles. Finding one's way around the downtown area is mystifying even to the experienced traveler, and one invariably searches for a street that disappeared on an angle intersection or circle. Apparently L'Enfant, the designer of the city, had more in mind than esthetics with this design. Such a street pattern would be particularly useful in the event of invasion by an enemy, who, like the modern traveler, would be easily confused. And a knowledgeable defender would have a tremendous advantage in knowing shortcuts and escape and attack routes.

Community design is also often related to economic considerations. As noted above, among certain cultures in Africa, livestock are important resources and are placed in the middle of compounds, whereas in other societies granaries are. In many medieval towns, marketplaces were in or near town centers, easily accessible to inhabitants. Shops were located along the main streets leading to the city gates and the marketplace. Furthermore, homes were also located as close to the main streets as possible (Saalman, 1968). In fact, well-to-do people in medieval towns lived on the main streets around the town square, and the poor lived away from the town center—the opposite of the pattern in many modern cities.

There are many other examples of city designs that are responsive to economic and commercial values. For example, the ancient Chinese city of Hang-chou was primarily a commercial center. Tuan (1974) described it as follows:

> The Southern Sung capital was established in Hang-chou, a city that gained commercial importance before it acquired its exalted political status as the seat of the emperor.
>
> The walls of Hang-chou were irregular in shape. It had thirteen unevenly spaced gates instead of the prescribed twelve. The principal pig market, rather than the residence of the emperor occupied the city's center. . . . By contrast with the sparsely used avenues of Ch'ang-an, those of Hang-chou teemed with pedestrians, horse riders, people in sedan chairs and in passenger carts. Besides roads, the city was served by canals, with their heavy traffic of barges loaded with rice, boats weighed down with coal, bricks, tiles, and sacks of salt. More than one hundred bridges spanned the canal system within the city walls, and where these were hump-backed and joined busy arteries, they caused traffic to congest into seething masses of carriages, horses, donkeys, and porters. . . . The streets of Hang-chou were lined with shops and dwellings that opened to the traffic. Off the Imperial Way, population density exceeded 325 persons per acre. The dearth of land forced the buildings to up to three and five stories. Commercial activity permeated the city and its suburbs: almost everywhere a visitor could see shops selling noodles, fruits, thread, incense and candles, oil, soya sauce, fresh and salt fish, pork, and rice. . . . The principal pig market was not far from the main artery. Several hundred beasts were butchered every day in slaughterhouses that opened soon after midnight and closed at dawn [p. 178].

How well this description might apply to some present-day cities, whose commercial activities seem to be of primary importance! In such communities growth and operation often seem unplanned and are directed largely at economic gain and commercial development—to the chagrin of citizen groups who fight, often unsuccessfully, against uncontrolled commercial growth. The importance of economic values is, to a great extent, a hallmark of modern American cities, whose governments and chambers of commerce readily adopt slogans that testify to the economic identities of the cities. American cities revel in their commercial identities: Milwaukee is the "Beer City"; New York is known as "Fun City"; Castroville, California, calls itself the "Artichoke Center of the World"; Phenix City, Alabama, is known as "Sin City"; Detroit is called the "Motor City"; Saint Louis is sometimes referred to as the "Gateway to the West."

The location of housing and workplaces is another aspect of urban designs in relation to economics. In the modern American city, most people do not live close to their work or to commercial centers. They commute long distances, and residential and commercial areas are often far apart. Downtown areas are dominated by office buildings and factories, with few residences. This arrangement is quite different from that in many traditional communities, where workplaces and housing were in the same or neighboring places. Even in larger cities, such as medieval towns, people lived very near their workplaces. And, as noted earlier, it was quite desirable to live close to the central marketplace, where much business was transacted. Similarly, in ancient Rome and Athens (Tuan, 1974) wealthy people lived adjacent to commercial establishments and directly alongside the poor. Nowadays we are more attuned to different "sections" of a city—for commerce, for certain ethnic groups, for the poor, for the wealthy.

Of course, the sectioning of cities is not unique to present times: it has existed in a variety of forms over the centuries. For example, the Chinese imperial city of Ch'ang-an (200 B.C.–220 A.D.) was divided into 100 or 200 wards, or sections, that were walled off from one another. Another example appeared in the British colonial period in India in the late 1800s (Rapoport, 1977). Here the British fostered city designs which separated them from the local populations and which perpetuated different living arrangements between caste groups in Indian society.

Religion, Cosmology, and World Views

A society's religious beliefs, cosmological beliefs, and world views are often salient in city and community designs, historically and cross-culturally. Many modern cities do not reflect such values, but traditional communities and those of earlier periods of history frequently included religious and cosmological values in their design.

An interesting interplay of political, religious, and cosmological values and beliefs appears in the village layouts of the South Nias Islanders of Indonesia (Fraser, 1968). For these people, religious values are organized around a series of polarities: sky/earth, sun/moon, male/female, upriver/downriver. These opposites are represented in two brother deities who complement each other and who are associated with the upperworld and the underworld. These cosmological and religious values are carried over directly into the social structure of villages, with the chief, a quasi-religious leader, associated with the upperworld and the ordinary people associated with the underworld. Furthermore, these values are explicit in village designs. South Nias villages are usually sited on hilltops, perhaps for defense but also because the village symbolizes the upperworld. Within the village a main street forms the axis of the community. The chief's house, typically decorated in an elaborate fashion, is located at the higher end of the street, as a symbol of his divine status and as a representation of the upperworld. As such, the chief's end of the village is identified with life, aerial animals, and the sun. The "lower" end of the village symbolizes and is decorated with animals representative of the underworld—snakes, crocodiles, lizards. The typical village is organized around a large plaza, at the end of which is a paved entrance to the community. Altars, columns, and stone seats dedicated to ancestors are often located in front of the homes of the important residents and face onto the main street. In planning a new village, a priest selects the site, performs certain rituals, and lays out the dimensions of the plaza, using pieces of the symbolic and holy "world tree" as markers and a central point, the "navel of the village," as the anchoring point. Thus, the siting, layout, and design of a South Nias village fits well with religious and symbolic values of this culture.

An example of the interplay of religious, cosmological, sex-role, and political facets of culture appears in the village design of the Dogon people of Mali, Africa (Fraser, 1968, 1974; Rapoport, 1969a). The ideal Dogon village is arranged in the shape of the human body. The "head" of the village contains the toguna, or men's meeting house, which is the first building constructed in the village, attesting to its importance. It is usually an open rectangular structure supported on eight stone or wooden posts and is intended to be both imposing and esthetic. The toguna is used by the council of elders, who meet in it in seated positions (it is too low to stand up in). According to Dogon values, a seated arrangement ensures rational and deliberate thinking. The toguna is also a place where young men are taught the important moral and cosmological values of the culture. Although women are not permitted to enter this building, their presence exists symbolically. The pillars supporting the toguna represent four female and four male ancestors, and it is believed that their spirits visit daily to renew the wisdom of the place.

The women's menstrual houses are located at the position of the "hands" of the village. These buildings are also erected early in the establishment of a village, and they are quite important to the community. The menstrual houses are round buildings whose entranceways are decorated with figures and sculptured forms. Women live in these huts during their menstrual periods, relatively isolated from the community. Men are usually not permitted to enter or even to repair the menstrual huts. However, as with the toguna council house, the spirits of dead men are believed to visit the menstrual houses. Furthermore, certain decorations on the building symbolize both male and female roles in the culture.

Other aspects of the design of Dogon communities are in accord with religious and cosmological values. For example, the homes of the village leaders are located at the "chest" of the community plan; religious altars are found at the position of the genitals; and the "feet" of the village contain religious symbols.

Religious and cosmological concepts have also affected the design of large communities, such as ancient Chinese and Middle and Near Eastern cities, as well as later cities of Europe and elsewhere. Wheatley (1971) posited a theory that urban forms in ancient history did not evolve mainly from political or economic factors, but derived from fundamental theological and cosmological values. He hypothesized that cities began as "centers," often in the form of shrines honoring deities and gods, priests, kings, or folk heroes. Such "centers" were symbolically marked, perhaps in simple ways at first. Gradually they became more elaborate and included platforms, temples, palaces, pyramids, and other structures. Many of these ceremonial centers were the residences of priests, kings, or rulers; others were simply shrines and monuments. For some cultures, such as the ancient Mayans and Greeks, these ceremonial centers were used only occasionally and were believed to be the homes of gods. In some instances a shrine was surrounded by residences and served both living and ceremonial functions.

The imperial city of Ch'ang-an in ancient China is a good example of the role of religion and world views in city design (Tuan, 1974; Wheatley, 1971). Although it did not meet all the ideal specifications of imperial cities, it met some. These general rules, set down in ritual books, were as follows:

> As prescribed . . . a royal city should have the following characteristics: orientation to the cardinal points; a square shape girdled by walls; twelve gates in the walls to represent the twelve months; an inner precinct to contain the royal residences and audience halls; a public market to the north

of the inner enclosure; a principal street leading from the south gate of the palace enclosure to the central south gate of the city wall; two sacred places, the royal ancestral temple and the altar of the earth on either side of the principal street. The meaning of the design is clear. The royal palace at the center dominates the city and, symbolically, the world. It separates the center of profane activity, the market, from the centers of religious observances. The ruler faces south in his audience hall, where he receives officials and conducts public business. His back is turned literally to the market [Tuan, 1974, p. 165].

Another example, later in the history of China, involves Peking of the 16th century, when it served as the imperial capital. In the following description, note the interplay of cosmological, political, and religious values and world views:

The Chinese imperial capital was a diagram of the universe. The palace and the principal north-south axis stood for the Polar star and the celestial meridian. The Emperor in the interior of his courts surveyed the southerly world of men. In Peking's Forbidden City the Wu or Meridian Gate pierced the south wall. The Emperor was borne through the Meridian Gate into the Forbidden City while civil and military officials entered by the east and west gates. The Four Quadrants in the heavenly vault became the Four Directions or Four Seasons of the terrestial grid. Each side of the square may be identified with the daily position of the sun or with each of the four seasons. The east side, with the blue dragon as its symbol, was the locus of the rising sun and spring. The south side corresponded to the sun at its zenith and to summer, symbolized by the red phoenix of *yang* ascendance. At the west side the white tiger stood for autumn, twilight, weapon, and war. The cold region of the north lay behind man's back, and was symbolized by hibernating reptiles, the color black, and *yin* element of water [Tuan, 1974, p. 167].

These examples show once again the interplay and close relationship of cognitions, perceptions, and world views, as discussed in earlier chapters, with the environmental places that people create.

Several modern cities also illustrate the role of religious values in community design. The medieval cities of Europe often had a church or cathedral at a central location. In Rome one finds churches and religious monuments throughout the city that serve as neighborhood focal points. Moreover, Rome has a separate holy city, the Vatican. This modern version of a temple city is analogous to the ancient Mayan, Aztec, and Incan cities of the Americas and to holy cities in Thailand, Cambodia, and elsewhere. Salt Lake City, Utah, was also designed with religious values in mind. The Mormon Temple is at the center of the city, it faces east toward the rising sun, and it is located on a square from which all other streets are designated.

AN OVERVIEW

In this chapter, just as for homes in Chapters 7 and 8, we described how community and city designs reflect a variety of factors—physical environment, politics, economics, cultural beliefs, and social systems. It is tempting to search for simple cause/effect determinants of community and city designs, as it was for housing. However, we approach community design as an extremely complex issue and one not understandable in terms of variables considered one at a time. Not only is there a complicated interplay of factors that contribute to community design, but there are shifts over time in the relative importance of various influences. As a result, it may be necessary to treat communities as complex unities closely woven into the whole fabric of society. For example, in many traditional societies and in smaller communities, social, economic, political, religious, and environmental factors all function in a unified way. Among the South Nias Islanders, the Bushmen of Africa, and other traditional societies, community design is visibly linked all at once with several facets of life. The location and layout of villages are based on longstanding traditions that incorporate political, religious, cosmological, and other variables within a single unity of design. Such factors are not separable; they operate together as a system.

Several characteristics of traditional societies may have contributed to such an integrated picture—the small size of these communities and cultures, their technological simplicity, the relatively unchanging quality of traditional cultures, and their subsistence level of existence. In more technologically complex, changing, and large-scale communities, one often sees the fragmentation and separate operation of political, religious, and other factors in urban design. Thus, some cities were originally designed as religious centers and were not geared for residential or commercial use. In other cities, commerce dominated; in still others, residential facilities have been most important. In addition, in large-scale communities, historically and presently, various factors may operate at different times to affect city design. For example, the political or religious values sometimes reflected in plazas and buildings are often vestiges of earlier periods of the history of a city. They may serve as landmarks of a bygone era, almost museum pieces.

If any quality is common to present-day cities, it is that many of them seem to serve primarily commercial and economic functions. New cities or redevelopment plans emphasize business districts and buildings and centers of commerce and industry. With the advent of mass-transportation technology—automobiles, rail and subway systems, freeways—cities are characterized by increasing separation between residential areas, business areas, and political and other centers. The lives of people in modern urban settings often involve a multiplicity of roles and places. People function as parents in one place, as businesspeople in another and as religious worshipers in still another. City and community designs often reflect these different roles through the physical separation of places, with commercialism and economics an increasingly visible urban function. Thus, perhaps because of their size and technological complexity and because of rapid cultural changes, modern cities do not always reflect a unity of factors in their design. New planned communities and futuristic cities, to be described in Chapter 11, have tried explicitly to achieve a unified set of functions in their design, at least in the minds of the planners. In any case, it is important to realize that city design reflects the complex interplay of religion, commerce, politics, and other factors; one cannot easily reduce the matter to one or even a few simple principles. Instead, communities and cities, like homes and other places, mirror a variety of influences, any one or any combination of which may be crucial in different cultural and environmental circumstances and in different historical periods.

SUMMARY

This was the first of three chapters that examine communities and cities from a cultural perspective. A central theme was that communities and urban settings embody a complex interweaving of a variety of factors, including environmental characteristics, religion and world views, politics, economics, and other aspects of social systems.

We described various cities and communities historically and cross-culturally and illustrated how they mirrored various environmental and cultural variables. Thus, an Indonesian village or a Cheyenne Indian camp circle could be described in terms of a variety of climatic, economic, social, and cultural variables. Similarly in larger cities; for example, in ancient China the emperor, a political and religious figure, was located at the psychological and physical center of the city, and elaborate attention was given to the design of streets and gates in accord with religious values, cosmology, agriculture, nature, and politics.

Modern cities, especially in the United States, do not seem to reflect so unified an interplay of such factors. Perhaps because of this nation's geographic isolation, political unity, and eclectic religious values, one rarely sees surrounding walls, religious values, or related factors as central to community design. In fact, modern U.S. cities seem more oriented to commercial development as a central value. Except for Washington, D.C., and the central location of government buildings in many cities, even the role of political values in city design seems minimal. Thus, in large-scale, complex, and ever-changing cities of the past and present, the contribution of various factors to urban design is quite complex, some factors assuming more importance in some settings and at different times in history than other factors.

The next two chapters continue the analysis of community and urban settings. Chapter 10 examines day-to-day life in modern cities and how people cope with, adapt to, and manage their lives in urban settings. Chapter 11 looks toward the future and presents some futuristic designs proposed by urban planners.

Chapter 10

LIVING IN CITIES

In this chapter we analyze the dynamics of everyday life in cities in relation to such questions as "How do people cope with and adapt to life in cities? What are the stresses and difficulties they face in urban settings? Is city life 'good' or 'bad' for the average person? What physical and psychological prices do people pay for successful or unsuccessful adaptation to urban life?" These questions have occupied the attention of scholars, laypersons, politicians, and social reformers for years. Unfortunately, there are no simple answers. Since the beginnings of modern sociology and psychology, scholars have offered a bewildering array of theories and data on life in cities and its impact on the well-being of people. At one extreme, some theories state that city life is bad for people. It is hypothesized to be stressful and to lead to crime, mental illness, and an assortment of social evils. At the other extreme, some theories argue that urban life is invigorating, stimulating, and growth-enhancing. In between are a variety of views to the effect that city life is sometimes good and sometimes bad, that it is all right for some people but not for others, and that it requires certain coping mechanisms to handle adequately stress, noise, and high population density.

The first part of the chapter examines representative theories about city life that social scientists have advocated at one time or another over the last hundred years. The second part describes some of the stresses and social pathologies that scholars and laypersons have examined in relation to city life, especially the problem of crowding.

The third part of the chapter presents a dialectic analysis of cities and communities. In this part, our thesis will be that city life involves an interplay of various oppositional forces: individuality/community, homogeneity/diversity, and order/disorder. And it is not that a particular amount of homogeneity or diversity, individuality or community, order or disorder is absolutely and unequivocally harmful or beneficial. Rather, we will propose that it is the ability of a person or a group to regulate each aspect of these dialectic polarities that bears on human well-being in cities. This theoretical perspective is similar to the analysis of privacy in

Chapter 4, where we reasoned that human well-being is related to a person's ability to regulate the level of interaction, not to have some absolute level of contact with others. Therefore, the question for us is not whether cities involve too much or too little contact with others, too much or too little diversity of experiences, or too much disorder or order in an absolute sense. Rather, it is whether people can regulate that stimulation, to obtain more or less homogeneity or diversity, individuality or community, or order or disorder when they desire it. But more on this later. First, we will examine some general theoretical approaches to life in cities that have been proposed over the past several decades.

THEORIES OF LIFE IN CITIES

Claude Fischer (1976), an urban sociologist, recently summarized three major sociological and social-psychological theories about life in cities. The oldest approach, *determinist theory,* states that urban settings act directly on their inhabitants and that certain characteristics of cities can lead to social and personality disorders and to deviant behavior. According to this theory, cities *cause* certain social pathologies. A more recent position, *compositional theory,* hypothesizes that urban settings do not directly affect social behavior. Rather, the crucial factor affecting behavior is the ethnic, national, or other qualities of subgroups in cities. Hence, crowding, city size, and other physicalistic variables are not as important to the quality of urban life as are culture, family organization, and neighborhood social structure. The third approach, *subcultural theory,* is an integration of the two preceding theories. Subcultural theory accepts the impact on people of urban size, diversity, and population concentration. And it recognizes that such physical factors facilitate the creation of new subcultures, affect existing groups, and also bring subcultures into contact with one another, generating a new blend of social structure. Thus, subcultural theory attempts to use both determinist theory and compositional theory. We now consider each of these approaches in detail.

Determinist Theories

Determinist theories of city life were first proposed by German sociologists of the late 19th century. Their central theme was that the large size of cities, the variety of people who were forced into contact with one another, and the diversity of urban experiences and stimulation had a marked impact on the lives of people—as individuals, families, and cultural groups. Determinist theorists believed that these features of city life often led to negative outcomes, such as alienation, poor physical and mental health, breakdown of the family, increased crime, and deterioration of the larger social system. According to determinist theories, cities and urban life acted *directly* on people, often in negative ways.

The German sociologist Georg Simmel wrote an essay on urban life that represents early determinist thinking (1950, p. 410). He said that an important factor in urban life involves "the intensification of nervous stimulation." This means, in modern parlance, that city dwellers are exposed to a tremendous variety and amount of stimulation, perhaps to the point of overload. According to Simmel, the tempo of city life is overwhelming, as people are bombarded with stimulation, noise, smells, and the hustle and bustle of activity. One potential result of this overload is interference with people's ability to cope with their day-to-day lives. A second facet of urban living in Simmel's analysis is that city life is built around business, exchange of commodities, trading, and other economic matters. Economics and money dominate people's lives, Simmel stated, and people become merely exchangers of goods and services, not whole personalities. Furthermore, Simmel theorized that city living requires a specific reorganization of day-to-day life:

> The relationships and affairs of the typical metropolitan usually are so varied and complex that without the strictest punctuality in promises and services the whole structure would break down into an inextricable chaos. Above all, this necessity is brought about by the aggregation of so many people with such differentiated interests, who must integrate their relationships and activities into a highly complex organism. If all clocks and watches in Berlin would suddenly go wrong in different ways, even if only by one hour, all economic life and communication of the city would be disrupted for a long time. . . . Thus, the technique of metropolitan life is unimaginable without the most punctual integration of all activities and mutual relations into a stable and impersonal time schedule [p. 413].

Simmel also hypothesized that the city-dweller must develop a "blasé attitude" in order to survive. He or she must react to others with coolness, detachment, and aloofness and with the head, not the heart. Thus, city-dwellers often ignore one another, avoid getting caught up in others' affairs, act independently, and assume an air of reserve. All this happens, Simmel stated, so that urbanites can survive in the complex, fragmented, high-stimulation environment of cities. Simmel also theorized that city residents act so as to become separate and distinct individuals. To establish their individuality, urbanites try to become specialists in their jobs, and they develop unique dress styles and behavioral mannerisms. One result of this quest for uniqueness, Simmel stated, is that people in cities run the risk of becoming less and less "whole" persons and more and more superficial role players and specialists. At the same time, Simmel also noted that urban settings have many positive features, including cultural stimulation, diversity of experiences, and opportunities for growth and change. However, the overall thrust of his thinking and of that of other determinist theorists of the period was that city life directly acts on people, and generally in negative ways.

The early German determinist approach was readily adopted by sociologists in the United States, and it dominated thinking about urban settings for several decades. For example, Wirth (1938) set forth the theme that urban life involved a stimulus overload, required extraordinary individual adaptations, and could eventually lead to various pathologies and aberrations. He stated that the density, heterogeneity, and high stimulation of cities forced people into impersonality, detachment, and disregard of others' welfare. And he believed that there were serious outcomes of such adaptation—anxiety, stress, mental illness, and breakdowns in social bonds and families. Furthermore, Wirth (and others) theorized that enclaves would develop in cities, with a consequent loss of community feeling and a weakening of the fabric of society. As the social cohesion of the family and community slips away, Wirth said, people become alienated, feel alone, and develop maladaptive behavior. Eventually larger-scale social pathologies appear, such as crime, juvenile delinquency, divorce, and mental-health problems.

The determinist view is still an important force in sociological and psychological theorizing about cities. For example, Milgram (1970) recently analyzed coping responses to the "psychic overload," or "stimulus overload," that presumably occurs in urban settings. He proposed a number of such coping mechanisms: (1) *Allocation of less time to each input,* resulting in people's being brusque with one another, resolving social contacts hastily, and not allowing extra time for civilities or leisurely interaction. (2) *Disregard of low-priority inputs,* or attending only to that which is important to oneself. Others are not helped readily; they are ignored, pushed, jostled, and treated almost as objects and not as people. (3) *Shifting burdens to others,* such as nondelivery of goods by stores, requiring people to perform their own services, and becoming more specialized on a job. (4) *Blocking off stimulation,* such as having unlisted telephone numbers, being unfriendly and not receptive to strangers or to those seeking one's services, and use of screening devices such as signs and closed doors. (5) *Diminishing intensity of stimulation by filtering devices,* such as keeping social contacts at superficial levels and cutting off those who attempt to be intimate. (6) *Creation of specialized institutions,* such as police and welfare agencies, that take care of people's problems and thereby protect citizens at large from being responsible for others. The result of all this, Milgram states, is a separation of people from one another and a tone to city life that fits the stereotypes of urbanites as cold, detached, and aloof.

In summary, determinist theories emphasize the following: (1) The density, heterogeneity, and hectic pace of cities act directly on people. (2) The effects of urban life are not always positive. In fact, determinist theories emphasize the deleterious qualities of city living. (3) City-dwellers cope with and adapt to urban settings by means of a variety of behavioral mechanisms, often involving impersonality, detachment, and lack of concern for others. (4) There are several costs associated with such coping and adaptation—personality disorders, anomie and alienation of people from one another, social disorganization such as crime and delinquency, and family breakdowns.

Compositional Theories

Compositional theories of city life have recently been proposed by a number of sociologists, such as Gans (1962, 1967), and by anthropologists, such as Lewis (1959, 1961). Their view is that people everywhere live and function in small primary and secondary groups—families, extended kin groups, neighborhoods, and small communities. Even in highly populated areas, where people have frequent contacts with strangers, the important parts of their lives are generally restricted to small groups of family members, neighbors, and friends. Compositional theories, unlike determinist theories, believe that such factors as city size, heterogeneity, and density have little direct effect on the average person: "It matters little to the average kith-and-kin group whether there are 100 people in the town or 100,000; in either case the basic dynamics of that group's social relationships and its members' personalities are unaffected" (Fischer, 1976, p. 34).[1]

Gans' compositional theory rests on two important points. First, people who live in cities are often different to begin with from those who choose to live in the country. Some people migrated to urban areas because they wanted what cities had to offer, such as freedom, stimulation, and economic opportunity. Therefore, differences between city and rural life may not be due so much to physical factors of size and density as to the types of people who elected to live in one place or the other. There is some evidence to support this compositional position in studies of rural-to-urban migration in the United States and elsewhere. For example, Chemers, Ayman, and Werner (1978) found that migrants to the city in contemporary Iran generally held positive opinions about such aspects of city life as social freedom, expanded women's roles, and job opportunities, while those who stayed in villages valued more traditional aspects of life, such as religious solidarity and extended family relationships. Furthermore, those who were disappointed by city life and returned to their villages expressed a desire for more traditional values.

[1]This and all other quotations from this source are from *The Urban Experience* by Claude S. Fischer. Reprinted by permission of Harcourt Brace Jovanovich, Inc.

A second aspect of Gans' thesis is that the stimulation, heterogeneous population, and high density of the city do not operate on people directly, as determinist theories say. On the contrary, Gans (1962) maintains, the city is a collection of "urban villages," or small, homogeneous neighborhoods that re-create village forms of association. Compositional theories do not state that physical factors have no effect at all on people's lives. Rather, they hypothesize that size, density, and stimulation have no *direct* effects on people. Instead, such factors may operate indirectly. For example, population size may make it possible for an ethnic group to develop its own economic and political power base in a community and thereby enhance job and other opportunities for individuals.

Fischer (1976) summed up the difference between the determinist and compositional views:

> Both emphasize the importance of social worlds in forming the experiences and behaviors of individuals, but they disagree sharply on the relationship of urbanism to the viability of those personal milieus. Determinist theory maintains that urbanism has a direct impact on the coherence of such groups, with serious consequences for individuals. Compositional theory maintains that these social worlds are largely impervious to ecological factors, and that urbanism has no serious, *direct* effects on groups or individuals [p. 35].

Subcultural Theory

The third approach described by Fischer (1976), and the one he espouses, is *subcultural theory*. This is an interactionist position that integrates the determinist and compositional theories. It agrees with the compositional view that the lives of city-dwellers generally occur within particular ethnic, occupational, religious, or other groups. Unlike compositional theory, however, subcultural theory argues that ecological aspects of cities—size, density, heterogeneity—also have an impact on people. There are, it is stated, complex interactions between various ecological qualities of cities and the functioning of subcultural groups. For example, Fischer (1976) hypothesized that large urban centers contribute to the formation of subcultures and neighborhood enclaves by permitting the development of a "critical mass" of people with common interests and values. Such a subcultural group becomes a network of social support and can provide close, emotional relationships for its members. Thus, cities give rise to all sorts of subcultures, based on ethnic, religious, occupational, and other characteristics. Some of these can be unusual subcultures—such as homosexuals, criminals, and religious sects—that might never arise in less populated places because of the absence of a critical mass. Fischer (1976) says:

> Sufficient numbers allow them to support institutions—clubs, newspapers, and specialized stores, for example—that serve the group, allow them to have a visible and affirmed identity, to act together in their own behalf, and to interact extensively with each other. For example, let us suppose that one in every thousand persons is intensely interested in modern dance. In a small town of 5,000 that means there would be, on the average, five such persons, enough to do little else than to engage in conversation about dance. But in a city of one million, there would be a thousand—enough to support studios, occasional ballet performances, local meeting places, and a special social milieu. . . . The same general process of critical mass operates for artists, academics, bohemians, corporate executives, criminals, computer programmers—as well as for ethnic and racial minorities [p. 37].

Urban subcultures often come into contact, sometimes enhancing one another and sometimes engaging in conflict because they compete for certain locations or services. Thus, the aloof, detached, impersonal styles of social interaction that determinist theorists described may indeed occur in relation to strangers and out-group members. However, subcultural theory reasons that warm, emotionally rich, personal styles of contact also occur, particularly among members of a subgroup.

In summarizing subcultural theory, Fischer (1976) stated:

> Subcultural theory is thus a synthesis of the determinist and compositional theories: like the compositional approach, it argues that urbanism does *not* produce mental collapse, anomie, or interpersonal estrangement; that urbanites at least as much as ruralites are integrated into viable social worlds. However, like the determinist approach, it also argues that cities *do* have effects on social groups and individuals—that the differences between rural and urban persons have other causes than the economic, ethnic, or life-style circumstances of those persons [p. 38].

Subcultural theory fits nicely with our thinking because it emphasizes the mutual impact of culture, environment, and social processes. We adopted the view that cultural and environmental factors influence each other and that they function as a unity. We would therefore expect that, as subcultural theory states, different cultures will evolve alternative life-styles and uses of the physical environment in urban settings.

The next section of the chapter examines a specific and popular problem of urban life—crowding.

CROWDING AND LIFE IN CITIES

For hundreds of years, social and political philosophers have speculated about how crowding in cities affects people's lives. In the past five decades, sociologists, geographers, and, more recently, psychologists have addressed this issue through empirical research.

The earliest empirical work on crowding was done by sociologists who were strongly influenced by the determinist theories of city life. Beginning in the 1920s, they tried to identify social pathologies that stemmed from population density, such as mental disease, crime, and various forms of social disorganization. For example, Schmid (1960a, 1960b) found high population densities and high crime rates in central-city areas of Minneapolis and Seattle and lower crime rates in the less heavily populated suburbs of the cities. In Honolulu, Schmitt (1957) found that population density was highly correlated with juvenile delinquency and adult crime. Data for mental illness, suicides, and density yielded similar results.

There are several problems with interpretation of these findings. First, the data on which they are based are correlational. That is, they involve statistical covariations between population density and indicators of social patholólgy, and one cannot properly conclude that density *caused* social disorganization. Alternative explanations could have accounted for the correlations. For example, density is not the only variable that distinguishes the center of a city from its suburbs. Factors such as the inhabitants' physical health, economic status, health facilities, and education also often differentiate central-city and suburban areas, and these factors might be related to social pathology. Therefore, although these studies are suggestive, they do not automatically point to the effect of density on social processes.

A second problem is that these early studies treated density in an undifferentiated fashion. Typical measures of density were persons per acre, persons per census tract, persons per nation, and structures per acre or per census tract—all of which involve relatively large geographical units. Only occasionally was density based on persons or families per dwelling unit. Such measures might have given insight into the relation among density, intimate face-to-face contacts, and the well-being of people.

A third feature of early research was its emphasis on social system *outcomes* rather than on social *processes*. Crime, mental disorders, death, and disease are outcomes, or end products, of a history of social experience. But what happens between people in high- and low-density situations on a day-to-day basis? In many respects early researchers approached crowding as a broad social system problem, not as an individual or interpersonal phenomenon. They focused on how the whole society was affected by crowding, with only secondary concern for how individuals and families coped with and responded to population concentration.

Beginning in the 1960s, sociological analyses shifted in methodological strategy, as exemplified in a study by Galle, Gove, and McPherson (1972). First, Galle and associates used a variety of population density indicators: (1) number of persons per room in a dwelling unit (the smallest and most directly interpersonal measure of density), (2) number of rooms per housing unit, (3) number of housing units per structure (for example, apartments per apartment house), and (4) number of residential structures per acre (the least directly interpersonal measure). Thus, they examined density indicators having different degrees of "closeness" to interpersonal relations. Second, this and other studies tried to account statistically for ethnic background, socioeconomic status, and other variables that in earlier studies might have obscured the relation between density and social pathology. Their results showed the highest association between *persons per room* and social pathology indicators—mortality, fertility, public assistance, and juvenile delinquency. Thus, the density measures that reflected social interaction most closely were the important ones. Galle and associates interpreted their results in terms of ongoing social processes that might have occurred in densely populated homes. For example, ill persons might not have obtained the quiet privacy they needed to recover, yielding high mortality rates; higher fertility might have resulted, in part, from difficulties in using birth-control techniques in dense homes; and children might have received less attention in larger families and might have had to rely more on peers for guidance, thereby contributing to juvenile delinquency. Although these were only after-the-fact interpretations and the results have not always been confirmed in other studies, the study is important because it focused on social processes that might mediate density/pathology relations: it tried to get closer to ongoing social interaction rather than treat population concentration as a vague producer of ultimate outcomes.

Other recent research has also given more attention to different measures of population concentration. For example, Marsella, Escudero, and Gordon (1970) examined the impact of persons per dwelling unit in Manila on psychosomatic symptomatology; Mitchell (1971) analyzed the relation between number of families per dwelling unit and marital satisfaction in Hong Kong; and Booth and Welch (1973) examined the relation of density to health and aggression in 65 countries.

In summary, recent sociological studies have taken a more sophisticated approach to the problem of crowding, and they have emphasized (1) differentiated analysis of density, with more attention given to the interpersonal, "micro" level of density, (2) interpersonal social processes that occur in high-density conditions rather than broad social outcomes alone, and (3) control of underlying variables that might account for density/pathology relations.

The upshot of this and other sociological research is that high population density may indeed be related to certain aspects of social pathology, but the effects are not simple, direct, or unequivocal. A multitude of other variables seem to be involved, there are many cases in which negative outcomes of high population density are absent or moderate, and the simple generalization that "crowding in cities is bad" is not universally substantiated. Furthermore, this work emphasizes the importance of treating population density as a complex variable that may operate differentially at social system, group, and interpersonal levels. For further discussion of sociologically oriented research see Altman (1975) and Fischer (1976).

There has also been a recent upsurge of research on crowding by psychologists in laboratory and field settings (see Altman, 1975; Baum & Epstein, 1978, for a summary of this research). In this work, attention has been given to the effects of crowding in face-to-face situations on stress, tension and discomfort, social interaction, and performance. This research is too voluminous to summarize here, and the effects of crowding are fairly complex, but one widespread finding of these psychologically oriented analyses bears on the theme of our analysis: people react to high density situations by means of a variety of coping mechanisms, whose successful or unsuccessful operation contributes to negative or neutral outcomes of high population density. This process is nicely illustrated in a series of studies by Baum and Valins (1977), who analyzed the reactions of college students who lived either in a crowded dormitory, where double rooms opened onto a common corridor, or in dormitories where six students shared a suite including living room and bathroom. Students in the crowded corridor arrangement not only showed more stress and dissatisfaction but used a series of coping mechanisms to regulate their social interaction in hallways and spent more time in their bedrooms, whereas suite occupants used their private lounge quite a bit. Corridor residents also indicated a greater desire to avoid social contact than suite residents did. In fact, corridor-dwellers more often avoided their dormitories and established friendships outside their residential setting, whereas suite residents tended to establish friendships within their dormitory.

A series of experiments also showed differences in social behavior outside the dormitory setting. For example, corridor residents sat farther away from strangers in a waiting room, engaged in less conversation, and looked at strangers less than suite residents did. This suggests that those living in the high-density situation had developed a general avoidance strategy toward others, even in situations outside their dormitory. Thus, crowding and excessive social contacts had apparently resulted in the adoption of coping reactions that were aimed at regulating contact with others. Baum and Valins also found that some corridor residents formed social groups in the dormitory and that these served to reduce stress and to make the living situation more acceptable.

From sociological and psychological research, only a small sample of which has been presented here, one can conclude that high population density sometimes does and sometimes does not have undesirable outcomes. The data also suggest that people often develop a series of mechanisms to regulate their interaction with others. In situations of high density, mechanisms may include withdrawal from others, avoidance of contact, and development of group structures to regulate interaction with others.

In some cases, the psychological and physical effects of regulating contact may be costly, consisting in longer-term stresses and strains (Altman, 1975). But how this happens and the exact circumstances under which coping mechanisms work or do not work are only partly understood.

How do people in different cultures respond to crowding? For the purposes of our analysis, an important set of coping mechanisms to regulate crowding involves cultural norms and behaviors. For example, several writers have suggested that Japanese society illustrates the skillful management of crowded living (Canter & Canter, 1971; Hall, 1966; Michelson, 1970; Rapoport, 1977). At an interpersonal level the Japanese have developed flexible use of their homes. With movable walls and partitions, the same area can serve several functions, whereas in the American tradition a room often has only one function. In traditional Japanese homes a room at different times can be an eating place, a recreation area, and perhaps even a sleeping place.

The Japanese also cope with limited space by miniaturizing parts of the environment and by fostering an attitude of pride in perfection of detail, as exemplified in their art and gardening practices—for example, bonsai. Japanese homes also shut out the neighborhood and city, which are often noisy and unkempt, by means of walls, careful siting of homes, and arrangement of interior spaces. Thus, a physical boundary is placed around a family group that literally walls off unwanted interaction, and the interior of the family environment is then richly differentiated by means of flexible use and decorative arrangements.

Rapoport (1977) also observed that Japanese cities have means for regulating contact with others and for controlling what appears to be a situation of stimulus overload. Some cities are divided into small neighborhood areas, perhaps to create a sense of scale with which people can identify. In these neighborhoods, places of eating, drinking, and entertainment are easily accessible and permit people to meet and interact on "neutral" ground, not in the extremely private residences. Somewhat similar mechanisms exist in other cultures. For example, in the Netherlands, a very densely populated small nation, Rapoport (1977) hypothesized that the distinct separation of towns from one another, with easily accessible open space in between, gives people a feeling that they can escape easily from densely populated areas. Rapoport also suggested that the Dutch customs of treasuring small things (like the Japanese custom), bicycling, and walking also reduce feelings of crowding, since the pace of life and rate of exposure to new information are markedly reduced.

In related analyses, Michelson (1970) and Mitchell (1971) observed that Hong Kong, a rather densely populated city, had a low incidence of social pathology, including diseases and family disorganization, as well as a relatively low death rate. They attributed this to styles of family functioning, social organization, and other cultural mechanisms for coping with high density. What might these cultural mechanisms be? Rapoport (1977) and others noted that many Oriental cultures have rather definite rules for interaction between men and women, high- and low-status people, and children and adults. Recall our earlier example of Chinese families in Malaysia (Anderson, 1972), where families who lived in communal arrangements had firm rules about access to each other's areas in the home and strict norms for children's behavior in relation to the other family, even to the point of punishing them for merely looking into the other family's space. Furthermore, people who were not in the immediate family could discipline others' children. In fact, this latter practice is quite common in many urban settings. One of us remembers the extremely crowded street of his childhood in New York City. Not only were games and other activities engaged in on the street, but it was an important place for socializing children. Almost any neighbor could arbitrate conflicts, reprimand a child, and serve as a liaison with a child's parents. Hence, in the midst of high population density, noise, and hustle and bustle, there were powerful mechanisms for controlling behavior and for teaching and enforcing social norms. Although an outsider might have viewed the street as chaotic and overcrowded, the residents saw it as a well-tuned, smoothly functioning subculture that had an elaborate set of rules, prescriptions, customs, and proper modes of behaving.

This is not to say that extremely limited space and substandard facilities are acceptable. Not at all. We mean only that in some instances cultural practices have evolved over the course of generations to permit people to cope with a variety of life circumstances, including population density. Such regulatory processes occur even in extreme circumstances. For example, Biderman, Louria, and Bacchus (1963) analyzed historical incidents of extreme overcrowding in slave ships, prisoner-of-war camps, immigrant ships, and elsewhere. They concluded that disease and social pathology were lowest where groups had a reasonable degree of social organization, often based on cultural practices. Cultural and other factors have an important mediating role in permitting effective coping with settings of high population density.

There has been other research on how individuals, families, and communities in different cultures develop cultural norms and practices for coping with highly dense settings. Rogler (1967) and Lewis (1959, 1961) used an anthropological perspective to describe coping reactions in crowded Latin American families. In certain city slums in Colombia and Peru, squatter families formed barrios (neighborhoods) by building shacks of scrap metal and by pirating electricity from neighboring areas (Rogler, 1967). Although they did not have community service facilities, formal civic organizations or a governance system, or sewage and garbage-collection systems, these small communities quickly developed their own social norms. Because the areas were densely populated, relationships among neighbors and matters of privacy became important. A norm of privacy gradually developed whereby people reacted strongly to others' noisiness or intrusion. In some instances children were kept inside, and families secluded themselves from others. Newcomers were received with extreme displeasure, often causing conflict and hostility even though no one had legal property rights. Lewis (1959) described a similar situation in a tenant community in Mexico, in which a norm developed that people did not visit one another's homes. This norm may have evolved because homes in the neighborhood were crowded or were not always nicely furnished. Or perhaps the norm was a way to cope with high population concentration and to provide at least one place to be alone with members of one's family and away from others. A similar practice exists in parts of India (Rosenberg, 1968), where small screened areas and corners are used by people who wish to be alone.

Munroe and Munroe (1972) and Munroe, Munroe, Nerlove, and Daniels (1969) studied three East African societies that varied widely in population density. The Logali had a density of 1400 persons per square mile; the Gusii, 700; the Kipsigis, 250. Questionnaires and psychological instruments revealed that the most densely populated group (1) had norms according to which holding hands with friends was avoided, (2) had the worst recall for interpersonal-affiliation words, and (3) tended to describe other family members in more negative terms. If one stretches the meaning of these data, the more crowded groups may have gradually developed cultural practices that involved avoidance of close contact with others, a devaluation of others, and a lowered desirability of affiliation activities—all of which reflect coping processes that may assist in controlling interpersonal boundaries, especially in response to heightened inputs from others.

Draper (1973) examined the effects of crowded living on the !Kung Bushmen of Southwest Africa. This hunting-and-gathering culture functions in loose kinship groups of about 150 people that are further divided into small bands of 15 to 40 people. The typical !Kung settlement has less than 200 square feet of living space per person, well below the "desirable standard" of 350 square feet in American culture. In village settings the huts of neighbors are so close that people can literally touch one another. During the day most of the people are in a small area, and social contact is quite high. Yet the !Kung seem to enjoy touching, close physical contact, and extensive social interaction. And they do not seem to suffer physically or psychologically from this high-density life. For example, the !Kung are quite free of biological stress indicators. Blood pressure is not especially high and does not rise with age, and blood-cholesterol levels are among the lowest in the world.

Draper (1973) attributed the seeming absence of stress outcomes to certain features of the social system. There is a norm among the !Kung that individuals or families may leave a settlement at any time to join another group or to establish a new group. The existence of social and family networks with other groups permits easy withdrawal, so that coming and going are not traumatic. Group affiliation is not necessarily permanent; the norm of free departure makes the handling of social conflicts an easy matter and gives people a sense of interaction control whenever necessary. Thus, interpersonal-boundary regulation seems to involve, in part, physical movement in and out of communities and contact with others.

In summary, our analysis of life in cities fits with many of the people/culture/environment linkages discussed throughout this book. The human ability to live successfully in a variety of physical environments—hot or cold ones, heavily or sparsely populated ones, mountains or deserts, or those poor or rich in resources—is a complex result of a variety of factors. To the extent that cultural practices exist to permit coping with circumstances, to the extent that people can regulate their contacts with one another, and to the extent that an appropriate blend of psychological, physical, and cultural processes can function, then people will mesh successfully with their environments. Accordingly, we view urban life as neither "good" nor "bad" in any universal sense. A satisfactory life in cities depends on a variety of factors—physical resources and facilities, space allocation within families, workable psychological and cultural coping mechanisms. Therefore, one must avoid simplistic conclusions of "good" or "bad" and instead conduct detailed analyses of the life circumstances of people in urban settings in relation to social, psychological, and cultural aspects of interaction. In this respect, then, we subscribe to the subcultural theory espoused by Fischer (1976). However, our thinking goes beyond this approach and also includes a dialectic perspective on urban life, described next.

A DIALECTIC ANALYSIS OF CITY LIFE

In examining urban living from a dialectic perspective, our basic thesis is that community and urban settings can be partly understood in terms of a dialectic interplay of a variety of factors. Just as for homes

(Chapters 7 and 8) and privacy (Chapter 4), we hypothesize a series of forces that function in an oppositional-tension system to yield a dynamic unity, these forces operating in a continually shifting balance in relation to one another. Sometimes these forces operate over long historical periods; sometimes they operate on a day-to-day basis or even within days. At times one side of an oppositional process may dominate; at other times the opposite pole may be more influential.

In particular, our analysis of city life will emphasize three dialectic processes: order/disorder, homogeneity/diversity, and individuality/community. Our hypothesis is that city living involves a continuous interplay of these (and perhaps other) processes, in which the strength of each dialectic opposite varies from one time and circumstance to another. Our goal, unlike that in many social science approaches, is *not* to undertake a unidirectional analysis that searches for the stable, unchanging qualities of cities. Rather, we hope to identify a few dialectic dimensions along which cities vary in a continual *process* of change and growth.

Order/Disorder

In the preceding chapter, we described how the design of some cities and communities throughout history and across cultures reflected cultural values related to religion, cosmology, politics, and the like. For example, the original design of Washington, D.C., specified a system of street coordinates originating at the Capitol Building, an expansive mall with stately buildings, and a blend of rectangular and angular streets, interspersed with circles and plazas, all orderly and planned in advance. To be sure, present-day Washington has such an image, at least to the tourists' and TV watchers' eyes. But modern Washington is simultaneously a place of disorder that in some respects borders on chaos. One sees unplanned growth, variety in living styles and homes, filth, and uncontrolled commercial development throughout the city—not only in outlying sections but in areas adjacent to the Capitol Building, the Supreme Court, art galleries, and other magnificent structures. Some neighborhoods are "jungles," where outsiders are in extreme danger; some residences, streets, and commercial establishments are in a state of disarray, and deterioration and slums abound. A person who visited these areas before other parts of the city would find it hard to believe that this was the Washington, D.C., whose image is conveyed as one of orderliness, planned design, and stately living. So, side by side, there are order and disorder—planned arrangements and life-styles coupled with uncertainty, confusion, and disarray.

Or consider the opposite side of the coin—for example, Los Angeles, California. This city is often depicted as chaotic, disorderly, and unplanned. In studies of its imageability (Chapter 3), no clear conception of Los Angeles emerged in people's minds (Lynch, 1960). It was perceived as a conglomerate of unregulated and unplanned sprawl. Its growth in the past 30 years reinforces this image, with community after community popping up here and there, with little focus or sense of order. However, there is an underlying quality of order amidst the disorder. Los Angeles is divided into smaller communities that have definable characteristics in the minds and activities of their residents. Many of these smaller communities have their own governance and tax structures, school systems, and police and fire departments. And their inhabitants, especially children and parent caretakers, tend to restrict their activities to the local community. Furthermore, the California freeway system, however chaotic it may appear to the outsider, actually structures the region, regulates access to its parts, and provides a kind of orderliness and stability to the whole area.

The same blend of order and disorder has occurred throughout history. For example, in Chapter 9 we described how many medieval cities of Western Europe were designed around a central square on which was located a church and/or a public building, with major streets coming out of the square, and with a wall surrounding the town. Furthermore, many of these towns had planners whose sole job was to ensure that additions and modifications to the community would be properly designed. All seemingly quite orderly and planned. But there existed simultaneously a substantial amount of disorder in the design and life-style of these medieval towns. For example, along major streets that connected the central square and the city gates, competition for commercial space was so extreme that buildings and shops were often jam-packed together and erected in helter-skelter fashion, some several stories high. Many such streets were dark and poorly lit, structures were often serious fire hazards, many buildings simply collapsed, streets were noisy, merchants erected large signs to attract customers that further blocked out light, waste products were often dumped into the streets without regard for sanitation, animals and children ran uncontrolled through the streets, rain turned the unpaved roads to mud, and noise was ever-present (Tuan, 1974). Chaos seemed to reign.

Even the design and arrangements of the walls, gates, and fortifications around medieval cities exhibited elements of disorder. Rothenberg, Germany, for example, has both inner and outer walls. As the city grew following construction of its first wall, homes and commercial activities sprouted up outside the city, often near the main gates and around the wall. Eventually an outer wall was built to incorporate what had grown up sporadically outside the original city limits. The inner wall was allowed to deteriorate, and some parts were actually knocked down. However, several sections of the old wall still exist and serve as monuments; other sections have homes attached to them in a haphazard way. And even the newer, outer wall has elements of disorder. Many of Rothenberg's towers have different designs to represent significant events in the city's history; certain parts of the wall serve as outside walls of dwellings. Furthermore, fortresses and battlements around the major gates that lead into the city grew in a topsy-turvy arrangement. So, although many medieval cities were planned to be compatible with certain cultural values and to exhibit those values in an orderly fashion, one also finds disorder, poor planning, and haphazard growth in these communities.

A similar pattern existed in the ancient cities of Athens and Rome. Alongside the beautifully planned layout of temples on the Acropolis of Athens and adjacent to the elaborate and well-defined Forum of Rome, with its temples, gardens, shrines, and monuments, one finds disorder and lack of community planning. Ancient Rome was a maze of poorly lighted streets, flimsily constructed, cold, damp, and dark homes, dirty streets, noise, confusion, and fire hazards (Tuan, 1974).

A combination of order and disorder also occurred in the ancient Chinese cities described in Chapter 9. For example, Ch'ang-an was carefully designed with the emperor's palace at the center, ceremonial streets, shrines and temples in particular locations, and city gates specifically planned in accordance with cosmological values. However, over the years orderliness gradually disappeared, perhaps as a result of changing politics. Busy markets intruded on residential areas, taverns, eating places, and houses of prostitution multiplied, and buildings and commercial establishments sprang up in an uncontrolled fashion (Tuan, 1974). Once again, side by side, we see the presence of both order and disorder in community design.

The order/disorder dialectic also applies to small, traditional communities, not just to large urban centers. As described in Chapter 9, the ideal design of Dogon villages in Africa is analogous to the human body. Although this pattern often applies reasonably well, aerial views of larger villages (Fraser, 1968) suggest considerable unplanned and disorderly growth. Homes are often scattered throughout the village, compounds and alleys arise in every direction, and the scene appears to be one of mass confusion.

Obviously there are exceptions to the dialectic interplay of order and disorder in community designs. These seem to occur especially among small, traditional communities—for example, among the Trobriand Islanders, the Haida Indians, and others described in Chapter 9. These communities appear to be orderly and stable, with everything in its place, little variation, and little disorder. It may be that small, relatively unchanging societies do not follow the order/disorder dialectic principle as dramatically as larger, evolving societies, which are more subject to technological innovation and social changes of all types. Or it may be that anthropological accounts of small, traditional communities simply do not depict the dialectic theme proposed here. These are questions that remain for the future.

The order/disorder quality of urban settings seems to be pervasive throughout history, among different cultures, and in a variety of communities. We might speculate that the shifting balance of order and disorder may even be necessary for the vitality of urban settings, that change and growth can come about only through oppositional forces of order or disorder in design and functioning of cities, and that each presses against the other to stimulate social evolution and change in a never-ending cycle. This is not to say that ghettos, slums, and poor, unplanned living arrangements are "good." Rather, the difficulties associated with such disorder eventually create pressure for change if an urban setting is to be viable. Similarly, planned and structured arrangements may contribute to a coherent image and a feeling of identification with a city. But if order and structure are carried too far in a rigid plan that does not foster change and growth, a general stagnation may result. Perhaps a constant interplay of order and disorder is necessary for the viability of a city, with each oppositional process shifting in its strength over time, so that each extreme is continually tempered by the other. If *either* order or disorder is carried too far, the result may be either stagnation and total resistance to change or chaos and anarchy.

This way of thinking does not assume an ultimate or optimal balance of order and disorder in city design and functioning. It may be that sometimes more disorder is "better" in that it facilitates social change, and that sometimes more order is "better" in relation to the solution of financial, economic, or other types of problems. Hence, we must avoid characterizing either end of this dialectic (or the other dialectics described below) as being "best" in some universal sense. Instead, it may be the dynamic and changing tension between opposites that is necessary for the viability of a community or city.

Homogeneity/Diversity

Cities and communities are a continuous interplay of homogeneity and diversity, or simplicity and complexity. This dialectic is reflected well in the reactions of first-time visitors to a strange city. Such an experience can be bewildering, and it often loads heavily on the side of diversity and complexity. If the city is in a foreign country, for example, diversity and complexity are manifested in a variety of ways. Traffic may flow on the "wrong" side of the street, automobile drivers may sit on the "passenger's side" of the car, signs may be unintelligible not only because of language differences but also because they often convey information in different formats and about strange places. Language is often incomprehensible, street noises are different, stores sell items with which one is unfamiliar, the stores themselves may be in unusual places or arranged in strange ways. Furthermore, living styles may be unfamiliar; for example, in some cities people use the street for many activities, whereas in other places people are rarely seen. A strange city may also be subdivided into sections that are not familiar, architecture is often different, eating places and hotels are sometimes located in unpredictable places, and there may be confusing customs regarding ordering of food, tipping, and relations with waiters and other employees. For many newcomers to a city, these and other factors convey a feeling of diversity, complexity, and confusion.

In time and with experience, however, a degree of homogeneity and simplicity about a city usually emerges. To facilitate this process, a visitor may take a guided tour of the city and study maps and guidebooks. Slowly, the initial confusion and diversity give way to a feeling of simplicity and homogeneity. The organization of a city around a plaza or downtown area emerges in the tourist's mind, various sections are put in spatial relation to one another, major monuments and sights serve as anchoring points, rules and customs about how to relate to pedestrians, automobiles, shopkeepers, and servicepeople become more understandable, and the city begins to take on a semblance of homogeneity and organization.

But this is not a linear process that always proceeds from diversity and complexity to homogeneity and simplicity. At another stage of experience, the visitor feels the need to seek out diversity within the established homogeneity of a city that he or she experienced. Out-of-the-way restaurants are sought, side trips are made to unique places that promise stimulation and unusual experiences. To the extent that such diversity is absent, a city can lose its fascination for tourists. Thus, some might say "Three days in Munich are sufficient to know it, but two weeks in London are barely enough." For some tourists, Munich's sights and experiences are appreciated in a much shorter time than London's, and this may result not so much from difference in size of the cities as from differences in homogeneity and diversity of experiences.

The qualities of homogeneity and diversity of cities do not apply only to the new visitor; they occur for the resident and are evident in the physical design qualities of cities and communities at all levels of scale. Rapoport (1977) gives several examples of the interplay of homogeneity and diversity in London and elsewhere:

> Color distinguishes various areas: the area around Pall Mall, Buckingham Palace, Eaton Square, etc., is white. At King's Road . . . the color turns to a warm red. . . . At that point this change in color coincides with a transition from the City of Westminster to the Borough of Kensington and Chelsea. West Kensington is gray and brown, Kentish Town is black, and so on. . . .

Activities also clearly distinguish places: on Saturday afternoons the West End is a scene of activity, people, color, noise, food smells and fast tempos whereas the city is quiet and dead. Finally, the residential squares can be understood as noticeable differences in the street pattern, striking examples being Russell Square and, particularly, Bedford Square from Gower Street. . . .

Another example is provided by Stone Town vs. Ngambo in Zanzibar. The former of tall, stone houses with narrow streets and alleys, is separated by an old creek from the latter with free-standing coral houses arranged randomly under a screen of coconut palms. The grain is different and one is inward turning, the other outward facing. The two areas are also inhabited by different populations and have very different street lives and activities, reinforced by sounds, smells, light and shade, temperature, air movement, and so on. . . .

. . . in Mexico City the avenue Cuahtemoc changes suddenly at Obrero Mundial. On the south of that intersection, there is a plantation, trees, changes in buildings and uses, from second-hand cars and car parts to "nicer" shops, restaurants and hotels; at the end of this part there is a large fountain in a park. There is a corresponding change in maintenance levels of sidewalks and buildings and all of these changes reinforce the transition [pp. 232–236].[2]

In Salt Lake City, homogeneity and diversity also appear side by side. To the casual observer, the city is laid out in a homogeneous, simple grid system, with straight streets organized in a coordinate system anchored at the Mormon Temple. But there are parts of the city where the streets wind in a mazelike way, following streams, gullies, and natural barriers, and this creates an atmosphere of diversity, mystery, and unpredictability. Furthermore, although Salt Lake has an overall image of having primarily modest, detached single-family homes on equal-sized lots, one also discovers neighborhoods of stately mansions and uniquely designed homes. And in spite of classic straight-line, shop-after-shop arrangements in the downtown area, one also finds a place called Trolley Square, a renovated Victorian trolley barn that has a maze of shops, restaurants, and galleries. Finally, alongside the seemingly homogeneous style of architecture and community design, there are nearby mountains that provide a unique diversity of possible experiences—dramatically different terrain, weather, and recreational possibilities. All these factors serve to create a diversity within homogeneity and homogeneity within diversity. We suspect that one will find a similar dialectical interplay in almost any community or city.

[2]This and all other quotations from this source are from *Human Aspects of Urban Form: Towards a Man-Environment Approach to Urban Form and Design*, by A. Rapoport. Copyright 1977 by Pergamon Press, Inc. Reprinted by permission.

Rapoport (1977) believes that people need an interplay of complexity and simplicity and that city designs should consciously include such oppositional processes. However, too much diversity and complexity is confusing and chaotic, and too much simplicity or homogeneity is boring. Rapoport states that the ideal community may be one that contains a blend of both polar opposites. But, once again, this does not mean a *fixed* level of diversity and homogeneity, but a continual and ever-changing tension between them, each dominating by turns or both existing simultaneously side by side.

How can this be accomplished? Rapoport (1977) offers a variety of suggestions:

1. Entertainment, downtown, and shopping areas might be designed to provide novelty and stimulation, whereas residential areas might be more unified and homogeneous.
2. Children's play spaces can be designed with open-ended features, to permit exploration and changes over time along with stable and predictable experiences.
3. Variations in color and texture from section to section of the city or neighborhood can provide a sense of both homogeneity and diversity.
4. A blend of simple and complex street layouts can produce homogeneous and varied arrangements.
5. Distinctive areas in cities, based on ethnicity, architecture, and commerce, can foster experiences of both diversity and homogeneity.
6. Variations in architectural styles, contrasts between greenery and the built environment, and so on can provide both diverse and unifying experiences.

Rapoport (1977) also suggests that simplicity/complexity, or homogeneity/diversity, can be implemented at many levels of scale, from regions to neighborhoods to individual streets. Because there are no singular solutions to achieve a blend of these dialectic opposites, his point, with which we agree, is that a city should be a dynamic, evolving place that complements the changing needs and values of its residents. Just as people change in their needs for homogeneity and diversity of stimulation, so communities should, ideally, provide a variety of experience and stimulation, from homogeneous and simple to complex and diverse.

Another point about homogeneity/diversity and order/disorder dialectics is that people will often create environments with such qualities whether or not they plan to. Throughout history and in different cultures, no matter how rigidly and homogeneously cities and communities had been planned, diversity and disorder gradually crept in as new sections grew, as different ethnic and cultural groups came on the scene, and as political, religious, and other values shifted. For example, London has had a dramatic immigration of people from Arabic and Middle Eastern countries over the past decades. Whole neighborhoods have been settled by these immigrants, with accompanying changes in the physical characteristics, life-styles, and images of such neighborhoods. Street life, shops, language, food, noises, and smells have created a diversity and contrast with nearby older, established neighborhoods. This migration pattern has certainly added to the diversity and complexity of London.

Conversely, no matter how diverse or disorderly a community or city may be, cultural values and practices are likely, eventually, to generate a semblance of homogeneity and order. For example, Rapoport (1977) and others described how squatter communities developed in many urban settings. These communities, especially prevalent in the larger cities of South America and Africa, are built out of scrap materials. They often initially give an appearance of bewildering diversity and disorder. There are no consistent architectural forms, streets and paths seem to go in every direction, a variety of building materials are used to construct dwellings, and there are no public services or apparent community organization. Complexity and diversity seem to predominate. But, as Rapoport (1977) pointed out, there is often a homogeneity and order to many of these settlements that exist side by side with their complexity. In Barranquilla, Colombia, for example, squatter settlements were designed in such a way that access to clusters of homes was controlled by an intimacy gradient that was evident in certain physical barriers that separated streets from individual homes. And in certain Asian, African, and Latin American squatter settlements, homes are clustered around cul-de-sacs, sometimes on the basis of kinship groups, with central commercial areas used for socializing, recreation, and meetings.

So community and city life reflect a dialectic tension between homogeneity and diversity similar to the interplay of order and disorder. Neither extreme of this dialectic opposition totally characterizes any community. Both forces always exist, although either one may dominate at a given time. And whether or not we consciously design diversity and homogeneity into communities, they may well arise in some form or another, perhaps because human beings themselves are dynamic and changing and will seek out both homogeneity and diversity in their lives.

Individuality/Community

We view the city, like the home, as involving (at a different level of scale) a dynamic tension between individuality and community.

The community side of the coin is manifested in many ways. In Chapters 2 and 3, we noted that many nations, cities, and small communities convey an "image" to their inhabitants and to outsiders that may be based on slogans, symbols, or architectural forms. When one thinks of New York City, any of several images comes to mind—skyscrapers, Times Square, the theater district, Wall Street, Central Park. For Washington, D.C., one might have an image of the Capitol Building, the White House, the Lincoln Memorial, or the Washington Monument. Thus, architectural forms and styles contribute to the identity of a community, such as the Saint Louis arch, the Vatican in Rome, the hotel and entertainment strip in Las Vegas.

A city's uniqueness can also grow out of activities, such as manufacturing, beer production, and recreation. Some cities have an atmosphere, or ambience, that serves as a symbol, such as the cosmopolitan quality of San Francisco or Montreal, the religious values of Jerusalem or Rome, the excitement of New York. So through architecture, visual effects, activities, and other means, cities and communities often have an air of being distinctive places. These symbols help give a sense of unity to a community, something that both its members and outsiders use to label and identify a place. These symbols are often used by outsiders to image a city and by residents to reflect and reinforce their identity with the community.

Certain activities also help create community feeling. For example, most large American cities have football, baseball, hockey, or basketball teams that are identified as the community's own team. These teams stand for the city, and sports fans usually support their own city's team, not those of other communities. Certain significant events—for example, when a city's team reaches the World Series in baseball or the Super Bowl in football—often generate a holiday atmosphere and sometimes set off communitywide celebrations. When the Denver Broncos achieved the Super Bowl in 1978 for the first time in the history of the team, Denver's citizens gleefully wore "Orange Crush" buttons, orange insignia, and orange shirts (the team's slogan and color). Other examples of celebrations that unify a city are the Thanksgiving Day parade in New York, the Rose Bowl parade in Pasadena, the Mardi Gras in New Orleans, and the Mummers parade in Philadelphia. The idolization of teams and various events contribute to a sense of identity with a community that often transcends ethnic, socioeconomic, and other differences among inhabitants.

The forces toward community identity involve more than symbols and activities: they can be embedded in the everyday architecture and design of a city. For example, the row houses and white stone steps of homes in Baltimore, the brownstones of New York, the sharp-pitched roofs and common façades of residences in medieval Germany, the step-roofed homes of Holland, the modernistic and sparsely decorated skyscrapers of New York, the pink and white stucco homes of Los Angeles, the adobe architecture of Albuquerque, and the systematic arrangements of villages in Africa and elsewhere contribute to a feeling of community identity.

Community ties also evolve from layouts and use of space. A key feature of community planning, from the modern city to the ancient city, from the large metropolis to the small traditional village, has been the idea of "center" (Wheatley, 1971). Thus, a central plaza, of one form or another, appeared in almost every community that we examined in Chapter 9. Such centers had a variety of forms—the marketplace or emperor's palaces of ancient Chinese cities; the temples of Egypt and the Middle East; the "city center" concepts of modern American cities that include downtown commercial areas, theater districts, and government buildings and complexes; the centrally located lodges of Cheyenne encampments.

Rapoport (1977) describes how the idea of center pervades every level of architectural scale in San Cristobal, Mexico. Homes are built around a central courtyard, groups of homes are clustered around local plazas, and neighborhoods are organized around a town plaza, all of which creates a nested hierarchy of centers. And in modern-day Rome, a highly populated city, local centers exist in the form of plazas and eating and shopping areas. Even in the squatter settlements of Africa and Latin America, homes are clustered around public spaces that are used for community activities (Rapoport, 1977). In fact, Rapoport (1977) and others have observed such clustering around central areas even in the absence of architecturally designed centers:

> For example, in the Chinese or Punjabi village people meet in the wide part of the main street, in North Africa it is the well for women and the coffee house for men. In the Bantu village the space between the animal pens and the walls of the living compound. . . . In the Puerto Rican New York neighborhoods the *bodega*, in South Chicago the stoop of the house for women and the elderly, the street for girls, the corners and taverns for men. In France it used to be the bistro and cafe, in Italy the piazza, galleria and cafe. In England it is the pub and street for the working class, the house and club for middle class. In Ancient Greece, it was the Agora, in Rome—the baths [p. 307].

In urban neighborhoods of Chicago and New York of the past 20–40 years, Jacobs (1961) described the streets as important gathering places that contribute to a sense of community identity. Our own childhoods in New York and Chicago show well how the street served as a community plaza or gathering place where all elements of the local society came together. On a summer evening, the following scene might take place: Boys played various games in the road—stickball, football, and modified forms of baseball. On the sidewalk and in the windows of apartments facing the street were observers—young, middle-aged, and elderly men and women. These bystanders took on a variety of roles as cheerleaders, coaches, referees, and critics. Women sat in chairs on the sidewalks, conversing, socializing, and disciplining one another's children. Merchants sold vegetables, ice cream, and candy. The street was alive with people of all ages engaged in a variety of activities—playing games, socializing, observing, monitoring children, courting, debating. Some streets had annual "block parties"; people brought food for all to share, decorated their street, and arranged for music, dancing, and entertainment.

Taken together, all these activities, symbols, and architectural design features suggest that people often have a sense of identity, imageability, and feelings of bonds with their community or city. In our framework, these represent forces toward togetherness and community identity.

However, city life also includes forces toward individuality, separateness, and apartness side by side with the forces toward unity. Individuality and separation exist in a variety of forms and at many levels of societal organization—the individual in relation to local community and to the city, groups and subcultures in relation to one another and to central authorities. For example, at the same time that groups or individuals feel a sense of identity with their community in regard to sports, religion, and other factors, there also may be attitudes and activities that tend toward separation—resentments and criticisms of government, hostility toward police, conflicts between ethnic groups who share facilities, separation of ethnic, nationality, and socioeconomic groups in different neighborhoods. In fact, as Fischer (1976) and others observed, there is a trend in many communities for ethnic, nationality, and socioeconomic groups to cluster in distinct neighborhoods. Such enclaves at once illustrate dialectic forces toward both unity and separateness. By living together, a group reinforces and demonstrates its internal unity as a subculture and simultaneously displays distinctiveness and separateness from others.

Such voluntary (or, ofttimes, enforced) separateness has occurred over and over throughout history (Fischer, 1976; Rapoport, 1977). In Sydney, Australia, for example, southern European immigrants clustered in inner-city areas and in the eastern suburbs; Dutch and German people lived in the outer suburban areas; Italians and eastern Europeans lived in the western suburbs (Rapoport, 1977). A city like New York is also a testimonial to the simultaneous unity and separateness of various groups. During the large-scale migration to America in the late 19th and early 20th centuries, each ethnic group initially lived on the Lower East Side of New York—Irish, Jews, Italians, Chinese, and others. With each new wave of immigrants the established ones moved out to more prosperous areas of the city. A similar process has occurred in recent years, as Black and Puerto Rican immigrants first lived in Harlem and on the East Side and gradually moved into neighborhoods in Brooklyn and the Bronx that were previously the enclaves of earlier European groups. Although internally cohesive, these communities were often seen, and saw themselves, as separate and often in conflict with other immigrant groups and with the city as a whole.

Many facets of a community's architecture and design also reflect individuality and separateness. In Japanese cities, for example, there are rigid separations between public and private life, with sharp boundaries between the public areas of large cities and the neighborhood and family residence (Rapoport, 1977; Tuan, 1974). Similarly, in the Middle East, homes present blank walls to streets, with a rigid demarcation between what is public and what is private.

Rapoport (1977) hypothesized that community and city life can be described in individuality/community polarities at all levels of scale, from homes to streets to neighborhoods to larger communities. For example, Rapoport (1977) and Fraser (1968) described the towns and activities of the Yoruba people in Nigeria as reflecting a combination of unity and separateness. The unity derives in part from the design of the whole community around the palace of the king, which is a huge compound that houses the king and his wives and also has a public plaza area. However, the people live in relatively individualized subgroups:

> The typical residential pattern developed in Yoruba towns consists of a localized segment of the lineage living together in a large, square compound having but a single entrance and bounded by mud walls seven feet high; long galleried rooms front on one another around a courtyard or impluvium. Each compound houses members of a single extended family [Fraser, 1968, p. 43].

Thus, in the midst of the unity provided by the king's palace and public plaza, there exist semiprivate neighborhoods organized around kinship lines. Similarly, among the Pueblo Indians (Rapoport, 1969b), we saw the simultaneous presence of a single community organized around a central plaza and separate family dwellings that fostered a sense of individuality and family distinctiveness.

Here again, as with the order/disorder and homogeneity/diversity dialectics, the viability of a city or community, or of its residents, is probably not conditional on one or the other extreme of the individuality/community dialectic. Rather, it may be a matter of achieving *both* community and individuality simultaneously or over a period of time. Total identification with a city may be stifling to individuals; total individuality without any sense of community may lead to anarchy. As with the other dialectics, the task of the individual in cities may be to weave his or her way through the individuality/community dialectic, to achieve a reasonable degree of both oppositional processes simultaneously and/or over the long run, and to develop a life-style in which individuality and community function in creative tension with each other. Thus, as before, we do not suggest that a fixed, permanently optimum balance of these dialectic opposites is desirable. Instead, a changing and dynamic relation between oppositional forces is probably best, with individuality dominating in some times or circumstances and community forces dominating in others.

Commentary

We described the dynamics of city life in terms of dialectical processes of order/disorder, homogeneity/diversity, and individuality/community. Our thesis was that life in communities and cities involves an interplay of these (and perhaps other) oppositional processes and that the shifting strength of each side of each of these processes lends vitality to life in communities and cities. In a sense, these dialectic processes provide the "motor" to urban life, much as they did at the level of homes.

It is important to reiterate that the operation of such dialectic oppositions may be "healthful" to the functioning of people in cities and communities. Just as "healthful" privacy regulation involves an interplay of openness and closedness, with neither pole ever completely dominating, so the viability of cities and life in cities may require an interplay of order/disorder, homogeneity/diversity, and individuality/community. It is tempting, as we shall see in the next chapter, to strive for "ideal" city designs that are orderly and homogeneous and where community identity is strong. But consider what it might mean to be a resident of a city that was totally organized around such goals. Role relationships between people might rigidify, little stimulation and excitement might exist, evolutionary growth might not easily occur as technology, values, and the composition of a community changed. But the other extreme is no better. Absence of planning, heterogeneity of design, total individuality of architecture, activities, and behavior could be anarchic and chaotic. Hence, cities and communities probably need to reflect a whole variety of cross-currents and oppositional processes that, over the long run, will permit change, growth, flexibility, and accommodation to shifting populations and demands.

One might even speculate that the plight of many modern cities is attributable to the overinfluence of one or the other side of certain dialectic processes. Los Angeles is sometimes described as not having been designed to provide a sufficient level of community or order; New York has been portrayed as having lost its sense of community identity and as having been subject to overly rapid social change and excessive diversity. What may be required in future city planning and redevelopment is not only attention to the usual issues of employment, physical renewal, economics, and politics but a careful assessment of the state of affairs with respect to order/disorder, homogeneity/diversity, individuality/

community, and other dialectic processes. Such an assessment may make it possible to incorporate interventions that restore a healthful oppositional tension between various forces. Thus, planning goals might include facilitation of oppositional tensions, not elimination of one side of a dialectic process.

The dialectic processes of order/disorder, homogeneity/diversity, and individuality/community have a common thread that can be characterized as involving a general *stability/change* dialectic.[3] That is, order, homogeneity, and community can be viewed as representing stability, continuity, or equilibrium of a social system. Disorder, diversity, and individuality all reflect the idea of change, instability, and unpredictability. Disorder represents a system in flux or in an unstable condition. Diversity implies variation, and individuality emphasizes the uniqueness and differences among people.

Thinking at the level of this underlying "superdialectic" of stability/change reinforces our preceding discussion about the viability of cities as requiring a satisfactory resolution of the order/disorder, homogeneity/diversity, and individuality/community dialectics. If these three dialectic processes reflect an underlying variation in stability and change, one might say that the viability of cities—and, indeed, of individuals in a variety of circumstances—requires an appropriate balance of stability and change regarding stimulation, experiences, and events. Equilibrium, homeostasis, or stability is necessary for human existence, to be sure, for without it cities and family and social relationships would be chaotic. Yet people also need stimulus variety, unpredictability, and change in their lives, else their existence becomes stagnant and they cannot grow beyond their immediate circumstances. So stability and change, in some appropriate dialectic tension, seem crucial for human functioning over both long- and short-term periods. Cities and other settings can provide the opportunity for such dialectic tension and can serve, therefore, as important vehicles for human growth and creativity.

Another point about our dialectic analysis of cities is that it is useful to think about a particular dialectic process, such as homogeneity/diversity, as being served by a variety of mechanisms, not just physical ones. Just as we viewed privacy, in Chapter 4, as a multibehavioral mechanism involving environmental, verbal, nonverbal, and cultural aspects of behavior, so we can profitably understand dialectic processes in cities as being manifested in a variety of ways. Homogeneity/diversity can be reflected in architectural design, cultural and other opportunities in a city, the range of ethnic groups and their various styles of life, the general pace of life in a city. Similarly, the other two dialectic processes can be seen in several dimensions of behavior and various qualities of communities. This will become more evident in the next chapter.

[3]We are indebted to Barbara Goza for suggesting this relationship.

One final note about our dialectic analysis: Our use of the dialectic processes of order/disorder, homogeneity/diversity, and individuality/community is somewhat arbitrary. These are processes that seem to us to run through the literature on cities and communities in one form or another. Some of these writers emphasize one or the other pole of a particular dialectic; some emphasize one dialectic process, others a different one. For us these three dialectic tensions and their underlying quality of stability/change seem to characterize well a range of community and urban settings. Undoubtedly there are other oppositional processes that can be used to characterize life in cities and communities, and we encourage you to develop your own ideas in this regard. Cities, communities, and, indeed, most aspects of culture/environment relations are complex and variegated and can be viewed from several perspectives. So we do not mean to imply that the dialectic analysis presented here is either complete or totally accurate. It is only one approach, and you should feel free to expand it and to apply your own perspective to this most fascinating topic.

SUMMARY

The present chapter examined the social and psychological dynamics of life in community and urban settings. In particular, we explored the stresses and strains of city living, population density and crowding, and coping and adjustment mechanisms used by people in urban communities. The chapter had three sections: a discussion of the major sociological and social-psychological theories of life in cities that have been proposed over the past hundred years; a review of selected research and theory on population density and crowding; and a dialectic analysis of urban life in terms of order/disorder, individuality/community, and homogeneity/diversity.

According to Fischer (1976), sociologists have proposed three general types of theories about life in urban settings. Determinist theories, the oldest, hypothesize that the large scale of cities and their high population densities often produce stimulus overload, and coping responses such as detachment, aloofness, and disregard of the needs of others. Determinist theories also reason that social pathologies of crime, disease, and family disorganization eventually result as people become more isolated and alienated from others.

Compositional theories discount city size and density as direct determinants of well-being. These theories hypothesize that people in cities spend the most important parts of their lives in families, extended kin groups, and local neighborhoods and that the quality of these groups is what affects the well-being of urban residents. If density and other factors play a role at all, they do so indirectly, by affecting economics, politics, and other aspects of life that, in turn, influence subgroups.

A third theoretical approach, subcultural theory, combines determinist and compositional positions. This approach agrees with the compositional view that life in cities generally takes place within the confines of various subcultures. And it agrees with the determinist idea that the heterogeneity, dense population, and large size of cities affect people directly. Subcultural theory also hypothesizes that city size permits the formation of new subcultures and may also increase the probability of conflict between subgroups as they come into contact and compete for space and resources. Thus, subcultural theory approaches life in cities as an interaction of ecological factors and cultural factors.

The second part of the chapter explored the topic of population density and crowding in urban settings. An analysis of sociological and psychological research suggested that population density in and of itself does not always impair human functioning. Our analysis focused on the theme that cultures develop a variety of behavioral mechanisms that permit people to regulate their dealings with one another, even in very densely populated situations. This analysis, compatible with our description of privacy regulation in Chapter 4, portrayed these mechanisms as a multimodal, culturally based system of behavior whereby people regulate and pace their contacts with others.

The third section of the chapter examined community and urban life in terms of the dialectic interplay of order/disorder, individuality/community, and homogeneity/diversity. Our analysis suggested that oppositional forces associated with these dialectic processes foster the potential for both instability and change in city life. The first dialectic, order/disorder, is reflected in the fact that many communities that were originally designed according to systematic plans eventually exhibited disorder and uncontrolled growth. And many communities that apparently had little initial planning or order gradually developed coherence and unity. The interplay of order and disorder may well create a vitality in city life and set the stage for change to meet the demands of new social, political, religious, and other factors.

Similarly, many cities convey a unity and homogeneity of image that is reflected in style of architecture, layouts of streets, and types of people and activities. Yet they are often places of considerable diversity in regard to such factors. Thus, diversity and homogeneity often exist side by side in urban settings. Again, such opposition not only may contribute to the stability of a city but can set the stage for change and evolution.

In regard to individuality/community, we noted that residents of cities often have a strong sense of identity with their community and with other residents. These feelings can be reinforced by slogans and symbols, architecturally unique factors, and community activities. But there also are forces in cities that create feelings of individuality and separatism, such as resistance to restrictions on individual freedom, conflicts among ethnic groups, and clustering of people into distinct and often rival neighborhoods.

We concluded the chapter with the theme that the complex interplay of dialectic opposites may well be necessary for the well-being and viability of a community and its citizens. Because order/disorder, homogeneity/diversity, and individuality/community imply forces toward stability and toward change, they may well serve as a system of checks and balances to ensure that different aspects of stability and change are represented in the physical environments of communities and cities. We speculated that problems can arise when one side of a dialectic polarity is overly dominant, with the result that certain issues receive less attention. For instance, overemphasis on laissez-faire commercial development may lead to a chaotic and disorderly community that pays insufficient attention to a sense of community and provides overly diverse stimulation. Unless these and other dialectic polarities are each treated as a unity, with some level of each oppositional force existing simultaneously and/or over time, adequate city functioning and individual well-being may be threatened.

Chapter 11

COMMUNITIES AND CITIES OF THE FUTURE

Having examined cities in relation to cultural and environmental factors (Chapter 9) and in terms of the dynamics of city life (Chapter 10), we now turn toward the future. This chapter considers some proposals offered by planners about "ideal" urban settings of the future. We will examine futuristic communities that already exist, along with some that are still dreams in the minds of radical futuristic planners.

We first describe idealized communities of the past, some of which have influenced present-day concepts. We then analyze an existing "new town," Columbia, Maryland, which will eventually have a population of 110,000. In addition, we will consider Habitat, a futuristic city that was erected at the Montreal Expo Fair of 1967. Finally, the futuristic proposals of Paolo Soleri are presented, including his plans for high-density, vertical cities, some almost a mile high.

We will not only describe the physical characteristics of these futuristic communities but also explore their cultural and philosophical values. Moreover, the dialectic concepts used in Chapter 10—namely, order/disorder, individuality/community, and homogeneity/diversity—will be applied to these new urban communities.

A HISTORICAL PERSPECTIVE ON "IDEAL" COMMUNITIES AND CITIES

During the 20th century we have come to believe in the importance of long-range planning in a variety of areas—population, agriculture, production, fiscal policies, resource management. So it is that the last 50 years have also had a good share of plans for communities and cities—urban renewal, new communities, and futuristic cities. This has even gone so far as to include the design of orbiting space colonies and settlements on other planets.

Interest in planned cities, however, is not unique to the present historical period. In Chapters 9 and 10 we described several ancient cities that were designed as ideal communities—for example, Chinese and

Middle Eastern cities, the towns of Greece and Rome, and the ideal city of the lost continent of Atlantis. However, unlike present-day futuristic concepts, many earlier designs were directed only at parts of a community, such as an emperor's palace, a religious temple, or a political or commercial center. Other facets of life, such as dwellings and transportation, were permitted to develop on their own, often in an uncontrolled way. Of course, there were some exceptions; for example, Clapp (1971) observed that, among the ancient Greeks, Hippodamus may have been one of the first total town planners. Not only did his designs pay attention to religious values, but he also spelled out details concerning street designs and locations of residences, marketplaces, and other facilities.

In the 20th century, comprehensive town planning came to the fore in many parts of the world. In the United States, Europe, the USSR, Israel, and elsewhere, there have been numerous attempts to implement "totally planned" communities that have the following characteristics (Campbell, 1976; Clapp, 1971): (1) The communities are often totally new ones, not additions to or modifications of existing areas. (2) The communities encompass many facets of life—politics and government, residential living, economics, religion, recreation. (3) They are often controlled by a single management company that regulates all aspects of development and land use. (4) They are usually designed to satisfy explicitly stated values, such as green space and recreation, residential living and city life, social and socioeconomic balance. (5) They are often self-sufficient economically, politically and otherwise. (6) Community designs are often restricted in population numbers and geographical size.

Following World War II, many new communities sprang up in the United States and Western Europe, often in suburban settings. However, many of these only provided more homes for a rapidly growing population, and relatively little attention was paid to broader social planning. The present chapter is not concerned with such unplanned communities; instead, our interest is in planned communities that try to meet most of the criteria listed above.

HOWARD'S GARDEN CITIES

One of the earliest and best-known city-planning concepts was proposed by Ebenezer Howard, an English environmental designer at the turn of the century. Howard (1965) stated his goals quite explicitly:

> Town and country *must be married*, and out of the joyous union will spring a new hope, a new life, a new civilization [cited in Fischer, 1976, p. 209].
>
> . . . a town design for healthy living and industry; of a size that makes possible a full measure of social life, but not larger; surrounded by a rural belt; the whole of the land being in public ownership or held in trust for the community [cited in Campbell, 1976, p. 19].

Howard's basic plan is shown in Figure 11-1. The ideal garden city was a circular community 1½ miles in diameter with about 30,000 inhabitants, surrounded by an agricultural belt. At the center of the city were a large park, community and government buildings, a hospital, theaters, museums, and other public facilities. This central area was surrounded by shops and stores. The remainder of the city was designed around a series of concentric rings. At the periphery were industrial areas and a circumferential railway. Residential sites were located closer to the center of the town. Midway between the outer areas and the town center Howard designed a parklike promenade that had recreational areas and schools, all of which were readily accessible to all residents.

The circular city was divided into six neighborhoods, or wards, by radial boulevards that cut through rings of the city like the spokes of a wheel. Each neighborhood was to have its own schools and parks.

Howard also developed a regional-planning concept that involved connections between garden cities and larger cities. Clusters of garden cities would be connected by roads and railroads, with agricultural areas in between cities. The smaller garden cities would be connected by rail to larger cities that had populations of about 60,000.

One of the first garden cities that still exists today is Letchworth, England. Although it was modeled after Howard's garden-city concept, some critics felt that the designers overemphasized the "garden" qualities of Letchworth and overplanted trees and shrubs, almost to the point of blocking out views and sunlight, and that too little attention was given to the built environment. More recent new towns in England, Finland, and elsewhere have sought a better balance between the rural garden image and the built environment (Tuan, 1974).

One of the most central cultural values in Howard's concept is that the ideal community should be a blend of rural and urban life. The countryside, in the form of greenery, parks, and agricultural areas, is to be close at hand. But people should also have easy access to schools, shopping, industry and government. Thus, the garden-city plan assumes that both cities and the countryside are important to people's well-being. Howard's design fits well with Tuan's (1974) description of 20th-century values as idealizing an organized blend of urban and rural life (see Chapter 2). Note, however, that Howard's goal was to have communities that were not *too* large or *too* urbanized; they were to be "garden cities," not large metropolitan areas dominated by the built environment with the rural environment is a secondary role. If anything, the reverse is true—they are dominated by the rural environment—and, as some critics noted, early designs may have overemphasized the "garden" side of the concept.

There are several other values in the garden-city concept. For example, the land and community were to be "for the people," not for political or religious leaders or ideals. The importance of education for the

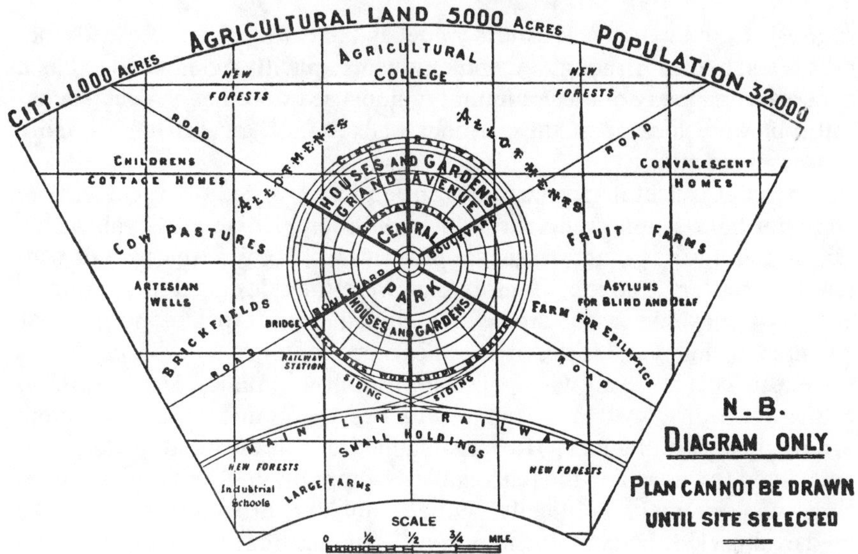

GARDEN CITY AND RURAL BELT

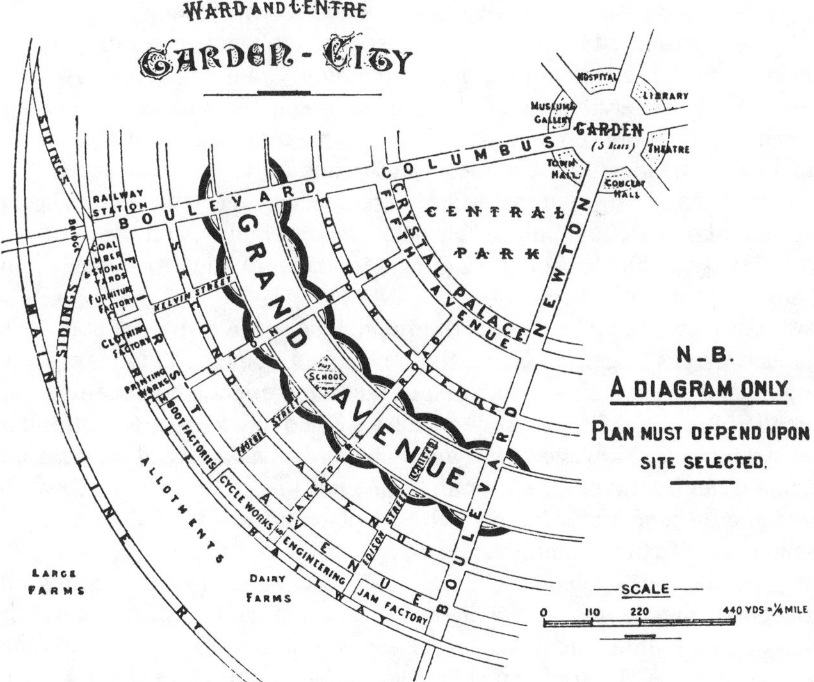

WARD AND CENTRE OF GARDEN CITY

Figure 11-1. Schematic diagrams of Howard's garden-city concept. From *Garden Cities of Tomorrow*, by E. Howard. Copyright 1965 by M.I.T. Press. Reprinted by permission.

masses, a 20th-century Western value, is also evident in the easily accessible schools. Although technology was explicitly acknowledged as a necessary mainstay of the community, industries were not physically central, but were located at the periphery of the city, away from the daily lives of residents.

It is also useful to note what garden cities were not. Clearly, they were not built around religious values, with temples or cathedrals at the hub of the city, as many medieval cities were. They were also not centered on powerful political figures, nor were they designed in relation to cosmological values associated with cardinality or seasons of the year, for example, as many cities described in earlier chapters were. Garden cities were also not designed with political instability in mind. There were no protective walls, watchtowers, or siting of the communities to protect against invasion. In fact, Howard planned a rail and road system that connected towns, all on the reasonable assumption that 20th-century England would remain politically unified, unlike European cities of the medieval period. Instead, the important values seem to be associated with a combination of green space and urbanity, services for individuals and families, and an attempt to enhance urban life within the political, economic, and technological values of a 20th-century democracy.

The garden-city concept can also be analyzed in relation to the dialectic polarities of individuality/community, homogeneity/diversity, and order/disorder. Howard clearly tried to achieve an acceptable blend of individuality and community. The organization around a community center and the location of schools, parks, and other facilities were aimed at creating a sense of unity in each garden city. Yet the emphasis on residential privacy, a home and garden for every family, and the variety of facilities available to people highlighted the individuality facet of the dialectic.

Garden cities also reveal the homogeneity/diversity dialectic. The similar designs of garden cities, the repetitive organization into neighborhoods, and the systematic location of facilities reflect a homogeneity and simplicity to city life, with few mysteries or novelties to cope with on an everyday basis. However, every garden city has a variety of services and facilities and a diversified population. One might, therefore, view the garden-city concept as having a blend of homogeneity and diversity in design and life opportunities.

On the third dialectic, order/disorder, it is clear that the garden-city concept came down heavily in favor of order and against disorderly, chaotic, and unplanned growth. The overall design and the detailed specification of the location of government facilities, residential areas, parks, and schools were clearly geared toward creating a planned and orderly environment.

The garden-city idea was also directed at promoting adaptation to modern urban life. Howard tried to minimize crowding stresses and to maximize health by providing people with privacy, a sense of community, availability of public and cultural resources, easily accessible transportation, and the opportunity to have a diversity of experiences. By accepting the inevitability of technologically oriented urban society, Howard sought to create an urban setting that would enhance people's lives in accord with 20th-century democratic ideals.

COLUMBIA, MARYLAND: AN AMERICAN NEW TOWN

In mid-20th century, the idea of planned communities took hold in the United States and elsewhere, and many of these communities were influenced by Howard's garden-city concept. (See Campbell, 1976; Clapp, 1976; Fishman, 1977; Moos & Brownstein, 1977, for descriptions of a variety of new towns and planned communities.) These communities were explicitly designed to prevent the perceived ills of city life—crowding, stress, crime, illness, impersonality. Many of these also were reactions against the evils of unplanned suburban growth that had followed World War II—sprawl, poor access to services, lack of community coherence, inadequate local governments, unsatisfactory schools and recreational facilities.

Although the new-town movement has had a longer history in Europe and notably in England, we will focus our attention on a U.S. city—Columbia, Maryland. Other new towns that you might wish to explore in the United States are Jonathan, Minnesota, Irvine, California, and Reston, Virginia. There also are many new towns in other parts of the world: in England, Israel, the USSR, Finland, Sweden, Denmark, and elsewhere.

Columbia is located 20 miles northeast of Washington, D.C., and 17 miles southwest of Baltimore, Maryland, with easy access to both cities by interstate highways. Columbia occupies about 14,000 acres, previously farm land, in Howard County, Maryland. In 1960 the population of Howard County was 36,000; in 1975 it was 108,000, with about 40,000 people living in the newly developed town of Columbia.

Columbia was the brainchild of James Rouse, a developer in the Washington-Baltimore area, who expressed his values as follows:

> Our cities grow by accident, by the whim of the private developer and public. . . . By this irrational process, non-communities are born—formless places, without order, beauty, or reason, with no visible respect for people or the land. . . . The vast formless spread of housing, pierced by the unrelated spotting of schools, churches, stores, creates areas so huge and irrational that they are out of scale with people—beyond their grasp and comprehension—too big for people to feel a part of, responsible for, important in. . . .

> I believe that the ultimate test of civilization is whether or not it contributes to the growth and improvement of mankind. Does it uplift, inspire, stimulate, and develop the best in man? There really can be no other right purpose of community except to provide an environment and an opportunity to develop better people. The most successful community would be that which contributed the most by its physical form, its institutions, and its operation to the growth of people [Hoppenfeld, 1971, p. 4].[1]

Beyond these general ideals Rouse formulated some specific objectives for Columbia: "First, to create a social and physical environment which would work for people, nourishing human growth; second, to preserve and enhance the qualities of the land as we build; and third, . . . to make a profit in the development and sale of land" (Hoppenfeld, 1971, p. 4).

These statements reveal several values of the Columbia concept. First, environments are for people, ordinary everyday people: individuals, families, old, young, middle-aged. There is nothing in these statements about Columbia's primarily serving religious, political, ethnic, nationalistic, or commercial goals. The value is also explicit that freedom of choice is important, as are opportunities for individual growth. In addition, there is the goal of providing all necessary services for residents. Finally, there is a clearly stated value that the land itself, the environment, is to be respected, nurtured, and preserved, both as an intrinsic conservation goal and as a vehicle to serve people.

Morton Hoppenfeld (1971), the planner of Columbia, stated some of these values pointedly:

> A good urban environment is not one only with high levels of sensual satisfaction and function efficiencies, it is also essentially a place of optimum choices where many of the needs and amenities of contemporary life are freely accessible. . . . Thus, our goal is a truly balanced community; a job opportunity for every resident; a dwelling for every job situation; houses and apartments in a wide variety of size and cost, and a chance to live, work, shop and play in the same place, i.e., a new living style, aimed at the current market—one out of ten from the one million people who in the next fifteen years will seek to live in the Washington-Baltimore corridor [p. 4].

In short, the focus of Columbia, Maryland, was to be on its residents—ordinary, individual citizens and their families. In fact, Columbia has been called "the people city" by its developers. This value is symbolized by a sculpture located at the center of town called "The People Tree." It is an abstract form which looks like a tree and whose

[1]This and all other quotations from this source are from "The Columbia Process," by M. Hoppenfeld. In D. Lewis' *The Growth of Cities*, Architects' Yearbook 13. Copyright 1971 by Elek Books, Ltd., London. Reprinted by permission.

leaves are small human figures as if to symbolize the central reason for the city's existence.

The Planning Process

The selection of Howard County as the site of Columbia was based on several factors: (1) accessibility to Washington, D.C., and Baltimore, Maryland, (2) the population growth in the region, and (3) the availability of enough undeveloped land where a totally new city could be established.

The land targeted for Columbia consisted of relatively small farms in predominantly rural Howard County. In mid-1962 the Rouse Company began to acquire parcels of land. By the end of 1963 over 14,000 acres of farm land had been bought (about 1/10th of the land in the county). This required some 140 separate legal transactions, a masterpiece of negotiation that undoubtedly required great skill, persuasion, legal expertise, and considerable "front money." There were, of course, some holdouts, and even today, one sees small plots of land in the middle of Columbia that hark back to earlier days.

Once the land had been acquired, there was a nine-month period of intensive planning and development of the master design concept of Columbia. The planning process was a unique venture, perhaps unparalleled in the history of town and community planning. Not only were the usual experts involved—architects, engineers, city planners, real-estate developers, and other technologically oriented groups—but the Rouse Company decided to bring in experts in government, family life, sociology, economics, recreation, psychology, housing, and communications. Over a dozen advisers from the social and behavioral sciences worked on the design team throughout the planning process. Following county approval of the master plan, construction was begun in 1966, and people began to move in during 1967. The goal was for Columbia to be completed by 1980 and to have a maximum population of about 110,000. It is now projected that achievement of that goal will be delayed several years. As of 1978, there were about 45,000 residents, with almost half of the planned dwellings already constructed.

The Design Concept

We now describe the physical plan of Columbia and some of its explicit and implicit cultural values. You might jot down what you think to be the cultural values expressed in the physical plan of Columbia as you read along. It might also be interesting to note those cultural values discussed in earlier chapters that are *not* salient in Columbia's design.

The long-range design of Columbia calls for 20% of the land to be allocated for natural open spaces, including woods, parks, lakes, golf courses, pathways, and school playgrounds. Another 20% is to be used for business and industry, including office space, industrial parks, and shopping malls. The remaining 60% is for residential space—homes, apartments, and condominiums. Specifically, there will be about 15,000 private detached homes, and 15,000 residential units including townhouses, condominiums, and rental apartment units.

The design logic of Columbia is summarized in Figures 11-2 and 11-3. At the center of Columbia is a downtown area that has commercial, recreational, and shopping facilities. Eight satellite "villages" will eventually surround the town center (see Figure 11-2a). Each village is a partly self-contained community and contains two to five small residential "neighborhoods" grouped around a village center. Thus, Columbia is organized around successively integrated social units, each of which has its own services and center and all of which are tied together in a hierarchically organized system. We next begin a description of Columbia at its smallest unit, the neighborhood.

Neighborhoods. The neighborhood is a basic building block of Columbia and has about 700 to 1200 dwelling units that house approximately 3000 people (see Figure 11-2b). Neighborhoods are functionally identical in several respects. For example, all neighborhoods have the same variety of housing—detached single family homes, cluster homes, condominiums, and rental apartments. Detached homes include moderate and low-priced development dwellings, which people select from existing models, and expensive custom homes that are individually designed. And multiple-family dwellings in every neighborhood range from federally sponsored low-cost apartments to expensive luxury apartments and privately owned condominiums. So neighborhoods are designed to include a variety of housing forms and socioeconomic levels and, presumably, residents who are culturally diverse. Because all neighborhoods have a variety of housing and people, there should be no rich or poor neighborhoods in Columbia, at least theoretically. Furthermore, on almost every street one finds a diversity of housing. Expensive custom-designed homes are located next door to low-cost development homes, and expensive condominiums can be found immediately adjacent to low-cost, federally subsidized rental apartments.

As shown in Figure 11-2b, a neighborhood is bounded on one side by a main thoroughfare—a village collector road that leads to the village center, to the town center, or to main access roads in and out of the city. Along these collector roads one finds higher-density apartments and condominiums. This arrangement minimizes traffic flow through streets that contain single-family dwellings, and it confines higher-density living units to certain parts of the neighborhood.

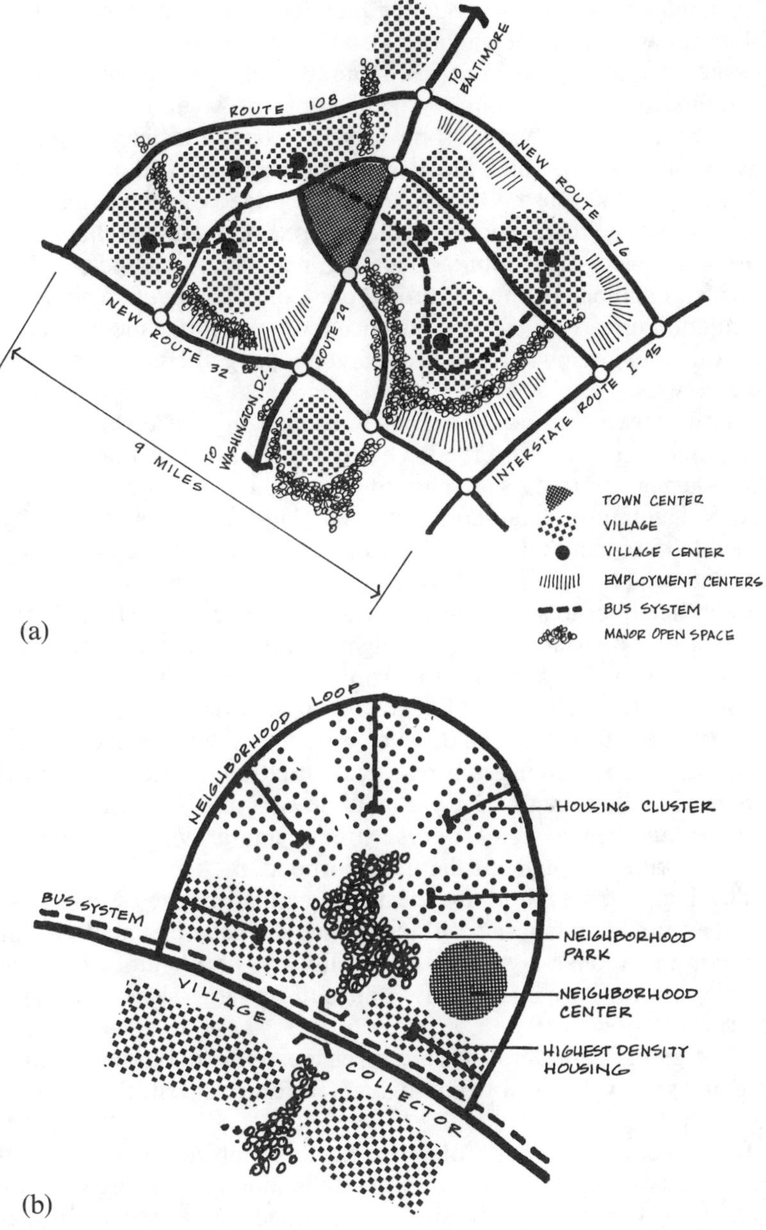

Figure 11-2. Plan of Columbia, Maryland. (a) City plan. (b) Diagram of a neighborhood. From "The Columbia Process," by M. Hoppenfeld. In D. Lewis' *The Growth of Cities,* Architects' Yearbook 13. Copyright 1971 by Elek Books, Ltd., London. Reprinted by permission.

A neighborhood is also bounded by a loop road that permits access to different parts of the neighborhood. Off the loop road are a series of cul-de-sacs that have 5 to 7 detached family homes, some modest, some very expensive.

At the center of many cul-de-sacs is a small cluster of trees and shrubs, at the edge of which are a basketball standard and a set of mailboxes arranged like post office boxes. The guide who took one of the authors around the town said that the mailboxes not only facilitated mail delivery but encouraged contact among neighbors. Cul-de-sacs with greenery and mailboxes appear throughout Columbia, even in apartment and condominium areas; in some instances we even found picnic tables in the central green area where, presumably, people gathered for meals and social activities.

Another feature of neighborhood housing is that, wherever possible, greenery and trees are preserved. Our guide informed us that, although outside housing contractors are permitted to build in Columbia, the Rouse Company maintains final authority over all plans and specifications. This is carried to the point that the Rouse Company decides which trees are to be retained on a home site and which ones may be removed.

Each neighborhood also has a neighborhood center within walking distance of every residential unit. Neighborhood centers contain a small food store and snack bar, a meeting room, a swimming pool, a park and picnic area, athletic fields, a child-care center for working parents, and an elementary school. People can drive or walk to neighborhood centers. In addition, there are walking and bike paths that connect all parts of the neighborhood. These paths lead from cul-de-sacs and high-density areas, go between and behind homes, cross streets, and provide an alternative network of routes throughout the neighborhood.

The logic of neighborhood design described above is carried out everywhere in Columbia, and all neighborhoods have essentially similar design configurations, layouts, and facilities. For identification, each neighborhood has its name clearly indicated on large signs at its major entrances.

What explicit and implicit cultural values reflected in the neighborhood concept have you noticed so far? Here are a few that we have identified:

First, we believe that Columbia can be analyzed in terms of the dialectic tension between forces toward community and forces toward individuality. The community side of the dialectic is evident in many ways. According to the design concept, neighborhoods are to be psychologically semiautonomous, identifiable, and coherent units. The idea is implicit that, if activities are focused around a neighborhood center, a sense of community will emerge. A related notion is that community ties can even be fostered at a smaller unit, such as the cul-de-sac with its community mailboxes and patch of common space in the center. Community values are also evident in the common design features of neighborhoods and in the quality control exerted by the parent company. The supervision of design and construction by the parent company attests to the importance of community rights, extending down to the design of neighborhoods and even individual homes.

The individuality half of the dialectic is also present in neighborhood design. People are given choices of homes that suit their financial statuses and personal interests—apartments, condominiums, detached dwellings. They can also choose from many styles and layouts. It is also possible for people to express their individuality in how they decorate and landscape their homes. Furthermore, there are individual choices with respect to recreational and cultural activities—swimming, parks, concerts, movies, educational programs. Finally, the design of neighborhoods permits every individual to have easy access to whatever is offered in the neighborhood—in terms of physical proximity and without special qualifications or social or economic standing. Individuality and community are, therefore, expressed in several facets of neighborhoods—designs of the physical environment, opportunities for selection of activities, access to different kinds of facilities. As we noted in Chapter 10, dialectic processes can be found in several dimensions, not just physical design.

A second dialectic that applies to Columbia is the interplay of homogeneity and diversity. There is a certain homogeneity, or simplicity, to Columbia's neighborhoods. All neighborhoods are alike: each has the same facilities, traffic flows, street arrangements, cul-de-sacs, and people. Yet there is also physical and social diversity within neighborhoods. Housing is different, even on the same street, and homes vary in form, design and cost. Presumably, this also introduces diversity in types of people in a neighborhood or on a street. Given the logic of neighborhood design, residents will almost necessarily differ in income levels, education, interests, politics, ethnicity, and general value systems. In addition, neighborhoods provide diversity in the form of a variety of activities from which people can choose. So Columbia's neighborhoods seem to offer both diversity and homogeneity of design, experiences, and people.

We also described cities and communities in Chapter 10 as reflecting a dialectic interplay of order and disorder. Clearly, neighborhood design in Columbia comes down heavily on the order side of the dialectic. Neighborhoods are planned to minute levels of detail, and all neighborhoods have a common planning concept. At the moment there is little evidence of disorderly development in Columbia. The overarching control over all aspects of community planning by the Rouse Company certainly militates against disorderly growth, at least for the near future. Whether it will occur in the future is difficult to say.

Ebenezer Howard's idea of a garden community, with its blend of green space and the built environment, is also evident in neighborhood design. In this way, Columbia fits Tuan's (1974) description of the present-day American ideal as including features of both urban and rural settings. These values are also evident in the names of neighborhoods and streets, all of which were assigned by the town developers. Consider the following street names: Wild Turkey Lane, Waterfowl Terrace, Marsh Hawk Way, Spotted Horse Lane, Grey Owl Garth, Wild Bees Lane. Clearly the animals of nature (even those that sting) are "good." But so are other aspects of nature, reflected in the following street names: Twin Rivers Road, Wind Stream Drive, New Moon Place, Rivulet Row, Morning Wind Lane, Rain Dream Hill, Fresh Air Lane. The implicit values of the rural life and natural landscape also appear in street names that recall literary figures of rural America: Faulkner Ridge Circle, Bryant Woods, Clemens Crossing. In fact, our visit did not reveal any street, neighborhood, or village names that reflected urban settings, religion, politics, or commerce. (The one exception was Wilde Lake Village, named after Mr. Wilde, the chairman of the board of directors of Connecticut General Life Insurance Company, the original financial backer of Columbia.)

Another cultural value explicit in the planning process was respect for the land. Hoppenfeld (1971), the town planner, stated:

> Choice locations for various activities such as schools, industry, low and high density housing, and lake sites were virtually dictated by the land and the critical economics of 'proper usage' (that is, harmony with nature).
>
> The same design attitude pervades today: Instead of the 5 foot contour suitable for general planning, 1 foot contours are checked in the field; roads are walked before final grades are set in order to minimize cuts of fill; trees to be saved are decided upon by size and species, and a road may bend or bifurcate to save a 30-inch oak [p. 5].

Thus, not only was the city intended to serve people, but it was to do so in a way that respected and accommodated to the environment.

Now, consider what the Columbia neighborhood is not. It is certainly not a wholly independent or self-sufficient community. Rather, it is a residential unit in a larger city, without extensive commercial or industrial facilities of its own. A clearly stated value is that the neighborhood is a place for families; its "center" is geared toward children and their families, not toward religion, politics, or commerce. To our knowledge there are no religious organizations or political units at the neighborhood level; these occur at the scale of the village and city.

The neighborhood is also not an ethnic or national enclave, as many cities described in earlier chapters were. In fact, Columbia is deliberately designed to avoid compositional clustering, through the variety of housing found in each neighborhood. Thus, there presently are no culturally distinctive qualities to different neighborhoods, as far as we could discern from written materials and firsthand observation. As discussed in Chapters 9 and 10, normally one can identify different sections of a city on the basis of architecture, layout, characteristics of the people, and culture. This is not true in Columbia; every neighborhood looks alike and has the same facilities, the same variety of housing, the same types of people, and the same general configuration. This certainly does not jibe with Fischer's (1976) subcultural theory (discussed in Chapter 10), which argues that effective urban communities often involve ethnic and other culturally homogeneous enclaves. Whether or not Columbia will eventually move toward such clustering is difficult to say.

Finally, concepts of directionality, verticality, or horizontality or other aspects of world views, discussed in Chapters 2 and 3, are not at all evident in the design of neighborhoods. Homes and streets are not oriented toward the cardinal directions; places do not seem to face in particular ways. The main criteria for design were to cluster residences around cul-de-sacs and the neighborhood center, to leave plenty of green space, and to preserve the land.

The village. Figure 11-3 outlines the organization of Columbia's villages. A village is composed of 2 to 5 neighborhoods and has 10,000 to 15,000 residents. When the city is completed, there will be eight villages containing a total of about 20 to 25 neighborhoods. At present seven villages are in various stages of construction. As shown in Figure 11-3a, the typical village and its neighborhoods are bounded by a major arterial road, and a local collector road permits auto access to and from neighborhoods (a bus system operates on major collector roads). A village may have any of the following recreational facilities: a lake for boating and sailing, a park, a golf course, a horse-riding facility. Although any resident of the city can use these facilities, major recreational sites are typically associated with the village unit.

In many respects the village is organized much like a neighborhood, only at a larger scale; that is, it has a variety of housing and facilities, and it clusters around a village center (Figure 11-3b). The village center is a larger and more elaborate version of the neighborhood center. It contains extensive shopping facilities, such as food, drug, and hardware stores, specialty shops, restaurants and fast-food places, a service station, a bank, and community service facilities, such as a library and community meeting center. The village center also has a "village green," with gardens and flowers, benches and tables, and a community bulletin board.

Recreational facilities are also located in and around village centers. There are athletic fields for baseball, basketball, football, and other

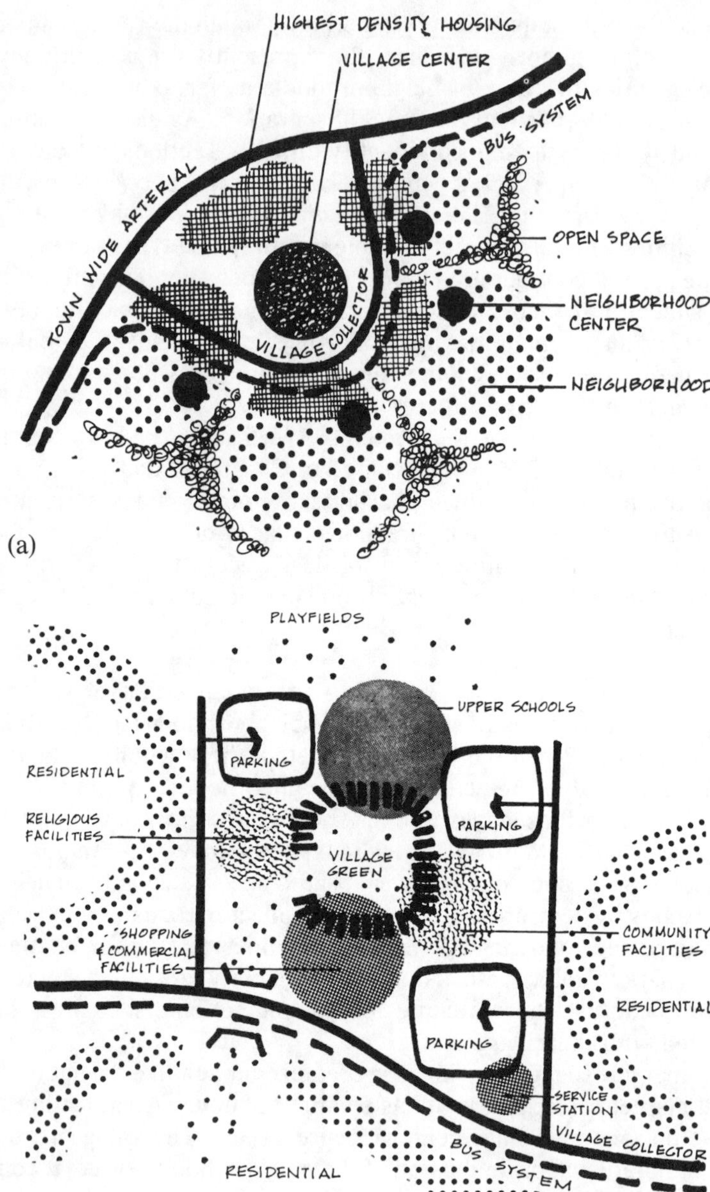

Figure 11-3. Plan of Columbia, Maryland. (a) Diagram of a village. (b) Diagram of a village center. From "The Columbia Process," by M. Hoppenfeld. In D. Lewis' *The Growth of Cities,* Architects' Yearbook 13. Copyright 1971 by Elek Books, Ltd., London. Reprinted by permission.

sports. Some villages have all-year swimming pools; others have bowling alleys, ice-skating rinks, tennis courts. In addition, village centers have commercial office space. Finally, around the periphery of most village centers are a middle school and a high school.

A fascinating aspect of life in Columbia concerns the place of religious institutions. Early in the planning process a decision was made not to sell land to individual religious denominations. Rather, a "Religious Facilities Corporation" was formed for the purpose of building interdenominational centers. Two such interfaith centers are presently shared by Catholic, Protestant, and Jewish congregations and are presently located in different village centers. Religious groups can also use the village community centers for meetings and services, and a few congregations operate out of churches that existed before Columbia was built. The sharing of facilities was an explicit planning decision, as stated in the brochure published by the interfaith group: "The bold new idea of different religious expressions working together where possible and having independent integrity when needed, began with the creation of Columbia. Thus from early on, Catholics, Jews and Protestants planned to live together in Columbia in creative tension to maximize their respective and collective interests." How well this arrangement fits with the modern American values of ecumenical relations between religions and the ofttimes less than central role that religion plays in the lives of many Americans! Contrast this with the salient place of religion in the design of communities and cities in other parts of the world and over the course of history, as described in earlier chapters.

In summary, the village is another step in the hierarchy of design that characterizes Columbia. Streets are microcosms of neighborhoods, neighborhoods are microcosms of villages. Each has its own central focus; each has its own service, commercial, recreational, educational, and community facilities; each is embedded in a higher level of organization.

What cultural values are reflected in the village and its center? Here again we can first apply the individuality/community dialectic. The concept of the village implies that people can (and should?) identify with a community larger than their street and neighborhood. An attempt is made to bring people together, not only for basic services, such as food and shopping, but also for community meetings, religion, and recreation. The assumption seems to be that there is a community identity that can exist at a level of scale larger than the neighborhood or street. In addition, there is an implicit value that it is desirable to locate community facilities in a common geographical area—for example, schools near shopping near religious facilities—and to create a center that is vibrant with all sorts of activities and all age groups. But the logic of the village design also implies that individuality is important. The opportunity for individual choice is evident in the variety of services and activities that are available to people—different shops, different types of restaurants, alternative recreational opportunities.

The organization of religious groups in villages also reflects the individuality/community dialectic. There is the attempt to have a unity of faiths which work together and which share the same facility. But there is also recognition that individual theological practices are worthwhile.

Another dialectic, homogeneity/diversity, also applies to the village, as it did to the neighborhood. All villages are basically homogeneous in their design and facilities. They all include neighborhoods clustered around a village center; they all have similar patterns of homes and locations of housing; the village centers all have similar facilities. Yet there is the intention to provide diversity in the form of different recreational facilities in different village centers and in a single village itself. While homogeneous in one sense, villages also provide their residents with diverse and complex choices for social interaction. Because a variety of facilities and people are available within and across villages, individuals and families should be able to choose from a diverse set of friends, activities, and services. Thus, the homogeneity of the basic physical design coexists with diversity of social activities and types of people with whom one can come into contact. Once again, dialectic processes need to be understood in terms of a variety of processes—physical design, social groups, activities, and facilities.

The village can also be described in terms of an order/disorder dialectic, just as we did for the neighborhood. Here too order and planning are central values. Everything in the village is planned under the guidance of the Rouse Company and no disorderly or unplanned design is evident in villages. So—for the moment, at least—the "order" part of the dialectic dominates village design and function.

Another value evident in village design relates to protection of the natural environment. Although the village center is a beehive of activity, structures are designed to blend in with the natural environment. Buildings are low, shrubbery is planted around the outskirts of the center, the village green is landscaped with flowers, trees, and shrubs. In addition, there are no billboards or tall signs anywhere in sight. Even gas-station signs are at ground level and are surrounded by shrubs and plants. Collector roads are also landscaped, open fields and park areas are carefully maintained, and there is a deliberate attempt to preserve the land and natural vegetation.

In summary, the village, like the neighborhood, idealizes a planned community where people can be part of a unity but still be individuals, where life is on a small scale but where there are choices among services and facilities. These and other aspects of the "good life" are intended to occur within a built environment that is simultaneously respectful of the natural environment. These values operate not only in the village and neighborhood but also at the larger-scale level of the city.

The downtown center. Downtown Columbia is designed according to the same logic used for streets, neighborhoods, and villages. Major peripheral arteries and internal collector roads permit easy access to any part of the city and downtown. There is also a bus system that connects neighborhoods, villages, and various parts of the town.

The villages of Columbia all cluster around the downtown area, which is a focal point for many activities. Downtown Columbia is dominated by a few key landmarks, which portray well some of the important values of Columbia. For example, one such landmark is a large man-made lake at the edge of the downtown area. This lake, one of three in Columbia, is used for boating and recreation. It is surrounded by rolling green hills and has a bike and walking path around it. On the lakefront at the foot of the town center is an open plaza used for concerts and plays. Immediately adjacent to the amphitheater are a picnic area and an open-air café. And nearby is the abstract sculpture that symbolizes Columbia—"The People Tree." Adjacent to these areas are restaurants and a movie theater. So one value that stands out clearly in the downtown area is to serve people in the areas of recreation, culture, and leisure.

A second aspect of the downtown area involves commercial interests, symbolized by a large, white office building, the tallest structure in the city. This building is located geographically and functionally at the center of the downtown area and serves as a central landmark. Nearby are several other office buildings and a motel. Thus, commercial and business interests are also intrinsic parts of Columbia.

The third focus of activities in the downtown area is an enclosed bilevel shopping mall that presently houses two department stores and over 100 shops, stores, and restaurants. The mall provides an array of services that are not available in village and neighborhood centers. It is analogous in design to the rest of Columbia. It has its own "center," a fountain and shallow pool, around which people eat lunch, rest, or watch the shoppers. The mall has skylights that provide a feeling of the outdoors as the natural light plays on the running water of the fountain. There also are growing trees throughout the mall, some 20 to 40 feet tall. Thus, in the midst of all the hustle and bustle of people shopping, there are symbols of nature—another example of Columbia's goal of melding the urban and natural environments.

The centrally located fountain is analogous to the neighborhood or village center. This image is made salient by a marketplace atmosphere. Around the pool are craftspeople with handcarts that display leather goods, jewelry, and other items as well as open-air restaurants and tables. The fountain area, the craftspeople, and the restaurants create an atmosphere very similar to that in marketplaces found in towns and communities all over the world.

Fast-food restaurants adjacent to the fountain specialize in diverse foods—Polish, Jewish, soul, Greek, Italian. Columbia's intention to have a diversity of values, interests, and people may well be reflected in this cluster of restaurants.

In summary, the town center of Columbia is organized around three major activities that were important values in the minds of the planners—commercial interests, recreational interests, and personal services to residents. Nowhere in the downtown area does one find religious symbols, buildings, or monuments; nor could we find readily visible governmental or political centers. The downtown area can also be analyzed in terms of the dialectical concepts of order/disorder, individuality/community, and homogeneity/diversity. As in other parts of Columbia, order and planned design predominate. The layout of the town center is systematic, any part of the area can be reached easily, and there is little that is spontaneous or disorderly in the design.

With respect to individuality/community, the pattern is similar to what we described for villages, neighborhoods, and streets. A sense of community is evident in the image of the downtown as the "center" of the whole city, a place where residents can go for recreation, business, and personal services. Furthermore, the focal points of the lakefront recreation area, the high-rise office building, and the mall presumably create community gathering places. But individuality also exists, in that the facilities of the town center are supposed to appeal to a broad range of individual preferences, from recreational opportunities and lakefront facilities to the shops and services in the mall. Thus, different individuals can presumably satisfy their unique needs in the downtown center.

Homogeneity and diversity also exist in the downtown area. Homogeneity is implicit in the analogous design of the town center with that of the villages, neighborhoods, and streets. The downtown, like other parts of the community, has outer access roads, centers and focal points, little mystery in location and availability of services, and the same commercial, recreational, and personal services (albeit more varied) as those found in neighborhoods and villages. Yet there is considerable diversity in the downtown area, with its variety of recreational opportunities, shops, restaurants, and services. So homogeneity and diversity exist side by side in the downtown area, much as they did at other levels of the community.

Other parts of Columbia. Columbia also includes a number of communitywide facilities located in different parts of the city. These include a hospital, a 110-acre campus of the Howard County Community College, and part-time graduate and undergraduate facilities of Loyola College—Baltimore, Antioch College, and Johns Hopkins University. In addition, there are a dinner theater and the Merriweather Post Pavilion of Music. The latter facility is located in a large park known as Symphony Woods and seats 12,000 people in a covered area and on a lawn. In addition, Columbia operates its own medical health plan with voluntary participation by residents.

Citywide recreational facilities also abound: three lakes, a game preserve, 1900 acres of parks, playgrounds, and open space, 28 miles of paths for walking, biking, and jogging, a central athletic club, ice-skating rinks, golf courses, roller-skating rinks, and tennis clubs. Many of these facilities are located in villages; however, all are under the jurisdiction of the Columbia Association, a private, nonprofit corporation supported by all Columbia property owners. Many recreational facilities are available to all members of the association, but certain ones require additional fees.

Columbia also has long-range plans for four industrial parks, located on the fringes of the city away from residential areas. These parks will emphasize distribution, office, and research-and-development activities, with only a small number of firms involved in manufacturing. As of 1977 there were 150 industrial firms located in the industrial parks, ranging from large companies such as General Electric and Toyota to small, private firms. It is anticipated that about 3200 of the 14,000 acres in the city will be used for industrial purposes.

There is obviously much more to Columbia than we have presented. (See Burby & Weiss, 1976, and Moos & Brownstein, 1977, for other analyses of Columbia.) However, for our purposes the features of Columbia that stand out are its emphasis on orderly planning, the central importance of the natural and urban environments, the concept of clustered and hierarchically arranged communities, and the idea of "centers" built around recreational, commercial, and service facilities. In addition, Columbia emphasizes the importance of diverse people living together in a common community, enjoying freedom of choice and individuality, side by side with community identification. Finally, Columbia is unique in its attempt to provide almost all of life's services to its citizens, under the benevolent control of a single management organization. All these features make Columbia a fascinating experiment in city design. While it is partly a city of the present, it is also futuristic in its ideals, and we will be interested in visiting it again some years hence, to see the match between these ideals and reality.

HABITAT, MONTREAL, QUEBEC

A strikingly different and smaller-scale futuristic community is located in Montreal on the Saint Lawrence River. The idea for this community, called Habitat, was proposed by Moshe Safdie, an Israeli-born architect, in connection with the International Exposition of 1967, which was held in Montreal. Habitat was to be a demonstration of a futuristic city design, variants of which Safdie believed could be used all over the world to solve many of the problems of urban life.

The physical design of Habitat originally called for a community of 1000 families, as an illustrative prototype of the concept. For other parts of the world, Safdie has developed conceptual designs of much larger communities (Safdie, 1970). One salient feature of Habitat is its three-dimensional design. Whereas Columbia is organized primarily on the horizontal dimension—that is, it spreads out over the land, and has relatively few high-rise structures—Habitat is exactly the opposite. It is a high-rise community that is built on a relatively small area of land. Because Habitat, Montreal, has only 158 dwelling units (financial problems made it impossible to build the planned 1000 residences), one cannot fully appreciate the concept of verticality unless one examines drawings of Safdie's plans for other cities. The vertical design concept derives from his conclusion that communities of the future will not be able to spread out horizontally, but that we will have to build upward, not just single buildings but whole communities where people will work, live and play. This general idea had also been part of several futuristic proposals offered in the 1930s by the environmental designer Le Corbusier, who undoubtedly influenced Safdie (Fishman, 1977).

A second salient feature of Habitat is its repetitive, boxlike character, with large, rectangular concrete modules stacked upon one another. Habitat, Montreal, does not have the smooth lines of the modern skyscraper, nor does it have an evident theme, like a church building. It is more like the terraced, modular design of the Pueblo Indians, with rectangular units piled up on one another. (In fact, Safdie stated that he was heavily influenced by the pueblo structures of the southwestern United States.)

Safdie also assumed that it would be desirable to provide many life services to the residents of his vertical cities, so that the ideal goal of Habitat is not only to include residences in the community but to have a variety of other readily accessible services. Although Habitat, Montreal, never achieved this ideal completely, the ideal is implicit in Safdie's approach.

Safdie also assumed that cities of the future, like those of the past, would grow and evolve. How could growth be permitted in a way that would avoid chaotic and uncontrolled development? His solution was to use prefabricated modular living units. If such units were manufactured elsewhere on a mass-production basis, they could be easily transported to the site of the community, lifted on cranes, and placed on top of existing units, thereby adding to the city or community. This would permit, theoretically, continual evolution and growth of a community through prefabricated units that would be compatible with the rest of the city. Furthermore, in Habitat, Montreal, the modules were designed as "plug-in" units, with all plumbing, wiring, and heating facilities built right in. All that needed to be done was to plug a new dwelling unit into existing plumbing and electrical systems. Even the bathrooms and kitchens of Habitat were built into the prefabricated units.

The basic building block of Habitat was a concrete module 38.5 feet long, 17 feet wide, and 10 feet high, yielding about 650 square feet of floor space. It was assumed that this space would be the minimum necessary for a one-bedroom house. Various-sized residential units were put together using one to three basic modules, either all on one level or on two levels, with each unit, however small, having a terrace, or open area, formed by the roof of the module below. With this modular system it is theoretically possible to create a large number of house plans simply by differential stacking and connecting of modules. Habitat, Montreal, modules are stacked 12 high at the highest point (120 feet above the ground). Safdie considered these residential units to be houses, not apartments, since they did not share walls with neighbors (except for terraces). Thus, people lived in physically separate dwelling units.

Habitat, Montreal, has public streets and thoroughfares, along with stairways, elevator lifts, and escalators. The outside streets are covered walkways, in response to the harsh winters of the region. Parking facilities and storage areas are at the bottom of the community, with elevators, plumbing, and services operating out of central core units.

The present Habitat, Montreal, does not contain the full-scale community facilities of Columbia, although it theoretically could. In addition to Habitat, Montreal, Safdie has designed similar communities for Puerto Rico, New York City, Washington, D.C., Israel, and elsewhere. The community in Puerto Rico has been at least partly constructed according to modular and vertical concepts, although its specifications differ from those of Habitat, Montreal.

A dominant value in Habitat is that the community is designed to promote and enhance the life of its residents. Throughout his book Safdie (1970) referred to a variety of human needs that his design was intended to satisfy—privacy, identity, community, stimulation, access to the outdoors, protection from the elements. Nowhere does one read about the community's being organized to serve religious, cosmological, or political values. Instead, the goal is to provide an environment that will enhance the lives of ordinary people—children, adults, and traditional family units. In this respect Habitat, Columbia, and Howard's garden cities share identical values about the importance of the individual and the nuclear family unit.

Another assumption concerns the desirability of access to both the urban and the natural environment. This is what Tuan (1974) described as the late-20th-century ideal, in which both the planned urban environment and the untouched natural environment are considered ideal. Safdie (1970) said:

> We want two extremes. We want the intensive meeting place, the urban environment, the place where everybody is together, and we want the secluded open space where we are alone in the country in nature. We need and want both. . . . The average North American's ideal is to go shopping in New York, to have a choice of going to theaters, concerts, operas, museums, restaurants, discotheques. . . . The ideal environment would have the variety of Manhattan's amenities and the recreation space of the sea coast or the open spaces of New England as part of daily experience, close enough so that you could enjoy both every day [p. 223].[2]

In another place he stated:

> We have two kinds of distinct feelings in the environment, one which we associate with being in the city, the other with being in the open country—the sensations of walking in the forest under branches and leaves swaying in the breeze. The contrast is recognized whenever we feel the need to withdraw from the urban environment and go back to nature, which restores in us a certain peace and stability. . . . I believe that as the man-made environment approaches the perfection of the form fulfillment of natural organisms, this separation between the man-made and natural will disappear, that we as men will be equally fulfilled in either man-made or natural environments [1970, p. 147].

Safdie described several factors that had given rise to the preceding values. First, during his boyhood in Haifa, Israel, he lived in an apartment but also raised chickens and goats in proximity to his home—a kind of simultaneous urban and rural setting that he hoped to re-create in Habitat. Furthermore, his analyses of the Aztec, Mayan, and Pueblo cultures reinforced the image of natural and urban environments existing side by side.

How did he plan to blend the urban and natural environments in Habitat? One strategy was to design the community so that people had terraces and gardens on the tops of residential modules, where they could be outdoors, where they could grow plants and vegetables, and where they could have a small symbol of the natural environment. In addition, Habitat had public gardens and green spaces even though there were many problems in developing adequate watering systems. Furthermore, the community was designed to have many windows and walkways that

[2]This and all other quotations from this source are from *Beyond Habitat*, by M. Safdie. Copyright 1970 by M. Safdie. Reprinted by permission.

permitted people to have visual access to the river and woods surrounding Habitat. For example, in addition to residential windows that faced outward, the protective concrete barriers around pedestrian streets and public places were designed with low and horizontal 3-inch slots every 20 feet so that children could see the surrounding environment.

Another assumption underlying the Habitat theory was that cities are "living things," almost like biological organisms. Safdie hoped to design cities that could continually grow and accommodate increasing numbers of people without losing their coherence. He said "The problem then is to develop a form in which increased density evolves naturally without the destruction of what has been built in an earlier stage" (Safdie, 1970, p. 55). To do this he worked from a biological and evolutionary model; that is, animal forms have been selected through evolution to generate an organism/environment fit, and cities can be designed to do the same thing. For example, he reasoned that cities could grow in the same way as a snail shell. A snail never outgrows itself but expands around a central core in an orderly and progressive way. Couldn't cities also be designed to grow in a systematic way, clustered around a core of central services, with new and old units maintaining their coherence in relation to the whole? Safdie viewed Habitat as a spirally growing place, like a snail and its shell, with core services, such as plumbing and electricity, more or less at the center and with modules added in an orderly, compatible, and evolutionary way.

The biological analogy was carried further, even to the design of windows.

> What we ideally require of a window is not unlike what the eye provides. The window should shrink or expand according to the quality of light and the time of day and season. It should move in and out of the wall in response to the sun's penetration and in the direction in which we are looking through it. Its transparency should vary, sometimes allowing all light through, sometimes very little. It should have the quality of becoming instantly opaque. It should expand and shrink like the shutter of a camera [Safdie, 1970, p. 148].

We can also examine Habitat in terms of the dialectic processes of individuality/community, homogeneity/diversity, and order/disorder, as we did for Columbia.

Individuality was a central value to be achieved:

> People want to feel that they can shape their own personal environment, they can change it, they can modify it, they can choose it, that it's not imposed on them, and they like to feel that it's not the same as everybody else's, because they are not the same as other people. In fact, the ideal would be dwellings that are as different from each other as human faces and personalities are different from each other [Safdie, 1970, p. 150].

Although Habitat's modules are identical, Safdie felt that their arrangement and stacking in a variety of combinations would permit people to put their individual stamp on the environment. However, the community aspect also appears in Habitat. The attempt was, ideally, to create a unity to the community by means of gathering places for community activities, a sense of common bonds, and a coherent identity with others through the vehicle of design. Community bonds were reflected in the inclusion of public meeting and socializing places, children's play areas, and public transportation systems that would permit people to go to any part of the city quickly.

Another dialectic reflected in Habitat concerns homogeneity/diversity of design and life-style. The fundamental design of Habitat is simple, repetitive, and homogeneous, the basic building block being a uniformly sized concrete module. And this standardization exists in built-in bathroom and kitchen fixtures, window designs, and other features, all yielding a sameness and homogeneity. But Safdie also sought variation in Habitat through the concept of "diversity in repetitiveness."

> Habitat tries to show that it is possible to have an environment that is not monotonous, one that has the possibility of identity and of variety, choice and spatial richness, and yet at the same time the use of repetitive mass-produced systems. . . .
>
> People visiting Habitat were reminded of a Mediterranean village. . . . [Such villages] consist of a vocabulary of repetitive components—for example, the Arab village with its cubical room, dome, vault, and court. These components are manipulated by the individual who builds his own house. . . . Habitat is in the tradition of spontaneous self-made environments, the beginnings of a contemporary vernacular [Safdie, 1970, p. 118].

How can diversity and repetitiveness be simultaneously achieved? Habitat's solution was as follows: use different ways of stacking modules, thereby creating varied visual and internal configurations of space; give people the opportunity to plan their own interior space; provide a variety of views through windows. In nature, Safdie theorized, there is repetitiveness of form in a species, but there is also variety. While all members of a species look alike in some ways, they are also quite unique. So it was intended that, within the simplicity of Habitat's design, people would have access to a wide range of designs and associated activities. Furthermore, it was hoped that Habitat, like Columbia, would have a broad spectrum of residents with respect to ethnic, socioeconomic, and other characteristics, yielding a diversity of social views from which people could sample.

Habitat and Columbia share similar qualities on the homogeneity/diversity dialectic, although they use different design concepts. In Columbia, diversity was achieved through variation of house types, people, and activities. Yet neighborhoods and villages were quite similar to one another, yielding simultaneous homogeneity and diversity. Habitat, in contrast, creates diversity by using different arrangements of the same structures, not different structures arranged in similar ways.

With respect to the order/disorder dialectic, Habitat, like Columbia, comes down strongly on the side of order and planning. Without such order, Safdie argues, urban life would be chaotic and not facilitative of human development. Here again, it will be interesting to see what happens in the coming years and whether what has befallen most cities and communities will occur in Habitat—namely, some degree of chaos and disorder.

A final quality of Habitat is its responsiveness to environmental conditions. Safdie proposed a number of design features in response to the harsh winter climate of Montreal. There are covered outside streets and street shelters, open slots at the bottom of outside railings that reduce wind velocity and snow accumulation, irrigation systems for watering public greenery, windows designed to minimize condensation and to handle the extreme winter/summer differential, and windows and dwellings placed so as to receive several hours of sunshine a day. In his plans for a 1500-dwelling-unit community in Israel, Safdie designed a domed window and shutter system for terraces, which could be adjusted to handle temperature conditions during hot summer days and cool nights and which permitted use of a terrace during the winter. So the Habitat concept, in its attention to human needs and well-being, not only focuses on psychological and cultural factors but also is sensitive to physical environmental factors.

In summary, beyond the interesting aspects of its physical layout, Habitat reflects several present-day values of Western society—the importance of the individual and the family, the need to weave together the built and natural environments, the desirability of orderly planning and growth, and the attempt to achieve an appropriate interplay of individuality/community and homogeneity/diversity of human experiences.

SOLERI'S CONCEPT OF ARCOLOGY

Habitat and Columbia are existing cities. Now we turn to an urban design concept of the distant future, which presently exists largely in the mind and vision of its planner, Paolo Soleri.

Soleri has done sketches and general layouts of more than 30 futuristic cities; these can be found in his book *Arcology: The City in the Image of Man* (1969). Although the particular configurations vary, Soleri includes a common core of concepts in all his city designs. One vivid example is the city of Hexahedron, shown in Figure 11-4.

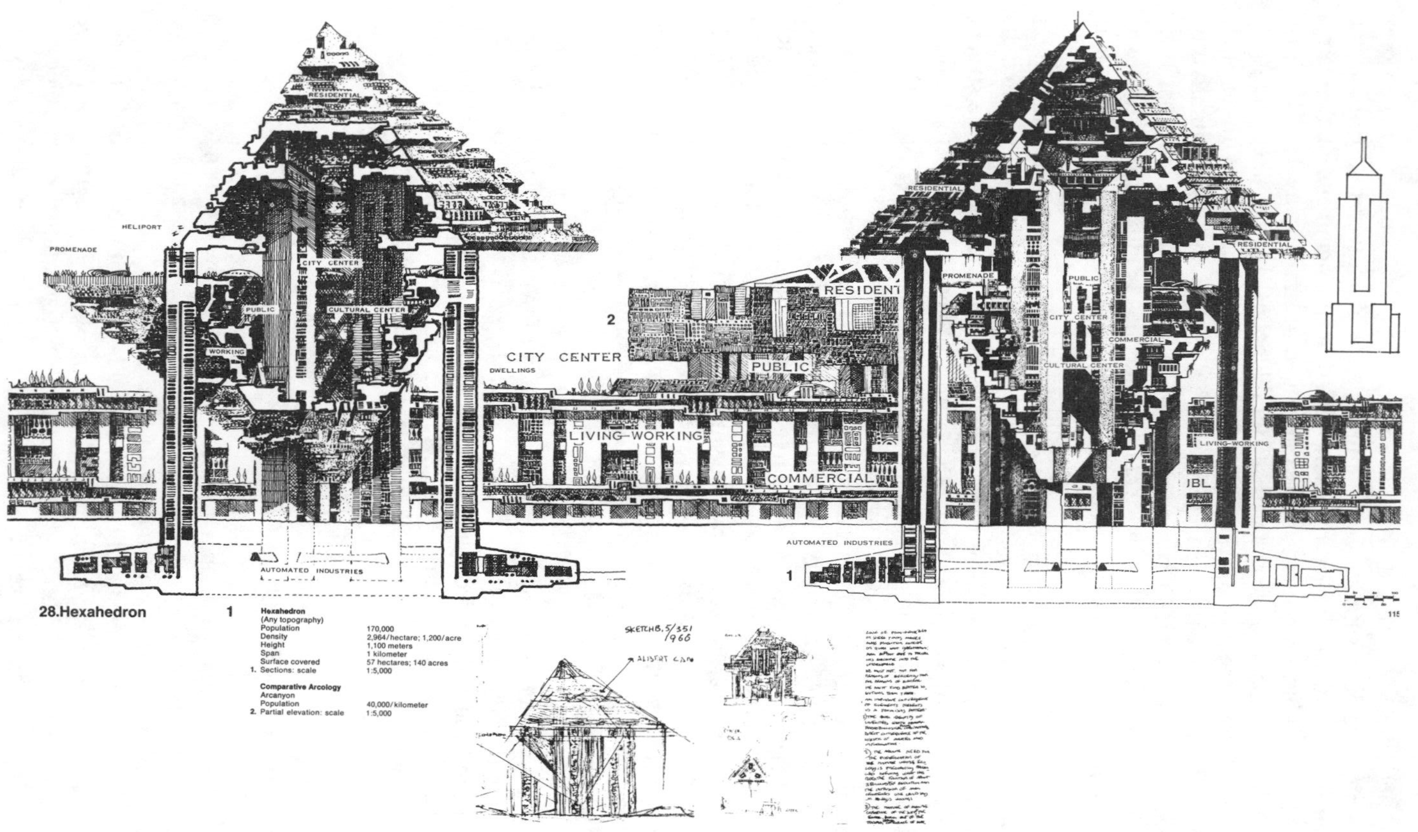

28.Hexahedron

1 **Hexahedron**

(Any topography)	
Population	170,000
Density	2,964/hectare; 1,200/acre
Height	1,100 meters
Span	1 kilometer
Surface covered	57 hectares; 140 acres
1. Sections: scale	1:5,000

Comparative Arcology

Arcanyon	
Population	40,000/kilometer
2. Partial elevation: scale	1:5,000

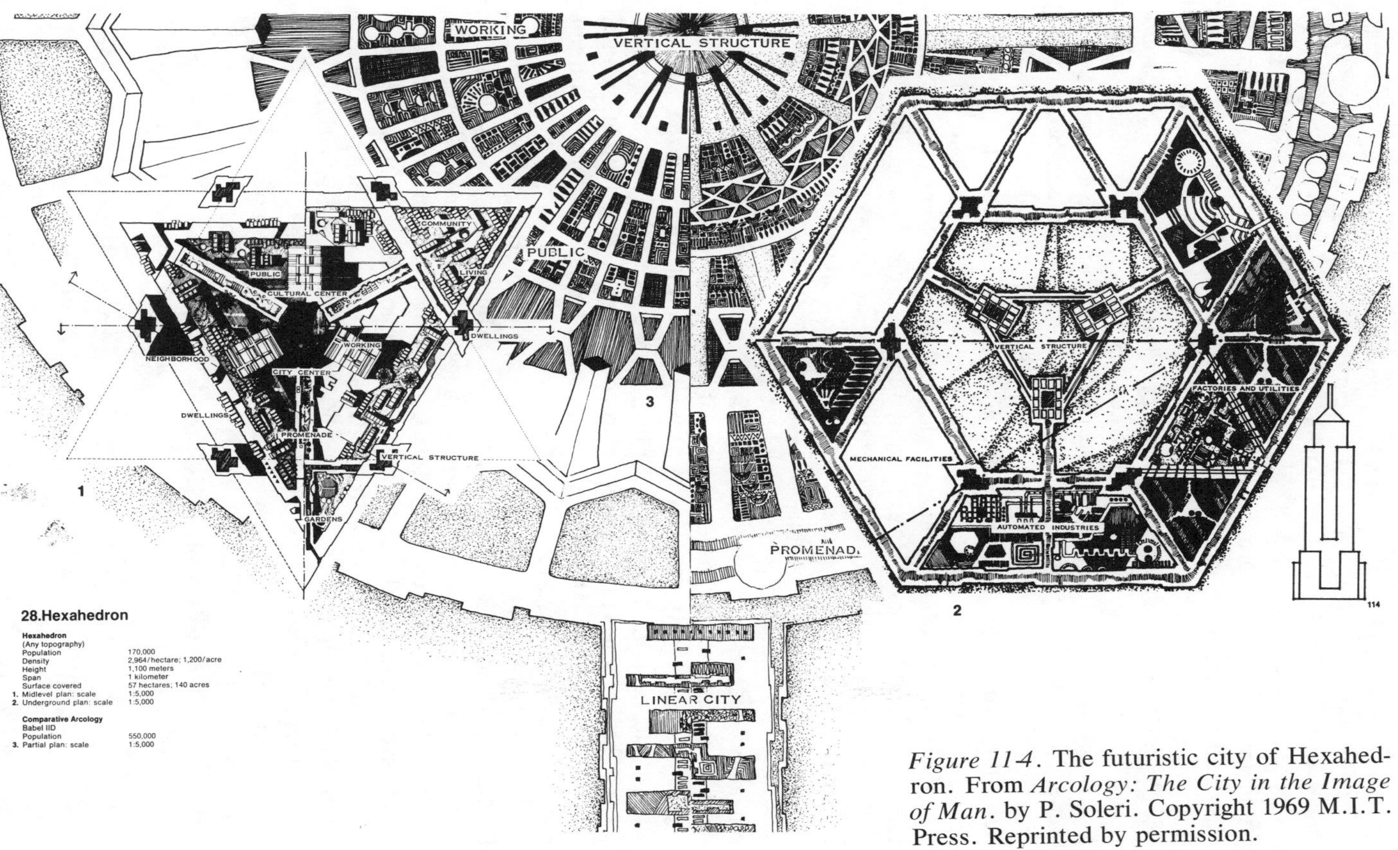

Figure 11-4. The futuristic city of Hexahedron. From *Arcology: The City in the Image of Man*. by P. Soleri. Copyright 1969 M.I.T. Press. Reprinted by permission.

A central feature of Soleri's approach is that cities of the future are to be three-dimensional. Like Safdie, but more dramatically, Soleri calls for vertically built cities. Hexahedron, for example, is designed to be 1100 meters high (somewhat less than a mile). Other city plans range in height from 300 to 400 feet to a mile, depending on population size. Cities also vary in the space they occupy; Hexahedron covers about 140 acres. With a projected population of 170,000, Hexahedron will have about 1200 people per acre—a rather dense place, even if one considers the distribution of people in the vertical dimension. However, as discussed below, Soleri believes that there are virtues in density, and he deliberately designed some cities to have high concentrations of people. Some of his cities will house up to 6 million people; others have as few as 1500. And, depending on the land, climate, and goals of the city, population density varies from a few hundred people per acre to over a thousand per acre.

Soleri's cities have common characteristics that are represented in the hypothetical city of Hexahedron. First, the city is conceived of "in the image of man" (as in the title of his book), and it has many features of the human body. The outer layer of the city is analogous to the eyes, ears, and skin and is in immediate contact with the world. It is on this outer surface that residential areas are located, facing the natural environment but also being part of the city. For Soleri, the natural environment of deserts, forests, and wilderness, as well as farm land, is to exist outside of the city, sharply distinct from it. However, people living in the city can and should have easy visual and physical access to the natural environment. The outer areas of the city also contain parks and recreational and other facilities, such as airports, but it is residential dwellings that dominate on the outer surface.

At the next layer of the city, toward the interior, there are public facilities such as offices, cultural centers, promenades, shops, theaters, and museums. These are community places where people obtain services, work, and use recreational facilities. According to the analogy of the city as a human organism, this layer houses the "mind" and "control centers" of the community. It is here that individuals come together and create a unity to the city that is more than their separate lives on the periphery. At the next layer of the city, deep in its central core, is the "plumbing" of the community, in the form of power plants, warehouses, and heavy industry. The central core area is analogous to the internal organs and digestive and vascular systems of the human body; it involves basic "life processes" that underlie the workings of the "mind" and the "sensorimotor" parts of the urban system.

Movement through Hexahedron is to be by high-speed transportation systems that will take residents from their homes to offices, shopping areas, cultural centers, and recreation areas within just a few minutes. Furthermore, because of Soleri's belief in the importance of the natural environment to human well-being, people will be able to go easily to the natural environment outside the city.

With its enormous population density and three-dimensional quality, coupled with what undoubtedly will be considerable visual, auditory, and other stimulation, one can easily imagine a life of extraordinary activity in a city like Hexahedron. However, homes will be separated from the hustle and bustle of the city's center, so as to provide people with solitude. Homes also are to be spacious; for example, one set of dimensions specifies apartments that are 60 feet long, 35 feet wide, and 20 feet high, a good bit larger than many homes.

Hexahedron is only one of many urban designs proposed by Soleri. Other cities are appropriate for oceanfronts, deserts, mountains, farming areas, and elsewhere. He has even designed a city called Asteromo, which is an "asteriod" on which 70,000 people can live in space. One can see that Soleri has not restricted himself to the present time or even to the planet Earth.

It is not possible to say much more about the actual design of any of Soleri's cities, because he does not provide the extensive details that were available for Columbia and Habitat. His proposals are at a conceptual stage and are formulated at such a general level that we are literally dealing with a "theory," not a plan for particular places.

Soleri, a former student of Frank Lloyd Wright, the visionary American architect, is now building his first futuristic city, north of Phoenix, Arizona. This city, Arcosanti, is to be a small-scale demonstration of his concept and will eventually house 1500 people. The city is being built by students and volunteers, and its construction has not progressed very far. You can visit or write to Soleri at Arcosanti and learn more about the project.

What are the philosophical and cultural values that underlie Soleri's ideas? He is sometimes explicit, but his statements about the goals and philosophy underlying his city plans contain many complex and elusive themes. Nevertheless, several themes stand out clearly and are implied in the title of his book, *Arcology: The City in the Image of Man*. The term *arcology* is a shorthand combination of *architecture* and *ecology*, and it conveys Soleri's idea that the built environment of the city and the untouched natural environment are both "ideal" and that together they contribute to people's well-being. People need the city for social, cultural, economic, and community reasons. But they also require easy access to the beauties of untouched nature. Both are good, and both are necessary for people's well-being. However, the concept of arcology also states that the built environment and the natural environment must be sharply separated from each other, not woven together. Although gardens and greenery in the city are acceptable, the city is the city and nature is nature, and they are to be distinct places, neither contaminating nor subverting the other's essence. This value system is clearly different from that underlying Habitat and Columbia, both of which blended the urban and natural environment in a single setting.

The subtitle of Soleri's book—*The City in the Image of Man*—conveys two other central facets of his theorizing. First, cities must serve individual needs. They are not designed primarily for religious, political, or economic goals. Rather, cities are to serve the needs of people and should facilitate the growth and well-being of ordinary individuals. As part of this value, Soleri believes that cities should be designed at a scale that an individual human can handle (for example, a person must have access to every part of the life of a city without stress or strain) and the city must attempt to serve all human needs—social, cultural, political, educational.

> The care of the citizen is the sap of the city. But one can care only for that which one loves. Lovableness is the key to a living city. A lovely city is not an accident, as a lovely person is not an accident. . . .
>
> . . . Metropolitan life means access to the source of economic well-being, to all the institutions that make up the culture of a country, to the institutions of health, education, leisure, play interaction, and to the noninstitutionalized aspects of private and collective life; short of this plentitude (access to it, that is to say), metropolitan life is not justifiable [Soleri, 1969, p. 7].[3]

This theme is, of course, totally congruent with 20th-century values and with the goals of Columbia and Habitat. Unlike many cities of the past and in other cultures, which often emphasized religious, political, and commercial institutions, Soleri's cities place ordinary people at the center of urban and community planning.

There is still another value implicit in the title *Arcology: The City in the Image of Man*—namely, Soleri's biological and evolutionary theorizing about city design. As noted above, the arcology concept calls for cities to be modeled on human and other organisms. Cities, like organisms, are to be three-dimensional, with the vertical dimension a crucial part of their structure, just as it is in all evolutionarily advanced organisms. Furthermore, cities are to have their sensory apparatus (residences) at the skin, or surface, and their cognitive, muscular, and skeletal apparatus partly in the interior (schools, offices, cultural centers). Finally, industry and power plants, which are analogous to the digestive, organ, and vascular systems of humans and other advanced organisms, are located deep in the interior of the city. So Soleri's cities are more than simple "images" of man; they are literal simulations of the human organism and higher forms

[3]This and all other quotations from this source are from *Arcology: The City in the Image of Man*, by P. Soleri. Copyright 1969 by M.I.T. Press. Reprinted by permission.

of life. In this respect arcology cities and Habitat are similar, and both are quite different from Columbia, which does not explicitly use such an analogy.

Soleri applies still other aspects of evolutionary concepts to city design. For him, evolutionary theory suggests that more advanced forms of life are characterized by *compactness,* or *miniaturization, implosion,* and *efficiency*. Here are some of his views on miniaturization:

> In its evolution from matter to mind, the real has been submitted to numerous phases of miniaturization so as to fit more things into smaller spaces in shorter times. This process, from haphazardness and dislocation to coordination and fitness, has been mandatory because each successive form of reality carried in itself a greater degree of complexity. Any higher organism contains more performances than a chunk of the unlimited universe light years thick, and it ticks on a time clock immensely swifter. This miniaturization process may well be one of the fundamental rules of evolution. Now that the inequitude of man is turned to the construction of the superorganism, which society is, a new phase of miniaturization is imperative. Arcology is a step toward it [p. 31].

Soleri's idea is that large, formless, unorganized cities, like certain species in the history of evolution (the dinosaur?), are not viable. Rather, species that have survived and evolved are highly differentiated and very compact. The human being and, in particular, the human brain exemplify the importance of differentiation and miniaturization, Soleri states, and there is little else to match the elegance of their operation. So it is in technology that miniaturization of computers and electronic systems has permitted us to harness energy for many complex activities. For these reasons, Soleri strives to achieve compactness and differentiation in his city designs. Instead of expanding, exploding, and spreading out cities on the surface of the earth, he suggests that we adopt a principle of *implosion,* or inward compaction and miniaturization, as a more appropriate evolutionary process. Thus, Soleri calls for increasing the density of cities, but in an *efficient* way that enhances people's lives and facilitates their personal growth.

How is this to be done? First, one must ensure that cities provide all necessary life functions, as described above. Second, and more important, one must do so efficiently, just as the human body is an efficient system. Efficiency is achieved in a variety of ways. For example, each person must function as an independent "cell or organ system," operating on his or her own, but also be tied into the whole community. On this score, Soleri says:

> An animal is an organism of one mind. The city is an organism of one thousand minds. This is the most significant difference between a biological

> organism and the city. Furthermore, those one thousand minds do not stay put. They are eminently peripatetic, but in clusters of three or four or so (the family) they tend to define a territory that is more static (the home). What confronts the planner is the organization of the body to the satisfaction of the thousand minds. One may say that while an inner center, the brain, is the center to which the body renders service biologically, urbanistically the epidermis made up of a thousand brains is the "center" to which the body is dedicated [p. 31].

In addition, efficiency means minimizing pollution and land waste and developing frugal but concentrated uses of energy. This can be achieved through miniaturization and a "high payload" per unit of energy. All these thoughts are captured in some of Soleri's own words:

> Both vegetal and animal life are possible only within a condition of relative denseness. The degree of liveliness is proportional to the degree of compactness of the organism. . . .
>
> Compactness is the "structure" of efficiency. Within compactness the energy flow is commensurate to the function that is being performed. . . .
>
> Richer is the life where greater is the complexity. Therefore, greater the need for energy and thus greater the need for compactness. . . .
>
> The compact city is a three-dimensional city. Its vertical dimension is congruous to its horizontal dimensions. . . . The city must be a solid not a "surface."
>
> The three-dimensional city is respectful of the earth's sensitized skin. It does not spread an inorganic crust . . . over the vital green carpet of the earth.
>
> The three-dimensional city, because of its true efficiency (frugality), is also respectful of the earth's ecological systems and its atmosphere. It does not pollute the earth.
>
> The three-dimensional city is respectful of man because it is the best instrument for a full private and social life. The three-dimensional city is an instrument of culture [p. 9].

We can also examine the concept of arcology in relation to the dialectic analysis applied to other futuristic designs. Arcology cities, like Habitat and Columbia, are heavily oriented to orderly planning and organization. In fact, the very ideas of compactness, miniaturization, and differentiation are almost the epitome of order, and, in Soleri's thinking, uncontrolled or disorderly growth is viewed as an anathema to human survival. Thus, order reigns.

The dialectic of individuality/community is also explicit in Soleri's theorizing. As described above, he believes that cities should be designed to enhance the growth of individual human beings and to satisfy their needs. Homes on the surface of the city are designed to permit individual expression and to allow people to be with their families or alone, separate from the community. And individuals have ready access to resources and facilities they need or want for their personal growth. However, the city is also a community of individuals who must be tied together as a unity; it is an integrated body of people who complement one another and who form a "superorganism." So the arcology concept incorporates the dialectic of individuality and community.

In addition, the homogeneity/diversity dialectic applies to Soleri's theory. There is a homogeneous quality to his city designs, modeled as they are after biological organisms with certain kinds of facilities in the same places, and with similarity in that they all obey principles of compactness and unity of parts. Just as Columbia was designed around hierarchically unified and homogeneous villages and neighborhoods, so arcology cities exhibit a certain homogeneity. Yet, within the unity and homogeneity, there is diversity of activities, functions, and places. Soleri argues strongly that cities should be diverse, rich, stimulating, complex places. He also states that diversity will be further enhanced by increasing density along with compactness and efficiency.

COLUMBIA, HABITAT, AND HEXAHEDRON

On the face of it, the three futuristic city designs just described are quite different, each representing its designer's vision of the "ideal" community and city. Columbia is a horizontal, spread-out community; Habitat and Hexahedron are vertical communities. Columbia has a low population density; Habitat and Hexahedron are high-density settings. Furthermore, Columbia and, to some extent, Habitat bring nature into the city; Hexahedron keeps the city and the natural environment sharply separated.

In spite of these differences, these design concepts share several philosophical and cultural assumptions. For example, all three approaches focus on the individual human and the family as central to city design. Congruent with present-day Western values, the worth of the individual is salient, and all designs are geared to the satisfaction of individual needs, desires, opportunities for growth, and freedom of choice. In addition, the focus is on ordinary people, not emperors, kings, priests, or high-status persons. These futuristic city designs are intended to help ordinary people live happily, grow personally, and achieve their individual potentials. As described in other chapters, this has not always been an explicit goal of city design in other cultures or throughout history. What guided the development of many cities was religious, political, and economic institutions, or agents of these institutions. But in the three futuristic concepts examined here, it is the average citizen who is at the center of the process.

Second, the three planning approaches are similar in their aspiration to incorporate and make available to people both the natural environment and the built environment. Although their particular design solutions vary, they all adopt a perspective that the well-being of people depends in part on access to natural environments. Columbia emphasizes the landscaped natural environment in the form of gardens, lawns, recreation areas, and parks. Habitat also includes these but does not exclude the wilderness. Hexahedron, while idealizing both the natural environment and the built environment, keeps them sharply separate from each other, although both are readily available to people. Thus, Columbia blends the natural and built environments, Hexahedron keeps them apart, and Habitat does a little of both.

Third, these futuristic designs all create "total communities," where people can live, work, and participate in leisure and cultural activities. These designs imply that the ideal city should provide such services to all its inhabitants, and one can almost be born, live, and die in such communities.

There is also the theme, differentially explicit in these futuristic concepts, that cities are "organisms," or integrated entities that have a unity of their own. This idea is most explicit in Hexahedron, where the analogy between organisms and the city is vividly stated. In Habitat, Safdie also viewed the city as an organism that could grow and function in an orderly way. One can also see the germ of this idea in Columbia, at least implicitly: the city is a nested hierarchy of smaller units that fit together in an integrated community concept and function almost as a distinct organism. Thus, although Columbia, Habitat, and Hexahedron have different "anatomies," the idea of symmetry, integration, differentiation of parts, and emphasis on the whole seems to pervade all three.

These communities of the future are also similar in their dialectic qualities of individuality/community, homogeneity/diversity, and order/disorder. In each design philosophy one role of cities is to facilitate the well-being of individuals and families, to give them control over their lives, and to help them grow in accord with their capabilities and interests. Simultaneously, however, there is the conception of people as members of communities and as contributors to the well-being, vitality, and operation of the whole city.

Furthermore, in all three cases we saw the blending of diversity and complexity with simplicity and homogeneity. Unified design concepts, similarity of housing, and repetitiveness of various features existed side by side with variation, stimulation, and access to a variety of experiences and choices.

Finally, in all cases, the overarching emphasis was on order, planning, and regulation. Organization, efficiency, and logic were the keynote qualities in all designs. Uncontrolled growth and disorder, so prevalent in present-day cities, were viewed as negative in the three futuristic plans.

In fact, neither Hexahedron nor Columbia incorporated any growth beyond the confines of the original plans. Rather, cities were expected to reach a given size and stay within a specified physical area, and no spontaneous growth was provided for beyond those limits. Habitat was different. It also called for order and unity, but it implied that continued growth might occur, as long as such growth fit within the general planning concept.

So, although these three futuristic concepts of city design vary in some respects, they are quite similar in relation to several central philosophical values. And these values are quite in accord with many 20th-century Western cultural views about the nature of "the good life." It seems that even "radical" futurists are creatures of their cultures and illustrate the interlocked quality of culture and environment, a theme that we have emphasized throughout this book.

SUMMARY

The focus of this chapter was on cities of the future. Our goal was to examine such "ideal" cities, communities, and new towns in terms of cultural and environmental issues and certain dialectic processes.

The first section of the chapter provided a historical background to the concept of "ideal" communities and town planning. The creation of ideal communities has been a dream of city planners extending far back in history, although many earlier plans were limited in scope. Beginning about 1900, town planning included a number of integrated elements: the development of totally new communities, holistic planning to encompass all facets of life, single management of all phases of planning, explicit statements of goals, and communities that were almost wholly self-sufficient in politics, economics, and other facets of life.

An early-20th-century concept of town planning was proposed by Ebenezer Howard. His "garden cities" were self-contained communities that blended the city and the country, with urban areas containing green park areas throughout the community. The size of cities was controlled. There were schools, government, industry, business, and transportation within the circularly designed city. The goal of the community was to benefit ordinary people and to provide them with life's amenities and opportunities. The focus on the individual and family and the emphasis on both the natural and the built environment have pervaded other idealized communities throughout the 20th century, as has the need for systematic and orderly planning of urban communities.

We analyzed three examples of "ideal" cities and communities proposed recently—Columbia, Maryland, Habitat, Montreal, and Soleri's arcology cities. Columbia is already functioning as a community; Habitat, Montreal, exists as a demonstration city; arcology cities are still largely on the drawing board.

Columbia, Maryland, is one of the most thoroughly planned new towns in the present-day United States. Located on 14,000 acres midway between Washington, D.C., and Baltimore, Maryland, it is a totally planned community designed to provide full service to its residents. In many respects it follows Howard's garden-city concept, with an emphasis on serving individuals, providing a blend of nature and urban resources, and serving almost all of life's needs—housing, education, culture, recreation, religion, health. Columbia is designed around a hierarchy of units that includes cul-de-sacs, streets, neighborhoods, villages, and the town itself, and each unit provides a variety of services to its residents.

The second ideal community that we examined was Habitat, Montreal. This planning concept, unlike Columbia, emphasizes high-rise, vertical planning and high-density urban areas. Dwelling units are prefabricated, modular concrete rectangles that are stacked in various configurations, all within a relatively small geographic area. The concept involves prefabrication of similar modules, "plug-in" electricity, plumbing, and other services, and the creation of a city with infinite variation based on repetitive building-block modules. Habitat also attempts to provide access to nature—visually, through gardens and terraces, and through public parks in the community. Like Columbia, Habitat emphasizes the importance of providing individuals and families with full community services and the opportunity to express their identity and freedom.

The third example of an "ideal" city is truly futuristic and is only in its earliest design stages. Hexahedron, a city form envisioned by Paolo Soleri, can accommodate from 6000 to 6,000,000 people. Like Habitat, this design is based on a three-dimensional planning concept, with some cities a mile high. The arcology concept involves several elements: the emphasis on compactness and miniaturization, modeling after evolutionary processes, and using human and animal bodies as an analogue for city design. Although arcology communities are radically different in design from Columbia and Habitat, they too emphasize service to the individual and family and the provision of facilities and resources of both urban settings and the natural environment.

We also examined these city concepts from a dialectic perspective, noting how each one involved an interplay of the dialectic processes of individuality/community, homogeneity/diversity of design and activities, and order/disorder of the planning concept. Furthermore, our analysis suggested that, in spite of physical differences, all these designs were intended to be dynamic and to provide people with opportunities for growth, self-enhancement, and freedom of choice. In addition, the three futuristic plans all accepted city life as necessary and even desirable, as long as physical designs involved organization and planning and a harmonious blend of the natural environment and the urban environment.

Chapter 12

RECAPITULATION AND PROSPECTS FOR THE FUTURE

The goal of this book has been to weave together information about *culture, environment,* and *psychological processes*—sometimes in relation to places such as homes, communities, and cities, and sometimes in relation to behavioral processes of cognition and perception, privacy, personal space, and territory. We emphasized empirical findings and theoretical perspectives bearing on these issues, and we documented our ideas by citing a variety of scholarly sources.

The first section of this final chapter describes the philosophical themes that guided our analysis. Some of these themes were stated explicitly throughout the book; others were more implicit. A second brief section discusses topics that we did not cover, such as natural, recreational, and wilderness environments and institutional environments such as hospitals, schools, and prisons.

The third section of the chapter considers environmental design in relation to culture, a crucial issue in North America and in other cultures and other parts of the world. How can we help create environments which support cultural values, which permit cultures to flourish in new environments, and which foster the growth and well-being of individuals?

SOME THEMES OF THE BOOK

Our most explicit theme has been that culture, environment, and psychological processes operate as a unified system. A second theme has been that understanding culture/environment relations requires a multidisciplinary style of scholarship and research. A third theme has centered on a dialectic orientation as a promising way to understand culture and environment. Other themes related to the advantages of cross-cultural analyses and the desirability of simultaneous examination of "places," such as homes, communities, and cities, and "processes," such as cognition and perception, privacy, territory, and personal space.

A Systems Orientation

A central theme of our analysis was that culture, environment, and psychological processes are best viewed as an interdependent and unified system of variables. Each is related to the others, and each affects and is affected by the others. Hence, simple notions of "*X* always causes *Y*" do not usually hold in culture/environment relations. Rather, sometimes *X* causes *Y*, sometimes *Y* causes *X*, and most important, *X* and *Y* often operate as a unity and cannot be teased apart easily.

This theme was particularly salient in our analysis of homes (Chapters 7 and 8). That is, homes are best understood as a complicated interplay of a variety of factors—climate and other qualities of the physical environment, and cultural variables such as social structure, religion, and cosmology. And these factors have often operated over the course of centuries, each affected by and affecting the others, to yield a whole whose parts are not easily separated.

This is not to say that factors operate in equivalent ways in all settings. Climate may be more important to the design of homes in arctic or equatorial than in temperate climates. Privacy regulation may not involve the built environment for desert nomads to the same extent as it does in modern Western societies. So a host of factors play a role in environment/behavior relations, and their relative importance may vary from setting to setting and culture to culture. This naturally makes understanding of culture/environment relations a difficult task, and it suggests that we must study *patterns of relations* among variables, not factors taken one at a time or in isolation from one another.

However, although one can speak of complex systems and multiple directions of causation at a theoretical level, it is still necessary to conduct analyses and research studies at a detailed and mundane level. Put another way, it is important to "think big," but one must also be willing to "work small." Accordingly, the studies reviewed throughout the book and our analyses of particular places and processes were done at a small-scale level, with specific questions, hypotheses, and goals in mind. Even if one's goal is to understand a total system and the interplay of a variety of factors in that system, it requires a number of detailed, minute analyses.

Given the preceding discussion, two errors must be avoided by the student of culture/environment relations. The first error is to ignore the systemslike quality of culture/environment relations. This error takes the form of becoming entrapped in the details of particular variables and relations and overestimating their role in the whole system. For example, trying to understand homes or communities solely in terms of environmental factors such as climate, on the assumption that such factors are the most important ones or that they play an equivalent role in all cultures, is apt to lead to a very incomplete or distorted analysis. This error amounts to "losing sight of the forest for the trees."

But the opposite course is equally erroneous—namely, "losing sight of the trees for the forest." That is, one must try to understand specific relations between variables (the trees), or else one cannot possibly understand the whole (the forest). So, even though one believes that a myriad of variables may affect home or community design, it is simply not possible to study all of them at once; they must be understood in limited sets even though one might wish eventually to understand their operation as a unified pattern of factors. Thus, a systems approach of the type we have espoused requires that one work both at detailed, specific levels of analysis and at more complex and global levels.

An Interdisciplinary Orientation

Another theme of this book is that the understanding of culture/environment relations requires an interdisciplinary perspective. Because such topics as housing, city design, environmental cognition, privacy, and territory touch on so many facets of human functioning, they cannot be understood from the perspective of any single discipline alone. For example, the analysis of cities and communities requires some appreciation of the *history* of city designs; *archeological, sociological, political,* and *economic* facets of city functioning; *environmental design* processes; the *anthropology* of the cultures within which cities are embedded; and the *psychological* factors associated with life in communities and cities. This is not to say that you must become an expert in each of these fields or that you cannot examine a specific question from the perspective of a particular discipline. On the contrary, investigation of a specific problem may require a narrow focus and adoption of the perspective of a given discipline. But, for the most part, you will need to have at least a general appreciation of the content and approach of different disciplines, and, wherever possible, it will be helpful to weave those different viewpoints into the fabric of your analysis.

Consider a few examples in which we relied on the research, theory, and approaches of different disciplines. In our discussion of environmental cognition and perception, we drew on work in psychology, geography, history, environmental design, and sociology. In our analysis of privacy, we found useful ideas in the fields of anthropology, psychology, philosophy, sociology, and history. Our discussion of homes tapped the thinking of architects, historians, interior designers, anthropologists, art historians, landscape architects, and psychologists. And our examination of cities and communities relied heavily on the writings of historians, geographers, archeologists, anthropologists, sociologists, social philosophers, city planners, land developers, and psychologists.

A multidisciplinary orientation is simultaneously exciting and frustrating. It is exciting in that one has the opportunity to examine a problem from many points of view. All too often research requires so much specialization that one runs the risk of too narrow a focus, as in the "forest and trees" analogy discussed previously. So a broader perspective coupled with one's special interests can contribute to an exciting and educational adventure. Furthermore, a multidisciplinary orientation keeps open bridges between fields and the possibility of achieving a unity of knowledge among disciplines. All this is very exciting.

But adopting a multidisciplinary perspective is not always smooth sailing. Many times it is downright frustrating, because the communication barriers between different points of view are not always easy to surmount. For example, the cultural anthropologist, who often deals with many facets of a culture all at once, such as religion, economics, politics, and family, and the psychologist, who usually investigates a single process, such as perceptual behavior, often cannot find a ground on which to communicate. One is global in approach and the other is very molecular, and it is sometimes hard for them to bridge the large gap between them. Another example is the environmental designer, who ordinarily adopts a practical, problem-solving orientation and who is confused by (and confuses) the social science researcher, who is not accustomed to applying knowledge to a specific social problem. Thus, differences in the goals and approaches of various disciplines can contribute to mutual frustration.

Another challenge to a multidisciplinary orientation is that one must learn whole bodies of new information. While this is certainly a marvelous opportunity, it can be difficult. It is hard enough to keep up with one's own field of specialization, let alone become proficient in a totally new area. How do you know what you need to know? Where do you find crucial material from the mountains of information that exist in most fields? How do you screen out the valid research and theories in a new field? There are ways to solve these problems, such as consultation with colleagues, reading, and additional course work, but the challenge is still a difficult one.

Another hurdle in multidisciplinary work is that information about culture/environment relations is not always easy to locate in other fields. For example, descriptions of the physical design of communities and cities are often embedded in historical, sociological, economic, and political analyses and are not always treated in a central way. Discussions of privacy and territory are often inserted in a secondary way into anthropological accounts of the religion and social structure of cultures. So, to study culture/environment relations, one must be willing to dig for information in a variety of places.

In general, despite the many hurdles to overcome in multidisciplinary work, we believe that the understanding of culture/environment relations calls for breaking out of the conceptual and empirical bonds of single disciplines. And the opportunity to learn, integrate, and synthesize knowledge and ideas from several fields far outweighs any frustrations and pitfalls.

A Cross-Cultural Orientation

Along with a multidisciplinary orientation, it is valuable to adopt a comparative, or cross-cultural, perspective. First, such an approach increases the likelihood of a proper balance of emic and etic orientations. As discussed in Chapter 4 in relation to privacy, all too often we interpret the behavior of other cultures only in terms of our own value systems, from an etic orientation. Although this may be appropriate in the search for general principles of human behavior, complete understanding of a phenomenon also calls for an emic orientation, in which we try to understand the phenomenon from the framework of the culture itself. Thus, to understand privacy, not only should we compare privacy-regulation practices of other cultures with our own cultural styles to see how they are alike and different (etic), but we also need to understand the functions and operations of privacy mechanisms within the culture being studied (emic).

Cross-cultural comparisons can also extend or change the explanation of a particular relation previously viewed from the perspective of a single culture. For example, the relation of ecological variation to the perception of certain visual illusions was discovered through cross-cultural research. Those findings helped to change our perspectives on the role of experience in perceptual processes.

Cross-cultural research is also a fertile source of hypotheses and insights. It is common among students and some social scientists to ignore or downplay ordinary and everyday events in one's own culture. On numerous occasions, students exposed in class to certain environmental phenomena, such as privacy regulation or the design of bathrooms, will say "That's obvious; why study it?" However, when they see how different cultures regulate privacy or how bathrooms and bathroom practices vary across cultures, they begin to realize that such everyday and ordinary phenomena can reveal a great deal about a culture. The study of other cultures provides a backdrop against which to examine one's own culture and also can help one appreciate behavioral processes that might otherwise be ignored or considered unimportant.

Another advantage of cross-cultural research is that cultural phenomena are usually robust or salient. For example, home design has usually undergone the test of history, has evolved gradually to present-day forms, and has become part and parcel of the everyday lives of people. Homes are evident everywhere, and they vividly convey the values of a culture. Although laboratory research is crucial to understanding behavioral phenomena, the study of culture/environment processes must also be done in natural environments, where phenomena exist on an everyday basis and where they have been responsive to years of influence, change, and development.

A Dialectic Orientation

In several places throughout the book environmental phenomena were examined using a dialectic perspective. This philosophical approach assumes that environment/behavior phenomena have three properties: (1) They involve oppositional processes, such as openness/closedness for privacy, individuality/community and public/private in homes, and individuality/community, homogeneity/diversity, and order/disorder in cities and communities. In each of these pairs of opposing forces, one or the other pole is "stronger" at different times or in different settings. (2) Oppositional forces function as a unity, and they give meaning to each other. Thus, within any environment there are forces on both sides of the coin, each lending meaning to the other and each defining the other. (3) Oppositional processes are in an ever-changing and dynamic relation. Each presses against the other, and their ever-present opposition generates change and growth. For example, within a city or community strong forces of disorder and uncontrolled growth may eventually generate opposite forces toward order and planning, resulting in redevelopment and redesign of communities. The poles chosen to represent a dialectic are, to some extent, arbitrary. The skein of culture is woven with great complexity, and the dialectic processes that we examined are just a few among many possible alternatives. The extraordinary complexity of human behavior must be reduced to a level that we can comprehend, and often the choice of concepts, like dialectic opposites, is somewhat arbitrary. The ultimate value of such reductions and abstractions is in how well they facilitate our thinking about the problems under study.

The dialectic style of thinking helped our analysis because it is compatible with the idea of culture/environment relations as involving the interplay of a variety of forces and because it assumes that culture/environment relations are in a continual process of growth, change, and evolution. A dialectic orientation also does not presume that people and cultures aim toward some ideal state of affairs. Instead, this philosophical position hypothesizes that culture/environment relations are a never-ending process of coping, adjusting, and readjusting. A dialectic orientation emphasizes the growth of people and cultures toward new stages of development according to an evolutionary process of change. As such, dialectic philosophy is a way of thinking that seems compatible with the array of issues associated with culture/environment relations.

A Process and Place Orientation

This book was generally divided into two sections: chapters that dealt with environmental processes or behaviors and those that treated places in the physical environment. Parts 1 and 2 (Chapters 2–6) examined processes and behaviors of environmental cognitions and perceptions, privacy, personal space, and territorial behavior. Part 3 (Chapters 7–11) dealt with places such as homes and areas within homes, small communities, and large cities. Neither a place nor a process orientation is necessarily the "correct" or "best" one. Rather, full understanding of culture/environment relations requires that *both* processes and places be examined. For example, we need to understand how territoriality works as a process, the general functions that it serves, and how it operates in relation to human motives and needs. But territoriality is necessarily embedded in *places,* and we must therefore try to understand how such a process operates in a particular setting and how it relates to other processes in that setting. Thus, a home is more than a territory—it is the locus of a variety of environmental processes, including privacy, personal space, and perception and cognition. Ultimately, our interest is not just to understand how certain processes work but also how places work, how places embed processes, and how places are different from and similar to one another. Finally, if we are to go beyond merely understanding culture/environment relations and contribute to the creation of better environments in the form of real places like homes and communities, it is essential that we focus our scientific microscopes on *both* places and processes.

These, then, are the major philosophical themes that have guided our analysis. We believe that these ideas not only apply to the issues discussed in this book but can be extended to other facets of environment/behavior relations. In many respects such philosophical issues are as important as the myriad of facts, data, and theories presented throughout this volume. While facts and figures are certainly important for you to know, the general themes that underlie specific bits and pieces of information are the key to future progress in the environment-and-behavior field, because they will guide the particular research you do and how you interpret the research of others. Of course, we do not expect you to agree completely with our particular philosophical stance. Instead you should consciously develop your own philosophical assumptions and adopt those of others that make sense to you. In many respects, the clear statement of your own assumptions and biases is as important as, if not more important than, the specific facts you learn or discover. This is so because your underlying philosophical assumptions will, in large part, determine what you study, how you study it, and what you learn from the subject matter you investigate.

OTHER CULTURE/ENVIRONMENT TOPICS

The field of culture/environment relations is quite broad, and we have not covered all areas of the field, nor have we discussed every topic in a comprehensive fashion. In fact, it would have been possible to write a separate book (or several books) about the subjects of certain chapters in this volume. Moreover, we did not discuss several areas that you can follow up on your own. For example, recreation, wilderness, use of the natural environment, noise, pollution, and energy are just a few topics that would have been fascinating to examine in a cross-cultural perspective. And there are a variety of settings and places that you might wish to investigate from a cultural perspective, such as educational environments, work environments, prisons, hospitals, and transportation systems. We did not treat these topics for several reasons. First, it would have lengthened this book too much. Second, not all these topics have been treated comprehensively from a cross-cultural perspective. Third, and perhaps most important, we felt that the topics we chose best illustrate the themes discussed above and the ways in which culture/environment processes mesh with environmental places that people have created.

THE DESIGN OF CULTURALLY RELEVANT ENVIRONMENTS

Our goal in this book was to present a scholarly treatment of selected issues on culture and environment, not to produce a manual for use in the actual design of environments. However, we certainly hope that some of the material can be applied to everyday environmental design problems in different cultures. So this last section of the book points briefly to potential ways that knowledge about culture/environment relations can contribute to the design of "real world" environments.

Policy and decision makers around the world are presently challenged with many difficult environmental problems. In technologically advanced societies they are faced with such questions as "How can we design or redesign urban and suburban communities in the light of growing populations, rapid technological change, financial difficulties, and in- and out-migration from cities and rural areas? How can we cope with the extraordinary decay of our major cities? How can we produce changes in behavior regarding energy, wilderness, and natural resources? How can we minimize pollution of the water, land, and air? How should we design service institutions, such as schools, hospitals, and prisons, to meet the demands of the coming decades?"

There are also many problems to be faced in less technologically developed cultures. All over the world cultures are in various stages of transition from small, stable societies to technologically developed, larger societies. Innumerable nomadic and small-scale agricultural cultures are being exposed to 20th-century technology and rapidly incorporating it into their social systems. The result often is a dramatic change in their relationship to the physical environment, with subsequent reverberations throughout their culture. Thus, nomads are beginning to settle down, small agricultural societies are increasing crop production, whole communities are being forced to relocate because of construction of dams and hydroelectric plants, young people are migrating to urban centers, and role relationships between husbands and wives and between parents and children that have existed in a stable form for centuries are being disrupted. Moreover, new occupational opportunities are opening up and many old ones are no longer available, populations are growing rapidly, and housing demand is accelerating.

These social and technological changes have direct implications for culture/environment relations. How can new homes, communities, and schools be designed to be compatible with cultural values? How can culturally relevant information be gathered, filtered, and integrated so as to facilitate culturally appropriate environmental designs? In short, the problem we face is to design (or redesign) environments in ways that will not violate or create turbulence in cultures, but will be compatible with a social or ethnic heritage.

All too often the problem of cultural relevance has received little or no attention—not out of malicious neglect but simply because environmental designers have not always appreciated or understood the intimate linkage of culture and environment. Perhaps more important, we have often been guilty of adopting a strictly "etic" orientation to environmental design. That is, just as in research, we have tended to interpret the world in terms of our own culture and our own experiences and standards. Consequently, we often force on others what is appropriate in our own culture, or we too quickly and too superficially interpret the behavior and customs of others from our own perspective. In environmental design, this often leads to misunderstanding and poor design. For example:

1. Relocated villagers in Iran refused to live in new homes designed by Western-oriented architects because the toilets faced Mecca—a serious violation of religious practices.
2. Navajo Indians in the southwestern United States would not use a school that had been designed in the shape of a hogan by architects from the eastern part of the country. Hogans, the homes of Navajos, are holy and religious places, and the design of a public building in their shape was sacrilegious.
3. Pruitt-Igoe, a low-cost urban housing development in Saint Louis, was a disaster for the residents and developers alike, partly because its design totally eliminated the street life which urban Blacks had evolved over decades and which aided in socialization, social interaction, and community ties. Built in the 1960s and praised as a model of low-cost urban

housing, it was razed in the 1970s because people would not live there, crime was rampant, and the physical facilities had deteriorated.

4. Relocation of agricultural and nomadic peoples in a single village in Egypt and northern Sudan because of the Aswan Dam project resulted in considerable intergroup conflict and disruption of each culture's internal social system.

How can we proceed in the face of such complex problems and contribute to the development of better environments?

The process of environmental design is complicated and worthy of a volume in its own right (see Zeisel, 1974, for a description of this process). All that we will do here is highlight briefly how sensitivity to culture/environmental relations can be applied at several stages in the design process.

1. Diagnosing and assessing cultural practices and needs. It is almost a truism that a home, community, school, or city should be responsive to the needs, practices, and styles of its users. And assessing these needs and practices is usually the first step in the design process. Those involved in environmental planning and design, however, sometimes only apply concepts or knowledge based on their own values and neglect to incorporate analyses of user needs and practices; for instance, they often adopt an etic orientation in their assessment of user needs and practices. Moreover, environmental designers often become specialists in certain areas, such as school designs, and they develop implicit assumptions about what is appropriate to such settings. Frequently they then use those unstated assumptions in the design process without questioning their applicability to new settings and cultures. It almost becomes traditional to use certain configurations with little systematic evaluation of the workability of the design. Although this may be acceptable in some cases, especially within one's own culture, it might lead to a disaster in another culture. Hence, it is crucial to adopt an emic orientation in the early stages of the design process; the environmental designer must try to learn the culture's values, norms, and behavioral practices—that is, understand the culture from *its* perspective, and not simply impose one's own etic orientation. If there is any lesson at all in this book, it is that cultures vary widely in their orientations to the physical environment—perceptually, cognitively, and behaviorally—and we cannot possibly design effective environments for others unless we have a genuine appreciation of their relationships with their environments.

The diagnostic stage of environmental design can be enormously facilitated by broadening the base of the participants in the process. All too often, environmental design decisions have been made primarily by technological experts—architects, urban planners, and engineers. Only rarely have consultants from the social and behavioral sciences been brought into the early stages of the design process. One notable exception was Columbia, Maryland, described in Chapter 11, where psychologists, educators, religious experts, and others played a central role in the initial design of the community. The input of many specialists is especially crucial in the design of environments for other cultures.

There is also a small but growing recognition of the potential contribution of the consumer, or user, to the design process. Those advocating consumer participation reason that the perspective of the user is no less important than the skills of technical and social science experts. Here again, the diagnosis of a particular culture in relation to the environment may be facilitated by an analysis of life-styles and needs from the vantage of the people themselves, not only from that of outside experts.

2. Development of design solutions. The second stage of the design process is the development of alternative proposals for the problem at hand. Theoretically, such proposals should take into account crucial cultural values, needs, and practices uncovered in the first stage. The process of developing design alternatives is gradual, with proposals formulated and reformulated over a series of cycles. Once again, it is essential that several types of participants contribute to the process. Although the environmental designer is necessarily at the center of proposed development, the researcher can evaluate and contribute to design ideas using his or her knowledge of the culture. In addition, the consumer can evaluate and help develop design proposals using his or her distinctive perspective on the everyday life of the people in the culture. Thus, the development of proposals should, ideally, involve a series of checks and balances from several vantage points, in order to enhance the compatibility of alternative environmental designs with the culture.

3. Implementing the design. Actual construction and initial use of an environment occur in the design process. Here too it is crucial that knowledge about a culture be used to help people adjust to and effectively use their new environment. Frequently the design process ends with the completion of a building, community, or facility; the environmental designer and other consultants rush off to another project before or soon after a physical structure is completed. It is essential that all participants in the design process continue to be involved before and after construction. Their talents can be applied to educating users about the characteristics and use of an environment and how it fits with cultural practices and values, even though it looks different from their traditional environment. People often need to be taught how to use a new environment, how to achieve the goals that are important to them, and how to fit and blend with the new environment in a viable way.

Environmental education is especially crucial in a cross-cultural context. For example, people in a culture in transition may be baffled by new environmental settings and facilities, but their confusion and problems in adjustment can be alleviated if they are shown how the new environment is responsive to their cultural values and practices. Thus, environmental design in a cultural context involves far more than the construction of physical environments. It also includes, as an essential component, the education of people to use their environments in productive and viable ways.

4. Evaluation of environments. The final stage in the design process is evaluation. This means that on both a long-term and a short-term basis we should try to determine how well environments work. How effective were they? In what respects could they have been designed differently? How have the people changed the environment to better suit their life-styles? How has the new environment altered the lives of the people?

Very often we have neglected to look back and ask how well an environment worked. The pressures of economics and the demands of new projects lure us away from the environments that we created and toward those in the future. But we must understand our past failures and successes so that future designs can profit by that experience. This seems obvious, doesn't it? But the fact is that evaluation is an infrequent process. Furthermore, given the complexity of cross-cultural problems, the need for evaluation is even more crucial. Here again, environmental designers, researchers, and consumers can function as a team.

A FINAL NOTE

The study of culture/environment relations is a fertile, fascinating, and barely tapped area. It touches on many fields, and it has promise for developing a broad-based understanding of human behavior. Furthermore, an appreciation of the dynamics of culture/environment relations can facilitate the creation of a better environment for more people. Perhaps most important, the study of culture and environment may help us better understand, respect, and accept the similarities and differences among people of the world.

REFERENCES

Aiello, J. R., & Jones, S. E. Field study of the proxemic behavior of young school children in three subcultural groups. *Journal of Personality and Social Psychology,* 1971, *19,* 351–356.

Alexander, C. *Houses generated by patterns*. Unpublished technical report, Center for Environmental Structure, Berkeley, Calif., 1969.

Alexander, H. H. *Design: Criteria for decisions*. New York: Macmillan, 1976.

Alkire, W. H. Porpoises and taro. *Ethnology,* 1968, *7,* 280–290.

Altman, I. *The environment and social behavior: Privacy, personal space, territory, and crowding*. Monterey, Calif.: Brooks/Cole, 1975.

Altman, I. Privacy regulation: Culturally universal or culturally specific? *Journal of Social Issues,* 1977, *33,* 66–84.

Altman, I., & Haythorn, W. W. The ecology of isolated groups. *Behavioral Science,* 1967, *12,* 169–182.

Altman, I., Nelson, P. A., & Lett, E. E. The ecology of home environments. *Catalog of Selected Documents in Psychology*. Washington, D.C.: American Psychological Association, Spring 1972.

Altman, I., Taylor, D. A., & Wheeler, L. Ecological aspects of group behavior in social isolation. *Journal of Applied Social Psychology,* 1971, *1,* 76–100.

Altman, I., & Vinsel, A. M. Personal space: An analysis of E. T. Hall's proxemics framework. In I. Altman & J. F. Wohlwill (Eds.), *Human behavior and environment: Advances in theory and research* (Vol. 1). New York: Plenum, 1977.

Anderson, E. N., Jr. Some Chinese methods of dealing with crowding. *Urban Anthropology,* 1972, *1,* 141–150.

Appleyard, D. Styles and methods of structuring a city. *Environment and Behavior,* 1970, *2,* 100–118.

Appleyard, D. *Planning a pluralist city*. Cambridge, Mass.: M.I.T. Press, 1976.

Ardrey, R. *The territorial imperative*. New York: Atheneum, 1966.

Argyle, M., & Dean, J. Eye-contact, distance, and affiliation. *Sociometry,* 1965, *28,* 289–304.

Aries, P. *Centuries of childhood: A social history of family life*. New York: Knopf, 1962.

Asimov, I. *The naked sun*. Greenwich, Conn.: Fawcett, 1972.

Atkinson, A. Bernese middle land farmhouses. In P. Oliver (Ed.), *Shelter and society*. London: Barrie and Jenkins, 1969, pp. 49–65.

Barnes, F. The biology of pre-Neolithic man. In S. V. Boyden (Ed.), *The impact of civilization on the biology of man*. Canberra, Australia: Australian National University Press, 1970, pp. 1–18.

Barry, H., Bacon, M., & Child, I. A cross-cultural survey of some sex differences in socialization. *Journal of Abnormal and Social Psychology,* 1957, *55,* 327–332.

Basehart, H. W. The resource holding corporation among the Mescalero Apache. *Southwestern Journal of Anthropology,* 1967, *23,* 277–291.

Bates, M. Human ecology. In A. L. Kroeber (Ed.), *Anthropology Today.* Chicago: University of Chicago Press, 1953, pp. 700–713.

Baum, A., & Epstein, Y. M. (Eds.). *Human response to crowding.* Hillsdale, N.J.: Erlbaum, 1978.

Baum, A., & Valins, S. *Architecture and social behavior: Psychological studies of social density.* Hillsdale, N.J.: Erlbaum, 1977.

Baxter, J. C. Interpersonal spacing in natural settings. *Sociometry,* 1970, *33,* 444–456.

Becker, F. D. Study of spatial markers. *Journal of Personality and Social Psychology,* 1973, *26,* 439–445.

Berry, J. W. An ecological approach to cross-cultural psychology. *Netherlands Journal of Psychology,* 1975, *30,* 51–84.

Berry, J. W. *Ecology of cognitive style: Comparative studies in cultural and psychological adaptation.* New York: Sage/Halstead, 1976.

Biderman, A., Louria, M., & Bacchus, J. *Historical incidents of extreme overcrowding.* Washington, D.C.: Bureau of Social Science, 1963.

Blatt, S. J., & Wild, C. M. *Schizophrenia: A developmental analysis.* New York: Academic Press, 1976.

Blaut, J. M., McCleary, G. S., Jr., & Blaut, A. S. Environmental mapping in young children. *Environment and Behavior,* 1970, *2,* 335–351.

Boal, F. Territoriality on the Shankill-Falls Divide, Belfast. *Irish Geography,* 1969, *6,* 30–50.

Bochner, S. The house form as a cornerstone of culture. In R. W. Brislin (Ed.), *Topics in culture learning* (Vol. 3). Honolulu: East-West Center, 1975, pp. 9–21.

Booth, A., & Welch, S. *The effects of crowding: A cross-national study.* Paper presented at the meeting of the American Psychological Association, Montreal, Quebec, September 1973.

Burby, R. J., III, & Weiss, S. *New communities U.S.A.* Lexington, Mass.: Heath, 1976.

Campbell, C. C. *New towns: Another way to live.* Reston, Va.: Reston Publishing Co., 1976.

Campbell, D. T. On the conflicts between biological and social evolution and between psychology and moral tradition. *American Psychologist,* 1975, *30,* 1103–1126.

Canter, D., & Canter, S. Close together in Tokyo. *Design and Environment,* 1971, *2,* 60–63.

Carpenter, C. R. Territoriality: A review of concepts and problems. In A. Roe & G. G. Simpson (Eds.), *Behavior and evolution.* New Haven, Conn.: Yale University Press, 1958, pp. 224–250.

Caudill, W., & Plath, D. W. Who sleeps by whom? *Psychiatry,* 1966, *29,* 344–366.

Cavan, S. Interaction in home territories. *Berkeley Journal of Sociology,* 1963, *8,* 17–32.

Cavan, S. *Liquor license.* Chicago: Aldine, 1966.

Chemers, M. M., Ayman, R., & Werner, C. Expectancy theory analysis of migration. *Journal of Population,* 1978, *1,* 42–56.

Cheyne, J. A., & Efran, M. G. The effect of spatial and interpersonal variables on the invasion of group controlled territories. *Sociometry,* 1972, *35,* 477–489.

Clapp, J. A. *New towns and urban policy: Planning metropolitan growth*. New York: Dunellen, 1971.

Clark, J. D. Human ecology during Pleistocene and later times in Africa south of the Sahara. *Current Anthropology,* 1960, *1,* 307–324.

Cooper, C. The house as symbol of the self. In H. Proshansky, W. H. Ittelson, & L. G. Rivlin (Eds.), *Environmental psychology*. New York: Holt, Rinehart & Winston, 1976, pp. 435–448.

Corden, C. *Planned cities: New towns in Britain and America*. Beverly Hills, Calif.: Sage, 1977.

Cox, D. R., & Zannaras, G. Designative perceptions of macro spaces: Concepts, methodology, and applications. In R. N. Downs & D. Stea (Eds.), *Image and environment: Cognitive mapping and spatial behavior*. Chicago: Aldine, 1973, pp. 162–178.

Cranstone, B. A. L. Environmental choice in dwelling and settlement: An ethnographical survey. In P. Ucko, R. Tringham, & G. W. Dimbleby (Eds.), *Man, settlement, and urbanism*. London: Duckworth, 1972, pp. 487–504.

Dasen, P. R. Cross-cultural Piagetian research: A summary. *Journal of Cross-cultural Psychology,* 1972, *3,* 23–39.

Dawson, J. L. M. Cultural and physiological influences upon spatial-perceptual processes in West Africa, Parts 1 and 2. *International Journal of Psychology,* 1967, *2,* 115–128, 171–185.

DeJonge, D. Images of urban areas: Their structure and psychological foundations. *Journal of the American Institute of Planners,* 1962, *28,* 266–276.

Downs, R. N., & Stea, D. (Eds.). *Image and environment: Cognitive mapping and spatial behavior*. Chicago: Aldine, 1973.

Draper, P. Crowding among hunter-gatherers: The !Kung Bushmen. *Science,* 1973, *182,* 301–303.

Earle, A. M. *Home life in colonial days*. New York: Macmillan, 1935.

Edney, J. J. Human territories: Comment on functional properties. *Environment and Behavior,* 1976, *8*(1), 31–48.

Eibl-Eibesfeldt, I. *Ethology: The biology of behavior*. New York: Holt, Rinehart & Winston, 1970.

Engebretson, D., & Fullmer, D. Cross-cultural differences in territoriality: Interaction distances of native Japanese, Hawaii-Japanese, and American Caucasians. *Journal of Cross-cultural Psychology*, 1970, *1*, 261–269.

Evans, G. W., & Howard, R. B. Personal space. *Psychological Bulletin,* 1973, *80,* 334–344.

Fahim, H. Nubian resettlement in the Sudan. Paper presented at the Conference on Psychosocial Consequences of Sedentarism, University of California, Los Angeles, December 1974.

Faron, L. C. Marriage, residence, and domestic groups among the Panamanian Choco. *Ethnology,* 1962, *1,* 13–38.

Firestone, I. J. Reconciling verbal and nonverbal models of dyadic communication. *Environmental Psychology and Nonverbal Behavior,* 1977, *2,* 30–44.

Fischer, C. S. *The urban experience*. New York: Harcourt Brace Jovanovich, 1976.

Fishman, R. *Urban utopias in the twentieth century*. New York: Basic Books, 1977.

Forston, R. F., & Larson, C. U. The dynamics of space. *Journal of Communication,* 1968, *18,* 109–116.

Francescato, D., & Mebane, W. How citizens view two great cities: Milan and Rome. In R. N. Downs & D. Stea (Eds.), *Image and environment: Cognitive mapping and spatial behavior*. Chicago: Aldine, 1973, pp. 131–147.

Fraser, D. *Village planning in the primitive world*. New York: Braziller, 1968.
Fraser, D. *African art as philosophy*. New York: Interbook, 1974.
Galle, O. R., Gove, W. R., & McPherson, J. M. Population density and pathology: What are the relationships for man? *Science,* 1972, *176,* 23–30.
Galt, A. H. Carnival on the island of Pantelleria: Ritualized community solidarity in an atomistic society. *Ethnology,* 1973, *12,* 325–341.
Gans, H. J. *The urban villagers*. New York: Free Press, 1962.
Gans, H. J. *The Levittowners*. New York: Vintage, 1967.
Godelier, M. Territory and property in primitive society. Paper presented at the Symposium on Human Ethology: Claims and Limits of a New Discipline. Werner-Reimers Stiftung, Bad Homburg, Germany, October 1977.
Goffman, E. *The presentation of self in everyday life*. New York: Doubleday Anchor, 1959.
Goffman, E. *Relations in public*. New York: Basic Books, 1971.
Gould, P. R. The black boxes of Jönköping: Spatial information and preference. In R. N. Downs & D. Stea (Eds.), *Image and environment: Cognitive mapping and spatial behavior*. Chicago: Aldine, 1973, pp. 235–245. (a)
Gould, P. R. On mental maps. In R. N. Downs & D. Stea (Eds.), *Image and environment: Cognitive mapping and spatial behavior*. Chicago: Aldine, 1973, pp. 182–220. (b)
Gould, P. R., & White, R. *Mental maps*. New York: Penguin Books, 1974.
Gregor, T. A. Exposure and seclusion: A study of institutionalized isolation among the Mehinacu Indians of Brazil. *Ethnology,* 1970, *9,* 234–250.
Gregor, T. A. Publicity, privacy, and Mehinacu marriage. *Ethnology,* 1974, *13,* 333–349.
Hall, E. T. *The hidden dimension*. Garden City, N.Y.: Doubleday, 1966.
Hansen, W. B., & Altman, I. Decorating personal places: A descriptive analysis. *Environment and Behavior,* 1976, *8,* 491–504.
Hart, R. A., & Moore, G. T. The development of spatial cognition: A review. In R. N. Downs & D. Stea (Eds.), *Image and environment: Cognitive mapping and spatial behavior*. Chicago: Aldine, 1973, pp. 246–288.
Hediger, H. *Wild animals in captivity*. London: Butterworth and Co., 1950.
Herskovits, M. J. *Man and his works*. New York: Knopf, 1952.
Hockett, C. F., & Archer, R. The human revolution. *Current Anthropology,* 1964, *5,* 135–168.
Hoppenfeld, M. The Columbia process. In D. Lewis (Ed.), *The growth of cities*. Architects' Yearbook 13. Letchworth, England: Garden City Press, 1971.
Howard, E. *Garden cities of tomorrow*. Cambridge, Mass.: M.I.T. Press, 1965.
Howe, I. *World of our fathers*. New York: Harcourt Brace Jovanovich, 1976.
Ittelson, W. H., Proshansky, H. M., Rivlin, L. G., & Winkel, G. H. *Introduction to environmental psychology*. New York: Holt, Rinehart & Winston, 1974.
Jacobs, J. *The life and death of great American cities*. New York: Random House, 1961.
Jones, S. E. A comparative proxemics analysis of dyadic interaction in selected subcultures of New York City. *Journal of Social Psychology,* 1971, *84,* 35–44.
Jones, S. E., & Aiello, J. R. Proxemic behavior of Black and White first, third, and fifth grade children. *Journal of Personality and Social Psychology,* 1973, *25,* 21–27.
Kaplan, S. Cognitive maps in perception and thought. In R. N. Downs & D. Stea (Eds.), *Image and environment: Cognitive mapping and spatial behavior*. Chicago: Aldine, 1973, pp. 63–78.
Kira, A. *The bathroom*. New York: Viking, 1976.

Kluckhohn, F. R. Dominant and variant value orientations. In C. Kluckhohn, H. A. Murray, & D. M. Schneider (Eds.), *Personality in nature, society, and culture*. New York: Knopf, 1953.

Knowles, E. S. Boundaries around social space: Dyadic responses to an invader. *Environment and Behavior,* 1972, *4,* 437–445.

Knowles, E. S. Boundaries around group interaction: The effect of group size and member status on boundary permeability. *Journal of Personality and Social Psychology*, 1973, *26,* 327–332.

Kroeber, A., & Kluckhohn, C. *Culture: A critical review of concepts and definitions*. Cambridge, Mass.: Peabody Museum, 1952.

Ladd, F. C. Black youths view their environments: Neighborhood maps. *Environment and Behavior,* 1970, *2,* 74–100.

Laird, D. A. The heredity of the modern bed and its weaknesses. *Scientific Monthly,* November 1935, pp. 409–420.

Lapovsky, E. J. *An examination of the concept of flexibility as a tool for the analysis of social systems*. Unpublished master's thesis, University of New Mexico, Albuquerque, 1962.

Lee, R. B., & DeVore, I. (Eds.). *Man the hunter*. Chicago: Aldine, 1968.

Leeds, A. Ecological determinants of chieftainship among the Yaruro Indians of Venezuela. In A. P. Vayda (Ed.), *Environment and cultural behavior*. Garden City, N.Y.: Natural History Press, 1969, pp. 377–394.

Lenski, G. E. *Power and privilege: A theory of social stratification*. New York: McGraw-Hill, 1966.

Lerup, L. Environmental and behavioral congruence as a measure of goodness in public space: The case of Stockholm. *Ekistics,* 1972, *34,* 341–358.

LeVine, R. A. Witchcraft and co-wife proximity in southwestern Kenya. *Ethnology,* 1962, *1,* 39–45.

LeVine, R. A., & Price-Williams, D. R. Children's kinship concepts: Cognitive development and early experience among the Hausa. *Ethnology,* 1974, *13,* 25–44.

Lewis, O. *Five families*. New York: Mentor Books, 1959.

Lewis, O. *The children of Sanchez*. New York: Random House, 1961.

Ley, D. The meaning of space in an inner city context. Paper presented at the meeting of the Canadian Association of Geographers, Vancouver, B.C., 1972.

Ley, D., & Cybriwsky, R. Urban graffiti as territorial markers. *Annals of the Association of American Geographers,* 1974, *64,* 491–505.

Little, K. B. Cultural variations in social schemata. *Journal of Personality and Social Psychology,* 1968, *10,* 1–7.

Lonner, W. J. The search for psychological universals. In H. C. Triandis (Ed.), *Handbook of cross-cultural psychology*. Boston: Allyn & Bacon, 1979.

Lorenz, K. *On aggression*. New York: Harcourt Brace Jovanovich, 1966.

Luce, G. G., & Segal, J. *Sleep*. New York: Coward-McCann, 1966.

Lynch, K. *The image of the city*. Cambridge, Mass.: M.I.T. Press, 1960.

Malmberg, T. *Human territories*. Netherlands: Nijhoff, 1977.

Marsella, A. J., Escudero, M., & Gordon, P. The effects of dwelling density on mental disorders in Filipino men. *Journal of Health and Social Behavior,* 1970, *11,* 288–294.

Martin, R. Concepts of human territoriality. In P. J. Ucko (Ed.), *Man, settlement, and urbanism*. London: Duckworth, 1972, pp. 427–445.

Martin, R. J. The ecology of a squatter settlement. *Architectural Review,* 1969, *145,* 213–214.

Michelson, W. *Man and his urban environment: A sociological approach*. Reading, Mass.: Addison-Wesley, 1970.

Miles, D. The Ngadju Dayaks of central Kalimantan, with special reference to the Upper Mentaya. *Behavior Science Notes,* 1970, *5,* 291–319.

Milgram, S. The experience of living in cities. *Science,* 1970, *167,* 1461–1468.

Milgram, S. Psychological maps of Paris. In H. Proshansky, W. H. Ittelson, & L. G. Rivlin (Eds.), *Environmental psychology* (2nd ed.). New York: Holt, Rinehart & Winston, 1976, pp. 105–124.

Mitchell, R. Some social implications of higher density housing. *American Sociological Review,* 1971, *36,* 18–29.

Moos, R., & Brownstein, R. *Environment and utopia: A synthesis*. New York: Plenum, 1977.

Morgan, L. H. *Houses and house-life of the American aborigines*. Chicago: University of Chicago Press, 1965.

Moyer, K. E. *The psychobiology of aggression*. New York: Harper & Row, 1976.

Munroe, R. L., & Munroe, R. H. Population density and affective relationships in three East African societies. *Journal of Social Psychology,* 1972, *88,* 15–20.

Munroe, R. L., Munroe, R. H., Nerlove, S. B., & Daniels, R. E. Effects of population density on food concern in three East African societies. *Journal of Health and Social Behavior,* 1969, *10,* 161–171.

Murdock, G. P. Correlations of exploitive patterns. In D. Damas (Ed.), *Ecological essays*. National Museum of Canada Bulletin No. 230, Anthropological Series No. 86, 1969.

Murdock, G. P. Cross-sex patterns of kin behavior. *Ethnology,* 1971, *10,* 359–368.

Murphy, R. F. Social distance and the veil. *American Anthropologist,* 1964, *66,* 1257–1274.

Murray, E. J. *Sleep, dreams, and arousal*. New York: Appleton-Century-Crofts, 1965.

Nash, R. *Wilderness and the American mind*. New Haven, Conn.: Yale University Press, 1967.

Neihardt, J. G. *Black Elk speaks*. Lincoln: University of Nebraska Press, 1961.

Newman, O. *Defensible space*. New York: Macmillan, 1972.

Nice, M. M. The role of territory in bird life. *American Midland Naturalist,* 1941, *26,* 441–487.

Noesjirwan, J. Contrasting cultural patterns of interpersonal closeness in doctors' waiting rooms in Sydney and Jakarta. *Journal of Cross-Cultural Psychology,* 1977, *8,* 357–368.

O'Neill, S. M., & Paluck, R. J. Altering territoriality through reinforcement. *Proceedings of the 81st Annual Convention of the American Psychological Association,* 1973, *8,* 901–902.

Orleans, P. Differential cognition of urban residents: Effects of social scale on mapping. In R. N. Downs & D. Stea (Eds.), *Image and environment: Cognitive mapping and spatial behavior*. Chicago: Aldine, 1973, pp. 115–130.

Ortiz, A. Ritual drama and the Pueblo world view. In A. Ortiz (Ed.), *New perspectives on the Pueblo*. Albuquerque: University of New Mexico Press, 1972, pp. 135–161.

Paine, R. Lappish decisions, partnerships, information management, and sanctions: A nomadic pastoral adaptation. *Ethnology,* 1970, *9,* 52–67.

Parke, R. D., & Sawin, D. B. Children's privacy in the home: Developmental, ecological, and child-rearing determinants. *Environment and Behavior,* in press.

Parker, A. C. Constitution of the Five Nations League. In W. N. Fenton (Ed.), *Parker on the Iroquois*. Syracuse, N.Y.: Syracuse University Press, 1968.

Parsons, H. M. The bedroom. *Human Factors*, 1972, *14*, 421–450.

Patterson, M. L. Compensation and nonverbal immediacy behaviors: A review. *Sociometry*, 1973, *36*(2), 237–253.

Patterson, M. L. An arousal model of interpersonal intimacy. *Psychological Review*, 1976, *83*, 235–245.

Peterson, N. Hunter-gatherer territoriality: The perspective from Australia. *American Anthropologist*, 1975, *77*, 53–67.

Price-Williams, D. R. *Explorations in cross-cultural psychology*. San Francisco: Chandler & Sharp, 1975.

Prussin, L. Fulani architectural change. Paper presented at the Conference on Psychosocial Consequences of Sedentarism, University of California, Los Angeles, December 1974.

Raglan, L. *The temple and the house*. London: Routledge & Kegan Paul, 1964.

Rapoport, A. *House form and culture*. Englewood Cliffs, N.J.: Prentice-Hall, 1969. (a)

Rapoport, A. The pueblo and the hogan: A cross-cultural comparison of two responses to an environment. In P. Oliver (Ed.), *Shelter and society*. London: Barrie & Jenkins, 1969, pp. 66–79. (b)

Rapoport, A. Nomadism as a people-environment system. Paper presented at the Conference on Psychosocial Consequences of Sedentarism, University of California, Los Angeles, December 1974.

Rapoport, A. *Human aspects of urban form: Towards a man-environment approach to urban form and design*. New York: Pergamon Press, 1977.

Reyman, J. E. Astronomy, architecture, and adaptation at Pueblo Bonito. *Science*, 1976, *193*, 957–962.

Reynolds, V. Open groups in hominid evolution. *Man*, 1966, *1*, 441–452.

Reynolds, V. Ethology of urban life. In P. J. Ucko (Ed.), *Man, settlement, and urbanism*. London: Duckworth, 1972, pp.401–408.

Roberts, J. M., & Gregor, T. A. Privacy: A cultural view. In J. R. Pennock & J. W. Chapman (Eds.), *Privacy*. New York: Atherton Press, 1971, pp. 199–225.

Rogler, L. H. Slum neighborhoods in Latin America. *Journal of Inter-American Studies*, 1967, *9*, 507–528.

Rosenberg, G. High population densities in relation to social behavior. *Ekistics*, 1968, *25*, 425–428.

Rosenblatt, P. C., & Budd, L. G. Territoriality and privacy in married and unmarried cohabiting couples. *Journal of Social Psychology*, 1975, *97*, 67–76.

Saalman, H. *Medieval cities*. New York: Braziller, 1968.

Saarinen, T. F. Student views of the world. In R. N. Downs & D. Stea (Eds.), *Image and environment: Cognitive mapping and spatial behavior*. Chicago: Aldine, 1973, pp. 148–161. (a)

Saarinen, T. F. The use of projective techniques in geographic research. In W. H. Ittelson (Ed.), *Environment and cognition*. New York: Seminar Press, 1973. (b)

Safdie, M. *Beyond Habitat*. Cambridge, Mass.: M.I.T. Press, 1970.

Scherer, S. E. Proxemic behavior of primary school children as a function of their socioeconomic class and subculture. *Journal of Personality and Social Psychology*, 174, *29*, 800–805.

Schmid, C. Urban crime areas: Part I. *American Sociological Review*, 1960, *25*, 527–542. (a)

Schmid, C. Urban crime areas: Part II. *American Sociological Review*, 1960, *25*, 655–678. (b)

Schmitt, R. C. Density, delinquency, and crime in Honolulu. *Sociology and Social Research,* 1957, *41,* 274–276.

Seligman, M. E. P. *Helplessness: On depression, development, and death.* San Francisco: W. H. Freeman, 1975.

Siegel, A. W., Kirasic, K. C., & Kail, R. V., Jr. The development of children's representations of geographic space. In I. Altman & J. F. Wohlwill (Eds.), *Human behavior and environment: Advances in theory and research.* Vol. 3: *Children and the environment.* New York: Plenum, 1978, pp. 223–258.

Siegel, A. W., & White, S. H. The development of spatial representations of large-scale environments. In H. W. Reese (Ed.), *Advances in child development and behavior* (Vol. 10). New York: Academic Press, 1975.

Shaffer, D. R., & Sadowski, C. This table is mine: Respect for marked barroom tables as a function of gender of spatial marker and desirability of locale. *Sociometry,* 1975, *38,* 408–419.

Simmel, G. The metropolis and mental life. In K. W. Wolff (Ed.), *The sociology of Georg Simmel.* New York: Free Press, 1950, pp. 409–424.

Smith, H. *The Russians.* New York: Quadrangle/New York Times Book Co., 1976.

Soleri, P. *Arcology: The city in the image of man.* Cambridge, Mass.: M.I.T. Press, 1969.

Sommer, R. Intimacy ratings of five countries. *International Journal of Psychology,* 1968, *3,* 109–114.

Sommer, R. *Personal space.* Englewood Cliffs, N.J.: Prentice-Hall, 1969.

Sommer, R. Peoples' art. *Natural History,* 1971, *80,* 40–45.

Sommer, R., & Becker, F. D. Territorial defense and the good neighbor. *Journal of Personality and Social Psychology,* 1969, *11,* 85–92.

Stea, D., & Blaut, J. M. Some preliminary observations of spatial learning in school children. In R. N. Downs & D. Stea (Eds.), *Image and environment: Cognitive mapping and spatial behavior.* Chicago: Aldine, 1973, pp. 226–234.

Stilgoe, J. R. Jack o'lanterns to surveyors: The secularization of landscape boundaries. *Environmental Review,* 1976, *1,* 14–31.

Sundstrom, E., & Altman, I. Field study of dominance and territorial behavior. *Journal of Personality and Social Psychology,* 1974, *30,* 115–125.

Suttles, G. D. *The social order of the slum.* Chicago: University of Chicago Press, 1968.

Suttles, G. D. *The social construction of communities.* Chicago: University of Chicago Press, 1972.

Tambiah, S. J. Animals are good to think and good to prohibit. *Ethnology,* 1969, *8,* 423–460.

Thrasher, F. M. *The gang.* Chicago: University of Chicago Press, 1927.

Tiger, L. *Men in groups.* New York: Random House, 1969.

Tringham, R. Territorial demarcation of prehistoric settlements. In P. J. Ucko (Ed.), *Man, settlement, and urbanism.* London: Duckworth, 1972, pp. 463–475.

Tuan, Yi-Fu. *The hydrologic cycle and the wisdom of God.* Department of Geography Research Publication No. 1. Toronto, Ontario: University of Toronto Press, 1968.

Tuan, Yi-Fu. *Man and nature.* Commission on College Geography Resource Paper No. 10. Washington, D.C.: Association of American Geographers, 1971.

Tuan, Yi-Fu. *Topophilia: A study of environmental perception, attitude, and values.* Englewood Cliffs, N.J.: Prentice-Hall, 1974.

Tuan, Yi-Fu. *Space and place: The perspective of experience*. Minneapolis: University of Minnesota Press, 1977.

Turnbull, C. M. *The forest people: A study of the Pygmies of the Congo*. New York: Simon & Schuster, 1961.

Turnbull, C. M. The importance of flux in two hunting societies. In R. B. Lee & I. DeVore (Eds.), *Man the hunter*. Chicago: Aldine, 1968, pp. 132–137.

Vayda, A. P. (Ed.). *Environment and cultural behavior*. New York: Natural History Press, 1969.

Vinsel, A. M., Wilson, J., Brown, B. B., & Altman, I. Personalization in freshman dormitories. Paper presented at the meeting of the Western Psychological Association, Seattle, Wash., April 1977.

Watson, O. M., & Graves, T. D. Quantitative research in proxemic behavior. *American Anthropologist,* 1966, *68,* 971–985.

Westin, A. *Privacy and freedom*. New York: Atheneum, 1970.

Wheatley, P. *The pivot of the four quarters: A preliminary enquiry into the origins and character of the ancient Chinese city*. Chicago: Aldine/Atherton, 1971.

White, L. A. The world view of the Keresan Pueblo Indians. In S. Diamond (Ed.), *Primitive views of the world*. New York: Columbia University Press, 1964, pp. 83–94.

Whiting, J. W. M. Effects of climate on certain cultural processes. In W. H. Goodenough (Ed.), *Explorations in cultural anthropology*. New York: McGraw-Hill, 1964, pp. 511–544.

Whiting, J. W. M., Kluckhohn, R., & Anthony, A. The function of male initiation ceremonies at puberty. In E. E. Maccoby, T. M. Newcomb, & E. L. Hartley (Eds.), *Readings in social psychology*. New York: Holt, 1958, pp. 359–370.

Whittaker, J. O., & Whittaker, S. J. A cross-cultural study of geocentrism. *Journal of Cross-Cultural Psychology,* 1972, *3,* 417–421.

Whyte, W. F. *Street corner society*. Chicago: University of Chicago Press, 1943.

Willis, F. N. Initial speaking distance as a function of the speaker's relationship. *Psychonomic Science,* 1966, *5,* 221–222.

Wilson, E. O. *Sociobiology: The new synthesis*. Cambridge, Mass.: Harvard University Press, 1975.

Wirth, L. Urbanism as a way of life. *American Journal of Sociology,* 1938, *44,* 1–24.

Wright, L. *Clean and decent*. London: Routledge & Kegan Paul, 1960.

Wright, L. *Warm and snug: The history of the bed*. London: Routledge & Kegan Paul, 1962.

Wynne-Edwards, V. C. *Animal dispersion in relation to social behavior*. New York: Hafner, 1962.

Zeisel, J. *Sociology and architectural design*. New York: Russell Sage Foundation, 1974.

NAME INDEX

SUBJECT INDEX